LIBRARY OF HEBREW BIBLE/ OLD TESTAMENT STUDIES

642

Formerly Journal for the Study of the Old Testament Supplement Series

Editors
Laura Quick, Oxford University, UK
Jacqueline Vayntrub, Yale University, USA

Founding Editors
David J. A. Clines, Philip R. Davies and David M. Gunn

Editorial Board
Sonja Ammann, Alan Cooper, Steed Davidson, Susan Gillingham,
Rachelle Gilmour, John Goldingay, Rhiannon Graybill, Anne Katrine Gudme,
Norman K. Gottwald, James E. Harding, John Jarick, Tracy Lemos,
Carol Meyers, Eva Mroczek, Daniel L. Smith-Christopher,
Francesca Stavrakopoulou, James W. Watts

THE JUDGEMENT OF JONAH

Yahweh, Jerusalem and Nineveh

Alastair G. Hunter

LONDON • NEW YORK • OXFORD • NEW DELHI • SYDNEY

T&T CLARK
Bloomsbury Publishing Plc
50 Bedford Square, London, WC1B 3DP, UK
1385 Broadway, New York, NY 10018, USA
29 Earlsfort Terrace, Dublin 2, Ireland

BLOOMSBURY, T&T CLARK and the T&T Clark logo
are trademarks of Bloomsbury Publishing Plc

First published in Great Britain 2022
Paperback edition published 2023

Copyright © Alastair G. Hunter, 2022

Alastair G. Hunter has asserted his right under the Copyright, Designs and Patents Act, 1988, to be identified as Author of this work.

For legal purposes the Acknowledgements on p. xxi constitute an extension of this copyright page.

All rights reserved. No part of this publication may be reproduced or transmitted in any form or by any means, electronic or mechanical, including photocopying, recording, or any information storage or retrieval system, without prior permission in writing from the publishers.

Bloomsbury Publishing Plc does not have any control over, or responsibility for, any third-party websites referred to or in this book. All internet addresses given in this book were correct at the time of going to press. The author and publisher regret any inconvenience caused if addresses have changed or sites have ceased to exist, but can accept no responsibility for any such changes.

A catalogue record for this book is available from the British Library.
Library of Congress Control Number: 2021951978.

ISBN: HB: 978-0-5676-7361-9
PB: 978-0-5677-0650-8
ePDF: 978-0-5676-7362-6

Series: Library of Hebrew Bible/Old Testament Studies, volume 642
ISSN 2513-8758

Typeset by Trans.form.ed SAS

To find out more about our authors and books visit www.bloomsbury.com and sign up for our newsletters.

*I offer this book to Maggie
in celebration of shared life
over many loving years.*

Contents

List of Illustrations	ix
Prologue	xi
Acknowledgements	xxi
Abbreviations	xxiii
INTRODUCTION	1
Chapter 1 THE FIRST PLACE: NINEVEH	24
Chapter 2 JONAH 1.1-3: THE CALL	46
Chapter 3 JONAH 1.4-6: THE STORM	62
Chapter 4 JONAH 1.7-10: THE LOTTERY	73
Chapter 5 JONAH 1.11-16: AN ETHICAL DILEMMA	85
Chapter 6 THE SEA, THE SEA	97
Chapter 7 MAKER OF HEAVEN AND EARTH: JONAH AND GENESIS	106
Chapter 8 JONAH 1.17–2.10: AN APPEAL FROM THE ABYSS	119
Chapter 9 JONAH, EXODUS AND PSALMS	152

Chapter 10
JONAH 3.1-10: AN INNOCENT IN NINEVEH 175

Chapter 11
JONAH 4.1-11: ON BEING ELIJAH THE TISHBITE 193

Chapter 12
THE LORD'S FONDNESS FOR LIVESTOCK 218

INCONCLUSIONS 234

Bibliography 253
Index of References 256
Index of Authors 268
Index of Subjects 269

Illustrations

Image 1. An elder from Nepal. Jenny Hunter.	xv
Image 2. A Nepalese man in flight. Jenny Hunter.	xvi
Image 3. Boat and crew from a Nepalese puppet show. Jenny Hunter.	xvii
Image 4. A dyspeptic whale. Jenny Hunter.	xvii
Image 5. A young Nigerian aristocrat. Jenny Hunter.	xviii
Image 6. A typical Indian ox. Jenny Hunter.	xix
Image 7. The worm Leviathan. Jenny Hunter.	xx

Prologue

This book is not a monograph: its aim is to bring together a range of familiar insights into Jonah in a way that I hope will lead to some distinctive insights. References are kept deliberately to a minimum, but the select bibliography should make it clear just how indebted I am to a long, distinguished and extensive history of scholarship. Such is the quantity of work on Jonah that it is nearly impossible to claim any idea as original or previously unexpressed; accordingly I make no such claims for what follows, and readily acknowledge what I owe to others.

Throughout I have used the designation Tanakh for what is variously known as the Hebrew Bible, the Jewish Bible, the Old Testament and the First Testament. The acronym Tanakh – standing as it does for Torah+Nevi'im+Ketuvim (Teaching+Prophets+Writings) – is the most neutral term I am aware of for the collection of ancient texts with which this volume is profoundly concerned. All biblical citations are from the New Revised Standard Version, unless otherwise indicated.

The allure of the book of Jonah is manifest. It has generated a large body of folk tradition, including at one time a whale skeleton in Mosul which was allegedly that of the fish that swallowed Jonah, sadly now no longer extant. Only the Garden of Eden myths match or surpass its cultural influence. It has spawned an equally vast quantity of secondary material in the form of commentaries and explanatory essays whose principal effect is to satisfy no-one and to leave all of the book's puzzles as inscrutable as ever. Despite its brevity it demonstrates tremendous literary, narrative and mythic skill, and its final words are unmatched as an enigmatic parting shot: Whatever you thought you had understood, you must now think again!

That said, why add another literary pebble to the exegetical mountain? Obviously, no scholar is immune to the fond belief that *this* time the key will be theirs to turn with the resulting academic acclaim. Less egotistically, the quest for 'truth', or at the very least for new light on old problems, is a persistent part of the intellectual's vocation, needing no further justification than the existence of human curiosity. Accidents of influence also play their part: I taught a course in the Hebrew text of Jonah in the University of Glasgow for a number of years, a process which cannot fail to stimulate one's own interest. One of my colleagues, Yvonne Sherwood, wrote a ground-breaking and well-regarded[1] study of the reception history of Jonah which I read with consuming interest, and another, Robert Carroll, lectured regularly on the book and worked towards a commentary which was sadly interrupted by his untimely death. Thus circumstances rather conspired to persuade me to enter into this crowded field. Time passed, as time does, and as if by some quirk of fate my own inheriting of Robert's contract fell into desuetude. I became disenchanted by my work on the volume, albeit it represented about 60% of a commentary – perhaps haunted by its pedigree, perhaps sensing the lack of need for another verse-by-verse treatment. My publisher kept gently reminding me of my obligations, and I kept promising to deliver; sadly with as much effect as Billy Bunter's long-awaited and never delivered postal order![2] Even guilt has its limits as a motivator, however, and it was only an insight offered by a young scholar, Marian Kelsey,[3] in a paper she gave at the summer meeting of the Society for Old Testament Study in Durham in July 2018, which suddenly sparked my interest and provided the impetus to take my reading of Jonah in a new direction.

I offer this pebble, therefore, by way of a treatment of Jonah not as a prophecy or a satire or a morality tale or fable, but as an intensely knowing literary squib designed to be detonated in the intellectual circles of the post-Ezra Jerusalem establishment. It makes explicit and complex use of the scriptures and traditions they would have been familiar with, and leaves no sacred cows (pun intended) untouched. A specific device intended to blow up in the middle of a particular clique twenty-four centuries ago – but one which we will find to be uncomfortably apt to our own political, ecological, moral and religious setting. The key role played by a city in what we now know as Iraq may be an accident, but surely serendipity has a proper role to play in the grand theatre of human folly. Caveat lector.

---

1. *A Biblical Text and its Afterlives* (2000). The book was certainly well received, and I would maintain that in the case the description 'ground-breaking' is no cliché.

2. Does anyone still remember Billy Bunter (the tiresomely non-pc 'Fat Owl of the Remove')? Are Frank Richards' books still read?

3. I acknowledge the specifics of her contribution at the appropriate point in Chapter 1 below.

The sense of place in Jonah is striking in that it involves journeys through extremes and provides unusual locations. From his (unnamed) home Jonah hot-foots it to Joppa, whence he sets sail for Tarshish – seemingly a random choice in terms of the narrative, but likely to have significance for both the author and the first readers, and perhaps also for the construct 'Jonah' at the level of metaphoric signification. Then he appears to engineer his immolation in the depths of the sea: at the very least he makes it as morally easy for the sailors as he can. His destination now is the abyss – very much a real place of fear in Israelite mythology, as I will show in my discussion of Jonah 2 and its roots in the traditions of the exodus and the escape through the sea.[4] Each of these journeys is clearly marked in the text as 'downward', using the Hebrew verb *yarad*,[5] but significantly each putative destination is thwarted: Nineveh through Jonah's choice, Tarshish because of the divinely instigated storm, and the watery abyss through Yahweh's intervention.

The mid-point of the book finds Jonah brought back up (*'alah*)[6] on to dry land courtesy of cetacean nausea, at which point the narrative breaks off, to resume at the beginning of Jonah 3 with the renewal of God's demand. Since Jonah had to go *down* to Joppa, it can be safely assumed that he returned *up* to his home. This time the prophet, having learned from experience, goes directly to Nineveh, seemingly at once and without incident. The uniqueness and strangeness of this journey is entirely elided in the text. While armies may have traversed the 600 or so miles from Nineveh to the Levant (supported by a commissariat and the facility to pillage *en route*), and exiles may have been force-marched in the opposite direction at unknown human cost, the utter implausibility of an individual making such a journey without support in order to demand repentance beggars belief. Furthermore Jonah is, I believe, the only biblical prophet who travels voluntarily (in the end!) to preach to a ruler far beyond his

---

4. See Chapters 8 and 9 below.

5. Throughout I shall cite Hebrew terms by means of transliteration, always indicating what their English equivalents are. Those familiar with Hebrew can fill in the blanks easily enough; others I hope will be able to gain some limited sense of the extensive, skilful and varied use of language by an author at the height of their profession.

6. Most of the transliterations should be self-evident; however a few Hebrew sounds are not directly equivalent to any in English. The two most problematic are two gutturals both represented by '. Readers may think of them either as glottal stops or as strong 'h' sounds in the middle of words, and ignore them completely at the beginning.

homeland. Certainly Amos the Judean travels north to Israel to make the Lord's feelings known – but that was hardly to an alien or distant culture. Jeremiah is taken to Egypt against his will, and while Ezekiel is based in Babylon, he went there as one of the company of exiles after 587, and in any case spend much of his energy berating his home country.

Jonah's final location finds him seated on a hillside outside the city in burning heat. We must assume that he ascended to that vantage point, from which he proceeded to take the moral high ground regarding Yahweh's actions. Just where that hillside might have been I will return to in Chapter 1. For now I will simply note that it is here that the remaining instances of *'alah* are found: the vine which grows up to protect Jonah (4.6) and the sun which arises the next day to torture him (4.7-8).

Of its nature a prologue is not a summary of content. Rather it serves as a means of signalling some of the key directions which will be taken in the body of the work, and as a kind of apology for the decision to undertake the project in the first place. I hope this prolegomenon will serve to whet the reader's appetite or arouse their interest. The introduction proper which follows will tidy up some preliminary material which might otherwise clutter the discourse.

In the meantime, I thank my reader(s) for persisting thus far and trust that their journey – unlike Jonah's – will provide personal satisfaction. Before continuing I wish to indulge a whimsy by offering, for no serious reason whatsoever, a list of the dramatis personae (in order of appearance). Some will of necessity be treated in more detail, and possibly with greater respect, in the body of this book. In the meantime I hope that something of the wit of Jonah's author will come through by means of this device. The illustrations are by Jenny Hunter, mostly based on sketches drawn during extended visits to Nepal and Nigeria. I find it rather satisfying to use these atypical images in place of the rather conventional portrayals commonly found in Bibles.

1. *Yahweh*

The thoughts and intentions of God are by definition impenetrable to mere humans – even (or especially) those designated as prophets. The most common form of the encounter with Yahweh is through the Word, God's audible but not visible emissary. The figure of the *sadhu* is, I think, an interesting way of summing up both the mystery and the self-negation of Israel's deity. Yahweh's track record is admittedly not good: unfair punishments, irrational readiness to forgive the unforgiveable and (despite many assertions to the contrary) a penchant for sudden reversals of policy without reference to the so-called covenant people.

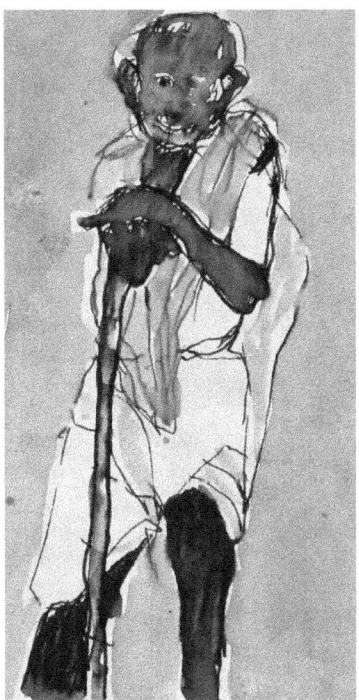

Image 1. *An elder from Nepal. Jenny Hunter.*

And while Yahweh's oneness, uniqueness and infinite superiority to all other would-be gods is regularly asserted, the records include numbers of instances of divine assemblies and councils, and the use of higher beings such as angels (in Hebrew 'messengers') and the notorious Satan (*shetan*) who seems to be employed in heaven as (forgive the inevitable pun) a devil's advocate. Confusing? Certainly. We can surely sympathise with Jonah's predicament, caught up as he is, without any say in the matter, in Yahweh's mad scheme to reform the Ninevites.

2. *Jonah*

The only significant prophet in Tanakh to have been named for a bird. His surname too is odd – *amittai* seems to be related to the word *'emeth* which means 'certainty', 'truth', 'honesty' and is itself derived from the verb *'aman* (from which, incidentally, the common responsive 'amen' in Jewish and Christian prayer is taken). Since many Hebrew proper names have meanings, a fact which the scriptures themselves are well aware of and which they often play upon, it is not unreasonable to propose that 'Jonah ben Amittai' is more than just a casual borrowing from 2 Kgs 14.25.

Image 2. *A Nepalese man in flight. Jenny Hunter.*

Anticipating a later more detailed review in Chapter 2, I simply note here that the term *yonah* has connections with a sacrificial bird, the sign of God's mercy as the flood recedes in Genesis 8 and the vulnerability of the individual under threat – especially Ps. 55.7 (I will return to this psalm at a later point). None of this is likely to be accidental, since we can be sure that the author of Jonah knew the scriptures and made frequent and subtle use of them.

3. *The Sailors*

Israel and Judah are not known to have been seafaring peoples. Their mythology regards the sea and the watery abyss as places of primal terror, as the psalm in Jonah 2 makes vividly clear. The technical terms relating to sea travel are to a considerable extent shared with Ezek. 27.8-9 and 25-29, part of an extended lamentation over the fate of the great trading island city-state of Tyre. It seems that the crews (including the captain or pilot) of merchant ships of the time were made up of slaves, and Ezek. 27.8-9 indicates the range of places from which such mariners may have come.

Image 3. *Boat and crew from a Nepalese puppet show. Jenny Hunter.*

Such crews would likely be of mixed origins – as is indeed true to this day of merchant shipping – and would have been particularly open to the need to respect whichever deities were operative in the course of their journeys. Readiness to honour whichever god served them well is hardly surprising, as Jon. 1.16 illustrates: 'Then the men feared Yahweh even more, and they offered a sacrifice to Yahweh and made vows'.

4. *The Big Fish / Whale*

It is customary in enlightened circles to treat with scorn those who naïvely imagine that a whale appears in Jonah, since they allegedly rarely appear in the Mediterranean, and in any case could not have kept a human being alive for thirty minutes never mind three days. Most of this scorn is wholly misplaced.

Image 4. *A dyspeptic whale. Jenny Hunter.*

I do not imagine for a minute that knowledgeable readers of Jonah thought his adventures were realistic; but in defence of the translation 'whale', the ancient world in general did not recognize a species difference, but certainly was aware enough of large sea creatures to formulate widespread legends featuring their participation. It is not unlikely that the author of Jonah was familiar with these. And, ironically, we moderns have been content to steal their terminology to describe our own improved taxonomy. The word 'cetacean' comes from the Greek *ketos* which, like leviathan, denotes a large sea animal; and a more specific term is *phallaina* (Latin *balaena*) leads eventually to the English 'baleen' whale.

5. *The King of Nineveh*

The designation 'King of Nineveh' is unique to Jonah in the Tanakh, and is not found in any extant contemporary literature. Everywhere else in scripture the expression 'King of Assyria' is used. This raises the question, why would the author of Jonah, who quite certainly knew the relevant texts, be guilty of such a solecism?

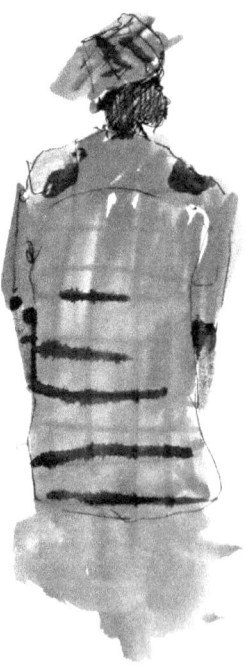

Image 5. *A young Nigerian aristocrat. Jenny Hunter.*

In my view, it is more than likely that this character, far from being a hitherto unheard of ruler from the eighth century, belongs to the array of symbolic features which characterise the book. It is more probable that a leader known to Jonah's author and readers is signalled. Who that might be will depend on how the signifier 'Nineveh' is to be understood: I will discuss this in more detail in Chapter 1.

6. *Cattle*

This is the point at which our interest in the actors in our little drama becomes somewhat surreal. Various sources suggest that the most likely species of domestic cattle in the ancient Middle East was the Zebu. Wikipedia summarises neatly (pun intended) the relevant information:[7] 'Zebu cattle are thought to be derived from Indian aurochs. Wild Asian aurochs disappeared during the time of the Indus Valley Civilisation from its range in the Indus River basin and other parts of the South Asian region possibly due to interbreeding with domestic zebu and resultant fragmentation of wild populations due to loss of habitat.

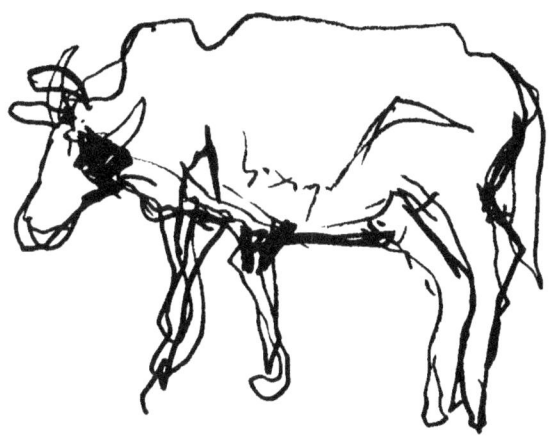

Image 6. *A typical Indian ox. Jenny Hunter.*

Archaeological evidence including depictions on pottery and rocks suggests that the species was present in Egypt around 2000 BC and thought to have been imported from the Near East or south.' Wikipedia

---

7. https://en.wikipedia.org/wiki/Zebu

and other zoological sources are silent on the matter of the likelihood of such creatures being content to be clothed in sackcloth, and their susceptibility to conversion. On these theological matters the book of Jonah is thus far our only ancient witness.

7. *The Worm*

A study in 2006[8] reported the discovery in Israel of a moth whose larvae eat the kind of plant which is often supposed to be the one which features in Jon. 4.6. I find this kind of obsessive devotion to the literal details of the story quaintly attractive, and therefore cannot resist introducing the *Olepa Schleini* larva to my cast of characters. It's really quite a cute little creature, and its taste for the *qiqayon* (or castor bean plant according to a speculative footnote in the NRSV) is hardly a crime. The illustration is not so cute – a snake-like creature of sinister appearance, perhaps linking the worm to the echoes of Leviathan in Jonah Chapter 2. Full marks to Yahweh for coming up with this one!

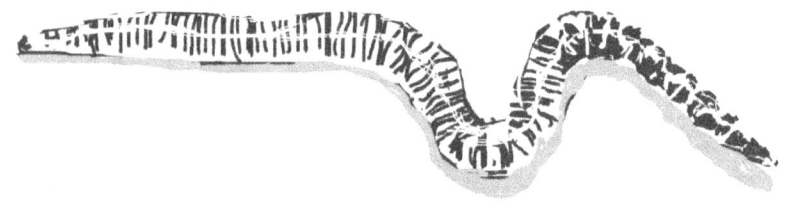

Image 7. *The worm Leviathan. Jenny Hunter.*

8. https://www.zobodat.at/pdf/MittMuenchEntGes_095_0005-0009.pdf

Acknowledgements

This work includes a deliberate homage to China Miéville, whose unique contribution to the Science Fiction genre over the last two decades has been nothing short of astounding. I will have more to say in Chapter 1 about the specific reason why I have chosen in particular to refer to his original *The City and the City*; for now I wish only to acknowledge a source of inspiration and a congeries of ideas – the coexistence in the same(?) space of two utterly different cities (Besźel and Ul Qoma), and the phenomenon of 'unseeing' which is a fundamental part of the existence and viability of the citizens of these two strange places.

I am grateful to the Brill and Bloomsbury for permission to make use of previously published material in an adapted form as follows:

Chapter 7: 'Creating Waves: Why the Fictionality of Jonah Matters', in *Sense and Sensitivity: Essays on Reading the Bible in Memory of Robert Carroll*, ed. A. G. Hunter and P. R. Davies (Sheffield: Sheffield Academic Press, 2002), 101–16.

Chapter 9: 'Jonah from the Whale: Exodus Motifs in Jonah 2', in *The Elusive Prophet: The Prophet as a Historical Person, Literary Character & Anonymous Artist*, ed. J. C. de Moor, OTS XLV (Leiden: Brill, 2001), 142–58.

'Inside Outside Psalm 55: How Jonah Grew Out of a Psalmist's Conceit', in *Psalms and Prayers*, ed. B. Becking and E. Peels, OTS 55 (Leiden: Brill, 2007), 129–39.

Chapter 12: 'An Awfully Beastly Business: Some Thoughts on *behēmāh* in Jonah and Qoheleth', in *Goochem in Mokum: Wisdom in Amsterdam*, ed. G. W. Brooke and P. Van Hecke, OTS 68 (Leiden: Brill, 2016), 82–94.

Finally, my thanks to my artist daughter Jenny Hunter for the drawings which illustrate the Prologue.

Abbreviations

AAJR	American Academy for Jewish Research
BCE	Before Common Era (equivalent to BC)
Bib	*Biblica*
CE	Common Era (equivalent to AD)
DCH	*Dictionary of Classical Hebrew*
ET	English Translation
HTR	*Harvard Theological Review*
ICC	International Critical Commentary
JPS	Jewish Publication Society (English Tanakh)
JSOT	*Journal for the Study of the Old Testament*
KJV	King James Version (aka Authorised Version)
KTU	*Keilalphabetische Texte aus Ugarit*
NEB	New English Bible
NIV	New International Version
NRSV	New Revised Standard Version
OTL	Old Testament Library
OTS	Oudtestamitische Studiën
RB	*Revue Biblique*
REB	Revised English Bible
RSV	Revised Standard Version
SBL	Society for Biblical Study
SJOT	*Scandinavian Journal of the Old Testament*
SPCK	Society for Promoting Christian Knowledge
UF	*Ugarit-Forschungen*

Introduction

The goal of this work is to tease out one possible reading of Jonah while at the same time displaying within a parallel commentary of a more traditional kind the polyvalence of this most intriguing of books. Over the last fifty years growing understanding has emerged that the book of Jonah – including the 'psalm' in ch. 2 – is a carefully constructed and expressed whole which comes from and is directed to literate and educated circles in the Jerusalem of its day. Two examples will suffice to illustrate this important consensus. First, Brichto (p. 68):

> My argument is that the Book of Jonah is from beginning to end, in form and content, in diction, phraseology, and style, a masterpiece of rhetoric. It is the work of a single artist, free from editorial comment or gloss; every word is in place, and every sentence. As aesthetic achievement the marvel of its creation is surpassed, if anything, by the marvel of its pristine preservation and transmission over a period of twenty-five centuries and more.

Secondly, Burrows (pp. 86–7), cites Feuillet's observation from 1947 that

> far from resembling a popular tale, the book manifestly comes from an educated Israelite, who conveyed his meaning by a masterly use of Scripture and a few items of folklore according to a well-considered plan.

Others have continued to echo this insight, which is now something of a consensus. However, the related question of what genre might best describe the book remains much more contentious, and I shall not engage with it beyond the personal observation that a work as sophisticated as the book of Jonah cannot be defined by the straitjacket of a specific genre. Many of the terms used – parable, ironic satire, parody, legend, didactic fable and so on – have partial relevance, but it is surely wiser to abandon the attempt at a single defining pigeonhole in favour of a more rhetorical approach which can take account of the sophistication of the author's work. This is not to deny the importance in particular of Edwin Good's opening salvo in his classic *Irony in the Old Testament* in which he risked a forthright account of the matter (p. 41):

> The Book of Jonah is a satire. It portrays the prophet in order to ridicule him. To be sure, the author clarifies his position by playing the figure of Jonah off against God. Hence it can be said with some justice that God is the central character in the story. But our attention is directed primarily to the prophet, and his attitude is the focal point of the tale.

There are important insights here, but it would be fair to say that the simple description 'irony' is no longer apt.

My starting point, therefore, while seemingly marginal, will I hope prove to be a fruitful key to one way of unlocking some of the mystery of Jonah's purpose or project. It is simply this: 'Why Nineveh?' Why has this remote city from the distant past been selected as the pivotal motif for whatever concerns lie behind this intriguing and frustrating book?

Any answer to this question must begin with an engagement with the traditional historical-critical questions of date, authorship and first audience; for whether we take Nineveh to be the actual place of that name contemporary with the book or regard it as a legendary place from the past serving the purposes of a much later period depends on these annoyingly pedestrian enquiries. These are matters which can never be finally resolved, but they are not for that reason to be avoided or shunted into the siding of 'yesterday's exegesis', safely parked and rusting away peacefully. At the very least I hope to offer a plausible historical framework supported by circumstantial evidence which will give comfort to my broader thesis. I submit that no honest commentator can hope to do more, and confess also that my own biases, shaped over decades of study of the materials, will undoubtedly be screamingly visible to most of my readers. But that too is the shared fate of all who propose to interpret ancient texts and uncover long-lost motivations.

Dating

Evidence pointing to a likely range of dates for the composition of Jonah has been reviewed repeatedly over the last century, starting with the ICC volume by Julius A. Bewer of 1912.[1] The results are remarkably consistent, varying only in the weight given to different criteria, indicating at the earliest ca. 500 BCE, and at the latest 200 BCE. The link between our Jonah and the figure briefly mentioned in 2 Kgs 14.25 is not held to provide any credible historical information beyond the possibility that

---

1. Most commentaries include an assessment of information relevant to the question of dating. I note those of Bewer (1912), Wolff (1986), Sasson (1990), Limburg (1993), Salters (1994), Cary (2008), Youngblood (2013).

it is the source from which the author borrowed the name of a marginal figure to serve his or her narrative purposes. That the prophet Jonah in this passage is supposed to have encouraged Jeroboam II to expand the borders of Israel is all we know of him, and that information has no obvious bearing on our Jonah's call to journey to Nineveh. Otherwise, the criteria most often cited are:

(1) Signs that the language of Jonah includes Aramaisms and features usually associated with Hebrew texts known to be later than 400 BCE.
(2) A wide familiarity with Tanakh writings up to at least 550 BCE, and – as Jonathan Magonet (1983) showed conclusively in his definitive monograph – a high degree of sophisticated intertextuality.
(3) More controversially, an argument that at certain points Jonah displays a specific connection with Joel. This depends on two points – the use in Jon. 4.2 of a form of the Exodus blessing (34.6) including the phrase 'and relents from punishing' which is only elsewhere found in Joel 2.13; and a phrase shared by Jon. 3.9a and Joel 2.14a ('who knows whether he will not turn and relent'). The dating of Joel is uncertain, but may be in the period 400–350 BCE. Were the direction of influence to be unambiguously from Joel to Jonah this would be helpful; however, it is clear that there is too much uncertainty in all of this to form any firm conclusion.
(4) The suggested end-date of 200 BCE is indicated by Sirach's reference to the Twelve Prophets (49.10) in the course of his celebration of famous men [sic]. While he does not directly name Jonah, there is no evidence of a version of any edition of the twelve prophets which does not include Jonah. Explicit references in 3 Macc. 6.8 and in some versions of Tob. 14.4, while later in date, further reinforce the sense of a late postexilic composition.
(5) The book's references to Nineveh are anachronistic, and geographically implausible, suggesting the use of a symbolic 'evil place' such as is found in other late prophets, and also interestingly in the Hellenistic world after 600 BCE. There is evidence that the Greeks knew that Nineveh was a sizeable city now in ruins, and that they regarded Nineveh (at least towards its end) as both opulent and licentious. Most commentators observe that the term 'King of Nineveh' found in Jonah was not used by the Assyrians, but is found also in Greek writings. The perhaps legendary and wealthy but witless Sardanapalus fits well the description of the king's antics in Jonah 3 (Bolin pp. 110–13, 118).

While none of these is conclusive, and each may be questioned to a greater or lesser degree, and while it is also true that the sum of five weak arguments remains weak, the broad consensus would seem to be plausible. I therefore conclude that, pending any other testimony, Jonah's composition may be placed in the admittedly broad range of 400–200 BCE.

The Use of Sources

Item (2) above deserves further explication, given the unusual character of the book of Jonah and the near-unanimous consensus regarding its use of sources in a highly erudite and imaginative fashion. This is relevant to questions of dating because it speaks to the matter of *when* and *in whose hands* this kind of meta-scriptural process might have been possible. Analogies with rabbinic midrash[2] take us some way – but what Jonah does with its sources is different from, and in some respects more artful – dare one say more subtle? – than what counts as later rabbinic exegesis. The author of Jonah, unlike, say, Jesus ben Sira or his namesake Jesus of Nazareth, is not a proto-rabbi. Ironically we can see this clearly by comparing the way that Mt. 12.38-42 uses the so-called sign of Jonah for its theological ends. The use in that passage of the specific detail of Jonah's three days and nights in the belly of the fish as a type of Jesus's post-crucifixion experience is much closer to rabbinic types of exegesis. Jonah never offers this kind of overt interpretation, preferring to let the reader be seduced by a seemingly naïve story with its bold, and rather odd, scenarios, all the time using a network of familiar words, phrases, tropes and myths quietly to bring about its effect. As we shall soon see, this is undoubtedly highly dependent also on the reader's background. Precisely because the story and its language are so tricky and allusive/elusive, what the work means for us is at an extreme level dependent on who we are and what we bring to it. That this is a truism of every reading experience does not detract from its specific and peculiar force in the case of Jonah.

The modern study which definitively set this ball rolling is Jonathan Magonet's *Form and Meaning: Studies in Literary Techniques in the Book of Jonah* (1976; re-issued in 1983 with some revisions and additions). Re-reading it now, some decades after I first encountered it, I remain hugely impressed by what Magonet achieved, and by the continuing

---

2. Magonet (p. 53) refers to the author as 'an excellent "midrashist"', though the accompanying note somewhat qualifies that evaluation.

relevance of its arguments and theses. For now, I want to emphasise its fourth chapter, which probes in detail the way that quotations, allusions and reminiscences of Hebrew scriptures are deployed. Magonet is quietly unequivocal in his assessment of the skills of the author, both in the deployment of scripture and the stimulation and provoking of the reader. For my purposes, perhaps the most significant explicit expression of this is the remark that '[t]he next step ... assumes both on the part of the author and his audience a mind fully conversant with other biblical texts, and an ear finely attuned to detecting similarities and differences in phraseology' (p. 68). For it seems to me that Jonah in its first context displayed virtuosity on the part of its author and demanded knowledge and dexterity on the part of its readers. In short, it belongs to educated intellectual circles on both sides. This in turn has implications for possible dating.

It will be helpful at this point to exemplify the extent to which these claims can be substantiated in the detail of Jonah's dependence on and reworking of the scriptures of Israel. I shall begin by summarising Magonet's case studies, then expand this with additional observations based on my own research. I do not propose to return to the subject of Jonah's intertextuality in detail in the body of this book; but that in no way should be taken to imply that the topic is not of central importance to the book of Jonah. Indeed, intertextual references will form a major part of the process of exegesis as I journey through the commentary element of this study, and they will further inform those chapters treating general matter, such as Chapter 9, 'Jonah, Exodus and the Psalms'. For now, I wish to offer my own readers the same courtesy given by the author of Jonah: an assumption that those steeped in and knowledgeable about Israel's scriptures can appreciate for themselves many of the sources and nuances with which the text of Jonah plays.

(1) The psalm in Jonah 2 was regarded with considerable suspicion when historical-critical investigation first became dominant, and for many years the consensus view held that it was an intrusive pastiche. That this is no longer the case is due in no small measure to Magonet's thoughtful analysis of the psalm in terms both of its imaginative use of traditional Psalms material and its function as an integral element of the developing narrative. He shows convincingly that the author used a carefully selected range of phrases from across the Psalter to root his psalm in familiar territory, all the time putting his own characteristic imprint on these pieces.[3] It is striking that there is an absence of such citations in the

---

3. Magonet (pp. 39–54, esp. p. 50) identifies phrases from Pss. 3.9; 5.8; 18.5; 22.6; 31.7, 23; 42.8; 50.14; 56.13; 69.2, 3, 16; 88.3; 102.2; 103.4; 116.1, 3, 16, 17, 18;

passage Jon. 2.5b-6a, which portrays Jonah's descent to the deepest abyss. Magonet interprets this as a mirror of the absolute isolation and despair experienced by Jonah before his rescue and the resumption of psalmic elements. I believe, notwithstanding, that these sentences also tap into scriptural loci relating to the trial of the sea crossing in Exodus; I shall discuss this in more detail in Chapter 9.

(2) From his review of other quotations (pp. 65–84) I want to single out a number of parallels which are particularly germane to my own approach. The connection with Elijah's experiences in the wilderness after the bloody debacle of the prophets of Ba'al is of course well known, and I shall return to the matter of Jonah's channelling of Elijah and his failed challenge to the ruling power in Israel in Chapter 11; suffice to note here that Magonet has made a strong case for the conscious and artful use of the relevant material from Kings in Jonah's concluding scene outside the city.

(3) Magonet points out (p. 65) that the verb used for 'to overthrow', when applied to cities, is in all but one other biblical instance used of the threat to Sodom and Gomorrah, or of threats to other cities using that explicit example. Further, the terms *ra'ah* and *chamas* used in Jonah of the wickedness of Nineveh are applied in Genesis to the generation whose behaviour brought about the flood. I will take these points up in my discussion of Nineveh in Chapter 1.

(4) Two specific terms which Magonet finds to be of intertextual importance are *yavasha* ('dry land'; pp. 65–6) and *tardemah* ('deep sleep', often sometimes associated with death; pp. 67–9). These will both receive further discussion in Chapter 7; for the time being I merely record them as aspects of the complexity and ingenuity of Jonah's use of sources.

(5) Not surprisingly Magonet (pp. 77–9) deals in some detail with the putative citing of Joel by Jonah. As most other commentators have observed, this is an impossible call, given that both works are likely to have originated in roughly the same period. His conclusion is that Jonah's use of the terminology in question is the more original, since it is more thoroughly integrated into the wider arc of the narrative. Perhaps; but

---

120.1, 11; 138.2; 142.4; 143.4-5; 145.19. The range is highly significant, suggesting as it does familiarity with the full Psalter – an entity which may well only have found its form at the very end of our putative time-frame.

surely one could equally argue that a novel addendum to the Exodus formula could have been introduced by Joel without any thought of its having wider implications, only to be seized upon by the author of Jonah in the same way that they adopted and bent to their own purposes so many other seemingly disconnected pieces – as Magonet himself argues convincingly.

Summing up thus far, we may add to the opening discussion of a possible date two further points of importance. Firstly, the author of Jonah is familiar with a wide range of Hebrew scripture, arguably across its whole spectrum including, for example, material from all five books of the Psalter. This surely pushes the date closer to the latest part of the possible range. And secondly, the exegetical and literary skills of the author and the likelihood that the intended audience had similar skills and experience of scripture, points to a time in later post-exilic Judah when we can postulate a sizeable scribal class with both resources and leisure, not to mention a context in which there are clear indications of rival schools of thought on the nature of Jewish life and belief and its interface with a wider world which impinges directly on their experience. I will therefore turn now to a brief discussion of these social desiderata.

Jonah's Scribe

In his interesting and important monograph, *Jonah's World: Social Science and the Reading of Prophetic Story*, Lowell K. Handy pays close attention to the character of the author of Jonah, based in part on the assumption of its origin in the Persian period of Judaean history.

> [I]t is ... most likely that the author of Jonah was at the very least: (a) a scribe; (b) trained in Jerusalem. (c) employed at something other than writing short stories; and (d) wrote down the story for others who were of a similar background to himself. (p. 30)

Handy then offers an overview of 'Scribes in Society' in which he describes scribal classes in the wider ancient Near Eastern world in general, tacitly assuming a broadly similar institution to have existed in Judah (Yehud[4]) during the Persian period (pp. 13–17). The coterie of scribes would have been an elite and privileged class, representing the

---

4. Yehud is the scholarly coinage for the political entity of Jerusalem and its hinterland during the Persian period (ca. 539–320 BCE).

perhaps 5% of the population which was literate, and using their skills to move in powerful circles. As such they would have been particularly attuned to any sectarian differences and alert to the significance of these for their own position. Landy comments 'it is almost a certainty that major divisions among "sectarian" groups existed not only in the period of the monarchies and in the Hellenistic Period, but in Yehud as well'. He does not pursue this theme in the rest of his work, in which he tends to conclude that Jonah (and therefore his author) was probably a scribal diplomat, free to travel and arguably directly familiar with the courts of the Persian administration. His clearest presentation of this theme can be best attested in his explicit discussion of 'The Jerusalem elite':

> Behind the short story of Jonah stands a vision of human society based on hierarchical structures, norms for how people ought to behave and a sense that the author's circle knows better than others what these are. ... Behind the story, the real wise person in Jonah is the circle of scribes telling and listening to the story. (pp. 124–5)

Handy goes on to insist that the 'story was written for literate elite in Yehud'. It is worth spelling out in more detail what this presumes, beginning with the phenomenon of intertextuality which as we have seen above is ubiquitous in Jonah. It functions in general on at least three levels. Firstly, the author must (a) be well versed in the traditional texts, (b) be knowing in his or her deployment of them, (c) most probably have access to a collection of these texts in written form, presumably in the Temple precincts, and (d) be more than merely functionally literate. It is beyond belief that the kind of detailed knowledge and use of texts displayed in Jonah could have been based on oral techniques. Secondly, there would be little point in producing such an elegantly shaped work for a readership – or audience – without the means to appreciate it. The repeating structure, the familiar sounding psalm, and the drama which infuses the narrative could well have had a superficial appeal. But the 'so-much-more', which readers through more than two millennia have perceived, is strong prima facie evidence that a popular audience was far from exhaustive of Jonah's contemporary reception. It seems likely that written versions would have circulated amongst and been appreciated by those able to dig beneath the surface, read between the lines, and understand the hidden message of Jonah's strange adventures. Thirdly, the character of Jonah is himself implicated in the skein of intertextuality, since much of that aspect of the book is expressed through Jonah's own words (1.9, 12; 2.2-9; 3.4b; 4.2-3, 8-9). This is no blunt prophet haranguing folk with divine threats, but a religious scholar using the texts he is deeply acquainted with to challenge God with reference to a number of central themes of Tanakh: creation, exodus, the temple cult, mercy and grace, justice, and human dignity. In noting this, I note also that there is no mention at all of the covenant. It is beyond credibility that the writer and their character would not have been familiar with that grand Deuteronomistic theme. Indeed, it forms part of the narrative in Nehemiah 9 which is one of Jonah's intertexts. The book's avoidance of this obvious key term must be significant, and we shall return to it in Chapters 9 and 13.

This is then not a story for Ninevites or indeed Persians or any other imperial rulers. 'Who cared about Jonah? A section of the elite of Yehud who could see themselves in some way connected to the person of Jonah.' Jonah's author, as a diplomat-scribe, would have been accustomed to having to communicate messages he neither believed in nor cared about 'to people he did care about, but negatively', a datum which goes some way to explaining the central conundrum of Jonah's response to his commission and his ultimate complaint against Yahweh (p. 125). Handy concludes (p. 126) with an intriguing proposal that

> this was not a text written to educate the population of Judaeans that Yahweh cared for other people. That was a given. The work may, however, reflect a desire on the part of the author to see Yahweh, on the other hand, equated with the ruling deity of the Persians, and to be acknowledged, even if only as one among many, as an important deity by the commoners of the wider world. Both religious desires would have placed small, truly insignificant Yehud on a worldwide stage in the minds of the Jerusalem elite. And many members of elite societies love to 'see and be seen' among the powerful.

While I am in agreement with Handy's portrayal of the character of the author as scribe, I shall not pursue this particular reading of the book. Furthermore, I want to raise a possible alternative to the Yehud dating which he favours, based on a recent review of archaeological evidence for the state – and status – of Jerusalem in both the Persian and the early Hellenistic periods. That said, it does seem to me that the proposal that the author of Jonah was an elite scribe, writing (for whatever reason) for an audience of similarly knowledgeable intelligentsia has much to commend it, and is one which I subscribe to. There are implications for dating; for in addition to the use of a very wide range of Hebrew scripture, already noted, we must now add the need for a social context in which such scribal activity could find space and the resources both to be produced and to be received.

Ehud Ben Zvi, in his important study of 'reading and rereading' in the book of Jonah, insists on the importance of a group he styles 'the literati' in the Jerusalem at the time of the book's composition. As he describes them, we might readily identify them with Handy's 'scribes'. On the matter of the resources necessary to sustain such a literate class, Ben Zvi comments (p. 6):

> Reading, rereading and studying books that claim, and were considered [*sic*], authoritative by a certain society are social activities. They necessitated a process of production of books that included writing, editing and copying. They also required a system of storage and retrieval of texts. All these activities demanded resources. Moreover, they required the existence of some educational system to produce bearers of high literacy who were able to read and study these texts, and at least a few who were able to write or edit them. Such a system required the allocation of resources.

He later includes the (fictional) character of Jonah as such a person, one with whom the literati could readily identify:

> Jonah is described as a person who is well educated in the corpus of religious texts accepted as authoritative for the Jerusalemite community .... The literati of Yehud, among whom and for whom the book was composed shared these attributes with the character Jonah. (pp. 108–9)

I shall turn to this aspect of the matter shortly; but first we should examine the character of Jonah as a would-be prophet.

Jonah the Prophet

Prophecy in the ancient Near Eastern is an important social context for Jonah. The fact that the book is arranged alongside the others of the twelve minor prophets implies that whoever was responsible for that placement thought it proper. Its precise position is fluid – after Obadiah in the masoretic[5] text; after Micah in the Septuagint, and at the very end in some Dead Sea material – so we are unlikely to find much help from that direction. However, a brief review of the narrative characterisation of prophets in the Hebrew Scriptures shows that Jonah fits the cultural and psychological profile very neatly. Because modern readers are accustomed to take the book as satire or pastiche it is often concluded,

---

5. The standardized Hebrew text; the name 'masoretic' is derived from the first-millennium group of scholars who vocalised the consonantal text.

without much debate, that Jonah is an anti-prophet, a joke at the expense of the tradition. I suggest that, whatever the book's ultimate appraisal of Jonah, he is presented perfectly seriously in that role, albeit with the expected accoutrement of 'oracles' largely stripped out, and with a series of discomfiting twists.[6]

First, Jonah has pedigree: 'The word of the Lord came to Jonah, son of Amittai, saying' (Jon. 1.1; cf. Isa. 1.1; 2.2; 13.1; Jer. 1.1-2; Hos. 1.1; Joel 1 etc). There is nothing untoward about this aspect of the opening of Jonah, and it is surely a deliberate move by the author who surely intended the connection to be made. However, given the subsequent behaviour and actions of our hero, it must be seriously considered that this is a deliberately misleading link. Thus the normative attribution is immediately unsettled by a quite *un*typical development: Yahweh orders Jonah to travel to Nineveh without much guidance about what he might say beyond the generic 'cry out against it, for their wickedness has come up before me'. The universal expectation in the prophetic books is to find an oracle directly attributed to Yahweh: nothing of the sort appears in Jonah. The closest we come is in 3.2, 'proclaim to [Nineveh] the message that I tell you'.

Second, Jonah is unhappy about his commission (1.3a): 'But Jonah set out to flee to Tarshish from the presence of the Lord'. It is not unusual for prophets and other leaders to be reluctant: Moses (at great length in Exod. 3.1–4.18), Gideon (Judg. 6.12-24), Isaiah (6.5) and Jeremiah (1.4-10) are familiar examples. It is as though – out of modesty perhaps? – it was incumbent upon the chosen prophet to proclaim their inadequacy. So far so good; but of course Jonah does not (at this point) verbalise his reluctance. He simply ups and leaves. Eventually we are given his considered rationale when, after the event, he indulges in a kind of 'I told you so':

> He prayed to the LORD and said, 'O LORD! Is not this what I said while I was still in my own country? That is why I fled to Tarshish at the beginning; for I knew that you are a gracious God and merciful, slow to anger, and abounding in steadfast love, and ready to relent from punishing.' (Jon. 4.2)

---

6. In an essay in which he takes seriously Jonah's role as a prophet, Abela (p. 2) 'proposes as a working hypothesis that Jonah is a prophetic writing involved in a metalinguistic discourse on prophecy itself'. He further observes (p. 7) that the 'clamorous absence of the "expected terminology" may be hinting at the narrator's strategy of dealing with the subject matter of his composition in an indirect manner'. This would explain the absence of the Hebrew term for 'prophet', perhaps by analogy with Amos's denial that he was a prophet or a prophet's son (Amos 7.14).

This is, of course, not a modest demurral but a direct challenge to Yahweh's ethical standards and moral consistency. Thus once more the outward conformity to a prophetic norm is subverted by the specifics of its application.

Third, the experience of victimhood is strongly represented in the book. Though it is often dismissed as self-pity, this aspect deserves to be taken more seriously in the light of similar experiences recorded in the lives (fictional or not) of a number of the mainstream prophets. Elijah may be the most pertinent, in that his experiences in the aftermath of his contest with the prophets of Ba'al on Mount Carmel are directly tapped for the closing chapter of Jonah (1 Kgs 18.17–19.18). Jeremiah is variously put in the stocks (20.1-2), threatened with death (26.10-11), imprisoned in a cistern (38.6), and taken into exile in Egypt against his will (43.1-7). Isaiah writes of the suffering servant, and might in part be tapping his own experiences. Daniel and his associates faced fiery furnaces and dens of lions, Hosea's family life was less than perfect, and Ezekiel's wife died (apparently) to provide God with a useful parable, while he was forbidden any signs of outward mourning (24.15-17). In Jonah's case, as with the other issues I have identified, the motif of victimhood is turned on its head. His 'denavistration' (if I may use a word coined from the Greek for ship by analogy with 'defenestration'[7]) is a direct consequence of Jonah's original disobedience, and is his own choice in order to save the lives of the crew. I will have more to say about this in a later chapter when I consider the text in closer detail; it is sufficient for now to note that 'victim' here is an ambivalent category. Similarly, in ch. 4, Jonah presents himself as victimised by a flighty deity, but only in the sense that he regrets the repentance of the city. Once again, a comparison with the closest model, Elijah, reveals the author's habit of upending norms: Elijah was genuinely threatened by Jezebel in consequence of his defeat of God's enemies; Jonah is threatened by no-one more sinister than a worm and a hot wind.

Jonah: Possible Worlds

The point of this seeming digression is to try to identify a plausible social context favourable to the production of a work such as Jonah. Of course that 'such as' begs a rather large question: what kind of book *is* Jonah?

---

7. I have found one Google reference to a use of this coinage, which admittedly I thought was unique to me(!): https://mob.indymedia.org.uk/en/2009/08/436968.html?c=on#c231285

Whether it is a targeted polemic, an instructive parable, or an ethical investigation (just three out of numerous possibilities) cannot easily be determined. But I believe that we can at least say with confidence that it is a major intellectual contribution relevant to its time and place and would have been certain to provoke critical (in both positive and negative terms) responses from its first readers. Assuming, as I do, that the book's origins are in the two centuries after 400 BCE, the only available polities are the period of Persian suzerainty which ended with Alexander's conquests, and the Hellenistic regime of Ptolemaic Egypt – one of the successor states to Alexander's brief-lived empire. These can be divided conveniently, if not with exact precision, around 300 BCE. Subsequently, after 200 Judah became a client state of Seleucid Syria, the second of Alexander's successor states in the Middle East.

Persian-period Yehud
There is now a considerable body of scholarly work, known informally as the 'Persian' school, which has, I believe, made a good case for considerable literary work on what became the Hebrew scriptures in the centuries following the exile.[8] The case rests on the assumption of an active scripture-producing scribal school – or schools – during the fifth and early fourth centuries BCE largely responsible for the creation of Tanakh. Their ultimate aim, building no doubt on popular traditions and whatever texts survived from before the exile, seems to have been to validate and support a preferred theocratic form of governance in Jerusalem. In the longer term the kind of programme indicated in the Deuteronomistic materials, and spelled out in the 'reforms' of Ezra and Nehemiah, was successful – as we can see in the Rabbinic form of Judaism which ultimately became the norm. The full extent of that endeavour is open to question, and a major weakness in the overall proposal is the lack of direct evidence either for such activity, and or for the physical conditions of and social structures in Jerusalem during Persian rule. But, even allowing for that caveat, the *fact* of post-exilic scripture-formation is undeniable, and the *fact* of inner-biblical intertextuality is also unassailable. We do not know if there were rival 'schools' in Jerusalem at that time, though the indication in Ezra and Nehemiah is that these reformers faced significant opposition. They chose to stigmatise their opponents as heretics (to use an anachronistic term),

---

8. Circumstantial support for this all-encompassing claim comes from evidence that much of the historical and prophetic corpus shows signs of post-exilic editing and/or completion, together with the fact that a number of individual works are clearly or almost certainly of a date later than 400 BCE.

unrepentant 'people of the land' (*'ammei-ha'arets*) who took 'foreign' wives and husbands and showed scant respect for the supposedly traditional values of social and ritual observance. There is room enough here, and to spare, for the construction of a more benign view of the people of the land: namely, those who remained in Judah after the Babylonian conquest and maintained a form of their traditional adherence to Yahweh in the most straitened of circumstances. Their resentment of incomers from Persia with their letters of authority from the great king would have been entirely understandable!

One interesting glimpse into the ruling classes in Jerusalem between 400 and 200 BCE concerns the family of Tobiah (also found in Greek form as Tobias).[9] There are tantalising occurrences of this name at various points in both biblical and extra-biblical sources, though whether they all belong to the same family must be left an open question. The striking thing about this strand of indicative evidence is that, contrary to the positions taken in Ezra and Nehemiah, there are few signs of an active proto-rabbinic establishment in Jerusalem during this period. We begin with Nehemiah, where Tobiah figures as an associate of Sanballat in the Samaritan opposition to Nehemiah's plans for the restoration of Jerusalem's city walls (Neh. 4–6 passim). Though he is described as an Ammonite, it seems clear from Neh. 6.17-19 that he was well-thought-of by native Judahites and was related to members of the restoration team (cf. Neh. 3.28-32). As we shall note below, a later individual of this name appears in the Zenon Papyri as governor of Ammon, which could explain Nehemiah's misrepresentation.

A Tobiah is also named in Zech. 6.10-14 as a supporter of the high priest Joshua, and is said there to be one of the returning exiles, and clearly a man of some wealth. This would place him, if Zechariah's dating references are reliable, in Jerusalem at the end of the fifth century, and so a putative ancestor of Nehemiah's opponent. While the risks of forming connections on the basis of similar names are well-known, the leading families amongst the returnees were probably limited in number and likely to have preserved the family name through the generations.

A reference in the Zenon Papyri from the reign of Ptolemy II (285–246 BCE) identifies a Tobias as leader of a military colony in Ammon in the mid-third century BCE, an individual who was involved in regular negotiations with the Ptolemaic government. The discovery of this archive brought about some rethinking of the account given by Josephus

---

9. A useful survey of this material is to be found in the form of an unpublished dissertation by Justin Huguenin at https://kb.osu.edu/bitstream/handle/1811/54608/The_Tobiads_and_the_Maccabees.pdf.

of the descendants of this Tobias in the early second century. Without buying into the more fanciful elements of Josephus's narrative, it appears that they were leading players in the struggle in Jerusalem at the end of the third century between supporters of the Ptolemies and those of the Seleucids. The conflicts up till then were largely to do with political differences – for example, a judgement as to whether tax-farming privileges from the Ptolemies or the benefits of a new, seemingly 'lighter touch' regime in Syria weighed greater in the scale of advantages. Following the religiously restrictive measures imposed by Antiochus IV early in the second century, the pendulum swung towards religious affiliation as the defining factor. Although it is beyond our date-range, it is of note that the kind of sectarian differences apparent in Judaea under the Romans have many of their roots in this period.

In short, the approach typified by both the family of Tobiah and the line of high priests[10] was one of rapprochement with the relevant ruling power and a broadly speaking laisse faire attitude to Judah's relationships with the external world. We know that the high priests towards the end of our period were just as involved in the realpolitik of juggling one power against another as were secular families. It is further apparent that there was little obvious animosity directed towards non-Judaeans, and – as the Elephantine Papyri indicate – broad tolerance of alternatives to the kind of strict Torah religion advocated by Ezra.[11] The establishment of a Jewish colony in Egypt with rather heterodox practices and its own temple was known to the authorities in Jerusalem and Samaria, to whom these colonists looked for advice and support. Indeed one of those to whom they appealed was the high priest Johanan ben Eliashib. If, as the majority of commentators affirm, the latest possible date for Jonah is 200 BCE, the case he is making seems to be directed not at the later rivalry between strict observance and laxity, but rather at choices between external governances. Indeed, such a scenario might help to explain the curious 'international' setting of the book.

Hellenistic Judaea
An alternative is potentially revealed in the Chronicler's emphasis on the royal cult and reinforced by the messianic and Zion-focused themes in the Psalms, especially those of Books 4 and 5, which point to some kind of

---

10. These were not entirely distinct groups – Onias the High Priest was a Tobiad.

11. Abela (p. 3) cites an opinion of von Rad's regarding Jonah which in his view is still valid: 'We have no knowledge of any "universalistic" opposition to the "particularist" measure taken by Ezra and Nehemiah, and the book itself contains no evidence to support such theory'.

divinely authorised kingship. A possible expression of this strand could be seen in the ultimately failed Hasmonaean dynasty. In 142 BCE Simon took on the role of High Priest and Prince, a double function carried on by his successor John Hyrcanus (134–104 BCE). This might be understood as a 'fulfilment' of the kind of expectations raised, for example, by Psalm 110 and cited in Heb. 7.17 as a characterisation of Jesus. Psalm 110 is of course an account of the nature of King David in Zion, portraying him as the priest-king Melchizedek; hence its peculiar relevance to this messianic hope and its putative fulfilments. The wave of messianic pretenders, perhaps including Jesus of Nazareth,[12] in the century after the demise of that dynasty in 63 BCE[13] further attests the influence and attractiveness of that messianic longing.

If the context of Jonah is to be found in the presence of rival sectarian groupings in Jerusalem, the most natural starting point is the Ezra–Nehemiah complex. Its key features for our purposes are (a) an extreme policy on intermarriage and other forms of association with neighbouring non-Judean peoples (Ezra 9–10; Neh. 13.23-31; cf. general segregation Neh. 9.2; 13.1-3); (b) a commitment to a Torah-based covenant in which the Levites have a specific role as teachers and interpreters, a responsibility given to the Levites by Moses in Deut. 31.24-29 (Neh. 9–10); and (c) the enforcement of Sabbath observance (Neh. 13.15-22). The other area, which is later associated with the Judaism of the Mishnah, is that of ritual purity; however, while that may be implied by the programme of segregation from the *goyim* and the annulment of mixed marriages (see Neh. 13.30), it is only explicitly referred to in relation to the duties of the Priests and Levites to purify themselves and those places and people involved in cultic events (Ezra 6.20; Neh. 12.30, 45; 13.9, 22). There is no sign of the detailed personal purification rituals to be found in the Mishnah and its predecessors. The question is: are any of these three sufficiently controversial to have produced disputatious sects in Persian or early Hellenistic Jerusalem?

It is appropriate to ask where the successors of Nehemiah and Ezra were to be found. They do not appear to be visible in the external evidence relating to the Persian period. For example, Ben Zvi (p. 9 n. 24) notes that 'there is no evidence to support that such a worldview [the attitude

---

12. Schweitzer is the principal progenitor of this proposal; however it is also clear from the Gospel accounts that a number of key actors in the passion narratives – such as Pilate and Judas – were of a similar opinion.

13. Pompey, as part of his annexation of Syria to the Roman Empire, put an end to Hasmonaean independence in 63 BCE, making Judaea a client state. The dynasty itself came to an end in 37 BCE when Herod the Great became Rome's client king.

to "foreigners" reflected in Ezra–Nehemiah] governed the Yehudite polity and its discourse for any substantial period', and remarks that, on the contrary, references to 'acceptable' mixed marriages are frequent in literature attributable to this period'. If we turn to the Hellenistic age, we should focus on those biblical and deuterocanonical books – other than Ezra and Nehemiah – which belong (as far as can be ascertained) to the period after 300 BCE. The most likely candidates are: Books 4 and 5 of the Psalter, Qoheleth, and Sirach, together with a few of the twelve prophets (Joel, Obadiah, Haggai, Zechariah and Malachi). Job and Proverbs might be relevant, but their dating is simply too uncertain. Even Sirach is marginal in that it is later than 200 BCE, but there is some consensus that it was completed shortly before the onset of the Maccabean wars and reflects conditions and attitudes in Jerusalem in the last quarter of the third century BCE.

Perhaps the most intriguing datum is the fact that the name of Phineas is honoured in two places: Ps. 106.30 – a clear reference to the notorious incident in Num. 25.6-13 – and also in Sir. 45.23-24, where the strange granting to Phineas of a 'covenant of perpetual priesthood' is celebrated. It is of course possible that Ben Sira only includes this item by way of some kind of completeness, without intending any contemporary consequences. However, other biases – such as the exaggerated attention to Aaron and the long passage in praise of Ben Sira's contemporary Simon the Just – suggest that the praise of the ancestors was indeed intended to have implications for the present-day reality of the readers of Sirach. Ezra's ancestry is traced to Aaron via the same Phineas (Ezra 7.5),[14] which might suggest that the ritual denunciation of exogamy in post-exilic Judah which is implied in Numbers has become something of an accepted attitude. Neither Psalms nor Sirach are commonly linked to any particular sectarian interest, which implies that, regardless of broader attitudes to political and economic dealing with the surrounding peoples and ruling empires, Jewish society after 300 BCE was by consensus endogamic. One flourish in Mal. 2.11-12 might be further evidence of this, when the writer laments that 'Judah has been faithless, and abomination has been committed in Israel and in Jerusalem; for Judah has profaned the sanctuary of the Lord, which he loves, and has married the daughter of a foreign God. May the Lord cut off from the tents of Jacob anyone who does this.' Echoes (or anticipations?) of the strict policies of Ezra and Nehemiah are perhaps to be found here.

---

14. The name Phineas occurs twice more in Ezra (8.2 and 8.33), this time as an ancestor of Ezra's fellow returners from Babylon.

The only other Psalms material which might bear some consideration is, not surprisingly, Psalm 119, the great hymn celebrating Torah. There is extensive evidence in the written sources that the religion of Judah in our period was founded on the idea of a covenant with Yahweh expressed in the record of God's dealings with Israel in the Pentateuch. It remained, surely, a temple-based cult expressed popularly in the form of regular festivals; and given the almost certainly low levels of general literacy, we should not think of this as in any way analogous to modern forms of 'Bible-based' faith. The kind of ceremony envisaged in Nehemiah 8 is perhaps the closest we can come to understanding how such a religious tradition might have been expressed beyond the circles of the scribes and any other literati. However, there are a few references within Psalm 119 which might hint at some sort of tension. I refer to vv. 23-24, 46, and 161 where the writer of the psalm hints at opposition from aristocratic circles. This may simply be standard rhetoric, but since we know that by the middle of the second century BCE a popular movement was under way in opposition to the increasingly Hellenised Hasmoneans – a movement which can be understood in proto-Pharisaic terms – these verses might hint at the beginnings of such a trend at an earlier stage. The relevant texts are:

> Even though princes sit plotting against me,
>   your servant will meditate on your statutes.
> Your decrees are my delight,
>   they are my counsellors. (vv. 23-24)

> I will also speak of your decrees before kings,
>   and shall not be put to shame; (v. 46)

> Princes persecute me without cause,
>   but my heart stands in awe of your words. (v. 161)

Whatever the import of these verses, they still speak to a literate community – as indeed does the whole of Psalm 119 whose intricate alphabetical structure and focus on the word of the Torah can hardly have been part of any oral tradition. One last example from this psalm hints at another aspect of the religious world of the time when we read in v. 164 that 'seven times a day I praise you for your righteous ordinances'. This *might* refer to some kind of pious ritual, but it seems to be an isolated instance and is perhaps better understood as a rhetorical emphasis on the high value the writer places on God's teachings. Seven is of course a significant number; but historically rabbinic prayer is called for just three times a day: morning, afternoon and evening.

Turning to the prophetic books which I have singled out, there is evidence that some of them influenced Jonah. I refer of course to Joel, as discussed above, and the interesting use of Nineveh as a model wicked city in several of these prophetic books at a time long after it had ceased to be a place of any importance. Other pertinent indications are slight indeed. Apart from Mal. 2.11-12 cited above, the only other one which might have a bearing is Hag. 2.10-14, where the prophet resorts to purity laws in a metaphoric fashion:

> On the twenty-fourth day of the ninth month, in the second year of Darius, the word of the LORD came by the prophet Haggai, saying: Thus says the LORD of hosts: Ask the priests for a ruling: If one carries consecrated meat in the fold of one's garment, and with the fold touches bread, or stew, or wine, or oil, or any kind of food, does it become holy? The priests answered, 'No'. Then Haggai said, 'If one who is unclean by contact with a dead body touches any of these, does it become unclean?' The priests answered, 'Yes, it becomes unclean'. Haggai then said, 'So is it with this people, and with this nation before me, says the LORD; and so with every work of their hands; and what they offer there is unclean'.

If this bears any relationship to contemporary practice, and is more than simply a picturesque use of the purity regulations in Torah, its closest parallel seems to be with the essentially Priestly and Levitical practices which are occasionally referenced in Ezra and Nehemiah. It hardly counts as evidence for the personal purity rituals of a later period.

I turn lastly to Qoheleth and Sirach. While they are both regularly classed as 'wisdom' literature, they have little in common in terms of style and content. The former appears to present Solomon's reflections at the end of his richly privileged life: but what follows is deeply unsettling, effectively undermining all the verities which the name of Solomon was assumed to signify. Its pessimism – or resignation or fatalism – seems contrary to the mainstream of Hebrew scripture, something which has led many to see Greek philosophical influences, particularly that of Stoicism – an influence which is also suspected for Sirach. What is more likely is that, rather than direct borrowing, both writers were working in an intellectual milieu in which Hellenistic influences were pervasive.[15] Unlike Qoheleth, Ben Sira represents a quite conservative approach to traditional wisdom tropes, though in at least two ways he expresses opinions which

---

15. Aside from Stoicism, many commentators have proposed that Ben Sira's hymn to wisdom (ch. 24) is modelled on Egyptian-Greek Isis aretalogies (sacred biographies in the first person celebrating the goddess).

from the perspective of Rabbinic Judaism might be thought radical. The first is his insistence that he himself belongs to the succession of those who originated Israel's scriptures, being inspired by the Spirit of God. His ambition is that what he writes will be added to that body of sacred literature. The second is his identification of Torah with Wisdom in ch. 24, and a personification of Wisdom which comes close to representing her as a divine force. The opening chapters of Proverbs 1–9 come close to the same quasi-deification, so Ben Sira is not entirely without precedent. Nevertheless one wonders how the leaders of the Great Synagogue would have responded to such an elastic approach to Israel's covenant with the one God Yahweh.

Regarding the particular points emphasised in Ezra–Nehemiah, Qoheleth is silent and Sirach largely so. However there are two points at which the latter prompts further investigation. I have already noted one: the celebration of Phineas as one of the glorious ancestors, a rather disquieting reminder that disapproval of marriage outside the boundaries of the people (the *'am*) was widely frowned upon, to put it mildly. The other seems to run counter to the implication of that disturbing emphasis. For at the end of his review of the twelve prophets (little more than a passing mention) he turns to those responsible for the rebuilding of the temple (49.11-12), saying 'How shall we magnify Zerubbabel' and also Joshua. Then, as a (grudging?) footnote comes v. 13:

> The memory of Nehemiah also is lasting;
> > he raised our fallen walls,
> and set up gates and bars,
> > and rebuilt our ruined houses.

This strikes a somewhat bathetic note, bearing in mind the significance of Ezra–Nehemiah for the future of Judaism. Ezra is entirely absent and Nehemiah is a kind of clerk of works, albeit an important one. Not only does Sirach having nothing to report about the social and religious concerns of these notable reformers, he seems to be magnificently unaware of them. This raises a possibility which has on occasion been considered: that the form of Ezra–Nehemiah which we now have is one which was an expanded version of an original narrative concerned only with the joint enterprises of the rebuilding of the Temple and the repair of the city walls. It seems unlikely that this speculation will ever be substantiated, but it would certainly help to explain what this brief resume seems to suggest: that generally speaking in the period 400 to 200 BCE, apart from a consensus about the importance of not marrying out of the community, the focus of the Jerusalem cult was a Torah-based popular religion centred on regular festivals, priestly-controlled sacrifices, and an awareness of the importance of Yahweh's lasting $b^e rit$ or covenant with Israel. There are no signs of the much more prescriptive personal religion of the post-Maccabean era, and there is no disputing the importance of working creatively with whatever greater power is for the time being the ultimate guarantor of Judah's security in return for a peaceable acknowledgement of the realpolitik. It is perhaps worth recalling in this regard that Ben Sirah was on his own account a diplomat who moved in high circles and was widely travelled. An agent of the Tobiads, perhaps? Or, given his compelling interest in cultic matters, a representative of the High Priest's office? It is within these parameters that we must somehow understand the rhetoric which lies behind the curious story of Jonah.

An Archaeological Footnote
I have one last piece to add to this jigsaw, based on the work of Israel Finkelstein. Finkelstein's archaeological work is rightly esteemed. He is a convinced exponent of the basic rule that when attempting to evaluate the historical material in the biblical texts, archaeological data should take precedence. He has a sharp eye for the vicious circle in which assumptions about the unassailability of the Bible are used to interpret sites on the ground, which then appear as support for the accuracy of said texts. In recent years he has been examining various aspects of historically testable material in Ezra, Nehemiah and Chronicles; these have now been published as a collection of seven essays: *Hasmonean Realities behind Ezra, Nehemiah, and Chronicles* (2018). If his findings are to be relied upon (and they have been tested over several years and numbers of reviews), they introduce startling evidence which bears indirectly but nonetheless pertinently on the matter of this chapter.

The essential archaeological material relates to evidence for settlement in Yehud in the Persian, and in the early and later Hellenistic periods. Finkelstein's particular accounts concern:

(1) The walls supposedly constructed under Nehemiah;
(2) The locations associated with the lists of returnees in Ezra and Nehemiah;
(3) The extent of Yehud on the basis of geographical lists in Ezra and Nehemiah;
(4) The identity of Nehemiah's adversaries;

(5) The historical reality behind the genealogical lists in 1 Chronicles 2–9;
(6) The list of cities ostensibly fortified by Rehoboam in 2 Chron. 11.5-12
(7) Accounts of the expansion of Judah in 2 Chronicles.

In all of these cases Finkelstein concludes that the archaeological evidence renders both the ostensible settings (that is, in the period around 400 BCE) and the historical information in Chronicles, improbable in the extreme. On the basis of his detailed surveys of settlement evidence he argues that Jerusalem was essentially a large village of some 400 people in the Persian period, with no more than 12,000 in Yehud as whole. Only in the Hasmonean period did population levels recover to those of the seventh century. He concludes that the data under discussion in the books in question are better suited to the period around the reign of John Hyrcanus. While he leaves open the origins of the earliest portions of the books, he nevertheless sounds a note of caution when he observes that the population prior to the Hasmonean period was unlikely to have sustained any significant literary activity.

It would be an understatement to say that Finkelstein's findings are surprising. If correct, they pose a stark challenge to many scholarly assumptions about the nature of the Judaean state in the Persian and early Hellenistic period, and force a rethinking of hypotheses regarding the cultural contexts for textual work in the second temple period. The implications are more radical than those proposed by those who have argued for an extensive enterprise of text formation, collection and editing in the Persian period; for if Finkelstein is correct, the earliest post-exilic era in which a sufficiently developed scribal activity can be realistically posited turns out to be some time after 200 BCE. This is not to rule out any such work at an earlier time, but it is likely to have been limited: little more, perhaps, than the care of (perhaps copying of) texts which survived the fall of Jerusalem or were brought back to the temple by those who chose to return from Babylonia. By contrast, we now have evidence both from the Dead Sea and (indirectly) from Ezra, Nehemiah, and Chronicles, of literary activity in the Hasmonean era.

A Tentative Conclusion
Certainly the foregoing observations are not the last word on questions of dating. The proposition of a school of scripture formation in the Persian period is by no means uncontroversial. My own position is that there are strong grounds in favour of it, but a serious evaluation is beyond the

scope this volume. Equally, the evidence for Hellenistic era textual work is persuasive though not conclusive, and the archaeological witness is difficult to assess. Finkelstein has been challenged robustly – and equally robustly responded. For the purposes of this study, it is enough to note that the end-point of 200 BCE is now rather porous, and the convention of a Yehud setting for much of the post-exilic scripture-forming activity will have to be re-examined, with a focus perhaps more on the fourth and third centuries BCE than on the fifth and fourth. What this implies for Jonah is a stronger possibility of an educated scribal author working in the relatively stable context of the late third century BCE, whose drama is certainly directed at identifiable circles in Jerusalem: a Jerusalem, however, where the big issues are probably political rather than sectarian. I propose, in short, a setting at the point where allegiances were being reviewed and the need to make canny decisions about the future external governance of Judah was urgent.

Chapter 1

The First Place: Nineveh

The selection of Nineveh as the object of God's wrath, and the prophet's commission to warn the city of its impending fate, constitute a significant mystery in the book of Jonah. Since the place itself was a ruin, or at best a small settlement, when the book was composed, its significance must be symbolic. But symbolic of what? Unlike Babylon, which is a frequent biblical metonym for all kinds of badness, Nineveh is not used in this way – with the significant exception of the Nahum and Zephaniah, of which more shortly. Whereas Babylon is also taken up by the New Testament, especially in the book of Revelation, and becomes in later Christian tradition a 'whore' who represents whichever faction one wishes to attack,[1] the only references to Nineveh in the New Testament are in Mt. 12.38-42 and its parallel in Lk. 11.29-32. Here the intention is not to point out the evils of Nineveh, but to draw a comparison between Jonah and Jesus as signs to 'an evil generation' (whether in ancient Assyria or contemporary Judaea). The fact that reference in the gospels to 'an evil generation' does not imply some distant malign entity, but rather the very people with whom Jesus engages, and with whose antagonism the early Christian community had to cope, suggests a possibility regarding Nineveh in Jonah which I will return to shortly.

Jonah's Sources and Nineveh: Nahum and Zephaniah

As we have already seen in the Introduction, the indications are persuasive that Jonah is rather a late composition, perhaps some time in the later Persian or early Hellenistic era – a deduction supported by the intensity of its intertextual engagement with many passages in all three of the

---

1. See https://en.wikipedia.org/wiki/Whore_of_Babylon for examples.

divisions of Tanakh. In turn this implies that the author likely knew Nahum and Zephaniah with their traditional prophetic rhetoric. Though the relationship (if any) between texts in the Bible can never be finally determined, the evidence of shared ideas and tropes can inform our discussion: thus a brief consideration of these two prophets will be helpful in trying to decode Jonah's use of Nineveh.

Nahum's brief collection of oracles announces itself unequivocally as *massa' nyn^{e}veh*, 'an oracle [literally, "something raised up"] of Nineveh'. Though the heading may well be a subsequent addition, it is clear from two references to Nineveh (2.8 and 3.7) and one to the king of Assyria (3.18) that a specific target is intended:

> Nineveh is like a pool
>   whose waters run away (2.8)
>
> Then all who see you will shrink from you and say
> Nineveh is devastated: who will bemoan her? (3.7)
>
> Your shepherds are asleep,
>   O king of Assyria:
>   your nobles slumber.
> Your people are scattered on the mountains
>   with no one to gather them.[2] (3.18)

The most obvious historical reference point would be the destruction of Israel in 721 BCE; the comparison in 3.8-10 with the fall of Egypt can perhaps be correlated with Assyrian attempts (not without success) to control Egypt in the first half of the seventh century BCE. However, Nah. 1.15 ('Look! On the mountains the feet of one / who brings good tidings, / who proclaims peace') clearly echoes a repeated motif in Isaiah (40.9; 41.27; and especially 52.7: 'How beautiful upon the mountains / are the feet of the messenger who announces peace'). The same passage looks forward to the restoration of Judah together with an afterthought on the subject of Jacob and Israel, suggesting a dating in the early post-exilic period.

> Celebrate your festivals, O Judah,
>   fulfil your vows,
> for never again shall the wicked invade you;
>   they are utterly cut off. (1.15b)

---

2. An interesting echo of Micaiah's warning to the king of Israel in 1 Kgs 22.17.

> For the Lord is restoring the majesty of Jacob,
>   as well as the majesty of Israel. (2.2a)

That being so, the same problem exists as with Jonah: Why Assyria, why Nineveh, at a time when its empire was long vanished? Even if there were an 'ur-Nahum' dating from the eighth century, why update it in an age when the most recent threat was Babylon, and even that was by then a fait accompli rather than an enemy to be confronted? Perhaps therefore there is a similar solution to both riddles, located somewhere in the realm of comfortably remote symbolic monsters being redeployed to damn contemporary miscreants.

Nahum sounds very much like the kind of oracle Jonah would have been expected to proclaim had he followed the regular prophetic job description. Fairly obviously, had a Hebrew prophet in the real world made it to Nineveh and unburdened himself of the rant that is Nahum, he would have been lucky to have escaped with his life, far less live to see the success of his preaching. This is of course part of the irony of the book of Jonah, the tale of a prophet whose success in this most unlikely of ventures is surely at some level satirical. Another reversal has been pointed out by commentators: the one clear shared intertext between Nahum and Jonah is that both refer to the classic definition of the mercy and love and faithfulness of Yahweh in Exod. 34.6-7. However, they each cite it partially, and to opposite effect. In Nah. 1.3 we read:

> The Lord is slow to anger but great in power,
> and the Lord will by no means clear the guilty

(One line is taken from Exod. 34.6 and one from 34.7). In Jon. 4.2, on the other hand, we find this:

> I knew that you are a gracious God and merciful, slow to anger, and abounding in steadfast love, and ready to relent from punishing. (Exod. 34.6)

Both citations add their own 'improvements': 'great in power' in Nahum, and 'ready to relent from punishing' in Jonah. Each undoubtedly signals the Exodus passage, but to quite opposite effect. A nice example from antiquity of the perils of selective citation of scripture!

The reference to Nineveh in Zeph. 2.13 is far less integral to that work, which actually focuses on the sins of Jerusalem and its elite. The introductory verse dates this oracle to the reign of Josiah, when Judah was caught up in the struggles between Egypt and Babylon over the putative corpse of Assyria. Josiah himself, as is well known, paid the price for backing Babylon prematurely, dying at the hands of the Egyptian forces at the battle of Megiddo (609 BCE). The vituperative tone of Zephaniah's preaching is somewhat at odds with Josiah's reputation as a great religious reformer (2 Kgs 22.1–23.30). It would be more apt as a condemnation of his successors. Or perhaps Zephaniah is witness to a different narrative about Josiah's reign, in which a faction disenchanted by his 'reforms' mounts a counter-offensive. Whatever the truth, the section on the laying waste of surrounding nations (2.4-15) is a not-inaccurate description of the general disruption brought about, almost incidentally, by the campaigns of the major political players Egypt, Assyria and Babylon leading to the establishment by 612 of the neo-Babylonian Empire as successor to that of Assyria. On a minor note, the use of the term 'Cushites' (or Nubians) in Zeph. 2.12 and Nah. 3.9 in passages dealing with Egypt perhaps displays awareness of the Nubian 25th Dynasty which was toppled by the Assyrians in 656 BCE.

This disquisition on two minor prophets perhaps only loosely associated with Jonah may appear to have little more than glancing significance for an understanding of the book. However, several aspects prompt a more structured connection. Firstly, the author of Jonah has sourced several pieces of his Jonah jigsaw from fairly marginal scriptures. We have already noted that the prophet's name is probably borrowed from a passing (and tantalisingly brief) note in 2 Kgs 14.25. The location of Joppa as Jerusalem's port is only mentioned twice, in Ezra 3.7 and 2 Chron. 2.16. Tarshish is a famously elusive destination, having perhaps exotic appeal. And the flora and fauna which populate three of the four chapters suggest a writer with a certain dilettante wit.

Secondly, the politically and cultically fluid situation in Jerusalem from around 550 to 400 BCE, which only began to be clarified with the activities of Ezra and Nehemiah, provides a plausible context for a series of works of a more or less polemical character supporting various templates for the future of Israel's communal life. The Deuteronomistic project and that of the Chronicler are two of the most obvious examples. Whether the strict Torah-based cult, and the social emphasis on ethnic purity and religious observance which seems to have been Ezra's agenda, was the last word may be open to doubt, as we have seen in the Introduction; but what is not in doubt is the combative and conflicting nature of many of the canonical texts which originated in the Persian and early Hellenistic periods of Judah's post-exilic history. It is not surprising to find texts such as Nahum, Jonah and others emerging from this creative melting pot. They should never be taken at face value.

Summing up these various points, I conclude on reflection that Zephaniah's reference to Nineveh, while interesting in the context of its own rhetoric, is not directly germane to Jonah. The Assyrian city constitutes just one example in an exemplary list of nations whom Yahweh has punished, by way of a warning to Judah of a similar impending fate. While it is undoubtedly noteworthy that this seems to be in the setting of Josiah's reforming regime, this is not a likely background for Jonah; moreover in Jonah the whole focus is on the fate of Nineveh.

Nahum provides a much more pertinent parallel. The whole oracle is focused on Nineveh, and is certainly, in the form in which it entered the canon, to be dated well into the post-exilic period, as the brief oracle relating to Judah and Israel in 1.15–2.2 shows, with its prophecy of restoration and its citation of Deutero-Isaiah. It also (as I noted above) deploys in a significantly partial way the famous self-description of Yahweh from Exod. 34.6-7. Each of these points is mirrored in one way or another in Jonah. His book too is wholly concerned with Nineveh (at least as far as Jonah's prophetic calling is concerned). It is surely late post-exilic – I have already indicated my personal inclination to a date at the earliest in the late fourth century BCE, and perhaps far later. And Jonah too makes use of part of Exod. 34.6-7. Nahum, perhaps conventionally, uses this passage to justify a well-deserved punishment for Nineveh; Jonah, perhaps unconventionally, uses the same passage to hold Yahweh to account for his wilful and arbitrary decision to spare the city. I think there are good grounds (supported more generally by Jonah's well-known deployment of many passages from Tanakh) to propose that the author of Jonah took a lead from Nahum in working out his story, but deliberately reversed it.

Jonah's Psychogeography[3]

For all that Jonah is supposedly about a prophet who journeys to a far distant land, there are many indicators of a much more localised context. Obviously the opening scene is somewhere in Judah. The putative source

---

3. Psychogeography was described in the 1950s as an exploration of urban environments emphasising playfulness and 'drifting'. In recent decades it has been adopted by British writers such as Iain Sinclair and Peter Ackroyd in relation especially to the flaneur-like exploration of London on foot (see https://en.wikipedia.org/wiki/Psychogeography). My choice of title for this book reflects the expression of that philosophy in China Miéville's *The City and the City*, or even more surreally in his *The Last Days of New Paris*. See, for example, https://www.lancaster.ac.uk/luminary/issue%207/Article%206.pdf. I am reminded also of Alasdair Gray's gothic metamorphosis of Glasgow as Unthank in his masterly *Lanark*.

in 2 Kgs 14.25 gives his town as Gath-hepher. One of many place names otherwise unknown, tradition locates this village in Galilee, though that identification is surely speculative. It is more than probable that the author of Jonah knew nothing of Gath-hepher and so quietly dropped it from the citation. Whatever his place of residence, which I will return to later, it was logical to use Joppa as the seaport for his flight from Yahweh's importunate demand.

When Jonah is asked by the sailors for some ID he responds in a somewhat unusual fashion. Avoiding a direct answer ('I'm Jonah, and I come from Gath-hepher') he uses a late form of ethnic self-definition ('I am a Hebrew') and specifies his religious affiliation ('I worship Yahweh, the God of heaven, who made the sea and the dry land') in a form clearly belonging to the Jerusalem cultus, but unique in its precise formulation. Neither the reader, nor evidently the sailors (whose responses indicate a knowledge of the God of the Hebrews), can have any doubt as to his ethnic and religious loyalties.

Jonah's prayer from his fishy refuge is remarkably intertwined with both the language of the Psalms and accounts of the Exodus from Egypt, in particular the crossing of the sea. But more significantly, the deepest loss felt by the prophet is the sight of the Temple in 2.4: 'How shall I look *again* upon your holy Temple?' (my emphasis). Later, his deliverance is achieved when his prayer 'came to [God], into [God's] holy temple'. We are being directed here to the thought that, in his everyday life, Jonah lives either in Jerusalem or close enough for regular visits to the temple.

After the delivery of his ultimatum to Nineveh Jonah repairs to a location east of the city from which he appears to have a view of the place sufficiently panoramic to enable him to watch its fate. While nothing is said directly about the elevation of this vantage point, it is not irrelevant to note that there could have been no such possibility in the plain where Nineveh was situated. However there is to this day a well-known view point to the east of and above the old city of Jerusalem which affords a clear sight of the city and of the temple area. To anyone familiar with the city this location by the Mount of Olives springs readily to mind as the setting for Jon. 4.5 and following.

In other words, I want to make the case that, since Jonah's travels are fabular, his destination has symbolic or psychogeographical rather than geographical significance. So far so uncontroversial. It is when we come to determine *what* that significance might be that things become more interesting. A supplementary question is: Are his two journeys incidental, merely a means to the symbolic end, or do they constitute part of that symbolism. The answer to the second question is unequivocally: Yes, they are profoundly meaningful to the overall intention of the book, and any proposal as to what that intention might be has to take this narrative process into account. In the course of the detailed commentary I shall show that, worked into the ongoing narrative, there are intimate and revealing explorations of a series of key aspects of Israel's *Heilsgeschichte* (history of salvation is the usual, perhaps too pious translation). It might be tempting, then, to go down the traditional route of reading the prophet Jonah as a kind of embodiment of Israel. But I want to resist that choice, not least because Jonah is certainly presented as a prophet, however unorthodox (see the Introduction), but also because taking Jonah to be a cipher for Israel has also too often resulted in the polarisation of Jonah/Israel/universalism versus Pharisee/Judaean/nationalism which has been responsible for readings which come perilously close to antisemitism.[4]

His experiences belong to the type of dramatic prophetic action which can be found in Isaiah, Jeremiah and Ezekiel, and in enduring them his function is to instruct the faithful – or more accurately the errant faithful. He himself is not changed by these events, nor is there any intention that he should be. Jonah's role, like that of all prophets, is to proclaim, and as such he is merely a vessel to be discarded when his usefulness is over. This is not to say that such prophets willingly accept this implication. Jeremiah's complaints, Elijah's flight and death-wish, and Jonah's sulk point to a human reluctance to be side-lined. But to little avail. Immediately after Elijah's vision on Mount Horeb his successor Elisha is introduced, and not long after that he is whisked off to heaven; Jeremiah's prize for his service of Yahweh is to be sent off to obscurity in Egypt; and Jonah is left alone on a hillside, bested by a beetle and a bovine herd. Moreover, it is not clear that their anguished questions to God are taken seriously, far less answered. On the other hand, figures who in some way embody the people of God such as Noah, Abraham and the Patriarchs, Moses, and David all experience God's blessing and are key players in the various incarnations of the divine covenant.[5]

Everything about Jonah's ordeals points to Jerusalem, where his careful readers must have been situated. His role as prophet is a familiar one, leading to an expectation that whatever its supposed target, what he had

---

4. See Sherwood (pp. 21–32) for a clear account of the reformation's trend towards antisemitism in respect of Jonah.

5. Should we count Ezra also amongst their company? That is unclear in terms of Tanakh, but surely a resounding 'yes' from the perspective of Rabbinic Judaism: Pirke Avot is a strong witness here as it traces the rabbinic succession all the way from Moses to the time of the Mishnah via the 'men of the great assembly' (a reference to Ezra) then Simeon the Righteous down to their present day (see Pirke Avot ch. 1). For the continuing importance of Ezra see, for example, https://www.chabad.org/library/article_cdo/aid/4166669/jewish/Ezra-the-Scribe.htm.

to say (either as the character Jonah or as the voice of the author of the book) was for their benefit. They could not have failed to 'read' Nineveh as a code for Jerusalem; its 'king' as the current ruling establishment. Therefore we need not tie ourselves up in knots about universalism versus chauvinism, or liberal versus conservative versions of Yahwism. Like virtually all of his comparators, past and present, Jonah the prophet does not direct his warnings to distant lands or remote peoples; nor do prophets generally travel to pronounce their warnings. Certainly many prophetic books contain oracles against various other nations, but these are not really calls on them to repent. Rather they are *either* self-indulgent descriptions of the inexorable fate of God's enemies, *or* salutary warnings to Israel. Though Amos journeys from Judah to Israel, that is hardly more adventurous than a trip from Carlisle to Glasgow; other exiled prophets such as Jeremiah and Ezekiel did not travel in order to preach – they took up their vocation where they happened to have been placed. In Jonah's case, that was surely Jerusalem, something which will become gradually clearer as I progress through the book. First of all, I want to examine in closer detail a number of parallels and intertexts that will contribute to my exploration of the question, Why Nineveh?

Genesis: Punishment of the Wicked

In the Introduction I referred briefly to Jonathan Magonet's proposal to link the warning that 'Nineveh will be overthrown' with other similar uses of the Hebrew verb (*hapakh*). His starting point was the observation that when used of the overthrow of a city this verb points firmly to the legend of Sodom and Gomorrah and its echoes in a number of biblical passages. He also notes another formulation with important connections to Genesis: namely the combination of two forms suggesting the presence of evil and violence (*ra'ah* and *chamas*) in Jon. 3.8. If these two can be substantiated as probable intertexts for Jonah important consequences follow. A brief consideration of each is therefore in order. Magonet's suggestion that the author makes use of the Sodom and Gomorrah legend and the flood narrative reinforces the sense of something stronger than merely echoes of traditional tales. Hence the fact that Jonah belongs to a rather select group of passages linking evildoing and violence points to deliberate device designed to be understood by the knowledgeable reader.

One further observation is apposite. The two legends of 'destruction of the wicked' in Genesis deploy, as I have remarked, two mechanisms: water and heat leading to different, but equally devastating, forms of barrenness. And in Jonah the prophet's two acts of rebellion are similarly punished: his flight to Tarshish ends with him drowning in the watery depths, only surviving because of the 'ark' in the form of the great sea creature, while his accusation that Yahweh is far too soft-hearted leads to his being afflicted by the scorching sun, burning wind, and a wild creature which devastates the only protection he has. Two further observations suggest themselves: a rather satisfactory parallelism between Jonah 1+2 and 3+4 in the light of Genesis; and a perhaps overly speculative thought that the curious case of the many cattle is a nod to the original ark which saved not just humankind but the whole of the (animal) created order.

Water

I begin with the flood-related pairing of evil and violence. The occurrence of these together is remarkably rare – I can find only six relevant instances – and in order to tease out the significance, if any, of these associations I must trouble the reader to bear with some rather tedious detail.

1. The combination of 'evil and violence' in close proximity in a semantically meaningful way is surprisingly uncommon. The locus identified by Magonet is the opening of the flood narrative in Gen. 6.5-13: here the word for evil occurs in v. 5, 'The Lord saw that the *wickedness* of humankind was great in the earth', prompting God's intention to blot them out. In the reiteration of this causal mechanism in vv. 11-13, the term for violence figures twice: 'the earth was filled with *violence*'.
2. In Exod. 23.1 we find a specific commandment which uses both terms: 'You shall not join hands with the *wicked* to act as a *malicious* witness'.
3. Isaiah 59.6-7, within a more extensive description of the many crimes of the people, includes the accusation that 'Their works are works of *iniquity*, / and deeds of *violence* are in their hands'.
4. An oracle in Jer. 6.7 employs both terms to describe the corruption of Jerusalem as a result of which Yahweh has condemned her: 'As a well keeps its water fresh, / so she keeps fresh her *wickedness*; / *violence* and destruction are heard within her'.
5. Ezekiel 7.23-24 has some resonance: 'For the land is full of bloody crimes; / the city is full of *violence*'. The next verse warns that they will be handed over to 'the wickedness of the nations'.
6. A brief oracle in Amos 6.3 describing the complacency of the leadership in Samarian and Zion may be noted: 'O you that put far away the *evil* day, / and bring near a reign of *violence*'.

7. Psalm 55, which will be the subject of a detailed analysis later (Chapter 9), has in my estimation important connections with Jonah. It is interesting then to find these terms bracketing the section in that song which appeals to the Lord to dispose of the psalmist's enemies: 'Confuse, O Lord, confound their speech; / for I see *violence* and strife in the city' (v. 9); 'Let death come upon them; / let them go down alive to Sheol; / for *evil* is in their homes and in their hearts' (v. 15).
8. Psalm 140.1-4. While the opening verses of Psalm 140 deal with a set of familiar complaints, as indeed does the passage discussed in Psalm 55, they share with that Psalm an interesting bracketing effect: 'Deliver me, O Lord, from *evil*-doers / protect me from those who are *violent* / who plan *evil things* in their mind' (vv. 1-2a); 'Guard me, O Lord, from the hands of the wicked, / protect me from the *violent*' (v. 4)
9. Proverbs 4.16-17 describes evildoers graphically as those who 'cannot sleep unless they have *done wrong*; / they are robbed of sleep unless they have made someone stumble. / For they eat the bread of wickedness / and drink the wine of *violence*.'

It is immediately striking that all of these deal with violence and evil *within* the body of God's people. Admittedly the flood narrative precedes the biblical origins of Israel as a specific entity, but it patently belongs to the timeline of the salvation-history narrative, and the fact that the first covenant is deemed to be that of God with Noah surely demands that we take this passage as part of that process. In the biblical perspective, of course, humankind was a single undifferentiated whole between Adam and Noah: only with the genealogy of Genesis 10 is the concept of peoples introduced – something which is indeed reinforced by the legend of the tower of Babel (Gen. 11.6: 'The Lord said, "Look, they are one people, and they have all one language"').

Regarding which of these might be prime sources for Jonah – apart from Genesis – I am inclined to put the two Psalms passages first, partly on the grounds of the discussion of Psalm 55 in Chapter 10, but more importantly because the whole focus of Jonah 2 is on psalms – including the song of the sea embedded in Exodus 15. A possible further cue might be found in Ezekiel 7, since a number of commentators have proposed influences from Ezekiel in Jonah 1. Magonet is somewhat dismissive of these, but they remain tantalising.

Fire

Regarding Sodom and Gomorrah and the verb 'to overthrow', the evidence is rather broader, but is still I think indicative of purpose. The foundational legend[6] as it is presented in Tanakh runs through Genesis 10 to 19, though the main focus in relation to Jonah is ch. 19 where the 'overthrow' of the various cities is spoken of in vv. 21, 25 and 29. Magonet points to a link between 'to overthrow' and 'cities'; however, I want to extend the scope somewhat to include reference to the four 'cities of the plains' which were subject to obliteration in Genesis 19. In passing it may be of interest that Yahweh, having promised at the end of the flood narrative never again to use water as a means of destruction, seems quite happy to resort to fire, pitch, sulphur and salt. My choice of relevant passages depends on two criteria:

(1) Jonathan Magonet's list of references where the threat to 'overturn' a significant centre of population is either cited or made. He explicitly excludes one (2 Sam. 10.3 = 1 Chron. 19.3) which reports the fear of the king of Ammon that David's ostensible desire to pay tribute to the new king's father is a cover for his intention to spy on and overthrow the city. I shall include it for completeness, but note that it is clearly an outlier, with little connection to the others. Magonet further observes that all of these either explicitly or implicitly refer to the fate of Sodom and Gomorrah.

(2) Other passages beyond Magonet's list including the citation of *either* 'overthrow' (*hapakh*) *or* one or more of the four cities in Genesis.

In parenthesis, before I explore further this network of scriptures, I want to emphasise that what is at stake here is not a claim that the book of Jonah explicitly adverts to them individually, but rather an appeal to the concept of *register* as a means recognising the way language functions not in terms of specific forms and genres but in relation to the social context(s) of the author and readers.[7] The term is perhaps rather generalised, and

---

6. As always there is uncertainty as to priority: it could be that underlying traditions surfaced in the references to these places in other scriptures, with the Genesis material a subsequent deployment for the purposes of the post-exilic Abraham material. For our immediate purposes this is not important, since we are working with the assumption that the author of Jonah knew a body of scripture rather similar to what later became Tanakh.

7. My immediate source for this concept is Vayntrub, p. 89.

has been criticised on the grounds that it can mean everything or nothing; nevertheless it offers a helpful way of describing how Jonah taps into an extensive set of shared references. Some of these are undoubtedly intertextual *sensu strictu*, but others belong to a more nebulous but still palpable range of familiar tropes available to the first readers. It is in this sense that I want to argue that both the flood legend and the Sodom and Gomorrah narrative are tacitly appealed to in Jonah in a way that would have resonated for them. In the following passages, significant terms and phrases are underlined.

A. *Magonet's List*

Gen. 19.21, 24-29

> He said to him, 'Very well, I grant you this favour too, and will not <u>overthrow</u> the city of which you have spoken.... Then the LORD rained on <u>Sodom and Gomorrah</u> <u>sulphur</u> and <u>fire</u> from the LORD out of heaven; and he <u>overthrew</u> those cities, and all the Plain, and all the inhabitants of the cities, <u>and what grew on the ground</u>. But Lot's wife, behind him, looked back, and she became a pillar of <u>salt</u>. Abraham went early in the morning to the place where he had stood before the LORD; and he looked down toward <u>Sodom and Gomorrah</u> and toward all the land of the Plain and saw the smoke of the land going up like the smoke of a furnace. So it was that, when God destroyed the cities of the Plain, God remembered Abraham, and sent Lot out of the midst of the <u>overthrow</u>, when he <u>overthrew</u> the cities in which Lot had settled.

As the foundation legend (though see n. 6 above) these verses provide the motifs which we should expect in further iterations: (a) the named cities of the plains; (b) the verb *hapakh*, 'to overthrow'; (c) the means of destruction – sulphur (*gafrit*), fire (*'esh*), and salt (*melakh*); and (d) the consequence of utter barrenness – implied rather than explicitly stated in this version, though arguably the note in v. 28 that Abraham 'saw the smoke of the land going up like the smoke of a furnace' leaves little doubt.

Deut. 29.22-23

> The next generation, your children who rise up after you, as well as the foreigner who comes from a distant country, will see the devastation of that land and the afflictions with which the LORD has afflicted it – all its soil burned out by <u>sulphur</u> and <u>salt</u>, nothing planted, nothing sprouting, <u>unable to support any vegetation</u>, like the <u>destruction</u> of <u>Sodom and Gomorrah, Admah and Zeboiim</u>, which the LORD <u>destroyed</u> in his fierce anger.

This passage from the series of curses and warnings of the consequences of unfaithfulness in Deuteronomy ticks all the boxes from Genesis 19: all four 'cities of the plain'; sulphur and salt; *hapakh* (translated as 'destruction' and 'destroyed' here); and explicit barrenness. The further item which we should expect is the target of God's wrath: in this case, the unfaithful in Israel.

Isa. 13.19-20

> And Babylon, the glory of kingdoms,
> > the splendour and pride of the Chaldeans,
> will be like Sodom and Gomorrah
> > when God overthrew them.
> It will never be inhabited
> > or lived in for all generations.

This is a somewhat less engaged iteration. It belongs to the tradition of oracles against nations, and lacks something of the visceral feeling which is perceptible in Deuteronomy 29. The target is Babylon, the two principal cities are named, *hapakh* is used, and barrenness is a permanent consequence.

Isa. 34.9-10

> And the streams of Edom shall be turned into pitch,
> > and her soil into sulphur;
> > her land shall become burning pitch.
> Night and day it shall not be quenched;
> > its smoke shall go up for ever.
> From generation to generation it shall lie waste;
> > no one shall pass through it for ever and ever.

There is a distinction to be drawn between oracles against distant powers, such as Babylon, Assyria and Egypt, and close neighbours who were surely perceived to belong to a similar cultural ethos. This threat to Edom is of that kind, though its use of the core legend is rather loose. It is her streams which will be turned (*hapakh*) to pitch (*zefeth* – a word only found in one other place as an element of the waterproofing of Moses' basket in Exod. 2.3), her soil to sulphur, and permanent barrenness is foretold. There is a greater sense of vitriol in the wording here, though the cities of the plain are only present by implication.

Jer. 20.15

> Cursed be the man
> > who brought the news to my father, saying,
>
> 'A child is born to you, a son',
> > making him very glad.
>
> Let that man be like the <u>cities</u>
> > that the LORD <u>overthrew</u> without pity

Though the legend of Genesis 19 is certainly present here, its application is at the limits of metaphoric distance, as it serves as a self-satisfying gesture by the prophet against his ever having been born. This is no doubt a feature of the Elijah and Jonah stories – but these both lack the trope of 'cursed be the bearer of news'.

Jer. 49.17-18

> Edom shall become an object of horror; everyone who passes by it will be horrified and will hiss because of all its disasters. As when <u>Sodom and Gomorrah and their neighbours</u> were <u>overthrown,</u> says the LORD, <u>no one shall live there, nor shall anyone settle in it</u>.

In an echo of Isaiah 34 we have here another 'local' oracle against Edom. The cities are named, they are overthrown, and barrenness follows. Perhaps we sense here something of the character of a gestural rather than visceral threat.

Jer. 50.39-40

> Therefore wild animals shall live with hyenas [in Babylon*], and ostriches shall inhabit her; <u>she shall never again be peopled, or inhabited for all generations</u>. As when God <u>overthrew</u> <u>Sodom and Gomorrah and their neighbours,</u> says the LORD, so no one shall live there, nor shall anyone settle in her.
>
> [*'In Babylon' is not in the Hebrew, but is implied by the context.]

An oracle against Babylon which, like Isaiah 13, reports rather than engages with the overthrow of Babylon and its barrenness. It is interesting to note that, where there might be geographical support for the tale of abandoned cities on the inhospitable shore of the Dead (Salt) Sea, the metaphor becomes largely symbolic in many of its subsequent iterations. It does of course segue ultimately into the exilic 'myth of the empty land' which populates many of the texts of that period. Thus we should make a distinction between the formal barrenness of the likes of Babylon and Edom and the theologically invested denaturing of Israel.

Amos 4.11

> I <u>overthrew</u> some of you,
>> as when God <u>overthrew</u> <u>Sodom and Gomorrah</u>,
>> and you were like a brand snatched from the <u>fire</u>;
> yet you did not return to me,
> says the LORD.

This is at the limits of meaningful usage, serving only as a loose metaphor for God's attempt to push Israel into some recognition of its apostasy with a view to redemption.

Lam. 4.6-8

> For the chastisement of my people has been greater
>> than the punishment of <u>Sodom</u>,
> which was <u>overthrown</u> in a moment,
>> though no hand was laid on it.
> Her princes were purer than snow,
>> whiter than milk;
> their bodies were more ruddy than coral,
>> their hair like sapphire.
> Now their visage is blacker than soot;
>> they are not recognized in the streets.
> Their skin has shrivelled on their bones;
>> it has become as dry as wood.

Only Sodom is cited here, but the writer takes an unusually graphic turn by offering us a pen portrait rather reminiscent (or, more accurately, anticipatory) of images of the fate of the inhabitants of Pompeii and Herculaneum, or those of Hiroshima and Nagasaki. The other feature which seems pointed in this account, and which might resonate with Jonah, is the focus on the pampered elite and their frightful transformation to, in effect, walking skeletons.

B. *Secondary Texts*

Deut. 32.31-32

> Our enemies are fools
> their vine comes from the vine-stock of <u>Sodom</u>,
>> from the vineyards of <u>Gomorrah</u>;
> their grapes are grapes of poison,
>> their clusters are bitter.

Apart from the use of Sodom and Gomorrah as code words for wicked places, there is nothing left here of the original story.

Isa. 1.7-10

> <u>Your country lies desolate</u>,
> > your cities are burned with <u>fire</u>;
> in your very presence
> > aliens devour your land;
> > <u>it is desolate</u>, as <u>overthrown</u> by foreigners.
> And daughter Zion is left
> > like a booth in a vineyard,
> like a shelter in a cucumber field,
> > like a besieged city.
> If the LORD of hosts
> > had not left us a few survivors,
> we would have been like <u>Sodom</u>,
> > and become like <u>Gomorrah</u>.
> Hear the word of the LORD,
> > you rulers of <u>Sodom</u>!
> Listen to the teaching of our God,
> > you people of <u>Gomorrah</u>!

[There follows a lengthy denunciation of Israel's cultic festivals and ceremonies]

Many of the key motifs are referenced here in a passage which makes creative use of the Genesis legend, turning it into a denunciation of the leaders and people of Jerusalem (cf. Lam. 4.6-8 above for a similar tactic). The extension into a denunciation of false ritual and worship shows the flexibility of the original as it is engrossed into a typically Isaianic oracle.

Isa. 3.8-9

> For Jerusalem has stumbled
> > and Judah has fallen,
> because their speech and their deeds are against the LORD,
> > defying his glorious presence.
> The look on their faces bears witness against them;
> > they proclaim their sin like <u>Sodom</u>,
> > they do not hide it.
> Woe to them!
> > For they have brought evil on themselves.

Another rather casual instance: at the very least uses of this kind illustrate the embeddedness of Genesis as a readily accessible and widely understood metaphor, and further support the contention that the kind of hints we find in Jonah would have been quote enough to trigger recognition of both the reference and its wider implications and applications.

Jer. 23.13-14

> In the prophets of Samaria
> > I saw a disgusting thing:
> they prophesied by Ba'al
> > and led my people Israel astray.
> But in the prophets of Jerusalem
> > I have seen a more shocking thing:
> they commit adultery and walk in lies;
> > they strengthen the hands of evildoers,
> > so that no one turns from wickedness;
> all of them have become like Sodom to me,
> > and its inhabitants like Gomorrah.

The links in this oracle are particularly interesting. Verse 13 references the turn to the prophets of Ba'al in Samaria – surely a hint of Elijah's notorious contest in 1 Kings 18 – but is then followed by an even stronger denunciation of the prophets of Jerusalem citing Genesis 19. Once again we find a ready combination of traditions which the reader (or hearer) could readily follow. Moreover, both of these traditions are part of the nexus of Jonah.

Ezek. 16.46-58

Part of a lengthy chapter excoriating Jerusalem and its abominations. In this section Jerusalem is portrayed as far worse than Samaria and her daughters to the north, and Sodom and her daughters to the south.

Hos. 11.8-9

> How can I give you up, Ephraim?
> > How can I hand you over, O Israel?
> How can I make you like Admah?
> > How can I treat you like Zeboiim?
> My heart recoils within me;
> > my compassion grows warm and tender.
> > I will not execute my fierce anger;

> I will not again destroy Ephraim;
>> for I am God and no mortal,
> the Holy One in your midst,
>> and I will not come in wrath.

Hosea is unique amongst the prophets in using the secondary pairing Admah and Zeboiim. Apart from that, he differs from others by proclaiming that Yahweh *cannot* punish the people with the same fate as those cities. His reason is interesting, since it alludes to the famous blessing in Exodus 34 which forms an important element of Jonah's response to God.

Zeph. 2.9

> Therefore, as I live, says the LORD of hosts,
>> the God of Israel,
> Moab shall become like Sodom
>> and the Ammonites like Gomorrah,
> a land possessed by nettles and salt-pits,
>> and a waste for ever.
> The remnant of my people shall plunder them,
>> and the survivors of my nation shall possess them.

Another application of the legend to local neighbours of Judah, similar in tone to Isa. 34.9-10 (the only missing element is the verb *hapakh*).

Ps. 11.5-6

> The LORD tests the righteous and the wicked,
>> and his soul hates the lover of violence.
> On the wicked he will rain coals of fire and sulphur;
>> a scorching wind shall be the portion of their cup.

My last example squeaks in because it vividly appeals to the Genesis legend through the use of a series of familiar expressions; moreover it adds a rider which resonates with Jonah 4: the scorching wind (not literally the same as that in Jonah) and the term 'portion' which is cognate with the repeated expression used in Jonah when Yahweh 'appoints' the various means by which Jonah is tested/tormented. The author of Jonah undoubtedly made much use of the Psalter, so this instance may have more importance that at first sight. Were it to be applied to Jonah himself, it might appear that he was tested *as one of the wicked*! An interesting thought.

Nineveh as Symbol

I have suggested that Nineveh in Nahum may be a stand-in for Babylon, a kind of misdirection should Babylonian officials come upon the text, but clear enough in its implications for a Jerusalem readership. After all, from a Judaean perspective, it was Babylon, not Assyria, which destroyed the city and the temple and marched its elite into exile. Not safe, perhaps, to damn them directly while many vulnerable Judaeans were in mourning 'by the waters of Babylon'. Might Jonah be interpreted analogously? But if so, what is a plausible referent for the symbolic 'Nineveh'? Apart from the use made of the name in Jonah, Nahum and Zechariah, it only appears again in two quite neutral settings: the – certainly fanciful – genealogy in Genesis 10 which is undatable, but probably part of the latest material in Genesis; and a note in 2 Kgs 19.36 (= Isa. 37.37) of Sennacherib's return to Nineveh after his defeat by 'the angel of the Lord'. Granted that the Deuteronomistic history is a post-exilic construction, this too offers nothing helpful for our understanding as to why Nineveh might be a useful symbol. It is, to put it bluntly, a hollow icon which brings no trail of pre-exilic menace such as is instinctive in the seemingly related terms 'Assyria' and 'Babylon'. These latter two feature prominently in historical and prophetic texts which are well aware of their fundamental – and disastrous – importance for the twin kingdoms of Israel and Judah, in view of which it would have been difficult for a post-exilic writer to use them in any kind of coded way.[8] I propose therefore that in the book of Jonah Nineveh must stand for a polity close to home. Everything about the detail of this clever parable is sharply focused on the religious identity of Jerusalem and the beliefs and traditions which characterise its practices.

The discussion above of the two Genesis sources identified by Jonathan Magonet provides a considerable body of evidence for the claim that in the register of its social context the most salient resonances of the flood and the fire legends are to be found rather close to Jonah's home. The former is almost exclusively an Israelite affair. The latter has more extended applications, but even so it finds its predominant, and certainly its most visceral applications to Israel directly (ten cases, including Jeremiah's lament at his birth) or her neighbours (five, including the origin story). Of the remainder, two speak of Babylon and one is indeterminate (Deut. 32.31-32).

---

8. By the time of the early Christian church this has changed: Babylon by then had faded far enough into the past to enable its symbolic use in Revelation as a signifier for Rome.

I sense that ancient readers of these oracles would not have been in any doubt that they were targeted directly to the home audience: something which Amos dramatized in his famous sequence of oracles in his opening two chapters. I want to suggest, therefore, that for the reasons presented in this chapter, we should see Nineveh as a symbol not of the long-vanished seat of Sennacherib's court, but of the very place that Jonah fled from precisely because he knew which great city was guilty of great wrongdoing and he feared the consequences of denouncing it and its culpable leaders – and so-called prophets. For if Nineveh is indeed to be identified with Jerusalem, and if the readers of Jonah were well aware that Nineveh was in ruins, what implications would they be forced to draw?

Others have of course made this connection – Qoheleth's observation that there is nothing new under the sun is peculiarly apposite to the study of the book of Jonah – but in the strong form which I want to endorse, it is rarely found. Ben Zvi (p. 118) hints at it when he writes:

> The fate of monarchic Jerusalem looms large over the book of Jonah. To be sure, in the minds of the Achaemenid period Jerusalemites, Nineveh was neither the only nor the first great city that most likely came to mind when they thought of a mighty city overturned by YHWH because of its sins. But in which way did the all-present knowledge of the fate of Jerusalem most likely inform the reading and rereading of Jonah at that time?

But my primary stimulus for the rereading of Nineveh as a stand-in for Jerusalem *in the reception of the book by its first readers* is the work of Marian Kelsey who devotes a significant part of the fourth chapter of her dissertation[9] to 'The Fate of Cities' and in particular to the significance of Nineveh. She comments (p. 104) that

> The depiction of Nineveh within the book of Jonah is similar to the traditional understanding of Sodom and Gomorrah. In the book of Jonah, Nineveh is a city which is wicked and sinful, but is not described, even by foreshadowing, as the destroyer of Israel. Thus, Sodom and Nineveh are closer parallels in the book of Jonah than would otherwise be expected from the broader biblical portrayal of Nineveh. Given the well-established comparison between Sodom and Jerusalem in prophetic warnings, and the portrayal of Nineveh in Sodom-like terms in the book of Jonah, one wonders to what extent Nineveh functions similarly.

---

9. Cited by kind permission of the author.

While these comments have their origins in Magonet's work, they considerably extend its implications. Thus, remarking on the supposed wickedness of Nineveh, Kelsey observes (p. 107) that 'Nineveh-of-Jonah is aligned with the wickedness of cities in general – or, if it is closest to the biblical account of any one city, it is that of Jerusalem/Judah in the prophets'. She draws the important conclusion (p. 114) that

> [t]he author of the book of Jonah has therefore chosen to describe Nineveh's wickedness in terms commonly, and sometimes uniquely, applied to Israel/Judah in other biblical literature. Sodom and Gomorrah were used in prophecy to serve as an example to Jerusalem. The description of Nineveh's wickedness in the book of Jonah, including the similarity between it and the Sodom tradition, suggests that Nineveh may serve a similar purpose in the book. The possibility is supported by various other hints at Jerusalem which appear throughout the text.

Encouraged by these insights, I suggest that the book of Jonah was never in reality about Nineveh, rather 'Nineveh'. Moreover 'Nineveh' is to be taken as the alter ego of Jerusalem – the city that repents; unlike Jerusalem as depicted in the Deuteronomistic historico-theology. Jonah's cities are psychogeographical manifestations, his travels journeys of the mind, and his findings not a thousand kilometres distant, but no further removed from his readers than that hilltop to the east of the city.

Coda: Unseeing Jerusalem

Miéville's conceit in *The City and the City* is that two urban centres of sharply contrasting character co-exist in the same geographical space, as the result of an event many centuries earlier. A fundamental consequence is that the citizens of both cities learn from early childhood to 'unsee' the people and structures in the other city. Moreover 'unseeing' is legally binding, and a shadowy organisation (known as Breach) exists to enforce this directive. The plot develops when a murder necessitates a detective from Besźel collaborating with one from Ul Qoma, thus temporarily negating the principle of unseeing.

The premise behind the conceit is that (all fantasy aside) we have as human beings an ability to blank out what we do not wish to see, or what we are accustomed not to notice. This is why, for example, Nathan's parable condemning David works. There was no way David could see himself in the story as it unfolded. Or, to take a much more contemporary example, residents of affluent areas of my own city, Glasgow, have an average life expectancy of around 80 years; in the deprived parts of the East End of the city that drops to 54. City of Culture, or City of Death?

The author of Jonah presents a city – Nineveh and a city – Jerusalem; the readers of Jonah may choose to 'unsee' the Jerusalem which overlays the fictive Nineveh, but it is there, nevertheless.

Chapter 2

JONAH 1.1-3: THE CALL

¹Now the word of the LORD came to Jonah son of Amittai, saying, ²'Go at once to Nineveh, that great city, and cry out against it; for their wickedness has come up before me'. ³But Jonah set out to flee to Tarshish from the presence of the LORD. He went down to Joppa and found a ship going to Tarshish; so he paid his fare and went on board, to go with them to Tarshish, away from the presence of the LORD.

Having set out my stall in the foregoing chapters, I turn now to a more detailed review of the text of Jonah. The purpose of this traditional verse-by-verse type of commentary is not to set out exhaustively all the historical- and text-critical positions hitherto enunciated, with the addition of my own proposals. Instead I shall adopt a somewhat impressionist approach, focusing from time to time on features of special significance for my overall thesis. There are already many fine commentaries on Jonah: there is no urgent need for another one.

By way of explanation, my reading in these 'commentary' sections is consciously naïve, in that I will often assume the role of the traditional reader/scholar rather than that of the presumed 'first readers' whom I have identified in the opening chapters. Where appropriate I will indicate how our received reading is either contradicted or nuanced when the latter presumption is entered into the exegetical equation. Moreover I will intersperse the commentary with chapters which develop certain general matters at greater leisure.

¹Now the word of the LORD came to Jonah son of Amittai

The book of Jonah opens with a puzzle: who is its hero or antihero? Does he have antecedents (as scholars have often suggested) in the mysterious character briefly introduced in 2 Kgs 14.25 who seems to have had something to do with predicting a successful enterprise on the part of Jeroboam II of Israel:

> [Jeroboam son of Joash] restored the border of Israel from Lebo-hamath as far as the sea of the Arabah, according to the word of the Lord, the God of Israel, which he spoke by his prophet Jonah son of Amittai, the prophet, who was from Gath-hepher.

This is attractive to our hankering after history, however sketchy, for it lends superficial credence to a view most of us publicly reject, but perhaps retain as a private vice: that there may be some kind of historical substance to the distant and disconcerting events set out in this short story. But the trouble with the intertextual relationship between Kings and Jonah, if that is what we are talking about, is that it cuts both ways. Perhaps the otherwise unknown prophet in Kings was plagiarised by someone who took Jonah (the book) way too seriously and lifted its central character as part of a misguided footnote to the history of Jeroboam II? On the other hand, it is widely accepted that the Elijah stories in 1 Kings 17–19 have influenced Jonah at various points, a datum I shall examine more fully in Chapter 11. The messages are decidedly mixed: Elijah is undoubtedly an influence on Jonah, and both Elijah and Jonah are found in Kings. However, while the Elijah material (as we shall see) is adopted in considerable detail, the reference to a prophet named Jonah is only used incidentally, and no reference is made to his supposed home town. The differences in the way these are separately applied leaves enough room to suggest two different redactional mechanisms. The first belongs to close intertextuality, while the second may well be an example of secondary redaction, perhaps on the part of someone who knew both books and wanted Jonah to have a secure provenance in a respectable locus in the former prophets.

Jonah has other curious features which have often been remarked on. It is a book that makes a habit of upsetting our normal expectations: pagan sailors who are more pious and observant than God's chosen servant; a prophet whose entire oracular opus consists of eight words in English (five in Hebrew), and who experiences the kind of dramatic success of which Isaiah, Jeremiah and Ezekiel could only dream; animals that fast and wear sackcloth – and, presumably, repent; a successful prophet who sulks under a vine and accuses God of being too merciful; a fish of uncertain gender (male in 1.17, female in 2.1); an entire population unsure of the difference between left and right (4.11).

To return to the eponymous hero, whether or not the man ever 'really' lived (and it must be admitted that this is highly unlikely) 'Jonah son of Amittai' suggests something meaningful, if not about the man, at least about the message he is made to convey. Both parts of the name merit more detailed consideration.

Apart from its use in Jonah and Kings as a proper name, the word *yonah* in Hebrew means 'dove'. It is often paired with a second word, *tor*. Whether the two refer to different creatures is not clear, and probably does not matter: they are both birds, by consensus belonging to the family of doves, pigeons and turtle doves (*columbidae*). In the references below, which cover all the occurrences of these two words, normal type is used for *yonah* and bold underline for *tor*.

(1) *Birds for sacrifice:* Gen. **15.9**; Lev. 1.14, **14**; 5.7, **7**, 11, **11**; 12.6, **6**, 8, **8**; 14.22, **22**, 30, **30**; 15.14, **14**, 29, **29**; Num. 6.10, **10**

(2) *The bird which shows the flood has receded:* Gen. 8.8, 9, 10, 11, 12

(3) *A bird which displays vulnerability, either of (a) individuals or (b) nations:* (a) Isa. 38.14 (Hezekiah's prayer); 59.11; Ezek. 7.16; Ps. 55.7; (b) Isa. 60.8 (Returning exiles; note reference to 'ships of Tarshish'); Jer. 48.28 (Moab); Hos. 7.11; 11.11 (Ephraim); Nah. 2.7 (Nineveh); Ps. **74.19** (Israel)

(4) *A metaphor for the beloved, in particular, his or her eyes:* Song 1.15; 2.14; 4.1; 5.2, 12; 6.9

(5) *Miscellaneous references:* 2 Kgs 6.25 (dove's dung); Jer. **8.7** and Song **2.12** (references to the seasons); Pss. 56 (title); 68.18 (a rich ornament).

If the prophet's name was meant to be meaningful, there is certainly a rich array to select from in the list above. It is slightly annoying that the one psalm (74.19) which speaks of 'the soul of your dove' as an expression clearly intending Israel uses *tor* rather than *yonah*. If nothing else, this accident might deter us from too ready an acceptance of the traditional interpretation which sees Jonah as a cipher for Israel, from whom we are expected to learn lessons about the folly of narrow nationalism and the importance of generosity to strangers and the universality of God's love.

It is clear that the more significant expression is *yonah*. The usage in Ps. 74.19 is the only case where *tor* in isolation is used in a meaningful metaphor; elsewhere it is for the most part one of a pair of terms for birds suitable for sacrifice (and of these, only in Gen. 15.9 does it occur alone). That aside, the two semantic groups which are particularly suggestive are 1 and 3: the bird used for sacrifice, and the bird which stands for vulnerability and oppression, but with the tantalising hint of a possibility of escape through flight – especially in Psalm 55. Other instances in the group 3(a) use the motif of the 'moaning' of the dove, and its location on mountainsides, to picture the despair of the oppressed individual. The examples in 3(b) treat the same theme, but on the level of nations rather than individuals. The Isaiah reference is noteworthy for its indication that the ships which will transport the exiles back are from Tarshish; Jeremiah uses the motif of the dove on the mountainside, but the subject is Moab; Hosea uses the dove to picture Ephraim (= Israel) as firstly foolish, then returning from exile 'like doves from the land of Assyria'; and Nahum is, of course, an oracle entirely devoted to the sins of Nineveh. Without labouring the point, it is clear that there are many echoes here of the character and experiences attributed to Jonah in the book that bears his name.

Jonah certainly sees himself as put-upon, and was literally made a sacrifice to the sea in ch. 1. Thus the usage in group 1 is arguably relevant – and it is presumably a connection that would be perfectly familiar to anyone who was in frequent attendance at the temple. As for group 3, the psalm in ch. 2 imagines Jonah's enforced exile from its precincts as a great sorrow; it is therefore more than tempting to suggest that the name encapsulates a poignant combination of the oppressed exile who has been sacrificed to God, yet who still retains a certain hope of ultimate freedom through flight. This is, of course, ironically subverted in the book, where Jonah's flight leads directly not to freedom and escape but to near death. Nevertheless, hints of both Tarshish and Nineveh in the references above serve to strengthen this speculation.

The dove which is sent out by Noah to ascertain the state of the flood is also a candidate for intertextual musing. His own near-fatal encounter with the flood (Jon. 2.3, though not the same term as that used in Genesis) fits into a wider Genesis creation context, which I will explore further in Chapter 7.

The examples in the Song of Songs do seem to be irrelevant, drawing as they do on the literature of erotic metaphors and similes with no obvious relevance to Jonah. Indeed, Song of Songs may well be later in date than Jonah, and was probably not part of the body of scripture which its author drew on for inspiration. I apologise to lovers everywhere, and to lovers of Solomon's Song, for this crass elision of a possible source, but I have not been able to establish any plausible connections in this direction.

One last point has some force. The name Jonah belongs to a small group of proper names whose meaning seems to relate to the narrative in which they are placed rather than to the usual range of theophoric possibilities. Similar examples are to be found in a number of places. The names of Adam and Eve, of course, representing 'earth' and 'life' are pointedly functions of the creation narratives; similarly Cain ('begotten?') and Abel ('emptiness') can be understood within the narrative structure of Genesis 4. Moses – often taken to be Egyptian in etymology – is interpreted by the tradition itself in terms of the legend of the basket. David may in origin have been a military title, if not related to the root 'beloved' (which is interestingly also the root behind Solomon's alternative name, Jedidiah, reported in 2 Sam. 12.25); and Samson – it has been speculated – might hint at a sun-god tradition.[1] Perhaps the closest in spirit to Jonah is the female judge Deborah ('wasp' or 'bee'): the same insect is used to refer to the military threat of Assyria in Isa. 7.18. Certainly the names Deborah and Jonah have a curious appropriateness to their characters' actions. Where Deborah ('the bee') implies a militarily successful woman, Jonah indicates the timid creature of flight so well portrayed in Ps. 55.6.

So much for the prophet's first name. His patronymic is also intriguing, because 'Amittai' seems to be developed from a root that means 'truth'. The compound word, as vocalized in MT, could mean something like 'my truths'. The likelihood that this is no accident has often been pointed out, and readers of a book like this will need no reminding (but I'll remind you anyway) that names in Tanakh are often meaningful. Sometimes the meaning is naturally present ('Isaiah' means 'Yahweh saves'). Sometimes it is the result of tortured etymology ('Abram' to 'Abraham' in Gen. 17.4-6). Sometimes it is the result of a pun: 'Adam' in Gen. 2.7 is formed by God out of the ground (*'adamah*); 'Isaac' is a name which is from the verb 'to laugh' (Gen. 18.12; 21.3-6). And sometimes names are meaningfully altered for political or theological reasons. One of Saul's sons is called Ishbosheth (which means 'man of shame') in 2 Sam. 2.10; in the corresponding passages in 1 Chron. 8.33 and 9.39 he has the much more likely name Ishbaal ('man of Ba'al'). It looks as though the writer of Samuel was keen to belittle the predecessor of his great hero, David. Good (p. 42) notes other examples such as *ben chayil* ('son of valour') in 1 Sam. 14.52 and *ben 'aw^elah* ('son of iniquity') in Ps. 89.22, and goes on to remark that 'Jonah, by analogy, is a "son of faithfulness or truth,"

---

1. It is plausible to associated the Hebrew *shimshon* with the name of the Sun God. A concise summary of the thesis is to be found in J. Alberto Soggin, *Judges*, OTL (London: SCM Press, 1981), pp. 231–2.

but he abandons his faithfulness at the first opportunity and speaks truth only under duress, even then not understanding it'. I endorse his view of the meaningfulness of the name, but do not share his interpretation. To sum up, we could say that the book begins as follows: 'The word of the Lord came to the Dove (oppressed Hebrew sacrificial exile), child of truth, saying …'.

While we are dealing with names, let us just note for completeness that 'Lord' is of course a cover for the personal name of Israel's deity, perhaps pronounced 'Yahweh', and possibly meaning 'The God who is or may be' (see Exod. 3.14 and many commentaries thereon). Finally, the 'word' (*davar*) is more substantial, more *meaty*, more of an entity than the English can convey. In 1 Kgs 19.9-11 (a passage whose importance for the author of Jonah as a kind of 'crib' is undoubted) when Elijah the fearsome prophet is skulking in a cave in the Negev, hiding from the even more fearsome Jezebel, the 'word' of the Lord speaks to him (v. 9) and alerts him to the fact that 'the Lord' is about to pass by (v. 11). That is a bold and dramatic device: the 'word' as a spokesperson for the Lord. So, here is our report on progress so far, in the form of a rewording of v. 1:

> So Word, speaking for 'Yahweh/who is or may be', came to 'Dove/ oppressed and exiled Hebrew', child of truth, saying …

What to make of the translation just offered is something yet again. It reminds us (as the name Yahweh does every time it appears) that there is always an element of uncertainty about him/her, and signals also that this is a god who is liable to use distancing manifestations (Word, Glory, Name, Holiness) to avoid direct encounters, and to employ citizens of unreliable character to carry out his/her wishes. Of course, so far we have no reason to worry about Jonah's reliability; on the contrary, the reference to truth implies the opposite. But truth itself is a tricky proposition, especially when it is Yahweh who won't confront it and the man of truth who has to point it out. The story of Jonah could well be read, though this would depart from more orthodox interpretations, as a parable about a man who insisted on pointing out the truth and was made to suffer for it. No one in power likes to be reminded of their flaws, their unreliability and their propensity to arbitrary actions; how much more so when the power is God.

By the way, and at the risk of seeming to be in league with the much-derided phenomenon of 'political correctness', I need to defend my use of the awkward formulation 'his/her' in the previous paragraph as a means of referring to God. There is no doubt whatsoever that Tanakh uses masculine gender for God, Yahweh, and all of the various names attributed to him/her. Translations more or less uniformly render 'him' in masculine form. However, when a modern writer makes reference to this being, he or she faces a secondary challenge. Notwithstanding the Hebrew convention, it is a moot point whether gender should be applied to, or is indeed relevant to, such entities. For many people this is a non-issue; I am not one of them, and it has been for many years my practice to try to avoid any gender specificity when speaking or writing about the Deity. This poses many problems, and I am not particularly fond of formulations like 'he/she', though I deploy them occasionally when there is no convenient alternative. That said, my first tactic is always to seek so to structure my sentences that the need for such neologisms does not arise. This is my practice, and is a purely personal choice. I hope the reader will respect it, just as I do not demur from those who retain the traditional, and undoubtedly scripturally supported, convention of masculine gender. It is of note regarding this dilemma that Ben Zvi (pp. 12-13) adopts the same convention, but on somewhat different grounds: namely, that the deity was *in Israel* conceived of being either a- or bi-sexual, fulfilling the roles occupied by both gods and goddesses in other cultures.

How did Word appear to Jonah? We are not told directly; indeed, Tanakh is often coy about the actual form of these communications. Prophets 'see' (*chazah*) oracles – thus Isa. 2.1: 'The Word which Isaiah ben Amotz saw concerning Judah and Israel', which would suggest an actual presence. This is in keeping with the reference we have already made to 1 Kings, and fits the naïve grammar of Jon. 1.1 in which 'Word' 'comes' and 'says' – though the Hebrew does not actually have the verb 'to come'; rather it uses the standard narrative introduction, 'it was' whose translation is quite vague, and might amount to nothing more than an indication of a past-tense narrative. We could settle for a sense of suddenness: one moment there is nothing, no mark on the page, no narrative; the next Word is *at* Jonah (who had previously been minding his own business, doing whatever prophets do when they're not condemning the world to eschatological doom), battering him with impossible requests. Donne famously welcomes this kind of approach to religion, in his memorable Trinitarian sonnet, 'Batter my heart, three-personed God'; Jonah, on the other hand, takes flight.

> [2]*saying, 'Go at once to Nineveh, that great city, and cry out against it; for their wickedness has come up before me'.*

We should move on, for I find myself eager to comment on the instructions actually given to Jonah. The verse begins with the kind of urgent imperative that features at the beginning of the Elijah legends. 'Get up and go'

(1 Kgs 17.9). This is a peremptory command, brooking no refusal; Elijah rushes off immediately to Zarephath for an appointment with a widow. It is a somewhat odd idiom, because it physically implies that the recipient is sitting down when the order comes. 'Hey, Jonah, get up off your ass and go…': a little crude, perhaps, but graphic. We might not unreasonably imagine our hero, sitting on the roof of his nice biblical mud-walled house, accessed by a picturesque flight of external stairs, dressed in some version of the Sunday School nativity tea towel. Perhaps he is drinking a mug of wine, contemplating the chickens and goats scratching around in the yard below, and the next-door neighbour's ox straying into the wrong field (again! see Exod. 22.5); perhaps he is meditating on the Psalms of David (not an unreasonable speculation given the song he will sing in the belly of the fish). The voice comes. He jumps up – carefully, for he's on the roof, remember – ready to go, just like Elijah, who (1 Kgs 17.10) 'got up and went'.

But the next part of the instruction is very strange, altogether out of the normal prophetic remit. Not, as they say, in the job description. We'd be looking to draft a new contract here, with considerably enhanced pay, pension rights, and holiday entitlement. For the destination is – wait for it – 'Nineveh, that great city'. The associations of Nineveh, at least insofar as it represents Assyria, are uniformly bad, unlike Babylon, from which city the messiah Cyrus came (Isa. 44.28–45.1), and where the Jews in exile did very well for themselves. It was influential Babylonian Jews who 'returned' from exile to create the post-exilic theocracy in Jerusalem, and interestingly, the key figures in the development of Mishnah (Hillel and Rabbi Akiva) are held to have been natives of Babylonia. Furthermore the authoritative edition of the Talmud is that which was produced by the Jewish rabbinic scholars of Babylonia between the third and the fifth centuries CE. Nineveh, of course, was the city of the Assyrians, whose principal activity, when not engaged in murderous internecine quarrelling, was the invasion of lesser states with the sole purpose of rape, pillage, depopulation and recolonisation. They became famous, amongst other things, for 'coming down like a wolf on the fold' (I refer to Byron's poem, 'The Destruction of Sennacherib', a favourite of school books of the distant past), which begins, in time-honoured galloping rhythm.

> The Assyrian came down like the wolf on the fold,
> And his cohorts were gleaming in purple and gold;
> And the sheen of their spears was like stars on the sea,
> When the blue wave rolls nightly on deep Galilee.

The northern kingdom of Israel fell foul of them in 722 BCE and its citizens, the legendary lost ten tribes of Israel, were sent packing. Unlike the later case of Judah (587 BCE) whose leading citizens were deported to Babylonia but treated relatively well, and enabled 'to return' in the later sixth century, the ten tribes were never heard of again. Like the Ark of the Covenant, which exists now only in the enjoyable Hollywood fantasies of Indiana Jones and the less charming fantasies of conspiracy theorists, the ten tribes have a curious afterlife in Mormonism and the beliefs of British Israelites. The Assyrians, it must be admitted, were good at what they did; so the very thought of a Jewish prophet hurrying off to their heartland to warn them of Yahweh's anger would have been seriously disturbing to the prophet in question, and of dubious legitimacy to a faithful Israelite. The sheer size of Nineveh is a theme which returns, in ch. 3, and is clearly designed to emphasise the gravity of the commission.

It is a little naughty of me to put scare quotes around 'returned' and 'to return' in the foregoing commentary. However, it is necessary to be aware of the ongoing debate about the precise status of the group which settled in Jerusalem some time after 540 BCE under the aegis of Cyrus the Great. It is unlikely that they were the same people who were exiled some fifty years previously, for obvious chronological reasons. They may even (given the youthful energy needed for such an enterprise) have been drawn from the second generation since Nebuchadnezzar. Moreover, the myth of the 'return' is closely tied to another, now discredited myth, that of the empty land; that is, the claim (found undoubtedly in scripture itself) that the exile completely depopulated Judah, leaving it prey to weeds and wild animals. That this was never the case is abundantly plain from other parts of scripture – and modern scholarship has dealt with this clearly; see for example Barstad (1996) and Lipschits and Blenkinsopp (2003). Thirdly, there is a presumption that the group from Babylonia were inspired to restore the ancient religion of Israel, whereas it is more probable that much of their agenda derived from the way that proto-Judaism was beginning to develop in the circumstances of exile, where there was no Temple and no sacrificial system, and a need to find new ways of affirming the ethnic identity of the community. Hence the renewed emphasis on Sabbath observance, dietary laws (see Dan. 1) and the preservation of the community from intermarriage (see Ezra 9–10). Hence also the new emphasis on the community as one which founded itself on Torah-observance, with the Torah now being defined within a set of physical written scrolls.

The task Jonah is given is simple enough, 'To cry against her [the city]', though precisely what he is to say is not revealed at this point. What we are told, because Jonah is told, is that the reason for his commission is 'their [the people of Nineveh's] wickedness'. You might well wonder why at this particular point in time Yahweh is suddenly exercised about the wrongdoings of a people who have for several centuries been a byword for cruelty. It could be a communications glitch, for what Jonah is actually told is that 'their wickedness has come up before me', as if up till now no information about the affairs of the Assyrians had reached the divine presence (the literal meaning of the term translated 'before me'). Perhaps there was just too much to deal with in other directions, what with hardening Pharaoh's heart, guiding a bunch of rowdy and disputatious Hebrews through the Negev, sorting out the fine print of the covenant, and damage limitation in respect of the monarchy. Perhaps, too, the Divine Council – Yahweh's lesser associates in the Kingdom of Heaven – who had been managing things on Yahweh's behalf decided it was time to bring the matter of the Assyrians directly to the Chief's attention. This is not an irrelevant/irreverent digression. One of Jonah's key complaints is of radical inconsistency on Yahweh's part, evidence that God manipulates the rules to suit what appear to be arbitrary divine choices. One way to square this apparent circle is via the clear evidence in Tanakh of a body which has often been referred to as The Divine Council.

There are a number of indications in the Tanakh that, at least at some time and in some quarters, Yahweh was understood to be the supreme being in a kind of heavenly assembly. The most striking examples of this phenomenon are in 1 Kings 22 and Job 1–2; other indications are to be found in Deut. 32.8-9; 33.2; Job 38.7; Pss. 29.1; 58.1; 82.1, 6-7; 89.6; 103.20-21; 148.2; Dan. 7.9-10. The curious piece of mythology in Gen. 6.2-4 may also have some connection with the ambivalence evident in Psalm 82 – in both of these passages the gods are deliberately brought down to mortal level as a punishment for their misdeeds.

I will confine my remarks here to 1 Kings 22 and Job 1–2, in both of which we find Yahweh engaged in what can best be described as highly dubious ethical practices in response to persuasion from less respectable members of the divine council. In the former, the prophet Micaiah reports a vision in which Yahweh seeks help in enticing King Ahab into a course of action which will lead to his defeat and certain death. Various suggestions are made, and then (here, Micaiah is speaking to Ahab and Jehoshaphat):

a spirit came forward and stood before the LORD, saying, 'I will entice him'. 'How?' the LORD asked him. He replied, 'I will go out and be a lying spirit in the mouth of all his prophets'. Then the LORD said, 'You are to entice him, and you shall succeed; go out and do it'. So you see, the LORD has put a lying spirit in the mouth of all these your prophets; the LORD has decreed disaster for you.

This turns out to be a self-fulfilling prophecy, for Ahab chooses to ignore Micaiah and to listen to the flattering words of the lying spirit. The point of interest for our purposes is the suggestion that Yahweh was either confused, uncertain, or duplicitous. This ethical problematic is reinforced in the well-known encounter between Yahweh and 'the *shetan*' – not, as later Christianity thought, a malevolent being from Hell called Satan, but a character more akin to the Jester or the Devil's Advocate familiar from Western literature and culture. Here again Yahweh is persuaded – possibly against his [*sic* Yahweh is a character in a folk-tale here, not a remote divinity] better judgement – to allow a grotesque series of disasters to befall the hitherto blameless Job. These occur in two stages, graphically set out in Job 1.13-19 and 2.7-8, with the very fact that Yahweh allows *shetan* two bites at the cherry only adding to the unpleasantness and the sense that God is at the very least pusillanimous, if not downright wicked.

Both of these stories are, of course, fiction or legend; but so is Jonah, and the point is that we are encountering the minds of ancient Hebrew thinkers and theologians who chose this mode of discourse to explore matters which clearly exercised them. Given that we know that Jonah makes serious use of 1 Kings 17–19, and that 1 Kings 22 is lodged within the overall Elijah corpus, it does not seem far-fetched to see in the God of Jonah another example of the well-attested Hebrew penchant for unbridled debate on the ethical nature of their deity. The seeming unreliability of the deity, and his or her susceptibility to the same kind of pressures that human beings encounter when faced with moral conundrums, raises the level of dramatic tension. Like Job, Jonah is a peaceable citizen quietly minding his own business. Like Job, he is quite prepared to challenge God as soon as he senses trouble; and like Job, he experiences a God who makes unreasonable demands, who appears to operate double standards, and who is systematically unpredictable – soft both on crime and on criminals, to borrow a slogan from modern politics. Like Job, Jonah is tormented by God (or God's agent). No doubt there is a difference. Job is portrayed as without blemish, while Jonah is disobedient. But his disobedience is not unjustified (this is the force of the citation in 4.2 of Exod. 34.6 with Joel 2.13). When Nineveh is awarded a blanket forgiveness on the basis of very little hard evidence, Jonah doesn't appeal to a divine doppelganger like the lying spirit of Kings or the *shetan* in Job; but the dilemma is similar, if perhaps more honest in that there is no overt attempt to excuse God.

There is a noteworthy play on words in this short briefing. The phrase for 'against her' and the verb which conveys the fact that the city's wickedness has 'come up' are very similar: *'aleyha* and *'al^{e}tha*, and the second word is a verb often used in the context of positive ascents – to Israel from Egypt, to life from death, to the sacred mountain from the valley. I shall argue that it is found in all of these senses in ch. 2, and again in ch. 4 where it refers to the rapid upward growth of the protective bush; for the moment we might content ourselves with the thought that this is the deliberate and blasphemous converse of a pilgrimage. Far from the faithful going up to the Temple to be in God's presence, this is the wickedness of a whole city daring to make itself known 'before him'. The crime of the Ninevites, therefore, is not just to have been wicked, but to have committed *lese majeste*.

There is a further significance to the instruction to Jonah to cry out *against* Nineveh. The verb used, *qara'*, is very common, but more usually takes another preposition, *'el* ('to'); indeed, when the instruction is repeated in 3.2 *'el* is used. I believe that the stronger form is used in 1.2 deliberately, as does Sasson (pp. 72–5). He further notes an emphatic character to the subordinate clause, so that we might render it something like: 'Proclaim against [Nineveh] that *indeed* their wickedness has made itself apparent in my very presence' (this is my rendering, not Sasson's). The weaker form in ch. 3 implies a less draconian instruction; Jonah is to preach *to* Nineveh, and that amelioration contains within it the seeds of Nineveh's salvation.

My reading so far has tended to the literal – as if Jonah had really been commanded by God to go to the historically extant city of Nineveh. Of course, trapped as he is within the confines of the narrative, Jonah has no option but to go with the flow (or, as we shall shortly see, against it). But we can stand aside and draw different conclusions. Even as early in the story as this we must surely be mistrustful, ready to bring to bear that most familiar of interpretive devices, *the hermeneutic of suspicion*. Can the author seriously imagine that we can take him/her literally? Does the author even want us to? The signs are there in plenty: the use of curiously symbolic names, the evidence of intertextuality in respect of the book of Kings, the egregiously improbable choice of Nineveh of all places to mount an evangelistic campaign, and the already evident playfulness in respect of the language itself. Might we be better to think of allegory, or pastiche, or satire – some literary form instinctively designed (as the text already is) to distance the reader from the ostensible narrative? Such a device is by no means unthinkable in a biblical writer, as we know from a number of examples. The parable Nathan told to embarrass David is a good example, as is the elaborate conceit which makes up the Song of Songs. More controversially, I might cite the evident historical pastiche which makes up Genesis 14 or the way that Qoheleth adopts the persona of 'King over Israel in Jerusalem' in order to explore the vanity of wealth and wisdom. I have already set out the case for an explanation of Nineveh as a symbol for Jerusalem: that will provide a context for my continuing exegesis.

> *³But Jonah set out to flee to Tarshish from the presence of the LORD. He went down to Joppa and found a ship going to Tarshish; so he paid his fare and went on board, to go with them to Tarshish, away from the presence of the LORD.*

Whereas Elijah's response to God's order was, as we have seen, that 'he got up and went', Jonah quickly displays a different mettle. Certainly this verse begins 'He got up' but his purpose was 'to flee' (a word which turns up again in 4.2, and has a homonym in ch. 2 which we shall consider further there) to Tarshish 'from the presence of Yahweh'. The last phrase is a blatant reminder of that same 'presence' which had been so defiled by the wickedness of the Ninevites. It's as though Jonah were in flight from Yahweh twice – literally, by heading off in the opposite direction, and metaphorically, by avoiding the numinous presence recently aroused to anger over Nineveh. Incidentally, as has often been pointed out, Jonah is not here engaged in the sort of naïve 'hiding' form God which Gen. 3.8 attributes to Adam and Eve. 'Much more likely, the phrase in 1.3 means to escape Yahweh's *cultic* presence where the prophetic oracle is vouchsafed' (Landes, p. 19), an observation which will find its fuller reference in our discussion of Jonah 2.

We should perhaps introduce a little theology at this point: the most obvious message of Jonah might be that flight 'from the presence of the Lord' leads not to safety but to the threat of death by drowning. There might be a corollary, that to embrace God's demands, even when they imply a journey to the most dangerous of known destinations, is the only 'safe' response. Unfortunately, Jonah's experiences in ch. 4 must cast a little gloom on this sunny conclusion, for we last see him waiting for death on a hillside outside Nineveh, and there is no word of his safe return home. This prompts the further thought that Jonah may well have been right to suspect the intentions of the God who sought to dispatch him to

Nineveh, since most of those who have *actually* journeyed to Assyria have found it to be far from reassuring (including both the lost ten tribes of Israel and, in recent years, a significant number of British, American and other forces). I am tempted to offer a further punning moral at this point, in anticipation of ch. 4, to the effect that Jonah, having liberated Iraq, finds himself under the protection of a bush (4.6) which sadly is immediately attacked by a worm and promptly withers the very next morning (4.7). Have we finally found the proof that Jonah belongs indeed with the prophets? Sadly not, for even though the prophets themselves were not above the odd pun,[2] it seems unlikely that the *qiqayon* of Jon. 4.6 can be etymologically connected to Dubya, pleasing though such an outcome would undoubtedly be.

There is a satisfyingly folk-tale aspect to v. 3, in that the information that Jonah is set on going to Tarshish is provided three times. He decides to 'flee to Tarshish', he finds a ship in Joppa which is 'going to Tarshish', and he pays his fare in order to 'go with them to Tarshish'. The verse is rounded off with a reiteration of the belief that in Tarshish a person might get 'away from the presence of the Lord'. I shall have more to say about Tarshish, and other marine matters, in Chapter 6; for now it is enough to note that it may simply be the representation of a mysterious destination to the west, just as Nineveh stands for a menacing destination to the east. Perry (p. 1 note 1) reminds us that the Targum 'unfailingly renders Tarshish, Jonah's supposed destination, simply as "the sea," thus suggesting that its particular identity is of less import than its symbolic value'. The use of 'the sea' is not a bad resolution of the problem, since Jonah flees seaward in order to avoid the overland journey to Nineveh where, ironically, he ends up in the desert contemplating the combined effects of his and the Lord's actions. The location of his viewpoint outside Nineveh is not precisely 'desert', but the conditions – arid, hot, with a searing east wind – justify the metaphoric use of that term. The ultimate irony, of course, is that the means of escape leads to disaster, while the trip to the dangerous east turns out well (at least for the Ninevites and their cattle, if not for Jonah and a certain cucumber plant – qv, 4.6).

Notwithstanding my endorsement of Landes' observation about the meaning of 'the presence of the Lord', it is tempting, in view of many other echoes of the opening chapters of Genesis to be found in Jonah (a subject discussed more fully in Chapter 7), to see here a witty reminder

---

2. E.g. Amos 8.1-2 and his basket of summer fruits – *qayts* – marking the end – *qets*, or Jer. 1.11-12 with his almond branch – *shaqed* – which reminds us that the Lord is watching – *shoqed*.

of the vain attempts of Adam and Eve to hide from God (Gen. 3.8). They hid 'among the trees' as if these items of God's handiwork could offer protection. The primeval couple complete a trilogy of futile resorts, adding the verdant garden to Jonah's deep sea and dry desert. In this context the *qiqayon* can perhaps be seen to symbolise the bringing together of all three, in that it is (of course) a plant, it grows in the desert, and it is almost certainly a species which encloses reservoirs of water in its fruit. But just as the trees could not shelter Adam and Eve, nor the sea bear Jonah to safety, so the mysterious plant fails also to provide cover. As we shall see in Chapter 7, the hints at creation and the absolute authority of God over the created order are not accidental: one of the important philosophical themes of Jonah is surely the integrity of creation and the indivisibility of its parts – something poignantly shown in the role of the animals of Nineveh and the fact that it is they who have the last word in the book: '*vubehemah rabbah* – and a great many cattle'.

One seemingly irrelevant point needs to be addressed: the curious note that Jonah bought his ticket for the journey (literally, 'he gave its price'). Perry notes that the Rabbis have suggested that the phrase tells us that Jonah hired the whole boat – which raises some problems for the lottery shortly to be held. For if Jonah was the only passenger, the outcome of the lottery seems rather predictable! In any case, the ticket incident is only one of a series of seemingly eccentric notes in the book; so what then can we make of the purchase of a ticket? I suggest just one reading: Jonah's paying of 'its price' anticipates the fact that the price he pays is much higher than he knows, for it is the price of life, his and the sailors. He was not forced on to the ship, he went willingly, and there is a ticket stub to prove it. A possible parallel is to be found in Exod. 22.15 in a context concerning the death or injury of animals on loan. NRSV reads 'If the owner was present, there shall be no restitution; if it was hired, only the hiring fee is due', but this is misleading, since the concluding phrase has a literal sense of something like 'If it was hired, it came with its fee [paid?]'. That is, blame is excluded because someone has already paid the price. The Hebrew of 'with its fee' uses the same idiom as that of Jonah's 'its price': there could therefore at a stretch be a case for the exoneration of the sailors on the grounds of Jonah's implicit acknowledgement of full responsibility.

Before leaving this verse it is incumbent on me to say something about the first appearance of a highly significant word for the message of Jonah: the verb *yarad*, 'to go down'. Up (*'alah*) and down are pregnant terms in Hebrew ideology, associated respectively with life and death, the promised land of Canaan, to which one goes up, and the dead land of

Egypt, whither one descends, the ascent of the mountain on pilgrimage and the descent into the pit which is Sheol. There is an excess of going down in Jonah: down to Joppa (1.3), down into the ship (1.3), down into the hold of the ship (1.5), down to sleep, and down, down, down to the bottom of the sea (2.6). Perry (pp. 5–7) emphasises the importance of this verb and notes a pun in the form *vayeradam*, 'he lay down to sleep', which echoes *yarad*. Curiously the opposite term, to go up, has a more ambiguous role. It first appears when the wickedness of Nineveh reaches such a pitch that it 'rises up' to God's attention (1.2), something we noted already. It next occurs in a positive sense when God raises up Jonah from the Pit (2.6), and then again positively when the notorious *qiqayon* sprouts up (4.6 – which incidentally includes the same combination of verb and related preposition which we remarked upon in 1.2). Finally, and negatively, the sun rises at dawn (4.8) to inflict itself upon Jonah as the final lesson in his masterclass in Schadenfreude, a lesson which reminds us, as it teaches him, that on at least one reading of the evidence Yahweh is a god who takes pleasure in the discomfort of human beings.

Chapter 3

JONAH 1.4-6: THE STORM

> ⁴But the LORD hurled a great wind upon the sea, and such a mighty storm came upon the sea that the ship threatened to break up. ⁵Then the mariners were afraid, and each cried to his god. They threw the cargo that was in the ship into the sea, to lighten it for them. Jonah, meanwhile, had gone down into the hold of the ship and had lain down, and was fast asleep. ⁶The captain came and said to him, 'What are you doing sound asleep? Get up, call on your god! Perhaps the god will spare us a thought so that we do not perish.'

⁴But the LORD hurled a great wind upon the sea, and such a mighty storm came upon the sea that the ship threatened to break up.

The action suddenly speeds up in v. 4. In the previous verse we saw Jonah safely on to the ship, presumably at anchor in Joppa, the prophet unpacking his overnight bag and taking out his reading material of choice (*The Adventures of Elijah: Prophet, Avenger and Vanishing Artist*, [Jerusalem, ca. 550 BCE] – a not entirely frivolous remark, given the close textual links between Jonah and 1 Kgs 17–22). Now all of a sudden we are at sea, and the full fury of God's anger is all too apparent. Two words in particular convey this atmosphere of terror: the verb 'to hurl' and the 'storm' (*sa'ar*) which hits the sea. Coupled with this theophanic panic is another note: an echo of the opening scene of Genesis 1, when 'a wind from God' sweeps over the surface of the waters in order to set in train the process of creation.

First the panic. Throughout Tanakh God's appearances or manifestations are accompanied by various forms of fear, ranging from a proper sense of awe to downright terror. The two extremes can be summed up in the shape of Moses on the one hand and the Israelites he led out of Egypt on the other. Moses is regularly permitted into the presence of God, and while he may remove his shoes and hide his face (Exod. 3.1-6), he is evidently a privileged witness (see also 24.9-11 and 15-18). The Israelites, on the other hand, experience pure terror, particularly in the aftermath of the declaration of the Ten Commandments. Thus Exod. 20.18-19:

> When all the people witnessed the thunder and lightning, the sound of the trumpet, and the mountain smoking, they were afraid and trembled and stood at a distance, and said to Moses, 'You speak to us, and we will listen; but do not let God speak to us, or we will die'.

And this, remember, is a benign encounter with a God who has just offered the people a favourable deal for a long-term relationship. Where God is angry, or wants to make a big impression, the whirlwind appears (*sa'ar[ah]*, mostly spelled with a *samekh*, but occasionally with a *sin* – both letters sound like the English 's'). It is out of the whirlwind that God grumpily challenges Job to explain his arrogance (38.1; 40.6); it is in a whirlwind that Elijah is caught up into heaven in the presence of a bemused and frightened Elisha (2 Kgs 2.1-12). The verb 'to be stormy' and the noun 'storm, whirlwind' are remarkably consistent in meaning in all of their instances in Tanakh. With the exception of just three examples – in 2 Kgs 6.11, Hos. 13.3, and Dan. 11.40 – they consistently have divine or theophanic significance. Sometimes the theophanic storm is simply a dimension or manifestation of Yahweh (as in 2 Kgs 2.1-12), but more commonly it is associated with God's determination to destroy the wicked, and in one case with the truth that *all* humankind will in the end be blown away (Isa. 40.24). There is also an interesting subgroup of cases which bear comparison with the personal threat faced by Jonah (a subgroup, because arguably Jonah is a sinner and therefore falls under the wider rubric of God's judgemental whirlwind). Here is a detailed breakdown.

Theophanic appearances of Yahweh

(a) *'Without prejudice'.* 2 Kgs 2.1, 11; Ezek. 1.4; Job 38.1; 40.6; Pss. 50.3; 148.8
(b) *Threatening punishment of the wicked.* Isa. 28.2; 29.6; 41.16; Jer. 23.19; 25.32; 30.23; Ezek. 13.11, 13; Amos 1.14; Nah. 1.3; Hab. 3.14; Zech. 7.14; 9.14; Job 27.20; Pss. 58.9; 83.15
(c) *God's wind that destroys all humankind in the end.* Isa. 40.24

Jonah-like passages

> Isa. 54.11 (note reference to Noah in v. 9); Jon. 1.4, 11, 12, 13; Job 9.17 (the 'innocent' Job crushed by a tempest); Pss. 55.8; 107.25, 29 (both of these psalms turn up in a comparison of Jon. 2 with other scripture – see Chapter 9).

It seems evident then that the use of this verb and its associated nouns in Jonah has a significance that would not have been lost on the book's first readers.

When this portentous storm is combined with the opening verb, the sense of doom is redoubled, for 'to hurl' occurs predominantly in quite sinister circumstances. In Jer. 16.13 and 22.26-28 it describes how God will 'hurl' the Israelites out of their land into an unknown territory, and in Isa. 22.17-18 a similar fate is meted out to leading families in Jerusalem. Since the effect of the hurling of the storm on the waters is to force Jonah, eventually, into an alien land, there is an interesting congruence of ideas. The other relevant occurrences of the verb are, first, in Ezek. 32.4, where God threatens to fish up Pharaoh and his people in a dragnet and hurl them on to the dry land as victims, and second, describing Saul's readiness to hurl his spear at David and Jonathan (1 Sam. 18.11; 20.33): an informed reader would certainly have picked up the sheer scale of God's aggression compressed into these few words – and would not have missed the point that they almost all refer to the punishment of Jonah's own people, not some remote ruined Mesopotamian city.

The great wind hitting the sea brings together two important features of Jonah's discourse: the frequent deployment of words for size, and suggestions of a background awareness of the creation story. The word for 'great' (*gadhol*) is repeatedly – almost indiscriminately – used of a long list of features and characters. Nineveh (1.2; 3.2, 3; 4.11), wind and storm (1.4 [×2]; 1.12), the sailors' fear (1.10) and fear of God (1.16), the fish (1.17), the great men of Nineveh (3.7), Jonah's anger (4.1) and his joy (4.6). One further instance is the verbal form, 'to make bigger', which is used of the growth of the *qiqayon* in 4.10. Fourteen occurrences in 48 verses, referring to nine different objects, certainly suggests a more than accidental feature; and if we note that there are no occurrences in the nine verses which constitute the psalm, the frequency is even more impressive, rising from one in four to more than one in three. Such density of linguistic choice supports the general thesis that the author of Jonah has very specific aims and provides highly visible cues for those informed readers who were the book's first audience.

One of the central issues in Jonah is the link between punishment and the collective: the seeming insensitivity of God to collateral damage or friendly fire, that oxymoronic invention of modern warfare. What had the sailors done to deserve Jonah's whirlwind? Were all the people of Nineveh equally guilty, including the children and animals? Perry (pp. 45–8) discusses both biblical evidence for solidarity between humankind and animals, and the rabbinic teaching that the latter must be capable of sin because (for example) they also perished in the flood. I will return to this question in Chapter 12. In the meantime, a more worrying issue is that the sailors are saved by what Perry suggests might be an assisted suicide (pp. 7–12) which leaves them by no means innocent (despite – or perhaps because of – their protestations in v. 11 and Jonah's complicity). Indeed, it is an ironic truth that their innocence was compromised by their being (innocently) made victims of the consequences of Jonah's disobedience. But then, when your ship 'begins to break up' – a phrase which preserves something of the assonance of the Hebrew '*chishbah lehishaber*' – you might be forgiven for clutching at whatever straws might be used to patch the leaks. In fact the phrase is odder still, since the first verb has the regular meaning of 'to plan', 'to think about' – as if the ship were personified and imagining its own response to the storm! – and all the other instances of the verb take a personal subject. In the spirit of preserving the assonance, I offer 'the ship considered collapsing' or 'contemplated coming apart at the seams'.[1] This is perhaps the first example in Jonah of a convention that sees inanimate things taking on a life and purpose of their own which serves to confound that of the participating humans – the others are the weed and the bars at the depths of the sea, the *qiqayon*, the east wind and the sun. If God is the creator, is this so outrageous?

One of the curious things about Jonah (the book) is that while its hero epitomises the infidel in his responses in each situation, those who would normally be classed as outsiders, as gentiles, behave with fidelity. It is this deliberate act of *ostranenie* (alienation) on the part of the author which has encouraged that unfortunate emphasis which takes the moral of the

---

1. This is a reading which a number of scholars have either advocated or at least noted as technically correct: for example, Brichto (p. 69) has 'the ship figured she was about to break up', and Sasson (p. 3) 'the ship expected itself to crack up'. It is symbolic of the cautious approach of the many 'approved' versions that none of them dares to represent what the Hebrew actually implies. Sherwood (p. 251) puts it nicely: 'The phrase "the ship expected itself to crack up" ... blurs the lines between physical disintegration and psychological disintegration, between breaking up and breaking down: so the ship, fearing her wrecking, becomes literally a nervous wreck'.

book to be support for liberal internationalism as against the supposed narrow nationalism of 'Judaism'. Yvonne Sherwood has ably catalogued this reading from its sources in (amongst others) the exegesis of Martin Luther – a man not renowned for his love of the Jews (pp. 21–32). I will not dwell on this *mis*-reading now, or on the inappropriateness of using the anachronism 'Judaism' in relation to the book of Jonah, beyond registering my own rejection of both as suitable terms of discourse. For what the book protests against is not, surely, a perceived infringement by God of a strict legal code, but rather the casual application of mercy where there is little if any evidence that it has been earned (4.2). I am reminded of Bonhoeffer's telling, if idealistic passage on cheap grace in *The Cost of Discipleship*, albeit in the context of specifically Christian commitment:

> Cheap grace is the grace we bestow on ourselves. Cheap grace is the preaching of forgiveness without requiring repentance, baptism without church discipline, Communion without confession, absolution without personal confession. Cheap grace is grace without discipleship, grace without the cross, grace without Jesus Christ, living and incarnate.
> Costly grace is the gospel which must be sought again and again and again, the gift which must be asked for, the door at which a man must knock. Such grace is costly because it calls us to follow, and it is grace because it calls us to follow Jesus Christ. It is costly because it costs a man his life, and it is grace because it gives a man the only true life. It is costly because it condemns sin, and grace because it justifies the sinner. Above all it is costly because it cost God the life of his Son. 'Ye were bought at a price', and what has cost God much cannot be cheap for us. Above all, it is grace because God did not reckon his Son too dear a price to pay for our life, but delivered him up for us. Costly grace is the Incarnation of God. (Bonhoeffer 1959: 36, 37; emphases removed)

On the other hand, note Perry's fascinating alternative reading of this motif, which removes it from the context of the forgiveness of the Ninevites to that of Jonah's personal relationship with God (pp. 137–41): he is not angry over God's fickle decision to forgive Nineveh, but because of his own failure to remember the truth about the nature of God which is enshrined in Exodus 34.

Of course Jonah's protest is questionable in terms of the covenant itself, which constituted an act of grace on the part of Yahweh ('It was not because you were great that I chose you'; it was an act of unmerited love: Deut. 7.7-8). Furthermore, that original act of grace depended subsequently on the willingness of the Hebrews to observe the terms of the covenant – but the likelihood of that could not be predicted in advance; hence the irony that Jonah, who explicitly disobeys God, and thus (presumably) stands to forfeit God's love, is ready to pre-judge others on the grounds that they were welcomed too readily into God's embrace. What he, and many commentators, fail to see is that there is nothing illogical in God's proposal to introduce a covenant based on repentance (indeed, that is clearly implicit in the prophetic corpus, even if it seems there to be confined to Israel) *with the same long-term condition: that the nations brought under its compass observe its terms.* The book of Jonah is therefore not a comment on the supposed failings of Judaism (supposing for a moment that it even existed at the time), nor is it a paean of praise to internationalism and the supposed superiority of gentiles. Instead it should be regarded as a thought experiment in which the writer imagines how a real threat (to the sailors) and the threat of a threat (to Nineveh) can engender in different ways positive responses to Yahweh. The rest of the story is left untold, as it must be. It is none of our business whether the sailors kept their vows or the Ninevites turned permanently from their evil ways, though we can suppose that in keeping with the strictures of Deuteronomy any relapse would have the same consequences for them as for the Israelites. What we should note, however, is that Jonah was never abandoned. The book ends with all of them – Jonah, the sailors, the citizens of the great city, and their children and animals, in narrative limbo.

> *⁵Then the mariners were afraid, and each cried to his god.*
> *They threw the cargo that was in the ship into the sea, to lighten it*
> *for them. Jonah, meanwhile, had gone down into the hold of the ship*
> *and had lain down, and was fast asleep'.*

The contrast in this verse between the sailors and Jonah is sharply drawn, and anticipates a similar, though less acute contrast between Jonah and the Ninevites in ch. 3. For the sailors all is action and bustle, epitomising the pragmatic combination of prayer and action which is advisable in situations of real danger. The cosmopolitan nature of the crew – a fact of the seafaring profession which has remained unchanged throughout the ages – is made very clear by the statement that 'each cried to his god'. We have no idea which nations were represented, but it seems likely that the gods at least of Greece, Tyre and Phoenicia were implicated, if not also deities from Italy and North Africa. Their collective impotence is one of the minor, but not unimportant lessons of the story: the author could hardly have chosen a better setting within which to demonstrate the unique power of 'the Lord, the God of heaven' who is ultimately confessed by Jonah. In this connection it is worth pointing to another significant contrast: the sailors' 'prayer' is in fact an inchoate cry of panic (*za'aq*), unlike Jonah's in 2.1 and 4.2, where the 'correct' term familiar from the psalms – *tephillah* – is indicated. Arguably Jonah, sinking to the bottom of the sea in the belly of the fish, might have been expected to respond with the same panicked yell that the sailors uttered. But Jonah perhaps was more laid back, certainly in the ship, if not in the fish. I suspect it is more likely that we are intended to grasp the same point about the superiority of Yahweh, a demonstration also found in 1 Kings 18 where the prophets of Ba'al call (*qara'*) upon their god, saying nothing more than 'Hear us, O Ba'al'. By contrast, Elijah 'speaks' to Yahweh, and his prayer consists of a coherent expression of specific desires, just as does Jonah's in ch. 2. The sailors are not mocked, unlike the prophets of Ba'al, whose god is jeeringly judged to be asleep, or in the men's room, while his prophets pray.

Another dramatic contrast is afforded by the story of Paul's shipwreck on the way to Rome, described in Acts 27. Almost everything here is reversed: there is an abundance of technical maritime detail; the distinguished passenger, far from being the cause of the storm, is the sailor's salvation (and the one who advised against setting sail in the first place); Paul is a prisoner rather than a willing passenger; and the outcome is the loss of the ship with no loss of life. Similarities include the throwing overboard of the cargo and the ship's tackle (vv. 18-19), and a process of divine intervention during which Paul, like Jonah, identifies his religious affiliation: 'For last night there stood by me an angel of the God to whom I belong and whom I worship' (v. 23). Did Luke set out deliberately to deconstruct Jonah? Given Luke's way with Tanakh models for his Gospel account (the various episodes in Luke 1 and 2 are heavily indebted to 1 Samuel 1 and 2) it is not unlikely that his account of Paul's adventure at sea bears a knowing resemblance to Jonah.

Despite these possible contrasts between Jonah and the sailors, we should note on the other hand that the verse opens with a verb strongly characteristic of the right attitude to God – that of fear (the verb is *yara'*) – and the cry of panic (*za'aq*) is associated in Isaiah's vineyard parable (Isa. 5.7) with the despairing cry of those who expected righteousness (or fair dealing – *tsedhaqah*) from God's chosen and were grievously disappointed. Thus while the sailors' cry is undoubtedly directed in the first instance to their own gods, the text plants for us a double expectation by the use of these two verbs: that proper awe of God will ensue, and that the responsibility that God's own have for the wider community will be enforced. It is no surprise, therefore, that the episode of the sailors ends in v. 16 with the declaration that 'they feared Yahweh greatly', and that the same words occur on an interim basis in v. 10 without an object: 'The sailors were terrified (literally, "feared greatly")'. These observations serve to qualify the rather stark contrast between the sailors' form of despairing appeal and Jonah's use of 'correct' liturgical terms which I noted in the previous paragraph, and his 'proper' use of *yara'* in v. 9. The author of Jonah is indeed a subtle operator.

Certain other turns of phrase are also of importance in this verse. The sailors 'hurl' the ship's implements into the sea, just as God 'hurled' the storm in the first instance, and as Jonah will in turn be 'hurled' into the sea (vv. 12, 15). It is tempting to understand this action as a form of sympathetic magic, the trick being to identify the object (or person) best fitted to placate whoever has caused the storm. At this stage that remains unclear, hence the desperate resort of throwing overboard whatever is not fixed in order to lighten the ship. The verb used here merits a comment, for its commonest meanings are 'to make light of', usually in a negative sense: thus, 'to despise' (Gen. 16.4, 5; 1 Sam. 20.30 etc.) or 'to curse' (on 76 occasions, including the related noun). It can also mean 'to make light of' – either people or situations. The use made of the verb here in Jonah is curiously limited: a (metaphoric) yoke is made lighter in 1 Kgs 12.4, 9, 10 (with parallels in Chronicles), and a burden is made lighter by being shared in Exod. 18.22; but only in Jonah is a physical object made (literally) lighter. One final, but highly significant instance should be noted: in Gen. 8.8, 11 it is the sea itself which 'becomes lighter', that is, subsides. The resonances between Jonah and the primeval narratives in Genesis are spelled out in more detail in Chapter 7; this coincidence serves to strengthen the connection in a suggestive way.

The sailors do not deliberately 'make light of' their plight, but by resorting to the same superstitious devices as (presumably) the Ninevites they demonstrate the futility of their beliefs and the impotence of their gods. Incidentally, there is a rather graphic aspect of this bit of business in the Hebrew which is lacking in English: what they actually seem to be doing is to lighten the ship 'from over them' (*me'alehem*); an odd turn of phrase which might conjure either the ship pictured falling down from the crest of a huge wave, or the ship envisaged as their enemy, but which also alludes to the verb 'to go up' which we have commented on above.

Jonah, meantime, sleeps the sleep of the just; or rather, he sleeps the sleep of the first man Adam when he fell into a trance in Eden while Eve was created. But first he has had to 'go down' two more times: down into the hold of the ship and down to sleep (*wayeradham*), a punning reference which I noted under v. 3. The implied reference to creation is not accidental, as Chapter 7 makes clear: the God of Jonah is conceived of as a creating God, and there may be an irony to be noted in the essentially barren and unproductive nature both of Jonah's sleep – which when enjoyed by Adam in the nominal form *tardemah* led to the birth of Eve – and God's 'appointments' in the form of fish, plant, worm and wind.

The 'hold' is in fact a Hebrew word (*yarkah*) usually used for particularly remote places. It is 'the ends of the earth' in Jer. 6.22, 25.32, 31.8, and 50.41; it is 'the far north', often with reference to God's location, in several places (Isa. 14.13; Ezek. 38.6, 15; 39.2; Ps. 48.3); it denotes remote locations in Ephraim and Lebanon (e.g. Judg. 19.1 and 2 Kgs 19.23); it is the innermost part of the house in Ps. 128.3 (where the wife goes about her work hidden from view) and Amos 6.10 (where fearful victims try to hide from their persecutors); and finally, Ezek. 32.23 uses it to describe the fate of Israel's enemies, Egypt and Assyria, whose dead are forever lost in the uttermost depths of the Pit. His words are sombre indeed:

> Assyria is there, and all its company, their graves all around it, all of them killed, fallen by the sword. Their graves are set in the uttermost part of the Pit. Its company is all around its grave, all of them killed, fallen by the sword, who spread terror in the land of the living.

Without wishing to make too much of this effect, it is clear that for Jonah to be in 'the uttermost part' of the ship is not simply a desire for solitude; it suggests absolute remoteness, a place either of infinite life or absolute death. Not a bad signifier for the challenge about to face Jonah.

> *⁶The captain came and said to him, 'What are you doing sound asleep? Get up, call on your god! Perhaps the god will spare us a thought so that we do not perish'.*

Up to this point in the story the relationship between Jonah and the sailors has been that of customer and crew: he had bought a ticket, their job was to deliver him safely to his destination, rather as modern travel has replaced passengers with customers and the sense of a shared (ad)venture with the rules of contract and compensation. A modern Jonah would, presumably, have been able to reclaim his fare from Ryanair along with an indignant five minutes of fame on YouTube regarding the deplorable lack of concern for safety on the part of cheap transport providers. To add insult to injury, presumably his own luggage formed part of the earlier sacrifice to the unheeding gods. But then, we all have tales of lost luggage, and they are supremely boring; sufficient explanation, perhaps, for this lacuna in the text.

Despairing of any hope of rescue, the captain (or *chief pilot*: see the discussion in Chapter 6) of the ship approaches – and reproaches – the sleeping beauty. He is, by the way, described as *rav*, which prompts an irrelevant but nonetheless tempting associating with the leadership cadre in later Judaism. No matter, his address to Jonah is understandably abrupt and impatient. 'What is it with you and sleeping?', followed by an echo of God's initial command: 'Get up', but this time to 'call upon your god'. Like many other passages in which foreigners refer to god, the Hebrew is careful to use the generic *'elohim* rather than the personal *Yhwh* who spoke to Jonah in v. 1, from whose presence he fled in v. 2, and who commanded the storm in v. 3. Jonah is a text which is hyper-sensitive to the presence of the other: its term of self identification for Jonah when he finally explains himself in v. 9 is Hebrew (*'ivri*), a term almost exclusively reserved for similar contexts, and it is clear that the sailors have to learn the name of his god – again, something which is evidenced in similar stories. I will explore these matters in more detail in the commentary to v. 9.

What the chief pilot asks of Jonah is limited. It amounts to little more than what the prophets of Ba'al did; namely, to call (*qara'*) upon his god. Significantly, the more technical term *tephillah* is not given to him or to his motley crew. And all that the cry seeks is that 'that god of yours' (a reasonable translation, I think, of *ha'elohim* following the reference to *'eloheyka*, 'your god') 'might pay us some heed'. The verb is reflexive, emphasising the self-absorption of the deity – something seen also in Elijah's mockery of Ba'al – and is preceded by a conjunction ('would that', 'perhaps') which suggests a rather abject note of pleading. Given the well-established links between Jonah and Elijah, the text of 1 Kgs 18.27 is particularly suggestive:

> At noon Elijah mocked them, saying, 'Cry aloud! Surely he is a god; either he is meditating, or he has wandered away, or he is on a journey, or perhaps he is asleep and must be awakened'.

The suggestion that the god is asleep or on a journey is particularly pointed, given than *both* are attributes of Jonah at precisely this point! The verse concludes 'that we might not perish', a verb which has a considerable back-story in scripture. Its predominant use is to express the fatal effects of divine judgement against both Israel and the nations, with a minor meaning of 'to be lost, to stray'. It is also used with reference to things and abstract qualities – again frequently in a situation of judgement. Its use here is a clear signal that the crew of the ship were well aware that the hand of 'god' (or 'the gods') is at work – a nuance equally evident in the repetition of the same verb 'perish' in 1.14 and 3.9, and even perhaps in the destruction of the *qiqayon* – as the direct result of God's action – in 4.10.

It is odd in the context of the narrative that the request that Jonah might pray to his god meets no response. There is no record at this point of his prayer to any god, nor does he explain his deep sleep. This is one of these silences, or aporias, so beloved of both rabbinic and deconstructive exegesis, begging for imaginative interpolation: did Jonah pray only to meet with silence; or did he simply keep silent himself, in his guilty knowledge that any prayer from him was unlikely to meet with success? And was it this avoidance by Jonah or silence from his god that forced the sailors into their resort to casting lots? But we know already that Jonah is not a man to take a telling: someone capable of distancing himself from Yahweh is hardly likely to pay much attention to the pleas of a mere ship's pilot. More seriously, on what basis might Jonah have uttered the requisite appeal? He knew perfectly well that he was an absconder, and (judging from his subsequent actions) he knew equally well that the predicament they all found themselves in was exclusively of his making. No mere plea was likely, at this point, to be effective; moreover, if Jonah had read his Bible – as his 'biographer' undoubtedly had – he knew with equal certainty that Yahweh's punishment of the guilty by no means included any effort to protect the innocent (witness the fate of Agag and the Amalekites in 1 Sam. 15, where Saul is damned not for genocide, but for his imperfect completion of the act under God's instruction). Perhaps silence was the only safe option at this stage. Maybe the sailors' seamanship might yet defeat the dark designs of the deity.

Chapter 4

JONAH 1.7-10: THE LOTTERY

⁷The sailors said to one another, 'Come, let us cast lots, so that we may know on whose account this calamity has come upon us'. So they cast lots, and the lot fell on Jonah. ⁸Then they said to him, 'Tell us why this calamity has come upon us. What is your occupation? Where do you come from? What is your country? And of what people are you?' ⁹'I am a Hebrew', he replied. 'I worship the LORD, the God of heaven, who made the sea and the dry land'. ¹⁰Then the men were even more afraid, and said to him, 'What is this that you have done!' For the men knew that he was fleeing from the presence of the LORD, because he had told them so.

⁷The sailors said to one another, 'Come, let us cast lots, so that we may know on whose account this calamity has come upon us'. So they cast lots, and the lot fell on Jonah.

The sailors now propose that they 'cause the lots to fall' (= the more prosaic English: 'cast lots'): a nice example of Hebrew's potential to introduce unintentional irony, in that a completely random process (casting lots) is defined by a causative form of the verb 'to fall' (*nafal*), as if some form of intention were involved. What they seek from this process is to 'know' (*yada'*) who is responsible for their present distress. Once again we encounter a verb used ironically in relation to the actual possibility of such certainty: modern readers (and some ancients) are – and were – well aware of the uncertainty attached to all forms of oracular information. The paradigm case of the Oracle of Delphi and the enquiry made by King Croesus is familiar enough, but the general principle is not new, and might well have informed the way that the author of Jonah deliberately manipulates his readers' naïvety. For, lo and behold, the lots when cast point to Jonah; an outcome which must have surprised no-one, since he seems to have been the only passenger, and hence the only unpredictable factor. In addition his distinctly odd behaviour surely marked him as a decidedly dubious character.

The lot is most commonly a device to share out either land or duties (this is its purpose in Numbers, Joshua, Chronicles and Nehemiah, with negative forms in Ezek. 24.6; Joel 3.3; Nah. 3.10; and Obad. 11). It is also, in parallel with the word for 'share' or 'portion', used with reference to what God will allocate – not necessarily a good thing! Thus Isa. 17.14; 34.17; 57.6; Jer. 13.25; and Ps. 16.5. None of these seem to be pertinent to what is going on in Jonah; but there are a few remaining instances which shed a little light. There is the mysterious 'casting of Pur' in Est. 3.7 and 9.24, which is linked to Haman's plotting for the downfall of the Jews; Prov. 16.33 offers the aphorism that 'The lot is cast into the lap, but the decision is the Lord's alone', which might explain the mechanism in Jon. 1.7; and finally – and perhaps most significantly – we have the use of the lot to select the scapegoat in the Azazel ritual in Lev. 16.7-10.

From all of this we might conclude, tentatively, that Jonah is being selected as a scapegoat to appease the elements, and that there is no chance of the lot falling on the wrong person, since its use in Hebrew is in fact quite different from our use of terms like 'lottery', whether applied to the unpredictability of life or of national lotteries. This reading is, however, difficult, since it is unclear who the second goat might be (the crew collectively?) and it seems to imply that the foe is some sort of demon, if that is what Azazel is in Leviticus.

Finally in v. 7 we turn to the phrase 'on whose account this calamity has come upon us'. There are two linguistic points of note: the word for 'calamity' is in fact *ra'ah*, which is the term used in v. 2 to identify Nineveh's 'wickedness'; and 'on whose account' uses a Hebrew form more typical of later Rabbinic syntax. The latter contributes to an overall argument about the date of Jonah, in tandem with the recognition of a number of possible Aramaisms, and need not delay us further at this point. The former might be a consequence of the range of meanings covered by the root in question, but a certain transferred significance should not be ruled out: because Jonah has fled from his responsibility to deal with Nineveh's wickedness, that quality of evil has transferred to others with whom he has contact. Significantly we find Jonah himself experiencing a similar 'evil' when God spares Nineveh – and is accused by Jonah of being soft on evil (4.1, 3). It is as if this *ra'ah* is a substance (rather like chewing gum or dog turd) which attaches itself to unsuspecting innocent feet once it has been discarded by its original host. Jonah passes it on to the sailors; at the end of Jonah's sea adventures it presumably returns to the Ninevites; their repentance frees them of the sticky substance, which proceeds to fasten once again to Jonah (4.1). At the end of the book, in a kind of ethical musical chairs, he is left with stuff on his shoes and no-one (not even the animals) to pass it off on.

> [8]*Then they said to him, 'Tell us why this calamity has come upon us. What is your occupation? Where do you come from? What is your country? And of what people are you?'*

Belatedly, perhaps, the sailors enquire into Jonah's antecedents, though even this is not entirely plain sailing (forgive the atrocious pun), as the mysterious remark at the end of v. 10 indicates. It may seem strange to modern readers, familiar as we all are with the bureaucracy of passports, visas and other red tape which restrict travel, that Jonah could just jump on a ship and set sail. On the other hand, would travel in the early Roman period in the Mediterranean have required documents, or simply enough money to provide the captain and his crew with a decent bonus at the end of the journey? (See further in Chapter 6.)

The question put to Jonah uses an emphatic form: 'Tell us, we beg you', stressing the point that the sailors want to ascertain as the most urgent priority just *why* the ship has run into danger, a problem that might be resolved once they discover who Jonah is and what his business. The NRSV translation at this point is less than felicitous, since it masks the intimate connection between Jonah himself and the 'evil' that has befallen them. Rather than the bland 'Tell us why …' we should read the much more expressive and intimate, 'Tell us, we beg you, on whose account …', a phrasing which makes it clear that far from being a routine cause-and-effect question, this expresses a search for the real existential character of Jonah, the only datum which might explain the extreme danger they all face. Four questions then follow: What is your business/occupation? Where are you from? (Literally, Where are you coming from?) What is your country? From which nation do you hail? Clearly the first of these continues the question posed at the beginning, since the answer to 'Why has this happened?' is likely to be bound up with an explanation of Jonah's business. It is, therefore, rather striking that Jonah gives no answer to either of these questions. In fact, assuming he was not a professional prophet, quite what his day job was remains a mystery. The only thing we can deduce is that he had the spare resources (and time) to contemplate lengthy journeys, whether to Tarshish or to Nineveh. Perhaps the author of the book has subconsciously modelled his anti-hero on Amos, a man of business and property who was also free to take time off the travel for God, and who was equally robust in denying he was any kind of professional seer. This is admittedly the merest speculation, but it is not without plausibility; certainly the denial of professionalism is something of a defining characteristic of the so-called writing prophets; that is, those after whom eponymous books are named. It is in marked contrast with the kind of sooth-saying for reward that would appear to have been the regular trade of the bands of prophets that roamed the countryside (see, for example, 1 Sam. 10.9-13; 1 Kgs 22.5-12; 2 Kgs 2.15-18, and the stories associated with Elisha in 2 Kgs 3–6), in both Israel and Judah, and the wider ancient Near Eastern.

The remaining questions, as we shall see in the next verse, are entirely ignored except for a single cryptic phrase 'a Hebrew I' (*'ivri 'anokhi*) from Jonah by way of explanation, and this constitutes a further authorial obfuscation. Not only do we not know what Jonah did, we have no idea where he lived; we do not even know whether he was an Israelite or a Judaean, a city dweller or a country lad. In short, the sailors' attempt to get hard facts out of Jonah, to locate him in space and time, and to clarify the position generally, are as doomed as are our own attempts to 'give to airy nothing a local habitation and a name'. There is a satisfyingly postmodern dimension to this: the sailors stand for the historicising preferences of modern biblical criticism as it has been practised since the days of Wellhausen, while the character of Jonah in the hands of his author deliberately confounds the desire for historical certainty.

Tanakh is good at 'embedded uncertainty', that is, of evading the straightforward answer to the plain question, something which is an endless source of frustration to dogmatists and systematic theologians. Right at the beginning the man and the woman in the garden try to wriggle out of their disobedience by their evasive answers to Yahweh's questions, 'Who told you that you were naked? Have you eaten from the tree?' Then in Genesis 12 Abram sidesteps the truth about who Sarah is in order to keep in Pharaoh's good books – and does so by getting Sarah to lie on his behalf. Abraham is again found to be less than straightforward when Isaac, on the verge of being sacrificed, asks him, 'Where is the lamb for a burnt offering?' Abraham mutters (in his beard?) 'God himself will provide the lamb for a burnt-offering' – a claim he had no grounds at all for believing to be true. Examples multiply in the repeated deceptions found in the stories of Jacob and Joseph – deceptions on which the very survival of the patriarchal line apparently chosen by God depends.

So it is not surprising to find the mother of all evasions at the point when Moses enquires politely of the Deity, 'When people ask who has sent me, what shall I say?' The exchange, in Exod. 3.13-15, merits being quoted in full:

> But Moses said to God, 'If I come to the Israelites and say to them, "The God of your ancestors has sent me to you", and they ask me, "What is his name?" what shall I say to them?' God said to Moses, 'I AM WHO I AM:' He also said to Moses, 'Thus you shall say to the Israelites, "The LORD, the God of your ancestors, the God of Abraham, the God of Isaac, and the God of Jacob, has sent me to you". This is my name for ever, and this my title for all generations.'

The phrase 'I am who I am' (in Hebrew *'ehyeh 'asher 'ehyeh*) is impossible to translate without ambiguity. NRSV itself offers as alternatives 'I am what I am' and 'I will be what I will be', and others have speculated further along the lines of 'I will become what I will become' and 'I will be what you will find me to be'. In other words, the definition opens up more questions than it answers, even if we can agree that it all centres on the verb 'to be'. Even the 'clarification' at the end of the passage which brings in Abraham, Isaac and Jacob adds nothing about the nature of God beyond the statement that the deity we are dealing with is Israel's deity – something Pharaoh (for whose benefit this is ultimately intended) could probably have worked out for himself.

> *⁹'I am a Hebrew', he replied. 'I worship the LORD,*
> *the God of heaven, who made the sea and the dry land'.*

Jonah's reply in v. 9 begins with a self-characterisation which is in fact unknown elsewhere in Tanakh. 'I am a Hebrew', he says; an *'ivri* – a term which is virtually exclusively used by others when speaking of Jews, and almost always in the context of foreigners. Nowhere else is the term used as it is here, as a form of *self*-identification.

Various attempts at its etymology have been made, including links with a mysterious ancient Near Eastern group known as the Hapiru (variously spelled), and proposals that it relates to the verb *'abar* which means 'to cross over', and might have echoes of nomadism in its semantic range. There is one nice example of the two words placed together, in 1 Sam. 13.7: 'Some Hebrews crossed the Jordan'. We might also anticipate a modest irony in Jon. 2.3, where the waters 'pass over' Jonah the Hebrew. But a health warning is in order at this point: the latter etymology does not meet with scholarly approval, and the former is so diversely interpreted by historians and archaeologists as to be virtually useless. Sasson (pp. 115–17), provides a useful summary of relevant information and the biblical usages can be summed up as follows:

(1) Abram is thus described in Gen. 14.13, the story of the invasion of Canaan by an alliance of four great kingdoms from Mesopotamia.
(2) In Gen. 39.14, 17 Joseph is described as a Hebrew by Potiphar's wife, then later, in 41.12, by the cupbearer. At one point Joseph himself, as if recognising this foreign usage, states that he 'was stolen out of the land of the Hebrews' – which incidentally leaves it a moot point whether he thought of himself as a Hebrew, and if so, what that might imply. It might indeed only indicate a geographical identity.
(3) There is a somewhat more confusing picture in the opening chapters of Exodus where the story of the midwives and the killing of the children makes particular use of 'Hebrew' to distinguish between Israelite and Egyptian midwives (1.15, 16, 19; 2.6, 7). The term is used next in 2.11, 13 in the story of Moses' interference in the quarrel between two 'Hebrews'.
(4) A key instance is to be found in Exod. 3.18, where the standard saying 'the God of Abraham, of Isaac, and of Jacob' (v. 16) becomes 'the God of the Hebrews' in the version intended for Pharaoh's ears (cf. 5.3; 7.16; 9.1, 13; 10.3). It would appear that God's instructions to Moses take account of the difference by explicitly using the term where Moses is given words to speak to Pharaoh, whereas the narrative – directed towards Jewish readers – uses 'Israelite'.
(5) In 1 Sam. 4.6, 9; 13.19; 14.11; and 29.3 the Philistines use the expression when referring to the Israelites.
(6) There are a few occurrences remaining in 1 Samuel (13.3, 7; 14.21) which might give the impression that the Hebrews were a separate group from the Israelites, one which aligned itself with the Israelites as a result of Saul's victories over the Philistines. It is not clear how much significance to accord this case – though it is tempting to recall that David, Saul's successor and rival, was at one time in the service of the Philistines.
(7) Finally, there is a completely different meaning given to the term in the legal material in Exod. 21.2, where it seems to refer to someone within the community who is caught up in debt-slavery.

However, in the light of its other occurrences, we might be justified even here in seeing the expression as one that described the more general population within which the Jews (or Israelites) formed a self-identified ethnos.

This would raise the even more interesting possibility that, at least in the texts which deal with the period prior to the establishment of independent states, there was no clear difference between the Israelites in particular and the 'Hebrew' population of Canaan in general. This possibility is strengthened by the fact that in Daniel, which in other respects has many similarities both of plot and of verbal detail with Joseph, the Babylonians are well aware that Daniel comes from Judah (cf. 2.25). In Daniel the term Hebrew is not used. Thus when we return to Jonah – and a likely date of composition not much different from at least the core traditions of Daniel – its use here seems all the more pointed. There is, in short, a deliberate emphasis on foreignness at this point. The sailors are foreign. Jonah is foreign to the sailors. They are headed for (foreign) Tarshish as an alternative to the definitively alien Nineveh. I suspect that Jonah is here presented as practising a certain dissimulation; for even the terms in which he describes Yahweh are somewhat unconventional, as I shall show shortly when I look more closely at the identity of 'Jonah's God'.

Jonah's response seems to have little if anything to do with the sailor's questions. It relates more to a deliberate signal to the reader that the god encountered both by Jonah and by us is the God of creation, or rather – to be precise – the Lord, the God of heaven, maker of both the sea and the dry land; the God, explicitly, of the second creation account in Genesis. This is the God who gets his/her hands dirty in the process of making and shaping, rather like the God of the book of Jonah who fussily provides for all kinds of minutiae of the natural world purely, it seems, in order to annoy our hero. If Jonah is trying to keep his distance from his divine pursuer by banishing him to the heavens, the author subverts that desire by choosing exactly that part of the opening chapters of Genesis which eschews the remote 'God said …' in favour of the more intimate 'The Lord God made …'.

The structure of v. 9 is interesting in itself, in that the syntax is oddly divided in such a way as to provide a kind of parallelism which offers information arguably absent from a surface reading of Jonah's reply. It reads, literally, as follows:

1 Then he said to them.
2   A Hebrew am I (*'anokhi*),
3   and the Lord, the God of heaven,
4   I (*'ani*) am in awe of –
5   who made the sea and the dry land

There are a range of parallels and contrasts in this short piece, not the least of which is the contrast between the term 'Hebrew' in its popular meaning of *nomad*, and the solid, fixed, heavenly identity of Yahweh, the God of whom Jonah stands in awe. There are the twin contrasts between heaven on the one hand and land and sea on the other, and between the sea and the dry land, and there is a relatively rare chiastic use of the first person forms in lines two and four which reinforces the sense of solipsism which surrounds the character of Jonah.

The only instances known to me which seem to have a similar structure are Exod. 17.7 ('Thus you will know that I [*'ani*] am Yahweh / behold I [*'anokhi*] will strike with the staff of my hand the water of the Nile'); Job 13.2 ('What you know I [*'ani*] also know / no less am I [*'anokhi*] than you'); Job 33.9 ('You say I [*'ani*] am clean, without transgression; / pure am I [*'anokhi*], and there is no iniquity in me'); and Isa. 45.12:

I (*'anokhi*) made the earth,

and humankind upon it created

I (*'ani*) – my hands – stretched out the heavens,

and all their host commanded.

Of these the Isaiah passage is the most tantalising given its subject matter which reverses the subject order: here God rules the first and third lines, humankind the second and the fourth.

With the luxury of hindsight, etymology, and a developed sense of context, we can draw out of this brief poem (for surely such it is) the poignant portrait of an insecure, rootless, self-absorbed individual who is well aware of the nature of the God from whom he is fleeing, and who is ironically able to apply the seemingly traditional language of Yahweh's creation of the world to the very specific and immediate predicament he and the sailors face: the desire for dry land and the life-threatening reality of the sea, combined with the desire for and simultaneous effort to avoid God. A further irony is to be found in the reference to the heavens, whence came the dreadful storm which caused their predicament.

The skill of the author is clearly seen in this verse, which communicates so much to us while concealing everything from its audience within the narrative. The sailors learn nothing useful – indeed, as we shall see, their reaction is so unexpected that we are given, at the end of the next verse, a fake gloss to see us through the impasse.

The key terms in Jonah's credo, as expressed in 1.9, are: the divine name Yahweh; the generic term Elohim; God's location in 'the heavens'; the verb *'asah*, 'to make'; and the two objects of God's making – the sea (*yam*) and the dry land (*yavashah*). Nowhere else in Tanakh does this precise collocation of expressions occur. This is not the only unusual feature, however, as the more detailed analysis which follows demonstrates.

The Title 'Yahweh, God of Heaven'
This phrase is found in a few other locations: twice in the story of Abraham's arrangements to identify a wife for Isaac (Gen. 24.3, 7); once (2 Chron. 36.23 = Ezra 1.2) on the lips of Cyrus when he issues his decree for the return of the Jews to Judea; and once uttered by Nehemiah (1.5) in a prayer. There are three instances, all associated with Nehemiah, in which the divine name Yahweh is omitted (1.4; 2.4, 20). It could be argued that all of these uses have a Mesopotamian connection – Abraham is supposed to have lived there, as did Nehemiah – which is rather fitting for the context of Jonah. As a footnote, it is only Jonah who uses the verb 'to fear'/'to be in awe of' to describe his relationship with this God.

God the Creator of Heaven and Earth: Citations Similar to Jonah 1.9
Jonah goes on to attribute to this deity the making of the sea and the dry land – and this also is unique to the book in the precise form it takes here. There are however examples of closely similar phrases, in all of which the objects of creation are 'the heavens and the earth'.

a. Subject Yahweh: Exod. 20.11; 31.17; Pss. 121.2; 124.8; 134.3; Jer. 32.17 (the verb is *'asah*)
b. Subject Elohim: Gen. 1.1 (the verb is *bara'*, 'to create')
c. Subject Yahweh + Elohim (in Chronicles + 'of Israel'): Gen. 2.4; 2 Chron. 2.12; Ps. 146.5-6 (the verb is *'asah*)
d. Subject El Elyon: Gen. 14.19 (the verb is *qanah*, 'to acquire')
e. Subject Yahweh + El Elyon: Gen. 14.22 (the verb is *qanah*)

God the Creator of Heaven and Earth: Citations Differing from Jonah 1.9
I add here for completeness a number of other passages in which the same description of God as maker of heaven and earth is found, but in language quite different from that of Jonah.

    a. Passages which are all broadly speaking wisdom formulae (see also Prov. 8.22-31 for a more extended treatment):
(Prov. 3.19) The LORD by wisdom founded the earth;/by understanding he established the heavens;
(Ps. 102.35) Long ago you laid the foundations of the earth,/and the heavens are the work of your hands.
(Jer. 10.12 = 51.15) It is he who made the earth by his power,/who established the world by his wisdom,/and by his understanding stretched out the heavens.

    b. Passages which use the characteristic vocabulary of 'stretching' and 'spreading' (see also Isa. 45.12):
(Isa. 42.5) Thus says God the LORD,/who created the heavens and stretched them out,/who spread out the earth and what comes from it,/who gives breath to the people upon it/and spirit to those who walk on it.
(Isa. 44.24) I am the LORD, who made all things/who alone stretched out the heavens,/who by myself spread out the earth;
(Isa. 51.13) You have forgotten the LORD, your Maker,/who stretched out the heavens/and laid the foundations of the earth.
(Zech. 12.1) Thus says the LORD, who stretched out the heavens and founded the earth and formed the human spirit within.

    c. General descriptions of God as creator of the heavens and the earth:
(Isa. 45.18) For thus says the LORD,/who created the heavens (he is God!),/who formed the earth and made it/(he established it;/he did not create it a chaos,/he formed it to be inhabited!).
(Neh. 9.6) And Ezra said: 'You are the LORD, you alone; you have made heaven, the heaven of heavens, with all their host, the earth and all that is on it, the seas and all that is in them.'

Clearly the formulation in Jon. 1.9 is entirely in keeping with late usage – almost all of the passages cited have a post-exilic or later provenance – and it is in keeping with the kind of language attributed to exilic circles. Nevertheless, in the final analysis and with regard to its specifics, the verse as a whole is strikingly original.

¹⁰Then the men were even more afraid, and said to him, 'What is this that you have done!' For the men knew that he was fleeing from the presence of the LORD, because he had told them so.

There is a lot of fear, awe, terror, and reverence in the first chapter of Jonah, with the same verb serving to represent a whole gamut of experiences. The sailors are 'afraid' in v. 5, Jonah 'respects' God in v. 9, the men 'fear a great fear' in v. 10, and the men 'fear a great fear of YHWH' in v. 16. By contrast, the concept does not reappear anywhere else in the book, despite the fact that many other terms in ch. 1 are deployed throughout the narrative and the psalm. The dual meanings in the root *yr'* are reminiscent of the slogan briefly used by the Pentagon at the start of the second Iraq war, 'Shock and awe' – a slogan which by coincidence disappeared rather quickly from official use. It is tempting to draw a parallel – just as the invasion slogan was dropped in favour of an attempt to win the hearts and minds of Iraqis, so the book of Jonah replaces the theme of the God of violence and fear with that of the deity who is ready to repent in the face of signs of remorse on the part of the Ninevites. Dare one extend the parallel by suggesting that, just as in modern Iraq there are deeply problematic issues relating to the real extent of any commitment to the Western democratic agenda, so one might legitimately question whether in the unwritten aftermath of Jonah's intervention there was any lasting change in the policies, practices and beliefs of the people of ancient Nineveh (or, for that matter, Jerusalem!).

The specific reference of the sailors' fear in this verse is, of course, their knowledge of Jonah's flight from God, 'for he had made this known to them'. This phrase is one of the oddest in the whole book, though it is nevertheless in keeping with the repeated use of gaps or aporia by the author. There is no previous hint that Jonah had said anything of the sort to them – indeed, it is much more likely that he would have kept quiet on the subject, since his purchase of a ticket on the boat would have been severely compromised had the crew known what a danger he might prove to be. Nothing earlier in this passage indicates that they had the slightest clue what was going on, though, from a pedantic point of view, the statement at the end of v. 3 that he had embarked with them 'to get away from the Lord' could be held to show that they *should* have known. This does open a narrow opportunity for an explanation, along the lines of their sudden realisation of what 'getting away from YHWH' meant. They should have known, for he had said – but only now does the full force dawn of who YHWH is and what disobeying him entails. This fits with the previous verses in which they ask Jonah to pray to his god (v. 6) and to give an account of himself (v. 8), for it is only then that Jonah makes explicit the connection between YHWH and the god who made heaven and earth. This explanation comes close to the legal principle that ignorance is no excuse. The fact that they had never heard of YHWH only compounds their predicament; the fact that the chapter ends with the sailors' fear of, sacrifice to, and swearing an oath before YHWH only serves to confirm the truth of this observation.

To sum up, the full horror of Jonah's guilt is now apparent, and in consequence the sheer enormity of what faces the crew. Hence their shocked exclamation, 'What on earth have you done?' – an idiomatic translation of 'What is this that you have done?' which I think picks up nicely the reference to YHWH as creator in v. 9 and anticipates their imminent futile attempt to row the boat ashore (literally, to dry land).

Chapter 5

JONAH 1.11-16: AN ETHICAL DILEMMA

¹¹Then they said to him, 'What shall we do to you, that the sea may quieten down for us?' For the sea was growing more and more tempestuous. ¹²He said to them, 'Pick me up and throw me into the sea; then the sea will quieten down for you; for I know it is because of me that this great storm has come upon you'. ¹³Nevertheless, the men rowed hard to bring the ship back to land, but they could not, for the sea grew more and more stormy against them. ¹⁴Then they cried out to the LORD, 'Please, O LORD, we pray, do not let us perish on account of this man's life. Do not make us guilty of innocent blood; for you, O LORD, have done as it pleased you'. ¹⁵So they picked Jonah up and threw him into the sea; and the sea ceased from its raging. ¹⁶Then the men feared the LORD even more, and they offered a sacrifice to the LORD and made vows.

¹¹Then they said to him, 'What shall we do to you, that the sea may quieten down for us?' For the sea was growing more and more tempestuous.

It is often said that the sailors' response to the realisation that Jonah is the cause of their trouble verges on the noble, on the self-denying. Perry (pp. 7–12) questions this in a subtle examination of the next part of the story, focusing in particular on the self-serving nature of their pleas to be forgiven (when all else fails) for having thrown Jonah to his death. He finds them guilty, at the very least, of assisted suicide. Nonetheless, the naïve reader cannot help but be moved by their attempts to avoid what in the end proves to be inevitable. For within the terms of the discourse and its obvious links to similar folk motifs we are surely directed by the author towards feelings of admiration. This is all the stronger for the obvious contrast we are invited to draw between the brave sailors who confront their fears and the coward Jonah who flees from his duty.

The fact that they are presented as asking Jonah what they should do with him in order to calm the sea is already significant: they know that the sea is getting angrier and angrier and they know their classical mythology, so the equation is a simple one. Perhaps their question is disingenuous – if Jonah himself tells them to do what all the folk-tales prescribe, they're safely off the hook, exonerated. But time is of the essence: the ever-increasing fury of the god-sent storm gives them little room for manoeuvre. The legend most often cited (see Handy, p. 172 n. 44) as a possible source for the sacrifice of Jonah to the sea/monster is the story of Andromeda. There is some evidence that this myth was associated with Joppa, but it would be far-fetched to propose a direct comparison. The myth itself concerns a princess (daughter of Cassiopeia and Cepheus) who is sacrificed to a sea-monster Cetus who is ravaging the kingdom in response to an unwise boast on the part of the queen. Andromeda is chained to a rock on the coast, but is rescued in due course by Perseus. A similar legend concerns the king of Troy, Laomedon, sacrificing his daughter Hesione to appease Poseidon and Apollo; in this case the heroic rescuer is Herakles. The sacrifice of a daughter is a sadly common theme in the ancient world – to the two already cited we can add, from Greece, the fate of Iphigeneia (Agamemnon's daughter) sacrificed to ensure the success of the Greek expedition against Troy, and from Tanakh the sacrifice of Jethro's daughter (Judg. 11.29-40).

The most obvious objection to all of these putative parallels is the fact that Jonah was no-one's daughter, and was for that reason a relatively free agent who chose his own fate, albeit under pressure from Yahweh and the sailors. However there is one other remote possibility in the Babylonian myth of Marduk and Tiamat which was almost certainly known in literary circles in post-exilic Judah (it may have influenced aspects of the creation account in Gen. 1), and which involves the heroic struggle by the young god Marduk to defeat the primal sea-monster Tiamat. There are echoes of this myth in some developments of the Exodus tradition in Tanakh – see, for example, Ps. 74.12-18, and my discussion of this (Hunter 1999, pp. 152–4, and Chapter 6 below). The struggle of Jonah to survive entombment in the whale, then, might be a bathetic reinvention of the Babylonian tale.

> [12]*He said to them, 'Pick me up and throw me into the sea; then the sea will quieten down for you; for I know it is because of me that this great storm has come upon you'.*

Jonah's response is immediate and unequivocal; as abrupt, indeed, as his later terse and effective words to the people of Nineveh: 'Pick me up;

hurl me overboard; that way the sea will subside'. It is no accident that the verb 'to hurl' here is the same as that describing god's initial sending of the storm in v. 4, and then the sailors' hurling of the ship's contents into the sea. Powerful sympathetic magic is hinted at, and the sailors can hardly have missed the point. But just in case they don't, Jonah goes on to repeat almost exactly the words of v. 7, though in first person: 'I know (I am perfectly well aware) that it is because of me that this terrible storm has beset you'. He replaces the more general 'this great evil' with the specific 'this terrible storm', but the replacement amounts to an acknowledgement by Jonah that he is fully aware of all the details of what has happened. This highlights an important aspect of the wider Jonah story: the extent to which he is presented as being aware of just what is going on. He knows God's nature (grand designer of heaven and earth, but too forgiving by far), he knows his own character (cynical, self-protective, a bit aggressive), he knows the rules (a primitive but ineluctable cause-and-effect) and he knows the Ninevites (not to be trusted, especially when they bring on the big repentance show for the benefit of an all-too-gullible deity). That Jonah has knowledge is something he shares with the mainstream prophets: what distinguishes him is that his knowledge is unashamedly current. He makes only one prediction – in 3.4, but that is little more than a throwaway conventional threat drawn from the repertoire of rent-a-prophet. Everything else belongs to the rather world-weary conventions of the man who knows that he serves an unreliable God within an entirely predictable framework of cause and effect.

These observations point to another important aspect of the book of Jonah. The combination of fear and knowledge in ch. 1 is of course a combination found also in the wisdom tradition, which regularly affirms that 'the fear of YHWH is the beginning of wisdom'. The term 'wisdom' is not itself found in Jonah (though its opposite might be implied in the famous concluding description of the Ninevites who 'do not know the difference between left and right'), but the sailors 'know' what Jonah is really about. Nevertheless, Jonah's knowingness might well be understood as a deliberate attack on the platitudes of wisdom, for while he begins with fear (v. 9) that fear proves to be the beginning not of wisdom but of rebellion and of pride ('I know you, God, better than yourself', to paraphrase 4.2b). That Jonah might belong, parodically, with wisdom, is not a new suggestion (see, for example, Wolff, pp. 80–8 passim); what is perhaps new is the proposal that it implies a God who favours those who are foolish. This brings us close to the territory carved out by Paul in 1 Cor. 1.18-25; the difference is that Paul meant it. No knowing (*sic*) reader of Jonah could have failed to see the irony that in the end

Nineveh was destroyed and its people vanished, their vapid repentance as hollow and ineffectual as the gourd that sheltered Jonah. This in turn raises the interesting possibility that Jonah was right, his assessment of the situation accurate, and that one meaning of the book is the futility of quick repentance and easy grace. We find ourselves, in the end, at one with Bonhoeffer's moral and somewhat daunting stringency, referred to above in our discussion of verse five.

> *[13]Nevertheless, the men rowed hard to bring the ship back to land, but they could not, for the sea grew more and more stormy against them.*

The response of the sailors in v. 13 is to redouble their efforts to break the chain of cause and effect by human means. Translators tend to interpret the simple Hebrew construction at the beginning of this verse as contrastive: thus NRSV has 'Nevertheless, the men rowed hard …'. The single-letter form *waw* which introduces this verse is the commonest connecting particle in Hebrew, used to join words and clauses. Its meaning is drawn from context, rather than from any predetermined definition, and it is variously translated as 'and', 'but', 'nevertheless', 'therefore', and so on. The contrastive reading is tempting, for it resonates with both the sailors' defiance of Jonah's plea and a rejection of the supernatural ordering of events. But it is not indicated grammatically (the contrastive form is often indicated where there is a clear negative thought in the second clause), and the narrative flows smoothly (unlike the sea!) from the previous two verses. I wonder if we would be better to read v. 13, therefore, as if it were describing an action simultaneous with the conversation in the previous two verses: it is, after all, unlikely that the rowers would have stopped their work while the captain and his officers questioned Jonah. If the ship was typical of those Greek and Phoenician vessels that plied the Mediterranean, the oarsmen would have been slaves or hired oarsmen who would certainly not have had any part in the dialogue between the crew and Jonah. Thus a better translation might be something like: 'Meanwhile the rowers kept on rowing, trying to reach the dry land; but they could not, for the storm grew ever more violent'. Incidentally, the verb used is not the normal one for rowing; its meaning elsewhere is 'to dig'. This offers a very dramatic image of the rowers *digging in* to the turbulent ocean, desperate to *dig* their way out of trouble.

The grammatical form used in the last phrase of this verse and at the end of v. 11, 'grew *more and more* stormy', is not uncommon – but there are two particular instances which might have special relevance to our story. One is to be found in Exod. 19.19, where the blast of the *shofar* announcing the advent of YHWH at Sinai goes on getting louder and louder. It is tempting to conclude that the author of Jonah, familiar with some form of Tanakh, is prompting the reader here, given that the storm also has a theophanic dimension. This possibility is reinforced, as we shall see, by the very detailed exodus references set out in Chapter 9, and by the links to Genesis discussed in Chapter 7. And that latter connection prompts the second pertinent example. In Gen. 8.3, 5 the same grammatical construction is used to describe the process by which the waters of the flood gradually receded. It is tempting, given that there are as we have already seen other hints of the flood story in Jonah, to identify a deliberate device at this point.

In the light of these remarks, the contrast between the honest endeavours of the rowers and the purposeful intervention of God is stark indeed, and reminds us of the multi-layered nature of the discourse. At the lowest level, characters who go about their business wholly unknowingly: the oarsmen, the citizens of Nineveh, the big fish, the gourd and the worm, and the famous cattle of Nineveh. One level up we find those who know there's something going on and imagine (delusionally) that they can do something about it: the sailors and the captain; the king and his court; the third level is populated only by Jonah, unless we include the whole body of prophets whose name he is probably taking in vain. This represents those who know what is going on, know what to do, and may or may not do it. From the point of view of kings and establishments, prophets are famously independent-minded, and have a corresponding tendency to go off-message: thus Micaiah in 1 Kings 22, Elijah and Jeremiah almost as a career choice, and Isaiah in his encounter with Ahaz (7.10-25). Only Jonah, however, goes off the *divine* message. Even to use the phrase 'off-message' is to beg another question: what *is* the message? – a puzzle which can be seen as one of the core themes of Jonah. At the top, of course, is God, who must be assumed to know what's what, to know what is to be done, and to be consistent in doing it. And yet … this is a God who refuses to punish the wicked, who seems willing to condemn an innocent crew in order to make a theological point, and who 'repents' far too often for the credibility of an omnipotent and omniscient being.

The moral layering is almost exactly inversely related to that of power and knowledge. Ethically there seems little to be said for God – perhaps a crude judgement, but almost forced upon the reader by the crude parodies in Jonah. Yahweh is portrayed throughout as arbitrary, self-interested, and without scruple. Jonah himself is a little better. He acts honestly on his assessment of the situation, and sticks to his guns right up to his moral high-point of urging the sailors to throw him to the waves. But he is also pig-headed and petulant, and seems to have little real concern for the Ninevites. Moreover, on one reading of ch. 2, he is a resounding hypocrite:[1] in the closing verses of the psalm he presents himself as devoted, honest and faithful to God – claims hard to reconcile with his behaviour in ch. 1. The captain and his crew have a better claim to respect on moral grounds. They cannot be blamed for their ignorance of Yahweh, and as soon as they become aware that something is wrong they take steps, within the terms available to them, to identify the problem and to put things right. As they leave the stage, the last thing we see them doing is making vows and sacrificing to Yahweh. Nevertheless, and whatever the caveats they enter in v. 14, they do throw Jonah to the waves, to his (as far as they know) certain death. They are, to a modern perception, guilty of murder, or at least of culpable homicide – a matter to which I will return in the discussion of the next verse. Finally, those at the lowest level are guilt-free. Galley-slaves or hired hands row to save their and everyone else's lives: they have no option. The citizens of Nineveh do what the court tells them – they have no choice, and in any case cannot tell their left hand from their right. And so on. In short, what Jonah gives us is a parable which spells out the problem of Eden: the more knowledge, the greater the moral responsibility; the more power, the less your chances of making the 'right' decision. This is an equation which appears to transcend all else, one to which God is as subject as any sentient being, and might well serve as one of the key explanatory modes for Jonah. But we are not yet done with ch. 1, and there may be more to say.

> [14]*Then they cried out to the LORD, 'Please, O LORD, we pray,*
> *do not let us perish on account of this man's life.*
> *Do not make us guilty of innocent blood; for you, O LORD,*
> *have done as it pleased you.'*

Loss of innocence could be the leitmotif of v. 14. The sailors can no longer claim they don't know Yahweh, nor can they pretend to be above the moral problems of the events they are caught up in. An unavoidable logic forces them to invoke the age-old theorem: it is fitting that one should die to save many (Caiaphas's advice in John 18.14 'that it was better to have one person die for the people'). They know they are guilty – hence their embarrassed prayer to a God they've only just met: 'Please, O LORD

---

1. But this, like almost every claim one can make about Jonah, is questionable – see the detailed discussion in Chapter 8.

[note their use of the special name of God reserved for Israel], we know we're about to kill someone who's innocent, but don't hold us responsible because, after all, you are doing whatever you please'. A classic of special pleading arising from a deeply atavistic fear that they are caught in an impossible situation whatever they do. To take no action would (they believe) lead to the death of everyone, including Jonah; to sacrifice Jonah offers at least the chance that others may survive, at the cost only of a death which is inevitable anyway. The arithmetic is elementary, but the morality is crude, on at least three levels. First of all we will never know, in the story's own terms, whether their initial assumption was correct. Perhaps the storm would have abated. Perhaps God was bluffing, testing them on a moral cusp. There is precedent for this interpretation, in the form of a rabbinic reading of the Akedah (Gen. 22) in which Abraham becomes convinced that God has instructed him to sacrifice his son Isaac.[2] This interpretation suggests that God was testing Abraham and that Abraham failed the test. He was meant to say no, to use his knowledge of God's nature to refuse an apparently divine instruction to commit murder. In the end, God had to save him (and Isaac) from his patriarchal stupidity, sacrificing an innocent ram for the purpose. (The same ram which gives rise to the *shofar* which sounds on and on in Exodus and reminds us of the storm which forms the present test.) By analogy, the sailors, tempted by their superstitious belief in sympathetic magic, hold that they have no option but to throw Jonah (whom, interestingly, they believe to be an *innocent* man – contrary to the reader's perspective) overboard. In this light their prayer is specious, a formalistic prophylactic rather than a genuinely moral move. (On this issue, see further Perry, pp. 7–12.) In this light also God can be seen for once as the most moral force: Yahweh saves the sailors, taking pity perhaps on their ignorance and naïvety, as God does in respect of other innocents in this book, and also saves Jonah by deploying (as in Gen. 22) an innocent creature for the purpose. We

---

2. *Genesis Rabbah* 56.8: Rabbi Acha said, 'Avraham started to wonder, "These words are only words of wonder. Yesterday, you told me" (Genesis 21:12), "Because in Itzchak will your seed be called." And [then] you went back and said, "Please take your son." And now You say to me, "Do not send your hand to the youth." It is a wonder!' The Holy One, blessed be He, said, 'Avraham, "I will not profane My covenant and the utterances of My lips, I will not change" (Psalms 89:35) – When I said, "Please take your son," I did not say, "slaughter him," but rather, "and bring him up." For the sake of love did I say [it] to you: I said to you, "Bring him up," and you have fulfilled My words. And now, bring him down.' Sourced from https://www.sefaria.org/Bereishit_Rabbah.56.9?lang=bi&with=all&lang2=en

don't know if this creature dies, but the survival prospects for a large fish (whether a whale or not) becoming beached and vomiting its last meal are not great.

Some of the details of the prayer itself are interesting, not least in the light of the other significant prayer-psalm in Jonah 2. Its language, like that of the psalm, is highly stylised ('Please, O Lord, we beseech you'; 'the life of this man'; 'innocent blood'; 'you are the Lord'; 'you have done what it pleased you to do'). It is also a prayer that, like that of Jonah, refuses to admit guilt or to accept responsibility. And it issues (in v. 16) in sacrifices and vows, just as does Jonah's. These similarities are surely not coincidental, though what they imply is less clear. Perhaps, hidden beneath the parody and playfulness of this book there is an appeal to formal religion, to the observance of the proprieties rather than needless fretting about deeper meaning. Just to test this mini-hypothesis, note that in addition to the formal prayers, vows and sacrifices we have already listed, there is Jonah's purely formulaic prophecy, the utterly formal response of the people of Nineveh, and the mysterious conclusion to the book which is nothing if not formal if it encompasses cattle in the redemptive process.

> [15] *So they picked Jonah up and threw him into the sea; and the sea ceased from its raging.*

After fourteen verses of lengthy debate and somewhat repetitive reflection on the issues, suddenly in verse fifteen the characteristically leisurely nature of one kind of Hebrew narrative is replaced by its opposite: a headlong rush to settle everything in the minimum space – seven words, on my count. 'Then-they-picked-up (1) Jonah (2) and-hurled-him (3) to-the-sea (4); whereupon-desisted (5) the-sea (6) from-its-raging (7)'. Admittedly, identifying what constitutes individual words is never easy, and is particularly difficult in Hebrew. The extensive use of both prefixes and suffixes, and of the connector *maqqef*, which functions in a manner similar to the hyphen in English, make this more of a subjective exercise than one might wish. A syllable count might give a more accurate picture: there are twenty-three in the Hebrew and twenty-one in NRSV – yet somehow the English still feels clunkier.

The succinctness of the Hebrew is hard to convey in English, which requires eighteen words – even though the syllable count is almost identical. Perhaps the issue is not one of essential difference, but rather of a failure of poetical nerve on the part of translators. The rhythm and assonance of the Hebrew are striking: the following is an attempt to set these out, first in transliteration, and then by means of a more 'poetic' English rendering (stress in both Hebrew and English is indicated in bold underlined).

vayis**su** et-yo**nah**	They **picked** up **Jon**ah,
vayiti**lu** el-ha**yam**	and **threw** him to the **sea**;
vaya'a**mod** ha**yam**	The **sea stood still**,
miza'a**po**	**rag**ing no **more**.

The stress patterns are quite different – those of the English give the passage an inappropriately jaunty feeling, in contrast to the sombre end-stress of the Hebrew – and the rhyme and half-rhyme of the Hebrew (*-su* : *-lu*; *-mod* : *-po*; *-nah* : *-yam* : *-yam*) is entirely absent; finally, the extreme terseness of the last line of the Hebrew is lost. No doubt the criticism could justly be entered that the failing is my own, that I am simply incompetent faced with the challenge of a difficult translation. The point, however, is that these nuances are lost in most of the standard English editions, and this loss, in the context of an attempt at a literary reading, is crucial. There may be ethical and theological loss as well, as I will now indicate.

Undoubtedly something of the urgency and rapidity of cause and effect does survive the translation: this is (it seems, or at least perhaps we are intended by the author to think) the justification of the process which the sailors, reluctantly or not, decided upon. It is an utterly pragmatic justification: it worked! It had the desired effect! Forget for a moment that we are in the territory of that most seductive of logical fallacies (*post hoc ergo propter hoc* – roughly translatable as 'If B follows A then B is caused by A'). Forget also that if this analysis of cause and effect is correct it entails a moral outrage. The power of the *language* is that it sweeps us along, rather as the sea had up until now swept the ship along, carrying us, willy-nilly, to our theological destination. The writer here is seen to have a powerful command of rhetoric, for once we are in the swim of things (ouch!) our critical and moral faculties are dulled in favour of a lazy kind of closure. And lest we should retain any doubts, or still hold to the vestiges of a hermeneutic of suspicion, the next few verses deliver conclusive and irrefutable proof that the moral and causal fabrics of the universe are intact: the dramatic 'conversion' of the sailors in v. 16, and the miraculous rescue of Jonah in v. 17 (see Chapter 8).

> [16] *Then the men feared the L*ORD *even more, and they offered a sacrifice to the L*ORD *and made vows.*

I have already (see commentary on v. 4) emphasised the importance of the word 'great' (*gadhol*) in Jonah. It is a pity, therefore, that it is omitted from the English NRSV rendering of the first phrase of v. 16 in favour of the anodyne 'the men feared the Lord even more' (this seems to be an isolated lapse: NIV, REB and JPS all use 'great' or 'greatly'). It is also regrettable that the sheer extent of repeated language in this verse is not represented. All of the verbs are reinforced by their associated substantives ('feared a great fear'; 'sacrificed a sacrifice'; 'vowed a vow') and the divine referent of these verbs (Yahweh) is given twice – five repeated words out of the total of eleven. The result is in the English a rather anticlimactic rounding off of what is surely one of the most dramatic chapters in Tanakh – a pedestrian signing-off rather than (as the Hebrew surely conveys) a bold and challenging theological Parthian shot. For it is in the personae of the pagan sailors that a genuine religious awe is presented. Their terror of the sea (v. 10) is now a powerful fear of Yahweh, transcending Jonah's formulaic claim to be a 'Yahweh-fearer' (v. 9) and his lip-service to the 'Maker of the sea and the dry land'. Their oath-taking and sacrifice (clearly entirely real and meaningful in context) anticipate ironically Jonah's questionable assertion in the last verse of the psalm (2.9) that 'I … will sacrifice to you; what I have vowed I will pay', particularly as it follows his denunciation by implication of the likes of the sailors (2.8: 'Those who worship vain idols forsake their true loyalty').

What this verse achieves is a transformation of two key ciphers – 'fear' and 'great' – from referents of weakness and dishonour into an expression of noble (if self-interested) sentiment. It resolves the first chapter in the direction of the book as a whole – an ironic contrast between Jonah's knowing scepticism and the willingness (and ability) of pagans to recognize the voice of the true God. It remains true to the hugely effective literary skills of the writer in its anchoring of its language in the semantics of the chapter as a whole. It leaves us with a deeply uncomfortable moral premise, that it is the sheer power of God and the naked use of terror by Yahweh which are best designed to persuade humans to direct their worship appropriately. And it finds in us a grudging respect for Jonah, whose doomed attempt to escape the hectoring voice of this monstrous god is perhaps more noble than we at first thought. Not that the author of this perplexing satire is, in the end, going to leave us with any respect for Jonah. But that is a matter for consideration in a later chapter.

Coda

Flight

Jonah 1 ostensibly presents a prophet fleeing from what he sees as a serious threat to his safety. His decision to flee to somewhere safely distant is, we have to assume, a rational response. The question not properly answered, however, is 'in what way does taking a ship from Joppa provide that security?'. It is irrelevant to Nineveh, which confronts Jonah with no perceptible hazard at this stage. It is irrelevant to Yahweh, for if there is one thing such a scripturally aware prophet/book as Jonah would have known is that you cannot hide from God. Not in Eden – as the first couple might be forgiven for thinking in their naïvety – nor in the wilderness of the Negev, as Elijah appears to have imagined; indeed nowhere at all, as Ps. 139.7-12 famously affirms:

> Where can I go from your spirit?
>   Or where can I flee from your presence?
> If I ascend to heaven, you are there;
>   if I make my bed in Sheol, you are there.
> If I take the wings of the morning
>   and settle at the farthest limits of the sea,
> even there your hand shall lead me,
>   and your right hand shall hold me fast.
> If I say, 'Surely the darkness shall cover me,
>   and the light around me become night',
> even the darkness is not dark to you;
>   the night is as bright as the day,
>   for darkness is as light to you.

There is no plausible interpretation of the kind of character Jonah is portrayed as, and the sort of text he belongs in, which could allow the idea that Jonah is trying to escape from Yahweh. There remains one obvious but surprising option: as we can see from the heartfelt prayer in ch. 2, Jonah's home is either in or close to Jerusalem. Flight to Joppa and hence across the sea is then, obviously but surprisingly, an escape from Jerusalem. The passionate nature of his prayer falls into place when we realize that he did not run from Jerusalem to escape God or avoid Nineveh, but because he understood the meaning of the great and sinful city, and feared the consequences of proclaiming to his own people a message that might effect a radical change.

Voices

Every narrative involves a hierarchy of voices, some more implicit than others. The search for a satisfying reconciliation of the diverse features of Jonah will in part depend on how we identify and characterise these speakers: a task I shall set in train now.

Taking 'speaking' literally, there are four voices on the same level (i.e. human characters) and two supernatural: the Word of the Lord and Yahweh, who are of course at this level of reading equally characters in the story. The human participants are Jonah, the ship's captain, the sailors, and the king of Nineveh: the last delegating his words to an unnamed speaker.

Next there is the narrator – who is, by the way, *not* to be identified with the author.[3] The narrator is just as much an invention of the author as are the characters already identified, but he/she/it is presented as a non-participant – or at least is commonly perceived as such by readers. Narrators are sometimes described as 'omniscient' (though see Pullman, p. 247, on this); a better formulation might be in terms of 'privileged' stance, since all sorts of information which would not normally be accessible to participants in events is ascribed to this figure. As an invention of the author, the narrator may be simply a device to convey information about the state of mind of other characters (something of course which no-one in real life can claim to possess). But narrators may also be biased or opinionated. Whether these biases or opinions are also those of the author is mostly unknowable.

Finally: the author. I have already explored this figure at some length in the Introduction at the level of access to literacy skills, professional experience, and knowledge of the scriptures. What I have not yet done is to consider what the author's intentions might appear to be in the way the narrative proceeds and the participants behave. Certainly 'intention' is a famously elusive (some would claim fictitious) quality; however with the deliberate omission of the adjective 'original' intention becomes a conceivable inference from the way the text is presented.

That should be enough theory for now. I will resume these musings in Chapter 13.

---

3. Philip Pullman, in his fascinating collection of essays, *Daemon Voices: On Stories and Storytelling* (Oxford: David Fickling Books, 2020 [2017]), adverts on a number of occasions to the matter of authors and narrators and the difference between them. To take one instance, he asks 'isn't the author the narrator? … No, is the answer. The narrator is a character invented by the author … I believe that the narrator is not actually a human character at all, and his or her relationship to time is one of the ways in which his or her uncanny inhumanness is manifest.' (pp. 245–6).

Chapter 6

THE SEA, THE SEA

This chapter is an admittedly frivolous digression which picks up some of the curious details of Jonah 1. Those uninterested in such diversions into minor pathways – the kind which are prone to end abruptly or peter out in a tangle of briars and brambles – may safely skip to Chapter 7.

Ships and Sailors

In a very brief compass Jon. 1.5-7 introduces a remarkable range of vocabulary for ships and sailors, or appears to. Three terms are used for 'ship': *'oniyah*, *chovel*, and *sefinah*. This last is a *hapax legomenon* – a word only found once in the whole of Tanakh, though it is also found twice in the correspondence of Bar Kochba in the second century CE. There are also two expressions for the crew: *mallach* (sailor) and *rav hachovel* (captain). However, the precise definitions of these expressions are difficult to determine.

The word *sefinah* may not strictly be a word for 'ship', since it seems to relate to a verb *safan* which means 'to cover', and is almost always found with reference to ceilinged rooms (cf. 1 Kgs 6.9, 15). Thus it may be better to translate the phrase *'el yarkithe sefinah* in v. 5 as 'to the remotest corner of the hold; that is, the deepest part of the vessel 'covered over' by the ship's superstructure rather than, as in NRSV, 'the hold of the ship'.

Apart from *sefinah*, there is a remarkable overlap of most of these terms with usage in Ezekiel 27. Magonet (pp. 80–1) is ambivalent about the likelihood of Jonah's author having explicitly referred to this chapter, but at the level I have been arguing for, of a wide and informed knowledge of the texts as a whole, the connection merits attention. The list of specific items is impressive:

'oniyah in vv. 9, 25, and 29
chovel in vv. 8, 27, 28, and 29
mallach in vv. 9, 27, and 29

Even if these terms had a wider currency in the Persian period, with the possibility of merely shared use of expressions, the fact that in Tanakh the grouping is only found in Jonah 1 and Ezekiel 27 is suggestive.

Translations of Ezekiel usually render *chovel* as 'pilot'; it seems inconsistent therefore not to render its use in Jonah in the same way. Accordingly I propose to use 'chief pilot' rather than 'captain'. There is support for this from Greek evidence:

> The *kybernetes* [helmsman] did carry over some of his original function, for he was the ship's navigating officer and in battle or storm might even handle the steering oars himself, although at other times he handed them over to quartermasters. This was only a part of his duties. He was the equivalent of the executive officer of today, and if the captain was absent or lost, he took over command. Indeed, as things were managed in the Athenian navy, more often than not he held the actual command at all times. (Casson, p. 86)

While this particular citation relates to the fifth century BCE, and to military vessels, the nomenclature and duties remain fairly consistent through time and for all forms of shipping. The Latin equivalent *gubernator* (clearly a latinate form of the same word) has the same meaning. Finally, since the Hebrew term belongs to a root which means 'to bind', with an associated noun meaning 'ropes', it is not unreasonable to imagine that the 'pilot-in-chief' was in charge of the steering of the ship.

The remaining term, *mallach*, is similar to the word for salt (*melach*); it too is confined to Jonah and Ezekiel 27. It is tempting to suggest a tradition similar to the English usage of 'salt' to mean 'sailor'. Sasson, sadly, pours cold water on this idea, pronouncing it a false etymology (p. 97). But if the English usage derives from the fact that the sea is salty, presumably sailors in Jonah's time were equally knowledgeable!

Regarding the crew, I have referred to them as either slaves or hired hands. Interestingly, and somewhat counterintuitively, Casson (p. 87) notes that military ships were crewed by free men for 'slaves were never used as regular members of crews: they were far too expensive'. However the merchant service was different, 'The crew, right up to and including the captain, were generally slaves'. But it is also the case that, while a 'shipowner might accompany his vessel on voyages, … he would leave its handling to the *kybernates*, his captain' (p. 114). Thus though their legal status was that they were slaves, we should not imagine that the crew were chained to their stations (as in Hollywood Roman epics) or lacked the freedom to make the navigational decisions necessary for safety.

Passengers

As for passengers, while there is no doubt that people travelled regularly by sea in the ancient world, evidence for fares paid by passengers is limited, and suggests that they were fairly arbitrary (Adams, p. 147). Passengers were only taken on incidentally – there were no passenger services as such – and they brought their own food and servants. They could be numerous: 'when Josephus, the Jewish historian, crossed in A.D. 64 he had no less [*sic*] than six hundred fellow passengers' (Casson pp. 192–3, 209). Ironically it seems that the book of Jonah is one of the few written sources from antiquity providing evidence for fare-paying sea-going passengers. Its fictionality does not entirely nullify the value of this report, though the sparing nature of the narrative gives the impression that Jonah, improbably, travelled alone. Did he have servants? What preparation might he have made for his trip? Typically of the author of Jonah we are left in the dark about such arrangements, just as the terse statement in 3.3, 'So Jonah set out and went to Nineveh', elides completely the serious practical difficulties associated with any such journey.

Youngblood (p. 71) comments on the evidence for travellers in ancient story traditions, suggesting that 'within the framework of the commission narrative, elements of another genre are detectable, a form commonly referred to as a travel narrative, or, more specifically, a maritime travel narrative'. He goes on to refer to two well-known Egyptian examples of survival at sea in pursuance of their divine appointment to some significant task: 'The Shipwrecked Sailor' and 'The Report of Wen Amun'.[1] These however seem to be remote from the context of Jonah, and it may be a moot point whether the book's author might have known them. The former seems to belong to the period of the Middle Kingdom (ca. 2040–1780 BCE), and the latter around 1000 BCE, and both are known only in single copies. Since both are reckoned to be fictional accounts it is possible that they circulated more widely. In sum, though they tell of diplomats *en voyage* facing storms at sea, there is little here of relevance to Jonah.

---

1. The simplest access to the text of these stories is through the following internet links: https://www.ancient.eu/article/180/the-tale-of-the-shipwrecked-sailor-an-egyptian-epi/ and https://www.ancient.eu/article/1087/the-report-of-wenamun-text-commentary/

Tarshish and Joppa

The two ports which feature in Jonah are Joppa (*Yapho*) and Tarshish. The location of the former and its historical reality are not in doubt, though Tanakh has little to say about it. The latter is better represented, but its whereabouts remain a mystery. Resolving such questions is of course not essential to an understanding of the book, but the reason for the author's use of these named destinations might be of interest.

Joppa

Yapho is mentioned just four times in Tanakh: Josh. 19.46; Jon. 1.3; 2 Chron. 2.16; and Ezra 3.7. The first of these occurs in an account of the possessions of the tribe of Dan, in turn part of a lengthy catalogue of the lands of the twelve tribes. Nothing of substance is said about the place. However, the references in 2 Chronicles and Ezra are of more interest because they provide confirmation that at the time of Jonah's composition Yapho served as a port for Jerusalem. The former occurs in the course of an account of how Solomon resorted to Tyre for the building materials he needed for the Temple; the latter similarly deals with the acquisition of timber from Lebanon for the post-exilic restoration of the Temple under the leadership of Jeshua and Zereubbabel. The significance of these is that the texts are firmly post-exilic, presumably fourth century BCE at the earliest. There is no parallel mention of Yapho in the account in Kings of Solomon's construction of the Temple.

Tarshish

The location of Tarshish is, sadly, not known.[2] There is a scholarly consensus (aka a guess we all subscribe to) that it may have been somewhere on the Mediterranean coast, whose length (I am informed by Google) is some 46,000 km. Not, therefore, a particularly helpful guess. An interesting example of the kind of argumentation to which those who want to narrow this range are driven is provided in an article by Brent Macdonald, who offers Utica in Tunisia as a solid candidate.[3] The broad hypothesis is not unreasonable, since the name is closely associated with shipping and has some connections with Tyre. The genealogical note in Gen. 10.4 identifies an eponymous Tarshish, one of the descendants of Japheth, with

---

2. Wolff (pp. 100-101) provides a detailed summary of scholarly data on the subject, as does Sasson (p. 79). Sherwood (p. 242 n. 138) places more emphasis on the legendary status of the town.

3. Posted by Macdonald in 2017 at https://notjustanotherbook.com/tarshish.htm

the coastlands – a connection which is repeated in references to the city found in Isaiah (23.6, 60.9 and 66.19) and in Ps. 72.10, which speaks of 'the kings of Tarshish and the isles'.

Many of the occurrences of the name are associated with ships – thus 1 Kgs 10.22; 2 Chron. 9.21; Isa. 2.16; 23.1, 10, 14; Ezek. 27.12, 25 (note that this is the same chapter in which Jonah's terms for ships and sailors are found) and Ps. 48.7 – and there is a brief narrative in 1 Kgs 22.7, paralleled in 2 Chron. 20.36-37, concerning a failed attempt by Jehoshaphat (king of Judah in the mid-ninth century BCE) to have ships built at Ezion-Geber to sail to Tarshish. Their subsequent wreckage at sea is seen, certainly by the Chronicler, as a punishment for hubris. In Psalm 48 it is the ships of Tarshish that are wrecked as the result of an east wind (*ruach qadim*) – a dangerous natural phenomenon which will feature later in Jon. 4.8.

It may be that Jehoshaphat was attempting to break into a lucrative market, for the other major aspect of Tarshish on which the sources are agreed is its business dealings. It was a source of silver and other precious goods, and appears to have been heavily involved in the transport of such items across the Mediterranean (thus 1 Kgs 10.22; 2 Chron. 9.21; Jer. 10.9; Ezek. 27.12; 28.13). In this respect its associations with another great entrepreneurial port, Tyre, are noteworthy (Isa. 23.1, 10, 14; Ezek. 27.12, 25). There is a possible pun in the text of Jonah which relates to this aspect of Tarshish: the word for business in the same context (Isa. 23.2, 8, 18; Ezek. 27.12, 15, 16, 18, 21, 26) is *sachar*, which is a near-homonym for the 'price' (*sachar*) which Jonah pays for his ticket.

All of this makes the city's elusiveness somewhat surprising, given that we know of both the existence and the location of many of the other Mediterranean trading ports of the time. Part of the difficulty is that, unless some form of the name has been preserved in local tradition, or the place was so significant that it figured in a range of ancient written sources, even if the site was excavated, showing that it was 'Tarshish' would still be challenging.

The last word on this subject goes to etymology, for in the absence of any other conclusion, attempts to explain the name as having coded significance will emerge. The most popular is a derivation from the Hebrew *rashash*, a rare word meaning 'to destroy' or 'to break up'. It only occurs twice – in Jer. 5.17 and Mal. 1.4 – and certainly (as we have seen) ships of Tarshish are known to be wrecked (in Ps. 48.7 and 2 Chron. 20.37). Unfortunately the much more common verb for 'to break to pieces' is used in both of these verses, while the use of *rashash* refers to the destruction of buildings and houses. Surely, had the ancient writers intended such a pun, they would have placed the two words rather closer together.

The best account of the significance of Tarshish that I have come across is that of Sherwood (pp. 250–1), which is worth quoting in full:

> But the *pièce de resistance* in this chapter is 'the ship going to Tarshish' – the first prop plundered from the tradition store-cupboard. Ships going to Tarshish are well-known structures ... and also something of a banana-skin of tradition, for a 'ship going to Tarshish' roughly culturally translates as 'the Titanic going out on her maiden voyage'. The analogy maps almost exactly: ships going to Tarshish are proud noble structures, carrying precious cargoes, and they are generically programmed to be 'shattered' by the 'east wind', and to promptly 'sink into the heart of the sea'. The 'ship of Tarshish' should be imagined as a familiar stage prop, built on a mechanism that ensures that it will inevitably tip over – for, as inexorably as icebergs and the Titanic in Thomas Hardy's poem 'The Meeting of the Twain', storm clouds and ships of Tarshish are simply, fatally, meant for each other.

A Big Fish

The 'big fish' which Yahweh appointed to swallow Jonah is the source of one of the most familiar images from the Bible – even making it into 'It Ain't Necessarily So' from Gershwin's *Porgy and Bess*. For a long time, as a youngster, I thought that the lyric ran 'Ol' Jonah he swallowed a whale'; I guess I imagined that scenario to be no more improbable that what the text(s) of Tanakh and Gershwin actually reported.

Much ink has been spilled debunking or supporting the factuality or not of Jonah's fishy adventure. For collectors of curiosities it might be of interest that the Nabi Yunus Mosque, in Mosul, is supposedly on the site of Jonah's burial place, and used to display on one of its walls the bones, allegedly, of the very whale which swallowed him. In a grim aftermath that mosque, with or without whale bones, was destroyed by the self-styled Islamic State in 2014 on the grounds that it was a source of apostasy. Incidentally, Jonah is the only one of the minor prophets to be mentioned by name in the Qur'an. Surah 10 is named for him, though it only refers elliptically to his story; there is a fuller account in Surah 37 (*Al-Saffat*: 'The Ranks') 139-148.

To return to Mediterranean sea-life, following the example of Greek legends we might have expected a dolphin, or a shipful of sub-Homeric heroes, or even Scilla and her horrendous pal Charybdis, for whom Jonah would have presumably been a tasty morsel. But a whale? This is perhaps the point to dispose of a long history of scholarly pedantry. Undoubtedly the text does not use a word for whale here; but it is unlikely that Biblical Hebrew would have possessed such a term. Modern Hebrew uses Leviathan, which describes a mythic sea-creature in Tanakh – one which I shall return to shortly. The dolphin (*delphis*) is certainly well-attested in Greek and figures in a number of legends: it is from ancient Greece that the image of 'the boy on a dolphin' is derived. There is much less certainty when it comes to whales, which may or may not have been identified by the Greeks.[4] One of the Greek words used is *ketos* (Latin *cetus*) which, like the Hebrew Leviathan, signifies a sea-monster, and leads etymologically to the Linnaean order of cetaceans. A more specific term is *phallaina* (Latin *balaena*, then eventually the English 'baleen'). There were certainly terms available in neighbouring cultures of Jonah's time to describe creatures like whales, and it is by no means impossible that the author knew of them without having to hand a technical term. For this reason it seems to me perfectly in order to use in English the term 'whale' as an interpretation of the author's famous plot device.

Even Bigger Fish

Lurking in the depths of Jonah lies Tanakh's equivalent of the Loch Ness Monster – a denizen of the deeps known variously as Tannin and Leviathan having dangerous associations with the myths of Canaan and Mesopotamia, Ugarit and Babylon. In Ugaritic mythology Tannin, a serpentine, possibly many-headed being, was defeated by Ba'al; similar myths attach to Lotan (the equivalent of the Hebrew Leviathan): the two appear to represent alternative versions of the same tradition. The Babylonian equivalent is Tiamat, sometimes thought to have etymological connections with the Hebrew *tehom* meaning 'the deep', part of the primeval chaos prior to creation in Gen. 1.1-2. The Babylonian myth of the defeat of Tiamat by Marduk and her consequent splitting into two to form the heavens and the earth are taken by some as the underlying legend informing the separation of the waters in Gen. 1.7.

Granted that the watery-chaos language of Jonah 2 has many parallels in Psalms in particular, it is somewhat surprising that more has not been made in the various commentaries of the possibility that the 'big fish' is a

---

4. On this question see the fascinating article by Deborah Ruscillo at https://www.academia.edu/4924462/A_ketos_in_Early_Athens_An_Archaeology_of_Whales_and_Sea_Monsters_in_the_Greek_World_2002_

stand-in for something much bigger, and even scarier. Hugh Pyper is one of the exceptions. In his discussion of the unique formulation 'the belly of Sheol' (pp. 345–6) he remarks that the psalm

> clearly locates [it] in the sea. … The writer of the prose of Jonah, then, … is faced with the following riddle posed by the poem's own account of the location of its speaker: What has a big belly, swallows people, swims in the sea at God's behest, and could play the role of rescuer while evoking Sheol? Psalm 104.26 gives the answer: Leviathan, who sports in the sea as God's plaything, and who yet in Ps. 74.14 is clearly identified with the destructive power of the sea. Leviathan is the one sent to the rescue.

He suggests somewhat tentatively that the presumed authorial decision to replace 'Leviathan' (with its hints of the Ba'al mythology) with 'great fish' has a parallel in Gen. 1.16 where the sun (Hebrew *shemesh*) is referred to as 'the great light'. Scholars have long since suggested that this too is an act of demythologising, since *shemesh* is one of the forms taken by the Canaanite sun goddess.

Sherwood too, though more elliptically, draws attention to the mythology of the engorging sea-monster which surely informs Jonah 2, stressing in particular (p. 254) the relevance of Jer. 51.34:

> King Nebuchadnezzar of Babylon has devoured me,
>   he has crushed me;
> he has made me an empty vessel,
>   he has swallowed me like a monster;
> he has filled his belly with my delicacies,
>   he has spewed me out.

The 'monster' here is *tannin*, which as we have seen has clear connections with the sea. Sherwood amends the NRSV – justifiably in my opinion – to read 'he has swallowed me like a sea-monster'.

The most detailed argument I have seen for the proposal that the author of Jonah was well aware of the allusion to Leviathan is in an article by Scott B Noegel which is available online at the University of Washington.[5] His starting point is the use by the Septuagint of the Greek term *ketos* for Hebrew *dag* (fish). Everywhere else the Septuagint uses *ichthus*, the regular Greek term, for *dag*; and equally significantly, used the expression *ketos* for both Tannin and Leviathan (p. 240). While it is not possible to date with any certainty the Greek translation of Jonah, this is certainly

---

5. http://faculty.washington.edu/snoegel/PDFs/articles/noegel-jonah-2015.pdf

evidence that by the first century CE at the latest a responsible translation could understand the *dag gadhol* as belonging to the category of Hebrew sea monsters.

Noegel then goes on to survey a range of potential allusions to Tannin/Leviathan within the book of Jonah. They are, I think, rather persuasive though probably not conclusive, and they fit very well with the idea adumbrated in the Introduction that the author of Jonah uses a register in which direct, indirect and allusive reference to a broad range of Tanakh texts is ubiquitous. To begin with (p. 243), he cites the image of the ship on the sea as pointing to Ps. 104.26 'There go the ships, / and Leviathan that you formed to sport in [the sea]'. After the (cosmological) storm 'hurled' by Yahweh breaks out, the figure of the *rav hakhovel* ('chief of the ropes') 'though in charge of the boat, …is no longer in control… The chaos of the sea and his inability to save it recalls Yahweh's question to Job from the tempest… : "Can you draw out Leviathan with a fishhook? Or snag his tongue with a rope (*khebel*)"?' (Job 40.25) (p. 244). The allusion here is perhaps less persuasive, that the 'ropes' responsibility of the ship's officer might call to mind the ropes which cannot tame Leviathan.

In the psalm in Jonah 2 the striking words of v. 3 describe Jonah's experience of drowning 'in the deep'. The Hebrew term used here, *mitsulah*, is important, and I shall discuss it in more detail in Chapter 9; for now I simply report Noegel's observation that one of its other rare occurrences is in Job 41.31: '[Leviathan] makes the deep boil like a pot' (p. 245). A further indication is to be found in the language of being *surrounded* by the watery threat (Jon. 2.3), implying the kind of twisting, serpentine motion of currents paralleling the root *lavah*, 'to twist, bend, be crooked', which underlies the name Leviathan. The same verb 'to surround' recurs in 2.6, 'The waters closed in over me, / the deep surrounded me; / weeds were wrapped around my head': here the deep is represented by *tehom* which I have already noted above as a likely Hebrew reduction of the Babylonian goddess Tiamat (see Noegel p. 247).

Chapter 7

MAKER OF HEAVEN AND EARTH:
JONAH AND GENESIS*

At various points I have noted already that there are important reminiscences, echoes and intertexts from Genesis in the book of Jonah. Some of these links were noted by Magonet, in particular language associated with the cause of the flood and the destruction of Sodom and Gomorrah, and I have considered these up to a point in Chapter 1 in relation to the symbolism of Nineveh. In this chapter I want to bring together these and other Genesis influences on Jonah, but with particular focus on the motif of creation in Jonah. This is not the first study to relate Jonah to the Genesis creation myth: Gerda Elata-Alster and Rachel Salmon (1989) discuss a possible interpretation of Jonah 4 as a reworking of the myth of Adam's expulsion from Eden, in which the creation and destruction of the gourd emulates the conditions first of Eden then of the world of weeds and thorns outside Eden.

The sites of principal influence (or correspondence) between Jonah and Genesis are, in order of their appearance in Genesis:

The creation myths (chs. 1–2);
The flood legend (6.5–8.22);
The destruction of Sodom and Gomorrah (18.16–19.29)

The argument which follows is not strictly (or even approximately) a logical one. Neither Genesis nor Jonah stand in any kind of binding causal relationship to the other, and I have no intention of making a historical- or text-critical case out of whatever intertextual networks may exist. Whoever wrote Jonah was free to do whatever they wished with the materials they found, without prejudice to whatever motivated whoever

* Material in this chapter is a development in part of Hunter 2002.

wrote the opening chapters of Genesis. The author was in consequence free to shape the source material in harmony with their own concerns. Nor does my analysis rest on any presumption about who borrowed from whom, whose work came first. Jonah, as we have seen, was most likely composed between 400 and 200 BCE, and the best guess about the opening chapters of Genesis is that they were the last to be composed. Hence the chronological question is in fact much more open than a naïve deduction from the relative positions of the two books might suggest. It is not outrageous to surmise that Genesis 1–2 could be later than Jonah, but my point is simply that it does not matter that much. It is *interesting* if Jonah is in fact dependent upon a collection of written scriptures which predate its composition; but the *fact* of intertextuality does not in itself resolve the question of priority. Nonetheless, while the range of other traditions with which Jonah interacts does strongly suggest a particular direction of dependence, what I want to insist upon is that the reader, lacking direct information about the intentions of the authors and the reliability (in historical, scientific or epistemological terms) of their work is forced, short of an arbitrary rejection of one book or the other, to read them together. The bizarre creative activities found in Jonah deconstruct the seemingly solemn business of Genesis 1 just as surely as the profundities of Genesis 1 force a similarly portentous reading of Jonah. We cannot laugh at Jonah 4 unless we are prepared to chuckle also as God manipulates the vast canopies of the heavens like so much celestial wallpaper; nor can we stand in awe of 'In the beginning God created the heavens and the earth' at the opening of Genesis without keeping some of that numinous feeling in reserve for the cucumber plant and the worm at the end of Jonah.

Creation

The first aspects of Jonah under consideration are those pertaining to the theme of creation, which is where my main focus will be. However, there is one motif – that of water and dry land – which belongs equally to the exodus and creation themes. Inevitably, therefore, there may be some overlap with the discussion in Chapter 9 on the Exodus motif; but since the biblical traditions themselves morph the two themes at various points (Isa. 43.1-21; and Pss. 74.12-17 and 89.5-12), this is hardly surprising. Creation–destruction–recreation represents a rather familiar biblical cycle, whether we view it in terms of the traditional *Heilsgeschichte* theology of the biblical theology school, or as an aspect of a more general *urzeit–chaoskampf–endzeit* literary and mythological pattern.

The connections between Jonah and the opening mythological chapters of Genesis are to be found both in terms of motifs and of specific semantic usage. The overall effect is to produce a set of resonances which persuade the reader to take seriously the possibility of a shared milieu, a common deployment of items, motifs and themes from what in all likelihood was a well-known body of myth. Psalm 8 is another familiar instance: most commentators perceive some kind of link between the second half of the psalm and the Genesis creation myth, but precise linguistic dependence is hard to establish. Similarly, Qoheleth's reflections (3.18-21) on the identical fate of men and animals, and some of his ruminations in the next chapter, have an affinity with the material in Gen. 3.14-19 and 4.1-16: I will return to this particular passage in Chapter 12. In none of these cases is direct textual dependence necessarily demonstrable; but the analogous example of Ben Sira, who does indeed seem to have worked with something like the Jewish scriptures later listed by Josephus, might point interestingly to a prevailing interest in creation myths which was to a greater or lesser extent informed by a body of written material. See also Deut. 4.15-18:

> Since you saw no form when the LORD spoke to you at Horeb out of the fire, take care and watch yourselves closely, so that you do not act corruptly by making an idol for yourselves, in the form of any figure – the likeness of male or female, the likeness of any animal that is on the earth, the likeness of any winged bird that flies in the air, the likeness of anything that creeps on the ground, the likeness of any fish that is in the water under the earth.

Both this passage, and Hab. 1.14 (discussed below) appear to refer to an explicit cultic formulation which is dependent upon the image/creation complex in Genesis 1, though it should be noted that the words for 'idol' and 'likeness' here differ from the term used in Gen. 1.26-27.

Lexical Parallels
I have commented more than once on the striking degree to which the book of Jonah exhibits the careful selection of direct and indirect quotation and the studied deployment of key terms and expressions designed to prompt a sense of recognition amongst readers. In this section and the next I shall describe these connections, dealing first with Jonah's use of lexically similar language, and then with its treatment of related themes.

(1) *'Dry land'* *(*yavashah*)* Jonah 1.9, 13. This noun, presumably from the common verb *yavash* ('to dry, dry up') has a limited semantic range, unlike its parent root, but one which is of considerable interest. In Gen. 1.9, 10 and Ps. 95.5 it belongs to the language of creation, representing the dry land which Yahweh creates by dividing the waters.

> And God said, 'Let the waters under the sky be gathered together into one place, and let the dry land appear'. And it was so. God called the dry land Earth, and the waters that were gathered together he called Seas. And God saw that it was good.
> The sea is his, for he made it,
>   and the dry land, which his hands have formed.

Its other principal use is in occurrences of the other 'dividing of the waters' theme – the Red Sea and the Jordan – in Exod. 14.16, 22, 29; 15.19; Neh. 9.11; and Ps. 66.6 with respect to the former, and in Josh. 4.22 where the Israelites' crossing of the Jordan is clearly presented as a reprise of the exodus experience. Apart from Jonah, the only other occurrences of this word are in Exod. 4.9 (×2) and Isa. 44.3-4. The former is in the context of one of the signs Moses is directed to use to convince the people of his qualifications to lead; the latter might be read as having an indirect connection to creation:

> For I will pour water on the thirsty land,
>   and streams on the dry ground;
> I will pour my spirit upon your descendants,
>   and my blessing on your offspring.
> They shall spring up like a green tamarisk,
>   like willows by flowing streams.

It does not seem unreasonable to attribute to Jonah a certain awareness in its use of this highly specified word. The fact that Jonah's sailors (1.9) fail to reach *this* kind of dry land, with its creative and redemptive echoes, is arguably no accident; nor is it a coincidence that the desired goal is reached only when a rapport with Yahweh is achieved, and the waters stilled. The theme of life-threatening waters is, of course, a major one in the primeval narratives of Genesis – and we shall return to it shortly. But it might be worth noting that, just as Noah sacrificed after the flood, so do the sailors once they are assured of reaching the dry land which represents their salvation.

I shall argue below that there is evidence of an anti-creation motif in some of the terms to be explored; the use of the *yavashah* in Exod. 4.9 (in the plague narratives) might figure as part of that destructive tendency – a possibility which would (remarkably) imply that only once does this word find a use other than in the themes pertinent to Jonah and Genesis.

(2) *The Fish (*dag*) Jon. 1.17 (×2); 2.10; (*dagah*) 2.1*. At first sight it would seem unlikely that the regular word for 'fish' would carry much specific semantic weight; but surprisingly we find that both the masculine and feminine forms of the word are rather narrowly deployed. Since there seems to be no semantic significance to the text's choice between the two forms (though, of course, rabbinic tradition finds a precise purpose: see the commentary on 1.17 in Chapter 8), for the purpose of this brief survey I have simply aggregated the uses. There are some 34 instances in total, of which only six are used with reference to *fish* in a semantically neutral manner (that is, without some pointers to theological or mythic motifs). A further four occur in the proper name 'the Fish Gate', leaving 24 in which we are forced to take note of motifs beyond the purely physical signified 'scaly creature which swims in the sea'.

All of these remaining instances fall under one of two headings – *creation* or *anti-creation* – which may be regarded as *oppositional* in traditional logico-critical terms, or *undecidable* in Derridean terms. Thus to the category 'creation' we can apply the four Jonah instances (since they refer to the creature which Yahweh specially 'appoints'), the Genesis references (1.26, 28; 9.2), and Ps. 8.8. Ezek. 47.9, 10 (×2) belong to a passage describing the sweet waters of the new Jerusalem – a 'new creation' motif – and Job 12.8-9 refers to the fish of the sea as part of a catalogue of created things which can testify that 'the hand of the Lord has done this'. The 'anti-creation' category takes off from the plague narratives of Exodus – specifically 7.18, 21, but see also the use of 'dry land' in Exod. 4.9 which we noted above. All of the other instances of this motif, bar one in the Psalms, are found in the prophetic literature. Some refer to the plagues (thus Isa. 50.2 and Ps. 105.29 directly, Ezek. 29.4 [×2], 5 indirectly), and the remainder to a kind of general destruction of God's work which will result from humankind's sinfulness (Ezek. 38.20; Hos. 4.3; Zeph. 1.3). There is a remarkable twist to this fishy tale in Hab. 1.14 which threatens wicked humankind with the fate of becoming 'like the fish of the sea, like creeping things which have no ruler' – a remarkable disintegration of creation for at least some of those born (according to

Genesis) to rule. There are in fact several very suggestive links between Hab. 1.14 and Gen. 1.26 which make it quite probable that the former is a deliberate undermining of the latter, as becomes evident when we set them out together:

> Then God said, 'Let us make (*'asah*) humankind (*'adam*) in our image, according to our likeness; and let them have dominion over the fish of the sea (*dag hayyam*), and over the birds of the air, and over the cattle, and over all the wild animals of the earth,' and over every creeping thing (*remes*) that creeps upon the earth'.

> You have made (*'asah*) people (*'adam*) like the fish of the sea (*dag hayyam*), like crawling things (*remes*) that have no ruler.

The Habakkuk passage uses a different term for 'ruler' than the Genesis text's 'have dominion'; but the other similarities, and the forceful substitution of 'in our [i.e. God's] image' with the demeaning 'like the fish …' signal a striking reversal of the optimistic theology of creation. And this is further strengthened by the contrast between noble humankind which has dominion in Genesis, and debased human beings like insects without rulers.

(1) *'Sleep,' 'To sleep'* (*tardemah, radam*) *Jonah 1.5, 6.* One of the most interesting direct linguistic connections is in the verb used to refer to Jonah's innocent sleep in the hold of the ship, a connection that Magonet (pp. 67–9) discusses in his chapter on intertextuality. Once again, like the terms for 'fish', this might at first seem insignificant; but it turns out that the verb and its associated noun are for the most part used in the context of divinely induced sleep, or sleep leading to visions or revelations. To the former category belong Gen. 2.21; 15.12; 1 Sam. 26.12; Isa. 29.10; and Ps. 76.5, and to the latter Job 4.13; 33.15; and Dan. 8.18; 10.9 (and again Gen. 15.12). There are two uses of the root to indicate laziness (Prov. 10.5 and 19.15), and it occurs finally in the macabre story of Jael's murder of Sisera when he was sleeping the sleep of exhaustion (Judg. 4.21).

Apart from Proverbs, it is clear that this kind of sleep has profound – sometimes fatal – consequences. Jonah's sleep, had it not been interrupted, would no doubt have been of that kind, just as Sisera's was, and (arguably) Saul's in 1 Samuel 26; this is the import, too, of the usage in Psalm 76. But the sense of laziness and dereliction of duty is also pertinent – Isa. 29.10 has a special resonance:

> For the Lord has poured out upon you
> > a spirit of deep sleep,
> he has closed your eye, you prophets,
> > and covered your heads, you seers.

No doubt this is a curious and obscure text, yet it has an aptness to Jonah that tempts me to make a connection: the 'deep sleep' sounds very like Jonah's senseless behaviour (in both meanings: being unconscious, and being imprudent) in the hold of the ship. If we then make the further connection to Genesis, and note also that the hold signifies the womb, as does the fish, we discover that the text introduces at least two fascinating subversions of the creation legend. Jonah's sleep is that of laziness and ignorance, where Adam's is divinely induced; and Jonah moves from womb to womb in a reversal of the Genesis episode in which the man becomes (uniquely) a womb while asleep in order to give 'birth' to the 'womb-an' who will henceforth have sole claim to the power to give birth.

Magonet teases out another aspect of this word by noting that since Jonah receives no revelation, the primary meaning is the sleep that presages death. He suggests that it could be the first intimation of Jonah's death wish (why else sleep so soundly in the midst of a storm?[1]) and then links this to the story of Elijah in 1 Kings 19. I will return to this theme in Chapter 11, but should note now that, despite the tempting parallel between this episode and Jonah's repeated wish for death in 4.3, 8, at this point the logic of the narrative militates against such an interpretation.

(4) *'Spirit', 'Wind' (ruach) Jonah 1.4; 4.8.* Obviously the ubiquity of the word *ruach* makes it difficult to attach any specific significance to its individual occurrences. We can hardly claim that Jonah uses it in direct reference to its role in Genesis. Nevertheless, its use in the primeval narratives of Genesis is quite restricted. We find it used twice in relation to water: first to describe the agency of creation (1.2) and then of re-creation, in the dissipation of the flood waters (8.1). Otherwise, it occurs in 6.3, 17 and 7.15, 22 with reference to the life of God in both humankind and animals where, in an interesting anticipation of Qoh. 3.19-21, each shares the one spirit – a matter which I will return to in Chapter 12. There is

---

1. It is tempting to counter with the question: Did Jesus have a death wish when he slept through the storm on the Lake of Galilee (Mt. 8.23-27)? Even as a pastiche of Jonah, this would entail the conclusion that neither Jesus nor Jonah was desirous of death.

one further occurrence, describing the weather as Adam and Eve strolled in the garden (Gen. 3.8) – a phrase often translated 'the evening breeze' which would be more accurately rendered 'in the day's wind'. The two instances in Jonah, then, take on a certain disruptive importance in that they both refer to the undoing of creation – the storm which threatened the sailors in 1.4 and the scorching wind burning Jonah in 4.8 – and a serious threat to the life of both Jonah and those around him.

(5) *'To the East'* (qedem). Strictly speaking this root belongs to Jonah 4, where it occurs three times, in vv. 2, 5, and 8, referring to his *haste* in fleeing to Tarshish, his sitting to the *east* of Nineveh to view events, and the hot *east wind* which beat down upon him. The same root, of course, is used three times in the famous phrase 'east of Eden' (Gen. 2.8; 3.24; 4.16). It has a further intertextual relevance, not related to the creation material, which I will consider in the discussion of Jonah and the Exodus in Chapter 9.

Non-Lexical Parallels
In addition to the preceding quite specific verbal links, there are also more general comparisons which can be identified at a broader level. I note three further themes which link Jonah and Genesis: the creation of vegetation (Gen. 1.11-12, compare the *qiqayon* or gourd in Jon. 4.6), the creation of creeping things (Gen. 1.24-25, compare the worm in 4.7), and the verbs for the act of creation itself (*bara'* and *yashar* in Genesis, and *manah* in Jonah).

The first two add to the sense of pastiche or subversive humour which hovers always over the surface of Jonah, like the spirit/wind of God hovering over the waters in Gen. 1.2, but in Jonah's case ready to bring chaos out of order, just as Yahweh caused turmoil in Jonah's (previously uneventful?) life by demanding the impossible. Compare, in this context, the opening of Jonah, 'the word of the Lord came to Jonah', with the first move in creation, 'God said'. In the former case the divine word sets in train a series of events which produce mayhem all around, in the latter order emerges from chaos (*tohu vavohu*). The faintly preposterous nature of the scene at the end of the book, with strange appearances and disappearances designed seemingly for the sole purpose of irritating the prophet, and the concluding bathos of 'and also many animals', confirms what the non-pious reader might already have suspected: that the big fish has a similarly ludicrous part to play. Of course the sense of playfulness and the confounding of norms through what seems to be ridiculous, are not the whole story. There is serious purpose behind Jonah's seemingly irreverent language, a subject on which I shall have more to say later in this volume. For the moment, however, I want to emphasise the note of *irresponsibility* implied in the book's subversive treatment of creation.

The final connection – or rather, disconnection – lies in the refusal by Jonah of the expected terms for create, and the use instead of a term which really has more to do with portions, allotted shares and the like (see also the commentary at Jon. 1.17 in Chapter 8). There are no obvious parallels anywhere in Tanakh to the way Jonah deploys this verb, though Ps. 61.7 in which the psalmist asks God to 'appoint steadfast love and faithfulness to watch over [the king]' certainly shares with Jonah the meaning of 'appointing something as an agent (of God) to carry out a particular purpose'. It is hard to resist the inference, given the explicit pointers to the wider creation tradition, that Jonah's selection of the verb *manah* here is a deliberate twist. These bizarre nonce-works are appointed, in a parody creation, to be Jonah's fate, his lot – to force him into the realisation that the God whom he thought he had sussed and whose ways he understood was in fact even more fickle and playful than his worst fears. Jonah feared that God was the kind who would show mercy to those who (in Jonah's estimation) did not deserve it. In the event God turns out to be one who does indeed forgive the undeserving, but just to rub salt in the wound, that same God further heaps misery on those who believe themselves to be faithful, like Jonah himself, who protests (2.8-9):

> Those who cling to false gods
> > may abandon their loyalty, but I with hymns of praise
> > shall offer sacrifice to you; what I have vowed I shall fulfil.
> Victory is the Lord's!

Of course, this protest is at first glance itself ironic, or self-deceptive, since everything else we read directs us to the conclusion that Jonah (the character) is precisely the opposite of everything implied in that pious piece of self-justification. We would do well to reflect on the level of hypocrisy involved here, and to consider whether God's taunting of Jonah in ch. 4 was not a rather appropriate 'victory' in the circumstances!

The Flood

Magonet (p. 65), citing Orlinsky, remarks on the significance of the pairing in Jon. 3.8 of 'wickedness' and 'violence' which are cited as the cause of the flood in Gen. 6.5, 11 and 13. I explored the significance of this in some detail in Chapter 1, suggesting that the broad structure of Jonah reflects God's two methods of destruction – water and fire.

While these specific terms form a potent link between Jonah and Genesis 6, there are furthermore broadly defined influences which are suggestive. First, the punishment for human wickedness and violence is to be visited on the whole creation. And so the act of redemption must equally apply across every order of creation. That is the reason for the Ark, and it is mirrored by the Ninevite cattle in sackcloth; further, it is shown to be part of God's ethical plan both in the taking of all animals aboard the Ark and in Yahweh's final word to Jonah: 'and also many cattle'.

Secondly, the Ark itself is, like the wilderness temple, built to a divine blueprint, as a place of refuge and of God's covenant (Gen. 6.13-22):

> And God said to Noah, 'I have determined to make an end of all flesh, for the earth is filled with violence because of them; now I am going to destroy them along with the earth. Make yourself an ark of cypress wood; make rooms in the ark, and cover it inside and out with pitch. This is how you are to make it: the length of the ark three hundred cubits, its width fifty cubits, and its height thirty cubits. Make a roof for the ark, and finish it to a cubit above; and put the door of the ark in its side; make it with lower, second, and third decks. For my part, I am going to bring a flood of waters on the earth, to destroy from under heaven all flesh in which is the breath of life; everything that is on the earth shall die. But I will establish my covenant with you; and you shall come into the ark, you, your sons, your wife, and your sons' wives with you. And of every living thing, of all flesh, you shall bring two of every kind into the ark, to keep them alive with you; they shall be male and female. Of the birds according to their kinds, and of the animals according to their kinds, of every creeping thing of the ground according to its kind, two of every kind shall come in to you, to keep them alive. Also take with you every kind of food that is eaten, and store it up; and it shall serve as food for you and for them'. Noah did this; he did all that God commanded him.

We know from Jonah 2 that Jonah felt particularly drawn to the temple: his prayer from the belly of the whale is a heartfelt longing to look once more upon its holy presence. From the depths of the flood he seeks its sanctuary: as it were, an Ark floating above the dark waters which threaten his life.

Two other points of perhaps lesser import can be noted: the 40 days of the flood ('Forty days more, and Nineveh shall be overthrown'), and the injunction against the spilling of human blood (Gen. 9.6) which is linked to humankind's creation in God's image, and may well at some level inform the scene where the sailor's plea their innocence of any such crime.

Sodom and Gomorrah

Both the flood story and the account of the destruction of the cities are in essence anti-creation narratives. That this is the case in the former is strikingly marked by the instruction given to Noah by God when the flood has subsided:

> Bring out with you every living thing that is with you of all flesh – birds and animals and every creeping thing that creeps on the earth – so that they may abound on the earth, and be fruitful and multiply on the earth. (Gen. 8.17; see also 9.1-7)

The Sodom and Gomorrah legend is more complex, not least because it is interwoven through the Abraham narrative in Genesis 12–19.[2] The fiery apocalypse in ch. 19 is the culmination of an extensive account which deals with at least three threats to the viability of the divinely chosen family. First, on account of the rivalry between two branches of the family: that of Abraham and that of Lot (13.3-13); second because of Sarah's infertility, leading to the emergence of a second line of descent: that of Hagar and Ishmael (ch. 16); and third, on account of the existence of urban centres whose people are 'wicked, great sinners against the Lord' (13.13) and whose existence threatens the land promised to Abraham. Genesis 13.14-16 summarises neatly the promise, and hence the implied threat:

> The LORD said to Abram, after Lot had separated from him, 'Raise your eyes now, and look from the place where you are, northwards and southwards and eastwards and westwards; for all the land that you see I will give to you and to your offspring for ever. I will make your offspring like the dust of the earth; so that if one can count the dust of the earth, your offspring also can be counted.

Just as the flood was set to end God's experiment with humankind before it had properly begun, so this three-fold menace could have eliminated the father of countless peoples before even one child had been born.

---

2. In historical-critical terms there is an argument to be made for seeing at least chs. 14 and 17 as subsequent additions to an earlier, perhaps more straightforward form of the history of Abraham. Not least of note is that in ch. 12 we have the first of three versions of a legend of Abraham's passing off his wife as his sister, and in ch. 16 the first of two versions of the birth of Ishmael and the fate of Hagar. These alone strongly suggest an elaborated narrative.

The resolution of these dramatic motifs is worked out over the full extent of this part of the tale of Abraham. The key features are:[3]

(1) Original promise of descendants, land and blessing (12.1-3).
(2) First threat from Egypt and Pharaoh (12.10-20): resolved by divine intervention.
(3) Second threat, from Lot's ambition: resolved by parting of the ways; Sodom and Gomorrah introduced (13.1-13).
(4) Second iteration of the promise (13.14-18).
(5) The first covenant between Yahweh and Abraham; 'deep sleep' (*tardemah*), including a third iteration of the promise (15.1-21).
(6) Third threat – the birth of Ishmael introduces a rival descent.
(7) Resolution: angelic visitation announces Sarah's forthcoming pregnancy (18.1-15).
(8) Fourth threat: Abraham's endeavour to thwart the destruction of Sodom and Gomorrah (18.16-33).
(9) Resolution: the destruction of the cities of the plain (19.1-29)
(10) Postscript: the incestuous birth of Lot's sons, the eponymous ancestors of Moab and Ammon (19.30-38)

The two features of this sequence which Jonah most directly hooks into are Abraham's vision in ch. 15, the result of a trance which leads to the first expression of the covenant,[4] and the overthrow of the violent and wicked cities. If these are valid connections, then we have a pointer to the third of the great mythic cycles from Genesis. Together these three dramas – creation, flood and destruction by fire – introduce us to the underworld of Jonah's story, the great epics of the Israelite scriptures which have both national and individual importance. For just as the place where Israel now stands is the result of these (and, as we shall see, other) potentially destructive experiences, so the individual's sufferings can be similarly expressed as a testing by earth, fire, wind and water: the earth, the *'adamah* from which *'adam* was formed; the fire (*'esh*) which consumes both the sacrifice and the guilty; the wind (*ruach*) which broke the formless chaos in Genesis 1 and sourced the breath (*nishamah*) of all that lives; and the waters (sea, deeps, flood) which are a constant threat to the precarious stability of the dry land (*yavashah*) without which all human life will perish. In one form or another Jonah endures each of these, and so at one level relives the history (the salvation history?) of his people.

3. Following on the previous note, I have omitted chs. 14 and 17 from this resumé.
4. A more detailed discussion of this point will follow in Chapter 10.

Coda: The Dog that Didn't Bark

But there is a mystery surrounding the dense intertextuality of Jonah, best defined by the Sherlock Holmes clue of the dog that didn't bark:

> Gregory [detective]: Is there any other point to which you would wish to draw my attention?
>
> Holmes: To the curious incident of the dog in the night-time.
>
> Gregory: The dog did nothing in the night-time.
>
> Holmes: That was the curious incident.[5]

I refer to the curious fact that Jonah nowhere invokes directly the central pillar of Jewish belief: the covenant ($b^e rit$). It is certainly present in the Genesis accounts I have identified: when the Ark is set up (Gen. 6.18), when life is renewed after the flood (the famous sign of the rainbow (Gen. 9.8-17), in the mysterious visionary sacrifice witnessed by Abraham (Gen. 15.18), and in Exod. 34.10-28 where the blessing formula shared by Jonah and Joel is to be found. While it is true that within the twelve there are relatively few references to the covenant, it remains curious that Jonah in particular, in which we find extensive references to and citations of many central features of Israelite religion and tradition, the covenant should have been, as it were, excised from the record. This too I shall return to at the end.

---

5. Conan Doyle, 'The Adventure of Silver Blaze'.

Chapter 8

JONAH 1.17–2.10: AN APPEAL FROM THE ABYSS

Note: In the Hebrew original, ch. 2 begins at what is 1.17 in English. Commentaries commonly follow the Hebrew convention and regard 1.17–2.10 as a single unit. I have followed this well-established rule, but in order not to confuse readers, I have refrained from the practice sometimes used of placing the Hebrew numbering in brackets. Those wishing to consult the Hebrew text should take 1.17 to be 2.1, and in all other references to verses in ch. 2, add one to the English numbering.

Verses 1.17–2.1

$^{1.17}$But the LORD provided a large fish to swallow up Jonah; and Jonah was in the belly of the fish for three days and three nights. $^{2.1}$Then Jonah prayed to the LORD his God from the belly of the fish,

^{17a}But the LORD provided a large fish

Not only did the Lord appoint a big fish, that same fish turns out to be of ambiguous gender. In 1.17 it occurs twice as *dag* (masculine grammatical gender), whereas in 2.1 it is *dagah* (feminine). It returns to masculine in v. 10 when it spews Jonah up on the beach. The significance of the fish is elusive, though explanations have been offered, particularly in rabbinic circles. Perhaps the best-known of these (Levine 1975, p. 71) is the proposition that Jonah was at first in a male fish, where he remained in (relative!) comfort for three days and nights. His circumstances being insufficiently harsh to move him to prayer, Yahweh transferred him to a female fish (*dagah*) which was much more cramped, owing to her being pregnant (there is a Hebrew verb *dagah* meaning 'to increase', found once, in Gen. 48.16, which might explain the play on words). Only then was he driven to pray for release, an explanation which if anything shows Jonah up in an even worse light than does the unadorned Hebrew text. While it would be difficult to out-do this rabbinic explanation, there is another interesting angle on the fact that it is while Jonah is inside the whale singing his psalm that it morphs from male to female.[1] I refer to the possibility of an appeal to metaphors of pregnancy and birth. As we shall see in Chapter 9, the psalm is replete with references to the exodus motif of the Red Sea with its associated theme of the 'birth of the nation' through the 'parting of the waters'. Of other instances of the term, the feminine form, and only that form, appears in Gen. 1.26, 28, though it is the masculine form in Ps. 8.8. The fish which die in the Nile at Moses' command are feminine: perhaps they have their revenge in Jonah!

The verse opens with that intriguing verb, *manah*, which I remarked on in Chapter 7. Amongst its meanings is that of 'to select for a particular purpose'. The grammatical form of the verb used in Jonah is quite limited in its occurrence – found three times in Daniel, once in Psalms and once in Job.[2] There may be a sense of 'to appoint as an agent' in this usage; though that interpretation does not quite fit the Daniel and Job passages. Sasson (pp. 147–9) is one of the few commentators to look more closely at the term; what he finds is worth reporting here:

(1) Each time the verb appears a different form of God's name is used: thus *YHWH* at 2.1; *YHWH-'elohim* at 4.6; *ha'elohim* at 4.7; and *'elohim* at 4.8.
(2) At each occurrence the agent commanded is from a different order of nature: a fish at 1.17; a plant at 4.6; an insect at 4.7; and a scorching east wind at 4.8.

In his discussion of Jonah 4 (p. 291) Sasson elaborates further on his observations on *manah*. He notes that the progression of divine names is from the most to the least personal, and that it is the two involving *YHWH* which lead to interventions beneficial to Jonah; the other two are to his discomfort. One final thought on this topic: the Hebrew for 'manna', the special 'bread' provided by God for the Israelites in the wilderness, is *man*, a word certainly within punning distance of *manah*. It is tempting, given the links that undoubtedly exist between Jonah 2 and Exodus, to

---

1. It is tempting, but probably unwise, to speculate on transgendering in Tanakh at this point.
2. Ps. 61.7; Job 7.3; Dan. 1.5, 10, 11.

wonder if the author's choice of this particular verb, and the virtually unparalleled use made of it, was prompted by a reminiscence of the miraculous bread that fed the wandering Israelites and saved them from certain death (Exod. 16.15, 31, 33, 35; Neh. 9.20). Perry (p. 58 n. 12) airs this possibility, offering as grounds 'since the manna of the desert is proof of God's loving care'.

Further creations in 4.6, 7 and 8 are deployed by God to play a part in Jonah's life: the 'cucumber plant', the 'worm', and the 'sultry east wind'. Like the 'big fish' they have uncanny properties, not least that they appear at precisely the right time and in the right place, and seem to have no intrinsic value: they are magical devices designed (perhaps entirely literally) to further the plot. There may be something to be said for translating the phrase as 'God produced a gigantic fish' where the verb reminds us of the conjuror 'producing' a rabbit out of a hat, and further emphasises the artificiality of what is happening. There is no serious attempt at verisimilitude: the author is surely knowing in the deployment of language which drives us out of the embrace of Clio, the muse of history, and into the clutches of either Calliope or Thallia (the muses, respectively, of epic poetry and comedy). For while the story of the storm, the shipwreck and the survival of the sailors could just possibly be rationalised into a believable narrative, no such option can be found in the story of a whale within which a man could live for three days. As a consequence we are driven to re-examine our take on ch. 1, and in particular the significance of the repeated 'great' (*gadhol*) applied there to the city, the storm, and terror or awe, but now just a measure of the size of the fish. The element of bathos is unavoidable, as is the conclusion that this is an essay in hyperbole, designed to drive its thesis to its absurd conclusion. We will return in the Chapter 10 to 'great' Nineveh and its 'great' people, followed at the beginning of ch. 4 by Jonah's 'great' rage.

17bto swallow up Jonah;

Given the densely intertextual character of the language of Jonah, the sinister implications of using the verb 'to swallow' (*bala'*) are certainly relevant. Out of about forty examples of the verb in Tanakh, all but three are negative. It is used of a range of human villains devouring their enemies (the victims are always Israel or the righteous); it describes the ground opening up its mouth and swallowing Korah and his associates (Num. 16.30-35; cf. 26.10; Deut. 11.6; Ps. 106.17-18). Several examples make it clear that the swallowing or devouring has a supernatural dimension: Nebuchadnezzar is like a sea monster (*tannin*); the robbers in Prov. 1.12 are compared to Sheol; in Ps. 69.15 it is the deep (*mitsulah* – the same word is used in Jon. 2.4) that the psalmist fears will swallow him; and in Jer. 51.44 Bel (one of the Babylonian gods) will be forced to disgorge what he has swallowed. In Pharaoh's dream, the withered ears of corn swallow up the ripe ones (Gen. 41.7, 24), while Aaron's rod (Exod. 7.8-13) transformed into a snake, devours the snake/rods of the Egyptian magicians – incidentally the term used here for snake is *tannin*. We have seen that Sheol is implicated by association in Prov. 1.12; and the idea of Sheol (see Jon. 2.2-3) either as the devouring monster or as the destination of those who are devoured is clear from other texts, most strikingly perhaps Isa. 5.14 and Hab. 2.5:

> Therefore Sheol has enlarged its appetite
> and opened its mouth beyond measure;
> the nobility of Jerusalem and her multitude go down,
> her throng and all who exult in her.
> …
> Moreover, wealth is treacherous;
> the arrogant do not endure.
> They open their throats wide as Sheol;
> like Death they never have enough.
> They gather all nations for themselves,
> and collect all peoples as their own.

Psalm 18.4-6 is also of importance, not least because of the range of vocabulary similar to Jonah that it deploys:

> The cords of death encompassed me;
>   the torrents of perdition assailed me;
> the cords of Sheol entangled me;
>   the snares of death confronted me.
> In my distress I called upon the LORD;
>   to my God I cried for help.
> From his temple he heard my voice,
>   and my cry to him reached his ears.

I will consider this passage again in Chapter 9; for now, I simply want to refer to the pairing of Sheol with Death which is present here, in the Habakkuk passage, and also in Prov. 5.5 and 7.27, two verses which express in slightly different language the belief that the fate of those who take up with the archetypal 'strange' woman is to go down to Death, to Sheol. They form, of course, a natural pair; yet surprisingly, though the author of Jonah uses both expressions, they are clearly separated. Jonah escapes Sheol (and therefore certain, though unstated, death) in ch. 2; it is then only in ch. 4 that the term itself appears, this time in Jonah's repeated expression of his desire to die. This separation may be an example of the 'dividing up of quotations' which is discussed by Magonet (pp. 73–6); at any rate it is a striking and original tactic.

It is clear from the foregoing analysis that the fate of Jonah at this precise point is far from favourable. I therefore disagree with those who explain the psalm of vv. 2-9, which is usually interpreted as the expression of a 'done deal', as the outcome of a sense of having been saved from the terror of the sea. On the contrary, as the language of the psalm makes clear, our hero's situation is still perilous: he is explicitly (v. 2) in the belly of Sheol, a destination from whence few, if any, return – a truth all too familiar from the Greek myths of the world in which Jonah was likely composed. And regardless of Rabbinic explanations of the gender of the fish (see above) which depend upon Jonah's accommodation in the first fish being overly commodious, it seems unlikely that at this point the story signals a happy ending.

The ancient world is not lacking in myths in which gods, demi-gods and unhappy human beings find themselves trapped in the underworld (Hades in Greece, Sheol in Israel). Perhaps the best known is that of Orpheus and Eurydice which tells of the failed quest by Orpheus to rescue his deceased wife from Hades. It was his fatal act of turning round before his mission was complete which condemned Eurydice: reminiscences of the story of Lot's wife (Gen. 19.24-26) are inevitable. A more successful rescue was that of Semele by her son Dionysus after she had been killed by her lover, Zeus.

One important aspect of this set of myths is that of the dying and rising god, exemplified in Greek mythology by Adonis who, having been killed by Ares in the form of a boar, is welcomed by Persephone (the goddess of the underworld). His lover Aphrodite seeks to release him, and a compromise is reached by which he will spend six months of each year on earth and six in Hades. There is probably a fertility dimension to this myth, forms of which are also found in Canaan (Mot, Ba'al and Anat), Egypt (Isis and Osiris) and Mesopotamia (Ishtar, Inanna and Tammuz/Dumuzi). The relationships are not always clear: Anat may be the lover or sister of Ba'al; Isis is the sister and wife of Osiris; Ishtar and Innana seem to be alternative names for the wife of Tammuz, who, in a complex legend, becomes (like Adonis) a fertility god who spends six months on earth and six in the underworld. In yet another form of the motif, Persephone, the daughter of the fertility goddess Demeter, is abducted by Hades to be his wife. After numerous adventures (some similar to those of Isis) an accommodation is reached to allow Persephone to spend eight (fertile) months of each year with her mother.

Apart from the quest to rescue family members or lovers from the clutches of death, some myths indicate a deliberate attempt to invade the underworld and take possession of it. This seems to have been Ishtar/Inanna's original intention, and only when that went badly wrong was Tammuz brought into the picture. There is a similar dimension, though at an almost comic level, in the adventures of Theseus in the underworld. Having been persuaded by one Peirithous to venture there to abduct Persephone, the two are trapped into sitting on enchanted chairs which hold them fast. It is only when Herakles, on one of his labours, sees Theseus that the latter is able, through Herakles's good offices, to escape.

It is perhaps unlikely that there are any direct parallels with the story of Jonah; nevertheless it seems probable that the author would have been familiar with at least some of these widespread myths, and the use of the sinister term 'swallow' and the highly unusual phrase 'belly/womb of Sheol' may encourage us to speculate that some knowing reference is there to be picked up by the educated reader.

> [17c] *'and Jonah was in the belly of the fish for three days and three nights.*

The stereotypical time-lapse of three days and three nights, which is proleptic in Christian typology of the death and resurrection of Jesus, has an existing track record in Tanakh. The number three has an established folktale role, as Olrik long ago pointed out – I have written more on this in my study of wisdom literature (Hunter 2006: 236–40) – and this accounts for some of the 'threes' in the Tanakh: for example, the dreams of the butler and the baker in Genesis 40, the three friends of Job and the three cycles of dialogues therein, the three days of darkness in the plague (Exod. 10.22); the three days, three men, three kids and three loaves of bread in the legend of the election of Saul (1 Sam. 9.20 and 10.3); and the multiple threes in the choice of punishments offered to David in 2 Sam. 24.12-13. There are examples of cultic significance in Tanakh: the fact that the journey to Sinai from Egypt took three days (Exod. 3.18; 5.3; 8.27; 15.22 – see also the three days' preparation for the theophany at Sinai in 19.10-11, and possibly the three days' notice of the crossing of the Jordan in Josh. 1.11); and the three great feasts recorded in Exodus 23. And finally there are arguably theological moments: it is on the third day that Abraham looks up to Mount Moriah on the occasion of the Akedah (Gen. 22.4), and in Hos. 6.1-2 the following must surely have influenced the New Testament's understanding of the length of Jesus's sojourn in Sheol:

Come, let us return to the Lord;
> for it is he who has torn, and he will heal us;
> he has struck down, and he will bind us up.
After two days he will revive us;
> on the third day he will raise us up,
> that we may live before him.

The general point is this, that there is ample precedent for the pregnant use of 'three days' in Jonah, and it is not improper to invest it with some significance. Matthew's interpretation is therefore perfectly fitting in principle, whether or not one recognizes his application of the idea as valid – an assessment which, like that of the various rabbinic explanations of aspects of the story, is entirely dependent on the group to which the reader belongs.

> *¹Then Jonah prayed to the LORD his God*
> *from the belly of the fish, saying*

By means of this verse the story turns literally in the space of a phrase from legend through bathos to the core myth of the exodus foundation narrative. It is not surprising, therefore, that precisely at this turn the heightened language of the Psalter is deployed, not as an awkward afterthought on the part of a later redactor, but as a deliberate 'knight's move' in the author's game of chess with the reader. Incidentally, the fatal flaw in theories which propose a later provenance for the psalm is that they leave a completely incoherent and truncated 'narrative' in the form of 1.17–2.1 and 2.10. To argue, as some do, that an earlier narrative was replaced by the psalm makes no sense: why would the later redactor wilfully destroy existing coherence when he could simply have added the psalm? The introduction to the psalm uses traditional language ('Jonah prayed to YHWH his God') but from an entirely unfamiliar locus ('from the belly of the "whale"'). The signs are clear: while we may superficially read the psalm in conventional terms, the context demands an awareness of the wider narrative. *What* the psalm means is inextricably bound up with *whence* it was uttered, and at what time – questions to which I shall return later in this chapter. Of course the place is not a real physical situation but a metaphorical locus. Thus to understand it requires that we attend to the possible meanings of that metaphorical place – which include death, sheol,[3]

---

3. Note that death, as annihilation, is not necessarily the same as sheol: see, for example, the witch of Endor's conjuring of Samuel's revenant (1 Sam. 28) and the Greek idea of what *hades* represented.

exodus, and the womb. It is to that strange, but in the end entirely coherent, poem that we must now turn.

Jonah's Psalm 2.2-9: Translation Issues

There are a number of translation cruxes in the poetic language of Jonah 2, which is commonly described as a psalm. Like all poetic language, ambiguity and occasional obscurity are part of its character, a fact which those who have ever ventured on translations of the book of Psalms are only too familiar with. In the case of Jonah there is an additional complication arising from the narrative character of this song. It is not, as many of the pieces in the Psalter appear to be, a free-standing composition. Jonah 2 is, I am convinced, closely related to the rest of the book. Far from being a later afterthought it has, as I hope to show, an important role in relation both to the events of Jonah 1 and to the overall sense of the book. That being so, rather than run the commentary through this passage as translated in the NRSV, as I have done in respect of Jonah 1 and will return to for Jonah 3 and 4, I propose to argue for and then present an alternative translation which I will then comment upon.

The Question of Tense
There is a long-standing difficulty with the apparent time-frame of the psalm which forms the bulk of ch. 2 of Jonah. It *appears* to be a thanksgiving after the event for the psalmist's rescue from peril, and this is how it is usually translated (thus KJV, RSV, NRSV, NEB, REB, NIV, JPS). The consequence of this not unreasonable translation is that the exegetical principle that the psalm was the *cause* of God's action on Jonah's behalf is difficult to reconcile with what seems to be written on the page. It is this disagreement which constitutes the most powerful case for the prosecution, that the psalm is an afterthought in the book as a whole. The difficulties are succinctly rehearsed in Salters (pp. 30–4). Limburg (pp. 31–3) defends the integrity of the psalm, but does not really address the problem beyond citing the once-popular explanation that the thanksgiving aspect is appropriate because it reflects Jonah's realisation that being alive inside a large fish is preferable to drowning – though we might argue that this is hardly motivation enough for such a paeon of praise as the climax in vv. 6b-9 (see further Bewer, pp. 21–4). Bewer is ultimately persuaded that the psalm is a later interpolation, though not a direct borrowing of pre-existing material, and that it was originally intended to follow v. 10. Wolff (pp. 78–9) also comes down in favour of a later interpolation, but by no means a simple borrowing from an

external psalm, while Sasson (pp. 19–20) broadly defends the book's overall coherence without dismissing the possibility of stages of growth. The most powerful defence of the psalm's being part of the original form of the book is provided by Magonet; see particularly his summary of the arguments (p. 54). I will follow Magonet in affirming the rightful presence of the psalm, though my arguments will not necessarily echo his. It is my conviction that a close attention to the tenses and verb forms in the psalm will help to elucidate this problem. This can be a somewhat technical matter, with which not all of my readers will be familiar. For those who are interested the next section provides some information on this topic which is not strictly essential to the argument, but which I hope will help to clarify it. Those who wish to may safely ignore the passage between the two §§ symbols.

§§

If there is one issue tailored to engender disagreement amongst Tanakh scholars more than any other it is that of tenses. In English these are represented by a wide range of forms enabling a very precise delineation of time and action: I am going, I go, I was going, I went, I have gone, I had gone, I will go, I will be going and so on – these eight forms (and the list is not exhaustive) have to be covered by a remarkably limited range in Hebrew. This is, of course, something of a simplification; but it will serve to illustrate the problems we face in Jonah's prayer from the fish. The starting point is that Classical Hebrew, unlike Modern Hebrew (Ivrit), does not *do* tenses in the manner of Indo-European languages. Ivrit does: it has regularised the so-called perfect as the past tense, the imperfect as future, and the participle as present. That whole convention is largely irrelevant to Biblical Hebrew, which has no simple correspondence between the *time* of an action and the *form* of the verb which expresses it.

The next point to make is that verbs are qualified by the addition of the conjunction (if that is what it is) *vav* which is the near universal means of linking sentences, paragraphs and ideas. The principal siglum for *vav* in English is 'and' – a singularly futile convention, for *vav* is above all a convention rather than a word. Wherever it appears the first question to ask is, what is the context? Here is the simplest example: where *vav* is followed by the negative particle *lo'* it is usually better to read it as 'but'. Further, where it links verbal clauses that have a consequential relationship (e.g. 'The king heard that his son had betrayed him *vav* he had him put to death') English conjunctions like 'so' or 'therefore' cry out to be used.

There is a further complication in the verb in Hebrew: there are two basic forms, the perfect (or 'complete') and the imperfect (or 'incomplete'),[4] which broadly conform to past and future tense. Note, however, that this convention may not always be apposite. Thus the perfect of the verb 'to age' (*zaken*) can mean both 'I was old' and 'I am old', since the former sadly and ineluctably implies the latter. Verbs like this are sometimes referred to as 'stative verbs' because they describe a condition, such as 'to be small', 'to be great' and so on. Returning to the main point, the addition of *vav* as a prefix to either form seems to 'convert' it to the other; thus if perfect equals past action (e.g. 'I said') and imperfect equals future action ('I will say') then, in certain circumstances, *vav* plus the perfect equals future action and *vav* plus the imperfect equals past action.

The key question is: how do we know when the convention holds? Is it a more or less general rule, or merely a syntactical convention with no predictable semantic consequence? The latter may seem strange, but a close consideration of almost any translation into English of Tanakh – particularly poetry and prophecy – will reveal that translators allow themselves extensive freedom in handling the Hebrew verb forms. In particular, interpreters of prophetic literature have frequently given themselves the widest possible latitude in the matter of the interpretation of these formal conventions in Hebrew. The result is, in effect, a ruling which distinguishes sharply between various forms of prose writing (law, narrative, history etc.) and poetry (psalms and prophetic oracles for the most part). There may be good grounds for this, but it does seem on the face of it odd for a language to use its verbal forms in such a diverse manner simply to accommodate poetic writing. I am suspicious of this scholarly deal, and will apply that suspicion to my discussion of Jon. 2.2-9 in the following pages.

§§

The first words of the psalm, as rendered by all the translations, thrust us right into the problem.

> I called to the Lord in my distress, and he answered me; out of the belly of Sheol I cried, and you heard my voice.

4. Grammarians nowadays prefer to use the terms QATAL and YIQTOL for these 'tenses', based on the actual structure of the forms rather than on an attempt to interpret their function. A further two emerge when the option to prefix the connector *vav* is included, producing in addition the terms VAYIQTOL and VEQATAL. Because this book is general in character and not a technical monograph I shall stick with the traditional terms *perfect* and *imperfect*.

The verbs are unequivocally in a form which is normally translated as past action; in the context they suggest that, at the very beginning of his dreadful experience, Jonah *has already cried out and been answered*. What can this mean? How can we explain it, without resorting either to the 'inserted psalm' theory or the 'fish better than drowning' hypothesis? But there is another possibility. The verb form 'he answered me' is the same as that of another verb, 'he caused me pain or grief'. Both have the same root, *'anah*, a form for which the *Dictionary of Classical Hebrew* lists no fewer than thirteen distinct meanings. The first in frequency, and by far the most common, is 'to answer' (385 in total), but the second, still with a significant number of instances (97), is 'to be afflicted'. While it might be natural to expect that a prayer to God will be *answered*, it is by no means improbable, given that the author of Jonah is at pains to demonstrate Jonah's uneasy relationship with Yahweh, that Jonah's prayer might be met not with an answer but with *affliction*. As we shall see this opens up the way to an instructive understanding of the point in the narrative to which this prayer refers and to its consequent meaning. I propose therefore the following reading of v. 2:

> I called to the LORD out of my distress,
>> but he caused me grief;
> out of the belly of Sheol I cried:
>> You heard me …

The concluding line leads directly into an account of precisely *how* God proceeded to afflict Jonah. Yes, God heard his voice, but not in a benign way.

There is a clue to this in vv. 3 and 5, in both of which we find that the verb translated 'surrounded me' in NRSV is actually an imperfect (without a prefixed *vav*), calling for a reading something like 'that the flood (or deep) might surround me'. This may seem a small point, but the fact that the writer uses this phrasing twice suggests intent, an intention which makes sense of the alternative translation I have proposed for v. 2. I must emphasise that this is not an arbitrary manipulation of the Hebrew: where an imperfect with no prefix occurs in a verbal clause its expected sense is *either* simple present tense, *or* cohortative form to be read as 'let it …' or 'may it …'. With that in mind, I observe that the opening conjunction *vav* in v. 3 is likely to convey a contrasting sense, since what happens thereafter is the opposite of what might be expected from the words 'you heard me' at the end of v. 2. Accordingly I propose to translate vv. 3 and 5 as

> ... but you cast me into the deep,
>> into the heart of the seas
>>> that the flood might surround me!
> The full force of your breakers and rollers swept over me.
> ...
> The waters closed in over me
>> that the deep might surround me!

I shall take up v. 4 in the next section, since there is a question there too about the translation of one word.

Small But Significant Words

All languages make use of seemingly insignificant words which often serve as qualifiers of the general sense of a clause. Translation of these can be frustratingly difficult, sometimes because they can display a diverse pattern of meaning making a specific choice tricky; but also occasionally because the available uses do not seem to fit the phrase in question. The temptation then can be to add another 'rare' meaning to facilitate the reading rather than struggle to comprehend a difficult original text.

An example of this kind of problem occurs at the beginning of the second part of v. 4. The Hebrew is *'akh*, which can mean 'surely', 'only', or 'however' – but not 'how' as an interrogative, as in the NRSV. This translation appeals to the Greek version of Theodotion for its reading; but his is an isolated witness, and it is fairly clear that the Hebrew we have is correct.[5] The temptation to follow that one alternative voice is that, on one understanding of the flow of the text, a question seems more apt at this point: 'How can I hope to look upon the Temple again, given my dire circumstances?' Other modern translations, such as the NIV, follow the Hebrew text, as does the King James. I shall follow their example and offer accordingly the reading:

> Then I thought,
>> 'I have been banished from your sight;
> Nevertheless I shall continue to look
>> towards your holy temple'.

The verb 'to say' can be used for inner thought or introspection; hence my choice of 'I thought' at the beginning. The variant 'continue to look' deals with another hidden problem with NRSV and other modern translations:

---

5. Sasson (pp. 179–81) provides a very full discussion of the problems both of the Masoretic Hebrew and the proposed emendation.

the verb translated 'again' is really an auxiliary verb signifying continuity of action. In other words, what the psalm suggests at this point is a man who, despite his contrary behaviour, remains devoted to and dedicated to his God and the holy places of Yahweh.

Spoiled for Choice
One last verse poses problems of translation which do not result from obscurity but rather from a surfeit of possible meaning. I refer to v. 8: 'Those who worship (*shamar*) vain idols (*hevel, shave'*) forsake (*'azav*) their true loyalty (*chesed*)'. Each of these five Hebrew words is a highly significant semantic term in the discourse of Tanakh, and this is the only instance in Tanakh where they all come together in one couplet. The closest similar ensemble is in Ps. 31.6-7a which reads:

> *I* hate those who pay regard to (*shamar*) worthless idols (*hevel; shave'*)
>   *so* I trust in the LORD.
> I will exult and rejoice in your steadfast love (*chesed*).[6]

A brief summary of their use in Tanakh will provide a context to enable those without Hebrew to appreciate the difficulties for translation. I have also provided a more extensive treatment of their importance in Tanakh set (as in the digression above) between the symbols §§ to indicate a passage which can safely be passed over.

shamar: to observe Yahweh's covenant and commandments (e.g. Exod. 19.5; 20.6); to watch over (Ps. 121.3, 4, 5, 7, 8).
hevel: breath or wind (Ps. 39.5, 11); vanity (Qoh. 1.2); idols (Deut. 32.21).
shave': vanity (Ps. 127.1, 2); lying, false (Exod. 23.10); perhaps idols (Ps. 24.4).
chesed: kindness, loyalty – perhaps the most frequently cited term in Tanakh for the relationship between God and humankind, and vice-versa. It is commonly, I believe erroneously, translated as 'loving-kindness' or 'steadfast love'. The key citation for our purposes is Exod. 34.6, 7 and its many parallels.
'azav: to abandon – *the* term of choice to describe the unfaithfulness of those who abandon Yahweh and their true faith to follow other (aka 'false') gods and alien traditions (e.g. Deut. 28.20)

---

6. I have made two small modifications to NRSV: the opening pronoun is 'I' in the Hebrew, so I have ignored NRSV's amendment to 'you'; in the second line I read the standard connecting particle *vav* as 'so'.

§§

Detailed Notes

shamar
This is a very common verb, so its significance must be based upon its predominant uses, unless very specific connections can be established between Jonah and any idiosyncratic instances. First, by far the most frequent meaning is to do with 'keeping' or 'observing' Yahweh's special instructions for Israel – the covenant, God's ordinances, word, person, and so on; these take up around 160 out of the 500 or so instances of the verb in total (to these could be added another 30 or so where *shamar* is followed by another verb and means something like 'to be careful to … obey', etc.). Then there are fifty dealing with God's protection of the faithful Israelite, and a few which relate to God's watching as it were to catch people out in wrongdoing (of these all but one are in Job). Another, more technical meaning, to do with being responsible for temple service, accounts for a further fifty, while festival observance is found in twenty instances. Most of the remainder (about 180) are more mundane, having reference to looking after things, guarding and serving as watchmen.

hevel
The most familiar context for this word is Qoheleth, where it occurs 35 times. There is no consensus as to its meaning in this book, but it clearly signals something pointless or vain. Of its uses outside Qoheleth, about 25 are in phrases where a meaning like 'vanity' or 'idol' seems appropriate. The former is the predominant sense (e.g. Job 9.29; Isa. 49.4; Jer. 2.5), but there are seven instances where the latter is indicated (Deut. 32.21, where it is paired with the expression 'no god'; 1 Kgs 16.13, 26; 2 Kgs 17.15; Jer. 8.19; 10.8; 14.22). The remaining ten occurrences appeal to what is perhaps the word's root meaning of 'breath' or 'wind' (Job 7.16; Pss. 39.5, 6, 11; 62.9; 78.33; 94.11; 144.4; Prov. 21.6; Isa. 57.13).

shave'
There is some semantic overlap between this term and *hevel*, though they only actually occur together in Jon. 2.8, Ps. 31.6, and Zech. 10.2. The predominant meaning is 'lies' or 'false witness': 24 examples, together with the repeated Decalogue injunction not to take God's name 'in vain'. A further 16 uses imply a meaning like 'vanity', and a final five require the term to signify directly 'idols' (Pss. 24.4; 119.37; Isa. 1.13; 30.28; Jer. 18.15).

chesed
This is one of the most theologically charged terms in the Hebrew vocabulary. It has suffered from the consequences of an early translation, 'loving-kindness', which has persisted despite overwhelming evidence that this is not the appropriate semantic field in which to place the word. The two main meanings of *chesed* are (a) 'loyalty' or 'faithfulness', when used in respect of an existing relationship – principally that between Yahweh and Israel; and (b) 'kindness' or 'mercy' when describing a free act of generosity between two parties not already in a relationship; the *Dictionary of Classical Hebrew* gives *loyalty* as the primary meaning. There is evidence that the root has something to do with loyalty and faithfulness, even with zeal: the related expression *Chasidim*, for example, is used of Jewish sects notable for their enthusiasm; the term has both a modern and an ancient reference in this usage.

'azav
While this verb can simply mean 'to leave' in the sense of leaving someone or something, it has two significant concentrations of meaning which constitute half of its occurrences. These are, (a) some 65 referring to the abandonment of Yahweh or Yahweh's covenant or instructions or prescribed way; and (b) 35 in the context of Yahweh either abandoning, or promising not to abandon, people.

To sum up, these five terms embrace a very important range of theological ideas: the keeping of Yahweh's covenant, or abandoning it; God's watchful protection, or God's warning that that protection can be withdrawn in response to unfaithfulness; two powerful expressions of the idea of vanity, lies, worthlessness and idolatry; and one classic word covering the highest forms of loyalty and generosity.

§§

Returning to v. 8, the first thing to note is that both structure and language are precisely chosen. The stanza forms a chiasmus of essentially four terms (the second and third words are bound by *maqqef* (Hebrew for 'hyphen') to form a single adjectival phrase *havle-shav^e* – something like 'vain idols' or 'empty vanities' – in which both the noun-phrases and the verbs are contrasted in terms of positive and negative theological value. The shape is as follows, using the NRSV language:

Those who worship	vain idols
Their loyalty	they forsake.

The form is a perfect chiasmus – the verbs are diagonally related, as are the noun phrases, while the crossed pairs are opposite in meaning. Given the precision with which this book is constructed and its keen sensitivity to other Tanakh texts, the chance that this is accidental, random, or unintended is vanishingly small. That being so, it is incumbent on us to try to decipher the purpose of this small but perfectly formed package of explosive theological material set at the literal and metaphorical heart of Jonah.[7] However, the language itself poses several problems which are exacerbated by many of the standard translations, whose only consensus seems to be that the final verb means 'to forsake'. I have set out five in addition to the NRSV text above – KJV, NIV, REB, JPS, and NJB – modifying the word order in each case in keeping with the chiastic structure:

KJV They that observe / lying vanities / their own mercy / forsake

NIV Those who cling to / worthless idols / the grace that could be theirs / forfeit

REB Those who cling to / false gods / their loyalty / may abandon

JPS They who cling to / empty folly / their own welfare / forsake

NJB By worshipping / false gods / their faithful love / some abandon

Summarising, *shamar* is taken variously to mean 'worship', 'observe' and 'cling to'; *havle-shave'*, 'false gods', 'worthless' or 'vain' idols', 'empty folly' and 'lying vanity'; and *chesed*, 'loyalty', 'mercy', 'their own welfare', 'faithful love' and 'the grace that could be theirs'. This confusion is not surprising, since both of the noun phrases in the chiasmus are seriously ambiguous terms, as we saw in the detailed analysis above. The disagreement over *shamar* is harder to understand, however, since of the meanings listed, only 'observe' seems appropriate. It seems that other interpretations have emerged in response to the rendering 'false gods/idols'.

It is necessary here to illustrate the challenges facing all translators by considering some of the criteria which might apply to our decision about how best to render this important but far from straightforward verse. Firstly, it is my conviction that we must retain the well-attested sense of 'to observe' or 'to keep' for *shamar*. Secondly, it seems indisputable that the context in Jonah is that of an existing relationship (even if we cannot

---

7. See below the addendum on 'the centre of Jonah'.

be sure as to the two parties involved) so that the meaning 'loyalty' is to be preferred for *chesed*. I come then to the rather puzzling phrase which appears at the end of the first line of v. 8. As I have already remarked, this is a hyphenated pair of terms one of which can mean 'emptiness', 'futility' or (in a concrete sense) 'idols', while the other encompasses 'futility', 'lies', or 'idols'. It is immediately apparent that the two terms enjoy a considerable semantic overlap. Assuming that the phrase is not a mere tautology, it is likely that we should plump for either 'vain or futile idols' or 'empty lies'. We have to make a choice – which at this point is arguably largely subjective. However, a certain direction emerges from the broader thrust of the narrative.

The choice of 'idols' has, I believe, two flaws. The first is that there is no precedent for an expression such as 'to keep / observe idols'; hence the resort to forms such as 'cling to' or 'worship' by those versions which prefer the interpretation 'idols'. The problem here is that the verb *shamar* does not really mean either of these things. It is interesting, incidentally, that the version which is closest to the Hebrew (in my estimation) is the King James. The second flaw – perhaps reservation is better – is that I do not sense that Jonah is particularly concerned with idolatry *per se*. Of course foreigners, like the sailors, and foreign peoples, like the Ninevites, worship gods that in Israel may have been regarded as idols.[8] But they do not abandon either 'loyalty' or 'kindness' in so doing. If, on the other hand, those under criticism are Jonah's fellow Judaeans, while both renderings are possible idolatry seems less likely to be a significant concern at the probable time of the book's composition. I propose therefore to adopt the translation:

> Those who are heedful of vain lies
>   forsake their true loyalty.

This version has the additional advantage that the chiasmus is better served. In the reading 'idols', while the verbs are clearly contrasted, it is not obvious that 'vain idols' and 'loyalty' form an opposed pair; in my version on the other hand there is a very clear contrast between 'vain lies' and 'loyalty' in addition to the overall contrast between the two lines.

---

8. There is considerable evidence that biblical warnings against other gods were based on a recognition that the temptation was real because these gods existed as dangerous alternatives to Yahweh.

Commentary on Jonah 2.2-9

Taking account of the foregoing discussion my full translation of the psalm follows:

> ²'I called to the LORD out of my distress,
>   but he caused me grief;
> out of the belly of Sheol I cried:
>   You heard me
> ³but you cast me into the deep,
>   into the heart of the seas
>   that the flood might surround me!
> The full force of your breakers and rollers swept over me.
> ⁴Then I thought, "I have been banished from your sight;
> Nevertheless I shall continue to look towards your holy temple"
> ⁵The waters closed in over me
>   that the deep might surround me!
> Weeds were wrapped around my head
>   ⁶at the roots of the mountains.
> I went down to the land
>   whose bars closed upon me for ever;
> yet you brought up my life from the Pit,
>   O LORD my God.
> ⁷As my life was ebbing away,
>   I remembered the LORD;
> and my prayer came to you,
>   into your holy temple.
> ⁸Those who are heedful of vain lies
>   forsake their true loyalty.
> ⁹But I with the voice of thanksgiving
>   will sacrifice to you;
> what I have vowed I will pay.
>   Deliverance belongs to the LORD!'

Having set out my preferred translation of the psalmic passage in Jonah, I shall now turn to a more detailed commentary.

> ²*I called to the LORD out of my distress, but he caused me grief;*
>   *out of the belly of Sheol I cried: You heard me*
> ³*but you cast me into the deep, into the heart of the seas*
>   *that the flood might surround me!*
>   *The full force of your breakers and rollers swept over me.*

Contrary to what may seem the natural interpretation, I regard this opening plea not as evidence of God's positive response to Jonah's despairing cry, but rather as a sign that worse was to come. The key question is: what point in the narrative prompted this prayer, and does the answer to that question help to explain its negative character? To resolve this puzzle we need first to return to the introduction, and to the way Jonah's *tephillah* (prayer) is introduced. Many versions begin 2.1 with the conjunction 'then' which immediately imposes a linear chronology upon the text, but no such explicit indication is present in the Hebrew. The JPS version simply reads, with no introductory link, 'Jonah prayed to the Lord his God', which is better, and leaves the decision about when he prayed to the reader. I think we can go further, especially when we note that the consequence of his prayer is that Jonah is 'cast into the deep', a fate which fits particularly well with an unnoticed silence in ch. 1. There is a point in that chapter where Jonah prays, at least by implication. There is a tendency to miss this incident in the overall thrust of the narrative, but it is undoubtedly there. I refer to the moment when the captain says to Jonah, 'Get up, call on your god! Perhaps the god will spare us a thought so that we do not perish' (1.6). Did Jonah pray at that point? And if so, what effect did his prayer have?

I propose that we read 2.2-3 in the light of that gap, and see it as combining Jonah's likely prayer *before* he was thrown to the waves, and Yahweh's response. This bending of the time sequence occurs more than once in Jonah: another clear example is the problem about the order of events in Jonah 4, which will be discussed later. In short, the author here uses the psalm to encapsulate more than one prayer by Jonah: the second begins at v. 4, and a third at v. 8. The whole prayer is certainly *presented* as emanating from the whale's belly, but the opening section is surely a report of Jonah's first response to the evidence that he had been found out. The result is to produce a remarkably precise connection between the events of ch. 1 and the subsequent experiences of Jonah in the sea as described in ch. 2. In other words, it is not until the middle of v. 6 that any answer to prayer comes – and it is not the opening prayer (presumably the one implied in 1.6) but a later prayer, that of 2.4, which is indicated. The selfish, intercessory prayer of desperation of v. 2a got the answer: No! It is only when a different kind of prayer is elicited from Jonah that his fortunes change. And it is interesting that this second prayer is *not* one of intercession, but (in my translation) an affirmation of either hope or determination: 'Nevertheless I shall continue to look towards your holy temple'. Incidentally, it is generally true of Hebrew prayer that to a surprising extent it eschews intercession. There is an old rabbinic story which makes this point very effectively: When you see a fire-engine in the street, do not pray that it is not going to your house. For if your house is on fire, the prayer is pointless, and if not, you are in effect praying for your neighbour's house to be on fire![9] One interesting further consequence of this reading is that we may perhaps understand the unique expression 'from the belly of Sheol' not as a metaphor for his incarceration in the whale, but as a reference to Jonah's attempt to use the hold of the ship as a place of retreat, of escape from the consequences of his actions. This interpretation sets up an interesting allusion to or echo of Ps. 139.8: 'if I make my bed in Sheol, you are there' (cf. also Job 11.8; 14.13; 26.6; Prov. 15.11; Hos. 13.14). Ironically, then, the hold of the ship – which seemed in human terms a good place of refuge – becomes a literally hellish trap, and the former (the slimy, fishy, dank and putrid gullet of the whale – in human terms a pretty good version of hell) turns out to be the source of redemption.

Turning to v. 3,[10] I want to make the point that the somewhat awkward use of 'your' in reference to the 'breakers and rollers' (and these are literal translations which share a serendipitous semantic parallel with English usage), which is almost impossible to turn into good English, is a deliberate device to link the fate of Jonah here with the actions of God and the sailors in ch. 1. This was in the worldview of the author no random storm, and each surge of the tormented sea is specifically designed by God to teach Jonah a lesson. There is of course much more to this than a literal account of a storm at sea, however personalised. Hebrew terms like Sheol and the flood (*nahar*), and the description of drowning, being overwhelmed by the waters, belong indisputably to the language of myth both in Canaan and in Israel, as evidenced by the Ugaritic texts and a wealth of parallel examples in Tanakh which have been frequently commented on (e.g. Pss. 29.3-4, 10; 74.12-15 and 124.1-8). Readers of the book would have been acutely aware of these resonances, so that the author's subsequent appeal to the imagery and terminology of the escape from Egypt through the waters of the 'Red' Sea would have been both natural and potent.

Incidentally, the portrayal of the experience of drowning in this verse and in vv. 5-6a is another instance of retrospection in Jonah 2: this was what it was like to face the terrors of the deep without any hope or prospect of rescue.

---

9. I cannot now trace the source of this moral.
10. Note: more material bearing on vv. 3-6 will be found in the extended consideration of the Exodus motif which is the subject of Chapter 9.

> *⁴Then I thought, 'I have been banished from your sight;*
> *Nevertheless I shall continue to look towards*
> *your holy temple'*

This second 'I said' reflects a further stage in Jonah's appreciation of his situation. As I have already indicated, I propose that we should understand the language of vv. 2-4 as a literary device analogous to the thoughts that a drowning person is conventionally supposed to experience ('my whole life passed before me in a flash'). Perhaps the most striking modern example of this device is William Golding's *Pincher Martin* (I will not elaborate further for fear of spoiling the book for those who have not yet read it); undoubtedly there is plenty of literary precedent for authorial permission to reveal to their readers thoughts attributed to characters *in extremis* which could never literally be knowable. It might be better, on reflection, to use 'thought' rather than 'said' in these circumstances; the fact that the personal pronoun is used together with the verb 'to say' at the beginning of v. 4 might increase the likelihood that *'amar* is being used in this interior sense. The earlier use, in v. 2, is much more formulaic, being little more than the conventional link to recorded speech or thought in Hebrew: 'Then Jonah prayed ... as follows' ('saying').

If the first part of the drowning man's response was a complaint (God had every chance to hear me, but instead chose to make things worse), the next stage is both nostalgic and ironic, and yet somehow hopeful: 'I have been banished from your sight; nevertheless I shall continue to look upon your holy temple (that is, the place where your sacred presence is to be found)'. The disingenuousness lies in the reader's perception that it was Jonah himself who chose to distance himself from God's presence; the irony in the fact that Jonah was never more close to God than when he was hurled from the ship and sinking to the bottom of the sea. The question of who may have banished Jonah and why will be taken up again in the coda to this chapter.

Two expressions here merit further examination. They are, the verb *garash* ('to dispossess / be dispossessed'), and 'your holy temple' (*hekhal qodhshekha*). The first of these is a remarkably forceful term. Just as the impact of being *swallowed* (*bala'*) in 1.17 goes far beyond the simple physical action, so *garash* has an overwhelming set of associations that must similarly have been called up in the mind of any scripturally informed reader. Its predominant use is to describe the driving out of nations and peoples, often at the hand of or instigated by Yahweh, in order to enable the establishment of Israel in the 'promised land' (see, for example, Exod. 23.28-31). Per contra, it can also, though rarely, be applied to the later displacement of Israel herself as a result of her sins and apostasy (thus 2 Chron. 20.11; Hos. 9.15). The Hosea passage is particularly relevant since it refers to God's intention to drive Israel out of God's house; that is, the Temple. In Gen. 3.24 and 4.14 Adam and Eve are *driven out* of Eden and Cain from the land, and the verb figures also in the tense relationships between Moses and Pharaoh (Exod. 6.1; 10.11; 11.1; 12.39): thus there are allusions to both creation and the exodus, the subjects of Chapters 7 and 9 of the present book. Sometimes individuals are driven out, or fear that fate: see Judg. 9.41; 11.2, 7; 1 Sam. 26.19 (where David expresses his fear that Saul will disinherit him); 1 Kgs 2.27 (Solomon banishes Abiathar from the priesthood, thus effecting the transfer of that institution from the house of Eli). There is also a technical usage to describe divorce, which has the effect of driving a wife away from her husband's household (Lev. 21.7 *et al*).

It is undeniable, therefore, that what Jonah protests here is that he has been driven out of his inheritance (even though he describes it in untypical terms, 'from before your [Yahweh's] eyes'). No-one else in Tanakh makes this claim, which seems tantamount to his believing that somehow his fate is analogous to that of Israel as a whole. Walsh (p. 226) makes an interesting point in regard to this sense of alienation when he observes that in ch. 2 'the dominant sense is of outward horizontal movement ... whether of the psalmist ["you cast me" "I am driven away" from before] or of the waves and breakers ["passed over me"] acting upon him. The overall effect is one of "distancing".' But who, or what, drove him out? At one level the narrative nudges us to answer: 'the sailors', especially as presented in the cameo at the end of ch. 1, where they appear to become the kind of faithful servants of Yahweh that Jonah arguably is not. This might in turn inform the protestations of Jonah in 2.8-9, which many have read as hypocritical, or at least an example of 'protesting too much, in that they could be understood as part of a turf war: a determined pitch by Jonah to reclaim his native traditions from those who have dispossessed him. But this is too superficial, since whatever we may think of the sailors' actions, no conscious displacement of Jonah from anything except the ship was on their minds. There are equally no good grounds for thinking that Jonah drove himself out, or went into voluntary exile; certainly the verb usually implies a relocation of the people or person banished at the instigation of a third party: there are no parallels to this theme of self-imposed exile. The use of the passive (*niphal*) form of the verb ('I have been driven away') relieves the author of the responsibility of identifying the people or god responsible; and it is further striking that this is the only occasion in Tanakh where this form of the verb is used.[11] Whoever was responsible, the entirely unprecedented nature of Jonah's banishment means that there is in principle no barrier to its being reversed – unlike those in most other scriptural cases. The sailors will return to their own lands and business, and Jonah himself, if he can get out of his present confinement, might well be able to reverse his banishment. Oddly enough, this fits with another view of Jonah, that far from being in denial, his true purpose was to save Yahweh from the full consequences of Yahweh's lamentable readiness to be merciful and to forgive sinners, a thesis proposed by Perry (p. xxix).

The end of this verse is also ambiguous, for it is not entirely clear whether it is a quality of God's (namely, 'holiness', to be found in the temple) or the 'holy temple' itself that is intended. While English translations to the best of my knowledge unanimously opt for the latter, there is something to be said for emphasising the personal nature of the quarrel between God and our damp hero. It is not just a holy place that Jonah longs for, it is the special place where the sacred essence of God is to be found that he is fixed upon, convinced that it is this ultimate essential nature of the divine which will bring about a reversal of his fortunes. It is also, ironically, the place of that from which he is said to have fled at the beginning, namely *p^{e}nei yhwh*, 'the presence of Yahweh'. The phrase itself occurs only six times outside Jonah in Tanakh – Pss. 5.7; 11.4; 79.1; and 138.2; Mic. 1.2; Hab. 2.20 – though possible synonyms such as 'holy place' are more common. In order to understand the use made by Jonah of this expression, it will be helpful to have before us these passages. They are, in order,

Ps. 5.8	But I, through the abundance of your steadfast love,
	    will enter your house,
	I will bow down towards your holy temple
	    in awe of you.

Ps. 11.4	The Lord is in his holy temple
	    the Lord's throne is in heaven.
	    His eyes behold, his gaze examines humankind.

Ps. 79.1	O God, the nations have come into your inheritance;
	    they have defiled your holy temple;
	    they have laid Jerusalem in ruins.

---

11. Two other possible instances, in Isa. 57.20 and Amos 8.8, are listed in the *Dictionary of Classical Hebrew* as coming from a secondary meaning of the root, 'to churn'.

Ps. 138.2	I bow down towards your holy temple
	and give thanks to your name for your steadfast love
	    and your faithfulness
	for you have exalted your name and your word above
	    everything.

Mic. 1.2	Hear, you peoples, all of you;
	    listen, O earth, and all that is in it;
	and let the Lord God be a witness against you,
	    the Lord from his holy temple.

Hab. 2.20	But the Lord is in his holy temple; let all the earth keep silence before him.

The salient points are: the striking idea in Psalm 11 that God keeps a close eye on humankind – the other side of the Jonah's desire to see God and his sorrow at being banished from God's eyes; the presence of the nations (aka the sailors) negatively in Psalm 79 and positively in Micah 1 and Habakkuk 2; and the conviction that God's holy temple is the focus of both awe and thanksgiving in Psalms 5; 138 and Habakkuk 2. All of these are part of the subterranean thought patterns of the psalm in Jonah, and indicate that the choice of this particular phrase, and its reiteration in v. 7 is no accident. Incidentally, while I would have to admit that only Psalms 5 and 138 lend any support to my alternative reading, they do so with more than a little force. Psalm 5.7 describes a progression, first into the 'house' (= temple) and then bowing before (a verb which elsewhere implies worship) 'your holy temple': surely 'the temple which houses your holiness' is better in this context? Psalm 138.2, 'I bow down towards your holy temple', uses exactly the same Hebrew as 5.7, and supports accordingly the same interpretation.

> *⁵The waters closed in over me that the deep might surround me.*
> *Weeds were wrapped around my head ⁶at the roots*
> *of the mountains. I went down to the land whose bars closed*
> *upon me for ever; yet you brought up my life from the Pit,*
> *O LORD my God.*

The Masoretic division of these verses between 5 and 6 is odd, since the phrase 'at the roots of the mountains' surely belongs with the preceding line. It is better to see vv. 5-6a as a single dramatic expression, taking Jonah down, down, down to the very depths of the sea and despair, enchained as it were for ever, before the dramatic reversal of his fortunes in the last lines of v. 6. It is a strikingly graphic passage, beginning with the same purposive clause that we met in v. 4, but this time with *nahar* ('the flood') replaced with the more sinister *tehom* ('the deep'): 'that the deep might overwhelm me', preceded by 'The waters closed in over me'. While the etymological connection between *tehom* and the Babylonian salt-water goddess *tiamat* may be debatable, as we noted in Chapter 6; what is certain is that there is in the account of Jonah's journey to the bottom of the sea an unmistakable appeal to one of the most fundamental nightmares of the ancient Semitic psyche, the fear of being cast helpless into the grip of the watery chaos that is Yam ('sea'), Nahar ('river, torrent') and Tehom ('the deep'), a downward trajectory from which (*pace* the myths of Ishtar, Osiris and Persephone) there is not even the slightest chance of return. The ticket Jonah purchased in Joppa is irreversibly one-way – no modifications are possible, even on payment of a supplementary fee.

Note also the dramatic effect of the escalation of terror between v. 3 and v. 5:

> You cast me into the depths (*mitsulah*) of the seas (*yamim*)
>   that the flood (*nahar*) might overwhelm me;

leads to:

> The waters (*mayim*) closed in over me;
>   that the abyss (*tehom*) might overwhelm me;
>   weeds (*suf*) wrapped around my head;
>   at the very roots of the mountains.

This is the stuff of horror. The vivid phrase 'the roots of the mountains' – incidentally an accurate insight into the geological truth that the mountain slopes visible above water continue relentlessly deep down into the ocean – conjures a terrible fate: to be ensnared in rope-like weeds growing from the inhospitable valleys at the bottom of the sea.

The end of this journey is then recalled by Jonah, together with its amazing sequel, in the last two lines of v. 6. Before I consider them, however, it is necessary to return briefly to the matter of Jonah's supposed location at each point in this journey. The broad trajectory is clear, and is signalled by the highly significant pair of verbs *yarad* ('to go down') and *'alah* ('to ascend'). Jonah goes *down* to Joppa (presumably from Jerusalem – this is surely implied by the references to the temple in ch. 2), to the hold of the ship, into the sea, and to the ultimate depths of *tehom*. From there he is brought up by God to suspended life, of a sort, in the whale, thence to the dry land (*yavashah*) of the seashore, and ultimately, we can assume, via Joppa back to Jerusalem (since at the beginning of ch. 3 he is back at his starting point).

Within the narrower confines of ch. 2, having taken the opening lines of the psalm (vv. 2-6) to be a dramatization of Jonah's 'drowning thoughts', vv. 7-9 then constitute his response to the miracle of having been rescued by the agency of the whale (or, more accurately Yahweh). It is in response to his whole-hearted expression of longing for the Temple that God enables the final stage of his journey back to life. To clarify: while the prayers and reflections in v. 1 through to the middle of v. 6 are part of the dying man's last-gasp, despairing cry, the final part of v. 6 constitutes the utterly unexpected record of God's rescuing him from, as it were, the precipice: the kind of last-minute snatching of victory from seemingly inevitable death that is the mainstay of many movies. We experience here the kind of sudden change of pace we encountered in ch. 1 (v. 15): the painfully slow descent into the depths, occupying all of vv. 3, 5, and 6a (five full lines), is reversed in just one line (five words in Hebrew):

> yet you brought me up alive from the pit, O YHWH my God!

The horrors of the pit (*shachath*) of death combined with the perhaps poetic justice of those imprisoning bars (the word is curiously similar to that describing Jonah's flight in 1.3, sharing the same three root letters) serve to enhance the miracle of God's rescue act, though Jonah might be forgiven for thinking that his deity had left it just a little late for comfort. I don't propose to enter into any discussion of the chances of survival for ten minutes, far less three days, in the digestive tract of a whale. A century ago Julius Bewer, in his ICC commentary, was clearly sceptical (p. 5); similarly Sasson (pp. 150–1) and Wolff (p. 132) are dismissive of literal interpretations. Nevertheless there are many reports of such experiences, most of them unsubstantiated, and the persistence of belief in them is curiously resistant to evidence. As it happens, I was regaled with one such account at a conference when I mentioned that I was engaged on this project. The reputed victim (a young boy) was freed within the hour, completely traumatised, and never spoke another word. The reader is advised to use Hume's test for miracles at this point, since the story was told to me by someone who had it from someone else, and as far as I know the boy's convenient silence eliminated the possibility of a first-hand account.

The author of Jonah, quite rightly, is indifferent to such objections. The amazing fish is but one fantastical item in a book which, for all its brevity, is uncommonly full of them. We are not required to justify them, nor yet to rationalise them; their purpose is to advance the Jonah project – be it satire, farce, morality tale or theological treatise. It is to be hoped that by the end of this study a somewhat clearer picture might be gained; but the reader is strongly urged not to cheat by looking at the conclusion in advance!

Verse six, with its juxtaposing of *yaradhti* ('I went down') with *vata'al* ('you brought me up'), undoubtedly marks the central turning point of the book. It is also very nearly, though not quite (and this would I suspect please the author enormously), at the centre in terms of verse count. Of course, this being Jonah, the turning point isn't going to lead to a traditional happy ending; rather it is a point of change to the next set of hazards which he must encounter. There is a more detailed consideration of the subject of the centre of the book of Jonah as an addendum at the end of this chapter.

> ⁷*As my life was ebbing away, I remembered the* LORD;
> *and my prayer came to you, into your holy temple.*

What follows now is on the face of it one of three things: an exemplary account of the repentance of a sinner and his return to righteousness; a piece of the most excruciating hypocrisy; or an instance of a common human failing: self-deception. But if this is, as I have suggested, to be understood as Jonah's prayer when he was first thrown overboard, as he sank to an inevitable death, might we in fairness wonder whether anyone would lie or lack self-awareness at such a point? Recall that we still do not know why Jonah left Jerusalem: it is possible that his actions were those of a faithful man, and that his despairing prayer was heard in the temple for perfectly good reasons.

I take the perfect form at the start of v. 7 as being roughly equivalent to the pluperfect in English, expressing in effect an explanation for the reversal of Jonah's fortunes in v. 6:

> [For] it was when I was at the point of death, that I had [finally] remembered
> Yahweh; my prayer rose up to you, to your holy temple.

The apparent reference here is to Jonah's earlier expression of despair in v. 4 of ever seeing God's temple again; however, if my alternative reading is adopted, that verse is not an expression of despair but rather of hope. And the natural question, why was it only at the point of death that Jonah thought to make the prayer which, presumably, was heard and answered, suggests a deliberate parallel with the behaviour of the sailors in ch. 1, who did everything they humanly could before resorting to their own propitiatory sacrifice and self-exculpating prayer. But the parallel is also a contrast, for Jonah strictly speaking does nothing – we are not given the content of his prayer, and there is no explicit indication of repentance or acceptance of his wrongdoing (if that is how we are to interpret his original flight to Tarshish) – whereas the sailors are shown to be devout, repentant, and explicitly aware of the dubious moral grounds on which they stand. So here is the first point of ambiguity: Was Jonah's silence that of the noble moralist, refusing to appeal to cheap grace, his punishment merited, even if unjust, and only *in extremis* would he utter that inchoate prayer for help that is the natural human cry in the face of the ineluctable? Or was he that other archetype: the stubborn fool determined to maintain his self-righteousness despite every piece of controverting evidence? Further, dare we enquire into Yahweh's motives in all of this: on the surface he is a benign deity eager to rescue a seemingly hopeless nation, thwarted by the pig-headedness of his chosen envoy. But he is also a ruthless tyrant, quite prepared to drown an innocent crew to teach one man a lesson, and complicit in reinforcing precisely the kind of superstitious stereotype (the propitiatory sacrifice) which would seem to be utterly at odds with the God of Exod. 34.6 ('merciful and gracious, slow to anger, and abounding in steadfast love and faithfulness'). Jonah's subsequent complaint that he resents God precisely *because* of his merciful nature is thus ironically at odds with the narrative in which this curious deity is an agent. The ambiguous nature of God is not unfamiliar to readers of the Tanakh; what makes Jonah different is the way that attention is drawn explicitly to this dimension of divine being and power. What we are to draw from this is not clear – perhaps admiration for the sophisticated nature of the writer's thinking about these matters, perhaps more explicitly a shared realisation of the unavoidably paradoxical nature of the combination of absolute power, pure free will, and the claim to be at one and the same time both loving and merciful, and just. Jonah the book dramatizes these issues; its bathetic ending is arguably the last word in a debate that can never be resolved; we will return to this in due course.

> [8]*'Those who are heedful of vain lies forsake their true loyalty.'*

Verse eight is terse, yet pregnant with meaning, and comes out as a bitter protest – against whom? – apparently unfitting in a man who has just been rescued, through no merits of his own, from a watery grave.

My considered judgement, at this stage of the debate, is that the core issue in Jonah is not which god one worships or makes sacrifices to, but how reliable are the words attributed to that god, or handed down by tradition. Jonah's flight was not occasioned by what God was, but by what God apparently wanted of him. It was what Yahweh *said* that occasioned his response. We might therefore venture the perhaps daring interpretation that Jonah understood his opening mission to be misleading – the kind of test that Yahweh sometimes sets for the faithful to see if they can discriminate between right and wrong. There is good rabbinic support for this possibility, which can be illustrated by two famous examples. The first is an interpretation of the Akedah, the story of Abraham's readiness to sacrifice Isaac in Genesis 22, which I discussed in Chapter 5; and the second is the story of the *bath kol* (literally 'heavenly voice' and so, 'voice of God') to which R. Eliezer appealed in an attempt to persuade his fellow Rabbis to disagree with Torah; the upshot being that the Rabbis cite scripture *against* Yahweh, and thereby end the argument (*Babylonian Talmud*, Bava Metzia 59b):[12]

> On that day R. Eliezer brought forward every imaginable argument, but they did not accept them. Said he to them: 'If the *halachah* agrees with me, let this carob tree prove it!' Thereupon the carob tree was torn a thousand cubits out of its place – others affirm, four hundred cubits. 'No proof can be brought from a carob tree,' they retorted. Again he said to the: 'If the *halachah* agrees with me, let the stream of water prove it!' Whereupon the stream of water flowed backwards – 'No proof can be brought from a stream of water,' they rejoined. Again he urged: 'If the *halachah* agrees with me, let the walls of the schoolhouse prove it,' whereupon the walls inclined to fall. But R. Joshua rebuked them, saying: 'When scholars are engaged in a halachic dispute, what have ye to interfere?' Hence they did not fall, in honour of R. Joshua, nor did they resume the upright, in honour of R. Eliezer; and they are still standing thus inclined. Again he said to them, 'If the *halachah* agrees with me, let it be proved from Heaven!' Whereupon a Heavenly Voice cried out: 'Why do ye dispute with R. Eliezer, seeing that in all matters the *halachah* agrees with him!' But R. Joshua arose and exclaimed: 'It is not in heaven.' What did he mean by this? – Said R. Jeremiah: That the Torah had already been given at Mount Sinai; we pay no attention to a Heavenly Voice, because Thou has long since written in the Torah at Mount Sinai, After the majority must one incline.

The interesting consequence is that Jonah now appears in a better light than Abraham, if it was his despairing attempt to dissuade Yahweh from the ill-advised project of offering cheap grace to Nineveh which set in train the sequence of events which led to his incarceration in the whale. The difference from Abraham is that God's rescuing of Jonah might then be seen as an admission, an acceptance that at some level Jonah was right,

---

12. Sourced at https://www.halakhah.com/babamezia/babamezia_59.html

and that (dare we suggest) the abandonment of *chesed* is a sustainable accusation against Yahweh. If *chesed* is indeed best understood as loyalty, what could be more disloyal than sending a Jewish envoy to carry out God's incomprehensible plan to redeem Nineveh? Which prompts an even more radical reading, that it is none other than God who has abandoned divine loyalty to Israel in pursuit of a vain attempt to win round the wretched Ninevites. So determined, indeed, is Yahweh that he inflicts a terrifying ordeal on Jonah only to rescue him at the last minute – a kind of divine waterboarding which is all too effective in that its victim 'sees the error of his ways' and joins the oppressor's camp. At the risk of compounding offence, there is a plausible parallel between God's doomed desire to impose Yahwism on Nineveh and the West's adventures in promoting democracy through invasion and military strength. There is no evidence that the Ninevites in the real world ever saw the light; it will be interesting to review the long-term effects of regime change in Iraq and Afghanistan;[13] certainly the medium term offers little by way of hope.

> *⁹But I with the voice of thanksgiving will sacrifice to you;*
> *what I have vowed I will pay. Deliverance belongs to the* LORD*!*

The structure of v. 9 is also distinctive. It opens with an emphatic form of the first person pronoun which establishes a clear disjunction with the preceding verse, and deploys the cohortative form of both verbs which is usually translated 'let me …'. What this establishes is a clearly contrastive declaration of intent: I am not like the disloyal described above: 'Given a chance I will be sure to express my thanks, pay my vows, and offer proper sacrifice to you'. This declaration of intent is important in the light of our analysis of v. 8, for it emphasises the keeping of vows – something surely lacking in those who are seduced by vain lies into abandoning their first loyalty. An ironic contrast is often seen here, on the grounds that Jonah's need of salvation was a direct consequence of his original disobedience; by contrast both the sailors and his fellow Judaeans are punctilious in their devotions – the former directly witnessed in ch. 1, the latter by implication since they remain in the vicinity of that very temple, separation from which is a key part of Jonah's cry from the sea. It will be clear by now that I do not support this understanding; nevertheless the extensive linguistic overlap with 1.16b is instructive. There the sailors sacrifice (*zabakh*) and

---

13. The resurgence in August 2021 of the Taliban, and their rapid recapture of much of Afghanistan after the withdrawal of Western forces, is sombre testimony to the pertinence of this aside.

make vows (*nadar*) to Yahweh; here Jonah promises to sacrifice (*zabakh*) and to fulfil (*shilem*) his vow (*nadar*) to Yahweh – almost as if he has a psychological need to upstage the upstart foreigners who threw him overboard and who are in danger of winning undeserved kudos for their opportunistic conversion (a theme which simultaneously anticipates the Ninevites behaviour in ch. 3).

Or is it Jonah himself who is being opportunistic, clutching at pious straws to persuade God to free him from his watery predicament? This would follow from the more popular trajectory of 'divine instruction–disobedient prophet–divine anger and punishment–humiliating rescue of bedraggled (and repentant) prophet' which is taken to explain the first two chapters of Jonah.

The final declaration, 'Deliverance belongs to the Lord!' (*yeshua' lyhwh*), has its closest parallel in Ps. 3.8 in which it represents the psalmist's deliverance from his enemies. It is usually included as part of Jonah's prayer, but it is also possible that it is the narrator's conclusion, celebrating Jonah's freedom from the effects of lies and deceit, and prompting the final resolution of Act Two of the drama.

Concluding Narrative

¹⁰Then the Lord spoke to the fish, and it spewed Jonah out upon the dry land.

And so the famous tale of Jonah in the whale reaches its denouement, when the creature, ordered (ordained) by God and now ordered (commanded) again by God, vomits our hero on to the talismanic dry land (*yavasha*) whose mythic significance we have already discussed in Chapter 7. Perhaps the fish was just sick of the whole business; perhaps, as someone else has proposed,[14] the fish had had enough of Jonah's psalm-singing. At any rate, what the best efforts of the sailors could not achieve has now been accomplished, and Jonah is back, potentially, where he started. The term for 'to be sick' is a single onomatopoeic syllable ending in a glottal stop (*qi'*) whose terseness acts as a symbol for the abrupt conclusion of this episode and the reversion to the starting point of the story.

Verse 10 and 1.17 form a satisfying inclusio for the chapter as a whole. At the start, God ordered (i.e. prepared – *manah*) a great fish (*dag gadhol*) to swallow (*bala'*) Jonah; at the end God orders (i.e. speaks to – *'amar le*) the fish (*dag*) to vomit (*qi'*) Jonah up.

---

14. Cited in Ackerman (p. 225).

Addendum: The Centre of Jonah

For those who relish the more pedantic approach to such matters, there are 48 verses in total in the Hebrew numbering of Jonah. The precise centre is between vv. 8 and 9 in the Hebrew of ch. 2 (seven and eight in English). Taking words as the metric, and bearing in mind the uncertainty of what constitutes a word, on my count there are 694, with the centre falling immediately after *havele-shave'* ('vain idols') in v. 8. Another authority (Christensen p. 22) reaches a slightly different word-count, but identifies a very similar centre-point:

> It is interesting to note that the center of the book of Jonah in terms of total word-count falls between the first and second words of 2.9 [ET 8], with 344 words on either side. This structural center focuses on an enigmatic phrase at the beginning of a puzzling verse, which in fact may be a proverbial statement.

Christensen further notes that Sasson (p. 160) 'separates this verse from the rest of Jonah's "Canticle from the Depths" (2.3b-10) by large dashes, as a parenthetical remark of some sort'. Sasson (p. 191) later comments that it 'may be accidental that the book of Jonah reaches its halfway mark in verse count just as it comes to the very strophe in which Jonah and God are in their closest proximity'. He is referring here to the Hebrew v. 8; in a footnote, he reports his own findings as to the centre on word-count, which appears to be in Hebrew 2.4 – a further illustration of the difficulty of precise delineation of 'words'!

There is something fitting about this coincidence, if that is what it is. The importance of the language of v. 8 cannot be ignored, and even if the precise centrality is accidental, in more general terms it comes at a central point of the narrative as a whole. Christensen's suggestion that this is some kind of proverb seems to me implausible: proverbs are not characterised by their use of major theological terms. But it could certainly serve as a coded message from the enigmatic author, itself enigmatic at a number of levels.

As an aside, if we were to date Jonah late enough, it might be possible to identify here an example of that Rabbinic love of word-play and the sheer enumeration of things which is so deeply rooted in Talmudic interpretation. The deliberate use of significant numbers is certainly not unknown elsewhere in the pages of Tanakh; thus, for example, the use of multiples of 11 or 22 verses, particularly in Proverbs – a simple significance based on the alphabet.

Coda

The Banished Prophet

In his second prayer Jonah complains that 'I have been driven away from your sight'. I remarked on the significance of this expression in my commentary above, and noted that the cause of that banishment is not easy to ascertain. While self-exile is a possibility which is certainly strengthened by the language of flight in 1.3, I would like to propose an alternative in line with my hypothesis that Nineveh might be understood as a representation of Jerusalem.

The narrative of Jonah has many gaps (the deconstructionist term *aporias* is tempting), seemingly a deliberate authorial device. Might there be such a gap between Jon. 1.2 and 1.3? We are accustomed to understand Jonah's words in 1.12, 'it is because of me that this great storm has come upon you', as a confession of guilt. But there is in fact no evidence for this assumption. The only other words he utters are a perfectly orthodox statement of belief (1.9) and his deep sleep in the ship's hold could be that of an exhausted but innocent man. To say that 'it is because of me' could also mean 'God has a vendetta against me' or, less opprobriously, 'like Job, I am fated to be pursued by God'. But why? What could God's purpose be? Here I return to suggested gap, and offer the thought that Jonah did *not* reject God's first instruction. Indeed he preached against Jerusalem, that great and wicked city, and was in consequence banished for his pains – a fate not unknown in prophetic experience. Verse 3 then should be read as 'So Jonah set out to flee …' rather than 'But …' (both are true to the Hebrew). The words of the psalm turn out then to be a true reflection of Jonah's experiences and an accurate depiction of his faith.

The Heart of the Matter

The verse at the heart of Jonah (2.8) then takes on a new significance both as to its content and its placement. This is a heartfelt plea, comparable with Job's anguished protestations of innocence: 'Those who are heedful of vain lies' are his enemies in the city, those who have been characterised by Yahweh as wicked, those who have refused God's call, those who persist in believing 'vain lies' and are therefore guilty of having abandoned the loyalty they owe to God.

What then follows in 2.9 is, on this reading, not an arrogant competition with the sailors, but a fundamental declaration of Jonah's loyalty. Like the sailors, he performs his commitment to Yahweh. Unlike them, he has never wavered in this.

Chapter 9

JONAH, EXODUS AND PSALMS*

Undoubtedly both the position and the character of the 'psalm' which constitutes most of Jonah 2 pose problems. My treatment of the subject in the preceding chapter has identified many of the features which make the psalm difficult to explain; I have, I hope, given a plausible explanation of these on the basis of its being integral to the overall narrative. This reflects my own position which assumes that, however the author composed the psalm, and whatever related texts have contributed to its composition, it is specific to and deliberately shaped for its present context.

In his brief overview of the psalm in Jonah 2 Sasson (pp. 205–7) refers to the wider phenomenon of poetic material included within prose narratives in Tanakh. In a monograph published in 1992 Watts examined in systematic detail the phenomenon of hymnic material inserted into Hebrew narrative, including a discussion of the psalm in Jonah. He regards this material as strictly speaking part of the narrative:

> The major literary conclusion ... is that, in the Hebrew Bible, the use of psalms in narrative contexts is a literary device used to achieve compositional (narrative) goals. (p. 186)

Scholars of Tanakh are not now quite so ready to fillet texts as they once were. There is no longer the same nonchalant attribution of apparent misfits to editorial activity, and only with reluctance are problematic texts explained away rather than explained. Though some commentaries still show signs of the source critic's love of the scissors in respect of famous cruxes like Jonah 2 and Job 28, there is an increased regard for more integrative and synchronic approaches, recognising the desirability

---

* The discussion on the Exodus in this chapter is a development of Hunter 2001.

of preserving in our readings the integrity of that which the ancients saw fit to present as a single composition. Thus in a survey of attitudes to the psalm, Bolin (pp. 98–101) showed that arguments *against* its integrity have become fewer in recent years. Brichto (p. 74) gives an eloquent defence of its aptness:

> Once we discern how fitting the psalm is in its context, there is no longer any reason to deny its composition to the narrator. The diction and style of this psalm is impeccable. It might hold a rightful place in the Psalter. Yet it contains not a single word or image which is original. It is a poetic mosaic, skilfully fitted together, each stone copied from one or another placement in the Psalter. And the composition as a whole and in detail is artfully contrived to serve the narrator's purpose: to bring into bold relief the absurdity of the prophet's plight and to contrast his behaviour with that of the pagan seamen.

The decision in principle to accept the psalm as integral does not, however, remove the problems it poses. Indeed it generates a surprising problem, which I have implicitly addressed in my discussion of Jonah 2: why is the 'fit' between psalm and narrative seemingly so poor? Inserted 'psalms' such as the 'confessions' of Jeremiah are often understood in terms of the use by an editor of material chosen from existing types to epitomise the words of an already defined character, and while the fit may not be perfect it is usually plausible. In Jonah, however, the psalm is awkward in terms both of content and of narrative improbability not least because the invented figure of Jonah is psychologically impenetrable. His motives are unclear and his status or profession wholly unknown. I have attempted to explore these issues in the Introduction and in Chapter 8, but they remain largely unknowable, in contrast with the insights we seem to have access to in the works attributed to the major prophets.

But I wonder if this is in fact a false knowledge, which might imply that Jonah is closer to the norm of Hebrew characterisation than we imagine. Much of the work on the prophets from the second half of the twentieth century onwards has revealed a series of standard tropes (call, reluctance, rejection, dramatic symbolic action, oracles against the nations etc.) which suggest not so much individual personalities with distinctive biographies as stock characters deployed by their anonymous editors/authors/inventors. If then we view Jonah not so much as a defined personality who must act consistently (essential a modern conception of human nature), but rather as the sum of his not necessarily predictable responses to his experiences, we may be closer to the way that pre-psychological and pre-romantic writers handled 'character'.

One standard answer to both of the problems of Jonah is an appeal to satire, and no doubt this is to some extent appropriate. The superficial contrast between the abjectly unprincipled Jonah of the narrative and the pious petitioner of the psalm can be seen to form part of the parodic effect of the composition – particularly when the rather hypocritical nature of Jonah's piety is taken into account. As an alternative, however, I have suggested that what the psalm highlights, amongst other things, is the problematic nature of God's original instruction to Jonah and the possibility that his flight might have been a principled one. Nevertheless it is still worth exploring, why *this* psalm and the particular themes it embraces? In an attempt to resolve this conundrum I will examine in detail the intertextual milieu of Jonah 2 and offer some tentative conclusions as a consequence. The most significant will be to affirm the psalm as the heart of the book, with the result that Jonah the character will emerge not as a work of imagination *inspiring* a poetic pastiche but as a fiction *necessitated by* a theological drama whose purpose is to shed a different light on a set of older theological traditions.

Intertext in Jonah 2

Sasson (pp. 166–215) lists parallels to the language of the psalm which he describes as 'illustrative passages' and Bolin (pp. 106–17) provides a helpful survey of the links between Jonah 2 and the Psalter. What is interesting is that the latter only rarely considers intertextuality between Jonah 2 and *other* parts of Tanakh. What I want to argue is that, while much of the psalm appears at first to be typical of the broad generality of the language of the Psalms, and does indeed make use of a patchwork of familiar language, it also contains a core of rather more specific words and phrases which can form the basis of a somewhat tighter approach to its use of other biblical texts. In my 2001 study I carried out a technical analysis of the key terms in ch. 2 on the basis of which I identified several passages which would repay further examination:

> A. *Genesis 8.1-12*. I have already considered this passage in Chapter 7 in connection with Jonah's links to the creation, flood and destruction motifs: the principal link here is with drying up (*yavash*) of the land after the flood and the use of the dove (*yonah*).
>
> B. *Numbers 16.30-34*. This passage finds its way into the list because of the theme of the earth/Sheol swallowing the damned Korahites – a significantly different motif which seems largely unrelated to Jonah.

C. *Isaiah 38*

D. *Psalm 18 (= 2 Samuel 22)*. Isaiah 38 and Psalm 18/2 Samuel 22 range metaphorically more widely than Jonah 2, and are concerned with two specific individuals (David and Hezekiah), which gives them a quite different resonance more closely connected to kingship psalms. No doubt the 'prayer of Hezekiah' is also one made from a situation of the apparent approach of death, but it has arguably more links with those psalms which are often characterised as representing prayers of David *in extremis*.

E. *Psalm 55*. This composition has a very suggestive – though speculative – connection with Jonah, and I shall treat it separately in a later part of this chapter.

F. *Exodus 15.1b-13*. A major source for Jonah, to be discussed in the next section under 'The Exodus Motif'.

G. *Nehemiah 9.9-11*. As we shall see, the verses from Nehemiah are heavily indebted to Exodus 15, suggesting that the two are related in a manner somewhat similar to that of Psalm 18 with 2 Samuel 22. Together with Psalms 69 and 107 a consideration of them will suggest a hypothesis concerning the use of exodus motifs by the author of Jonah.

H. *Psalms 69.1-3, 13-15*

J. *Psalm 107.23-32*

The Exodus Motif

I begin this section with the two relatively minor witnesses, Psalms 69 and 107, after which a detailed examination of Exodus 15 will show just how central the Exodus motif is to Jonah.

Psalm 69.1-3, 13-15

The main reason for the inclusion of this passage is the occurrence of *metsulah* ('the deeps') twice, and *bala'* ('to swallow') in vv. 2 and 15. Undoubtedly these are both relatively rare words, and their use in this psalm is echoed in Jonah (bearing in mind that there it is the *fish* which swallows Jonah). There is a general metaphorical relationship between Psalm 69 and Jonah, but arguably no literary dependence. This is perhaps most clearly seen in the vocabulary used in the psalm to describe how 'the floods sweep over me' (v. 2; cf. 15) and the reference to the pit in v. 15 which is reminiscent of Jon. 2.2, 6, though different Hebrew expressions are used. I conclude, therefore, that although there is nothing to suggest anything beyond a general similarity of figurative language, the *tone* of these verses from Psalm 69 has important similarities to Jonah: they belong to the same register. Magonet (p. 47) is inclined to see a deliberate borrowing here; Sasson (pp. 183–4) includes vv. 1-2 in his list of 'illustrative passages' (he is reluctant to use the language of borrowing), and notes also (p. 152 n. 17) that v. 15 'tells of the progressively dire situation of a God-forsaken poet':

> Do not let the flood sweep over me,
>> or the deep swallow me up,
>> or the Pit close its mouth over me.

I want only to add to this important observation two further dimensions: the archetypal Israelite fear of the mythic forces of the watery depths, and a likely allusion to the Exodus experience in which the Israelite survive the waters, while the Egyptians are drowned. Note in particular the words at the end of v. 14, 'let me be delivered *from my enemies* and from the deep waters' (emphasis added), which give this psalm a national reference.

Psalm 107.23-32
Unlike Psalm 69, we find here both a significant lexical content and an interesting narrative connection with the events of Jonah 1 in the form of the somewhat stereotyped experiences of 'those who go down to the sea in ships'. The key expressions shared with Jonah are 'storm' (*se'arah*, 1.3, 11, 12, 13), 'occupation' (*mela'khah*, 1.8), 'to quieten' (*shataq*, 1.11, 12), 'to swallow' (*bala'*, 1.17), 'billows' (*gal*, 2.3), and 'the deep' (*mitsulah*, 2.4; *tehom*, 2.5) – a somewhat denser frequency than in the case of Psalm 69. The 'story' is of course not specific, being one of a series of examples which the psalmist presents in support of the celebration of Yahweh's *chesed* ('loyalty') in vv. 1, 8, 15, 21, 31, 43, a term which is itself important in the rhetoric of Jonah (2.8; 4.2), and which was discussed more fully in Chapter 8. However, the close narrative connection with Jonah 1 (including the 'sacrifices of thanksgiving' of v. 22 – compare Jon. 1.16; 2.9) does bear closer examination. It would be foolish to make confident claims for the direct dependence of Jonah on Psalm 107, but it would be equally irresponsible to ignore what is a very strong set of parallels. Sasson hints at this by quoting Ps. 107.23-30 at the beginning of his discussion of Jon. 1.7-12 (p. 107), but neither he nor other commentators take it any further, and Magonet does not include it in his list of influences: it is

strange how little discussion there has been of this subject. I have been able to find only a few references even to the interesting verbal parallels. In view of other substantive links with the Psalter, I will return to this psalm later in this chapter, in formulating some broader conclusions about the literary development of the book of Jonah.

Exodus 15.1b-13
I have already remarked that this passage has very close links with Neh. 9.9-11; I will therefore treat the latter when we come to it more as an adjunct to the Song of the Sea than as a separate item. What makes Exodus 15 particularly interesting for the purposes of our immediate study is the presence of a few quite remarkable lexical items in common with Jonah 2. In order to spell out their significance I shall treat them in some detail.

(1) *'Dry Land'* (yibbashah, yibbesheth). There are just 16 occurrences of these related terms of which the less common *yibbesheth* only occurs twice. The relevant passages are:

> Gen. 1.9, 10; Exod. 4.9 (×2); **Exod. 14.16, 22, 29; 15.19**; Josh. 4.22; Isa. 44.3; **Jon. 1.9, 13; 2.10**; Pss. 66.6; 95.5; **Neh. 9.11**

Half are in the three passages we have already listed (indicated in bold type). Genesis 1.9, 10 is, of course, within the Priestly creation account – the relevance of which was noted in Chapter 7 – and its substantive links with the language of Exodus 14–15 are patent ('And God said, "Let the waters under the sky be gathered together into one place, and let the dry land appear." And it was so. God called the dry land Earth, and the waters that were gathered together, he called Sea'). Psalm 66.6 is a direct reference to the exodus, and 95.5 to the creation; Josh. 4.22 is in the context of a tradition (the crossing of the Jordan) which is evidently modelled on the exodus. Given that the only exception to this pattern is Isa. 44.3 ('I will pour water on the thirsty land / and streams upon the dry ground'), I consider it safe to conclude that the use of this term in Jonah is a strong and perhaps intentional signal that the exodus/creation theme is present.

(2) *'The Sea of Reeds'* (yam suf). The proper name *yam suf* occurs in the following places (those indicated in **bold** type are direct references to the exodus tradition):

> **Exod. 10.19**; **13.18**; **15.4, 22**; **23.31**; Num. 14.25; 21.4; 33.10, 11; Deut. 1.40; 2.1; **11.4**; Josh. **2.10**; **4.23**; **24.6**; Judg. 11.16; 1 Kgs 9.26; Jer. 49.21; **Pss. 106.7, 9, 22**; **136.13, 15**; **Neh. 9.9**.

The noun *suf*, meaning 'reed', is recorded in Exod. 2.3, 5, Isa. 19.6 and Jon. 2.5. Both Exodus and Isaiah explicitly refer to the reeds growing in and around the Nile, and there can be little doubt that this is the meaning the word would convey for readers of Jonah familiar with the traditions.

(3) *'The Deep'* (mitsulah). This expression is not so clearly specific to the exodus material. Apart from Jon. 2.3, its distribution is as follows (**bold** type indicates direct reference to the exodus tradition, *italic* indicates its use in relation to the cosmic fear of death in the depths, associated with the sea or the 'pit'):

> **Exod. 15.5**; Mic. 7.19; Zech. 1.8; **10.11**; Pss. *68.22; 69.3, 16; 88.6*; 107.24; **Neh. 9.11**; Job 41.31

Zechariah 1.8 is a linguistic crux for which emendations have often been proposed, and may, I think, safely be discounted. Micah 7.19 is rather interesting in that it occurs in a brief concluding passage which also takes up the theme of the mercy of God from Exod. 3.6 (see also above, in the note on Ps. 107), and reads like a brief historical summary:

> 'Who is a God like thee, pardoning iniquity
>   and passing over transgression for the remnant of his inheritance?
> He does not retain his anger for ever
>   because he delights in steadfast love.
> He will again have compassion upon us,
>   he will tread our iniquities under foot.
> Thou wilt cast all our sins into the depths of the sea.
> Thou wilt show faithfulness to Jacob
>   and steadfast love to Abraham
> as thou hast sworn to our fathers from the days of old.'

It does not seem far-fetched to associate this instance also with the exodus tradition. Those psalms which use the depths as a metaphor for death are, I would argue, in touch with a clear dimension of the exodus myth which is plainly employed in Jonah 2. Thus the only instances of *mitsulah* which fall outside this single complex are Ps. 107.24 and Job 41.31. We have considered the former already, and noted how that psalm might relate to Jonah; the specific usage both here and in Job, however, seems to be as a non-mythic or metaphoric synonym for the sea. These two apart, we have once more a highly significant term whose presence in Jonah is likely to have prompted echoes of exodus.

(4) *'The Deep'* (tehom). This familiar term, which is found at the beginning of the creation account, is found in the following passages. To clarify the argument, I have rendered in bold type those passages (the instance in Jonah is not listed here) which make explicit reference to the exodus traditions, in *italic* those which associate the term with the creation, and by underlining those in which the *tehom* is a violent threat to the safety of the individual or the nation.

> Gen. *1.2*; 7.11; 8.2; 49.25; **Exod. 15.5, 8**; Deut. 8.7; 33.13; **Isa. 51.10**; **63.13**; Ezek. 26.19; 31.4, 15; Amos 7.4; *Hab. 3.10*; Pss. *33.7*; 36.6; 42.7; 71.20; 77.16; 78.15; *104.6*; **106.9**; 107.26; *135.6; 148.7*; Job 28.14; *38.16, 30*; 41.32; *Prov. 3.20; 8.24, 27, 28*.

We have already observed a connection between the motifs of creation and exodus, and between the exodus water experience and the experience of despair in the face of death. Thus these three aspects of *tehom* which belong together in our survey account for 23 of the total of 33 occurrences. While the proportion is not quite as conclusive as for the first three terms, this still represents a remarkable consistency, and strengthens the probability that the reader will recognize what Jonah points to.

(5) *'The heart of the sea'*. Variants of the same basic phrase are found, in addition to Jon. 2.3, only in Exod. 15.8; Ezek. 27.4, 25, 26, 27; 28.2; and Prov. 23.34; 30.19. Its meaning in the Ezekiel and Proverbs passages is in relation to seafaring and to its attendant risk of shipwreck, which makes its use in Jonah obviously relevant. However, it occurs not in the near-shipwreck passage of Jonah, but in the psalm which, as we have already noted, has striking connections with the exodus myth. That the author of Jonah places this striking phrase in ch. 2 and not in ch. 1, together with its unique occurrence in Exodus 15, cannot but reinforce the already strong bonds between Jonah 2 and Exodus 15.

These selected studies are by no means the whole story, for we could note also the presence of further key terms from Jonah 2 which, while lacking the rather tightly circumscribed occurrence pattern we have analysed in the above cases, are nonetheless significant. Thus, for example, Pharaoh's army, like Jonah, *goes down* into the sea (Exod. 15.5; Jon. 2.6); the poem celebrates Yahweh's granting of *salvation* from peril (Exod. 15.2; Jon. 2.9); and we learn (Exod. 15.13; Jon. 2.4, 7, 8) that the return to the realm of God's *holiness* is as a result of God's *steadfast love* (or, as I would prefer, *loyalty*). In short, there is a very strong case for the thesis that at the heart of Jonah lies a commentary – albeit a very off-beat one – on the cherished exodus myth which lies at the heart of Israel's belief in itself as a people specially covenanted to God.

4. *Nehemiah 9.9-11*

Some mention should be made of this passage, which forms part of a narrative historical recital similar in content to Psalms 78 and 105. The key words which Neh. 9.9-11 shares with Jonah are 'dry land', 'the Red Sea', and 'the deep' (*mitsulah*). Beyond the strict limits of the passage itself, *chesed* ('loyalty, steadfast love') is used in v. 17, in the context of the familiar refrain from Exod. 34.6. The links are fewer in number than those shared between Exodus and Jonah; however, there are in addition several explicit references to Exodus – some predictable, like Egypt and Pharaoh, others which are more likely to indicate direct influence. These include the verb 'to cleave' (Neh. 9.11) used in Exod. 14.16, 21 of the dividing of the sea; 'to pursue' (Neh. 9.11) describing Pharaoh's pursuit of the Israelites when he regrets having let them go in Exod. 14.6, 8, 9, 23; 15.9; and the rare phrase 'like a stone' (Neh. 9.11; Exod. 15.5) whose only other occurrence is in Job 41.16 where it is used quite differently. Given that none of the latter group is found in Jonah, while the former are all in Exodus, we may conclude that Nehemiah is probably familiar with the Exodus material – and that references common to Nehemiah and Jonah result from Jonah's familiarity with the Exodus material.

To sum up so far, I have identified several passages which deserve further consideration in our exploration of the character of Jonah 2, each of which has a connection – sometimes explicit, sometimes implied – with the exodus motif. They are Pss. 69.1-2, 13-15 and 107.23-32, in each of which the motif is oblique; I will return to these two Psalms later in this chapter. In Exod. 15.1b-13, as I have just demonstrated, the motif is explicit.

Poetry as Narrative

To say that poetry often has a narrative function is to state the obvious. However, when it comes to the book of Psalms, and exemplars elsewhere in Tanakh, a rather sharp division tends to be drawn between those poems which are overtly 'historical' and the remaining majority which are mostly defined as cultic, confessional, or celebratory. I think that this boundary is rather more porous than we might think, and that Jonah 2 offers an example.

My starting point is that, contrary to some of the more dismissive treatments of Jon. 2.2-9, the poem is far from mere pastiche: it has clear narrative structure, uses powerful imagery and highly specialized language, and is replete with striking theological motifs. In the translation usually provided (e.g. NRSV) it represents an individual psalm of thanksgiving in which an opening résumé (v. 2) is followed by a detailed account of salvation (vv. 3-7) leading in turn to an affirmation and exaltation of God (vv. 8-9). The language is, needless to say, metaphorical, drawn from a reservoir of familiar images. Embedded in the brief legend of the fish (just as Jonah himself was interred in the creature) it becomes both literal (Jonah is indeed under threat from water) and ironic (the life-threatening event which is the immediate cause of the psalm's utterance is at the same time the life-*saving* wonder which enables Jonah to pronounce this psalm of reminiscent thanksgiving). We might take this encircling image one stage further: the story begins (1.15) with Jonah in the sea which surrounds the fish which will surround Jonah when he celebrates his metaphoric redemption from an earlier 'water ordeal' – an interpretation proposed forty years ago by McCarter (1973). He argued then that there is evidence for the language of a river ordeal in Tanakh similar to that familiar from Mesopotamian materials. Jonah 2 and Psalms 18 and 69 are the three examples he singles out, and it may not be without significance that these two psalms are both linked to Jonah in our current comparison.

Those who defend the integrity of Jonah point to both structural and (in a more limited degree) linguistic features which bind the psalm to the rest. Insofar as these are plausible, they are neutral as to priority; that is, they do not in themselves answer the question 'which came first?' However, they do add to the need to provide an explanation which takes account of the overall integrity of the work. It seems to me that accounts of the psalm which rely primarily on pastiche or cut-and-paste fail to deal with this simple point. The text of 2.2-9 is neither an idle copy nor a lazy crib; it was placed where it is with deliberation, it did not fall accidentally into a gap in some scribe's attention.

There is another, more general point to be considered: namely, the linguistic and chronological relationship between poetry and prose. It is well beyond the compass of this study to enter into what are major fields of study, but a few remarks are in order, particularly in the light of the study by Watts already mentioned. I begin with an obvious and perhaps naïve question: what are the differences of language which indicate that a passage is prose rather than poetry? Key sources for an understanding of this distinction are to be found in major studies by James Kugel, Adele Berlin, and most recently F. W. Dobbs-Allsopp.

Essentially, poetic language displays considerable density of parallelism (the repetition in close proximity of semantic forms, verbal ideas, and grammatical structures), a ubiquitous preference for concision of expression (eschewing for the most part the succession of clauses and narrative sequences found in prose), and to some extent the use of vocabulary not regularly found in prose. The last of these has proved tempting to those who focus on the second factor – the chronological relationship (if any) between the two forms.[1] Since it has often been claimed that the primary narrative forms are poetic – that people most naturally tell their tales in ballad form and preserve their traditions lyrically rather than in prose[2] – it is deceptively easy to tag distinctive poetic language as *therefore* characteristic of older stages in the development of Hebrew. From this a closed circle ensues, in which the date of poetic material is deduced from these same differences.

However more recent work on orality and the development of language has cast doubt both on the simple equation 'poetic form = earlier/more primitive language' and on the general assertion that oral performance is essentially distinct from written texts. As Vayntrub shows (pp. 19–35), the deployment of poetic performance within narrative in the Hebrew tradition is an authorial device for putting language in the mouths of actors in the drama and therefore cannot be assumed *prima facie* to come from identifiable oral traditions. It follows that passages such as Jonah 2, Exodus 18 and 2 Samuel 22[3] should not automatically be regarded as afterthoughts or artificial insertions in a smooth narrative process. Their function is directly related to the actors in whose mouths they are placed and the presumption ought to be that they are a good fit, even if superficial problems present. Moreover, even in cases like Judges 4–5 and Exodus 14–15, where a prose narrative is followed by a poetic section covering similar ground, they are not redundant repetitions; for the mere fact of their being placed in the mouths of characters, rather than the distanced reportage of the unknown narrator, forces us to read them with a radically

---

1. Incidentally, perhaps the raw division into 'poetry' and 'prose' is misleading. What, for example, do law codes and instructions for building temples have in common with story-forms? Are doggerel and popular proverbs in the same camp as elegiac and epic verse?

2. Closer to home, European ballad traditions have inspired subtle prose compositions. A recent novel by Andrew Greig, *When They Lay Bare* uses a Scottish border ballad as the inspiration for a fascinating and many-layered novel.

3. That 2 Samuel 22 is almost identical to Psalm 18 does not offer a disproof of this thesis, There is no definitive reason to rule out the possibility that this composition was first located in Samuel.

different attitude. This is why the psalm in Jonah is so problematic: it is precisely *because* we understand it to be Jonah's words that these words seem at first sight to be out of kilter.

Part of the reason why Jonah 2 is so discombobulating is that we instinctively read it as narrative and therefore expect it to cohere *narratively* with the rest of the book. This is both a proper instinct and a misleading one. Proper because poetry (and in particular Psalms) tell stories. Not always – and perhaps less often in the formalist types of poetry prevalent since the mid-twentieth century – but frequently enough for the expectation to be roused. What's more they do so most effectively. Psalm 132, for example, is a strikingly dramatic re-enactment of the quest for the Ark; Psalm 73 takes us through a dark night of the soul, and Psalm 82 presents a divine court-room scene which leads inexorably to judgement and death. And Psalm 55 is a vivid song of betrayal and recovery of trust (see further on this below). I have indicated already that Jon. 2.2-9 should be seen as a representative of this class of dramatic narrative poems. It is not, therefore, a mere *adjunct* to the prose context; nor is it the straightforward poetic alternative to a prose version. We cannot therefore understand it in terms of the development from oral to literary forms of transmission. This is in any case what we might expect, given the strong probability of a post-exilic composition date. What we have, rather, is a sophisticated poetic drama set in a prose context with which it has highly ambiguous and subtle relationships. Both the poem and the prose narrative reveal an author whose knowledge of a familiar body of Hebrew scripture is extensive and impressive, and who employs that knowledge in a highly imaginative way.

Commentators have regularly identified significant parallels elsewhere in Tanakh for the themes in the narrative chapters of Jonah, though it is important to emphasise that none is a simple imitation. Thus ch. 1 can be linked to the shipwreck scenes in Psalm 107 and Ezekiel 27; both ch. 1 and ch. 4 use key motifs from the account of Elijah in the wilderness (1 Kgs 19); Jonah's explanation for his flight (4.2) is given in terms of the familiar 'mercy of Yahweh' theme in Exod. 34.6 etc.; and Magonet (p. 65) shows that ch. 3 can be meaningfully related both to the Sodom and Gomorrah traditions and to the wickedness of the pre-flood generation, a relationship which I have examined in greater detail in the Introduction and in Chapter 7. When we turn to Jonah 2, however, the principal connections have hitherto been made in relation to liturgical phrases rather than narrative motifs. What I want to propose is that the poem is equally definitively influenced by what might be called *epic* motifs – specifically the river ordeal and the exodus escape through the sea.

Themes in Jonah 2

I believe that McCarter has made a good case for the existence of the river ordeal in Hebrew literature, and for its presence being particularly noticeable in Psalms 18 and 69 and in Jonah 2. My own discussion above has established an equally strong case for Jonah's explicit reference to the themes of the 'Red Sea'. Thus we find two themes combined – uniquely, as far as I am aware – in Jonah in such a way as to render personal and individual the national experience of the exodus. A third component can be added to this potent association of ideas: namely, that of the life and death journey *down* to Egypt and the redemptive return *up* to Canaan. Wyatt (pp. 375–8) suggests a punning interpretation of the sea of exodus as *yam sof*, 'the sea of extinction' (*suf*, 'reeds', and *sof*, 'to end', are very similar in Hebrew) and comments on the prevalence, especially in the Joseph material in Genesis, of the verbs 'to go down' and 'to go up' in relation to travel, always applied respectively to the journeys to Egypt and to Canaan. This implies a metaphoric parallel between Egypt and Sheol which explains the continuing horror of the thought of exile to Egypt in the biblical tradition – a horror, interestingly, which is *not* expressed in relation to the exile in Babylon. See in particular Gen. 37.25-28 where traders going 'down' to Egypt lift Joseph 'up' from the pit, but then take him ('down', implied; cf. 39.1) to Egypt, and Jacob's response to Joseph's presumed death in v. 35, 'I shall go down to Sheol to my son' (compare the similar sentiment in 42.38 and 44.29, 31).

There are five places other than Jonah 2 where these two verbs ('to go down' and 'to go up') are combined in relation to Sheol: 1 Sam. 2.6; Isa. 14.14-15; Amos 9.2; Job 7.9; and Ps. 30.3. In order to highlight the significance of Jonah's use of Sheol, *yarad* ('to go down) and *'alah* ('to go up'), the possible parallels are set out in full, indicating by means of italics where vocabulary from Jonah is present.

> The LORD kills and brings to life;
> he *brings down* to *Sheol* and *raises up*. (1 Sam. 2.6)

> 'I will *ascend* to the tops of the clouds,
> I will make myself like the Most High.'
> But you are *brought down* to *Sheol*,
> to the *depths* (*yarkethe*) of the Pit. (Isa. 14.14-15)

> Though they dig into *Sheol*,
> from there shall my hand take them;
> though they *climb up* to heaven,
> from there I will *bring them down*. (Amos 9.2)

> As the cloud fades and vanishes,
> so those who go down to Sheol do not come up;   (Job 7.9)

> O LORD, you *brought up* my *soul* (*nephesh*)
> from *Sheol*,
> *restored me to life* (*chayah*) from among those
> *gone down* to the Pit.   (Ps. 30.3)

It turns out that only one of these (Ps. 30.3) has persuasive parallels with Jonah 2. Moreover, none of these passages makes any reference to Egypt or hints at the exodus, though it is noteworthy that Isa. 14.15 uses the same expression for 'depths' as that found in Jon. 1.5 to describe the hold of the ship. In the first two passages there is expression of the moral belief that it is God who brings down to Sheol the proud and those who get above themselves (literally in the case of Isa. 14 which refers to the downfall of *hellel ben shakhar*, 'Day Star, son of Dawn', in NRSV; 'Lucifer' in KJV). The Amos citation is, like Ps. 139.7-12, concerned to demonstrate that there is no escape from God, neither in heaven nor in hell. Job 7.9 simply states the truism that there is no return from death.

It turns out that the conflation of the motifs of descent and ascent, the threat of Sheol, and the language of the Exodus is unique to Jonah 2: it is not even found in Exodus 15. It would not be an exaggeration to claim that this constitutes a drama of the utmost originality and of high theological significance. Moreover, when we recall that there are echoes also of the creation myths (the special term for 'dry land' and the implication that God's 'appointing' of the fish is an act of creation; see already Chapter 7) we begin to see that here we have encapsulated much that lies at the heart of Israel's covenant mythology. In short, Jonah 2 recapitulates Genesis and Exodus in a profoundly personal way.

Narrative and Poetry: A Tentative Exploration

It is in the light of these findings that I venture to suggest a shift in perspective towards the dramatic poem in Jonah as of the most profound significance to the wider prose drama, and certainly much more than a mere illustrative appendage to it. Indeed, a case might even be made that the poetic composition came into existence before the composition of the book we now have. I cannot claim to have *proved* that this is even probable in terms of the actual process which produced the book. But I believe that I have established that it is both *possible* and *fitting*, not least in that it gives proper place to what is evidently the high point of the book.⁴ How might this work out if we develop it further? In particular, how does the prose narrative *follow from* the poetic drama? For a start, it is interesting that the two journeys made by Jonah are in the two opposing directions implied by the mythology of the exodus. His flight is westwards, to wherever Tarshish may lie, in defiance of God – just as the journey to Egypt is seen as an effective departure from God's realm – and that flight is *downwards*: down to Joppa, down into the ship, and down into the waters. Having been *brought up* out of the waters, his second journey is eastwards, to Mesopotamia whence, in truth, much that came to form Judaism emerged (Ezra and Nehemiah, Hillel and Akivah, the Babylonian Talmud). We do not find the verb 'to go down' again, though 'to go up' reappears in the growth of the plant which God 'appointed' to provide shade for Jonah.

The ordeal theme which is found in the poem is also dramatised in the narrative – in the form of ordeal by water in ch. 1, and ordeal by heat or fire in ch. 4. The motif of creation is explicitly found in Jonah's self-identification – 'I am a Hebrew; and I fear the Lord, the God of heaven, who made the sea and the dry land' (1.9) – and more indirectly in the repetition of the significant word 'dry land' in 1.13 and 2.10, and the use of the verb *manah*, 'to appoint', in respect of the fish, the plant, the worm and the wind (only in Jonah is this verb used of living things). Finally, the mercy of God is revealed in narrative terms through the rescue of the sailors (1.15-16) and the forgiveness of Nineveh (3.10), and explicitly when Jonah sets out the grounds of his grievance in 4.2.

What I seem to have arrive at, curiously, is the probability that in its context Jonah was indeed something like an allegory (even, perhaps, a mini-*bildungsroman*) designed to lead the reader, if not the central character, to some realisation of the practical meaning of the exodus experience. In older tradition the exodus was an ordeal of the birth of the nation; in Jonah it becomes an ordeal associated with the coming to maturity of Israel as a means to the enlightenment of all nations. A drama, in short, characterising the fulfilment of the vision of both Isaiah 2 and Micah 4.

---

4. Hugh Pyper (pp. 339–42) acknowledges the propriety of this suggestion. Asking whether case might be made for the Psalm as the *source* of the prose narrative of Jonah, he proposes a number of questions pertinent to such a thesis: (1) What evidence is there – or could there be – that the prose of Jonah is dependent on the psalm rather than the other way round? (2) Could the Jonah-psalm have had an independent existence? (3) How does the book of Jonah relate to 2 Kings 14? (4) Last but not least, what good does this mirror reading do us as biblical readers? This is not a proposal with much ancestry, though he does note one early source for the idea of the priority of the psalm (J. G. A. Muller, 1794).

Psalm 107

If this may seem far-fetched, there is a possible prototype in one of the other psalms which I identified as having substantial intertextual links with Jonah 2, and which I have not thus far returned to: Psalm 107. Most commentators interpret this psalm as a series of thanksgiving hymns in response to rescue from a variety of threats and dangers, and this is fair enough. Its position in the Psalter is rather intriguing in that, while it seems to be the third in a series of 'historical' psalms (105–107), it is placed at the beginning of Book 5 rather than the end of Book 4, as though the editor wanted somehow to set it apart. Indeed, when we look more closely at the three, both 105 and 106 are *specifically* historical in that they provide personal names, places, and clearly identify episodes in Israel's history. Psalm 107, on the other hand, renders its 'history' entirely anonymously – no names, no places, no clear references to recognisable events. It looks as though it represents a deliberate attempt to universalise biblical episodes in such a way as to give them a wider relevance. I don't want to exaggerate this point: undoubtedly there are signs that this is a Hebrew psalm speaking to the descendants of Israel; nonetheless, the feeling that 'everyman' is present in these verses is palpable.

My principal focus will be on vv. 23-32, but a few comments on the way that other parts suggest familiar themes will help to contextualise these verses. The psalm is punctuated by various forms of a refrain (vv. 1, 8-9, 15-16, 21-22, 31-32, 43) which effectively divide it into a series of scenarios thus:

1 + 2-3	Introduction
4-7 + 8-9	Scenario One
10-14 + 15-16	Scenario Two
17-20 + 21-22	Scenario Three
23-30 + 31-32	Scenario Four
33-42 + 43	Scenario Five

The introduction, acting as kind of scene-setter, would have been readily understood in Jerusalem as a reference to the return from exile ('the redeemed…gathered in' from east, west, north and south) albeit somewhat exaggerated and glamorised. Scenario One hints at both the journeys of the patriarchs and the forty-year desert wanderings of the Israelites, but there are no specific markers, though the rather infrequent verb *ta'ah*, 'to wander', is used in Gen. 20.13 of Abraham, in 21.14 of Hagar, and in 37.15 of Joseph – all well-known biblical desert wanderers. Scenario Two similarly hints at various episodes: Joseph's imprisonment in Egypt, Jeremiah at the hands of his enemies (Jer. 38.1-6), and Daniel, But the fit is not good – none of these is portrayed as having 'rebelled against the words of God'. Scenario Three touches on a theme common in the Psalter and perhaps central to Job: the link between physical suffering, the threat of death, and sinfulness. No connect with any specific individual can be convincingly made. Scenario Five sums up the mood of the psalm using the language of eschatology – both the destruction and the renewal to be expected in 'that day: the day of the Lord'.

Scenario Four, vv. 23-30, bears a considerable superficial resemblance to the plot of Jonah 1, though my brief account of the rest of this psalm provides a reminder that no direct dependence is to be expected. I have underlined those expressions which are matched in the vocabulary of Jonah:[5]

²³Some <u>went down</u> to the <u>sea</u> in <u>ships</u>,	(1.3, 5; 2.6); (1.4, 5, 9, 11, 12, 15); (1.3, 4, 5)
doing <u>business</u> on the mighty <u>waters</u>;	(1.8); (2.5)
²⁴they saw the deeds of the LORD,	
his wondrous works in the <u>deep</u>.	(2.3)
²⁵For he commanded and raised the <u>stormy wind</u>,	(1.4, 11, 13); (1.4)
which lifted up the <u>waves</u> of the <u>sea</u>.	(2.3)
²⁶They <u>mounted up</u> to <u>heaven</u>,	(1.2; 2.6; 4.6, 7); (1.9)
they <u>went down</u> to the <u>depths</u>[6];	(2.5)
their <u>courage</u> melted away;	(1.14; 2.5, 7; 4.3, 8)
in their <u>calamity</u>	(1.2, 7, 8; 3.10; 4.1, 3, 6)
²⁷they reeled and staggered like drunkards,	
and were at their wits' end.	
²⁸Then they cried to the LORD in their <u>trouble</u>,	(2.2)
and he <u>brought them out</u> from their distress;	(4.5)
²⁹he made the <u>storm</u> be still,	
and the <u>waves</u> of the <u>sea</u> were hushed.	
³⁰Then they were <u>glad</u> because they had <u>quiet</u>,	(4.6, 6); (1.11,12)
and he brought them to their <u>desired</u> haven.	(1.14)

---

5. I have not included instances in Jonah which are clearly irrelevant, and where a term is repeated in Psalm 107 I have only listed the Jonah references the first time.

6. In Hebrew a different word from 'deep' in v. 24.

If Psalm 107 is formed of a sequence of allusive references to known episodes and themes, it is conceivable that there is a nod in the direction of Jonah in these verses, rather than a *source* for Jonah. It is by no means improbable that Psalm 107, as part of Book 5, belongs to a late stage of composition – it could certainly have been composed after 200 BCE. It is notable that Magonet makes no reference to this psalm, suggesting that he at least does not detect citations.

Psalm 55
One tantalising possibility is that the dove in Psalm 55 can be seen as the basis of an alternative 'Jonah' tale. The psalmist longs (v. 7) to have wings like a dove ('Jonah'), to fly away and to rest (Jonah flees from Yahweh and sleeps in the boat). The psalmist seeks a shelter (v. 8) – i.e., a place for a fugitive to hide! – where he will be safe from the tempest. Likewise the fugitive Jonah seeks shelter, and is endangered by the same tempest. The next section (vv. 10-12) describes the wickedness rampant in the city (Nineveh, aka Jerusalem!); and immediately afterwards we have a passage (vv. 13-15) where the psalmist complains that he could bear the insults of an enemy – but it is his close companion who has deserted him. We remember how Jonah accuses God of betraying him. In two places (vv. 16, 24) we read of the fate of the wicked who will go down to the pit; and Jonah himself speaks of that dreadful experience. And of course, when the psalmist calls to God (vv. 17-20) he is heard and saved.[7] In line with my comments on Psalm 107, I will set out the evidence which might indicate another Jonah-like narrative psalm. I admit at the outset that the specific details are by no means irrefutable; however, I contend that there is an accumulation of date sufficient to suggest an interesting comparison, just as we found in Psalm 107.

A. *Direct links between Psalm 55 and Jonah.* The mere coincidence of the occurrence of the name 'Jonah' in both Psalm 55 and the book is, of course, not enough to justify any more far-reaching thesis. At least some indication of more specific linguistic links would be desirable. They do exist, but in a somewhat scattered and impressionistic manner. I note for the record the following groupings:

---

7. A fuller account of this thesis is to be found in Hunter (2007). The linguistic data which follows is set out fully therein.

1. The storm and the wind
   Jon. 1.4, 11-13   Ps. 55.8
2. Wickedness, the city, its lawlessness and its size
   Jon. 1.2; 3.2, 3, 8; 4.1, 10, 11   Ps. 55.9, 12, 15
3. The plea to be heard and for salvation to be granted
   Jon. 2.1-2, 9   Ps. 55.1-2, 16-19
4. The threat to life associated with being cast down to Sheol or the pit
   Jon. 2.2-3, 6   Ps. 55.15, 22-23

One preliminary observation is worth making at this point: the examples found in (1) and (2) correlate most closely with those in Ps. 55.6-15, while (3) and (4) relate more closely to Ps. 55.1-5 and 16-23. The significance of this distinction will become apparent shortly, when we look more closely at the structure of Psalm 55 itself; for the purposes of reference, I will label these three sections of the Psalm as A (1-5), B (6-15) and C (16-23).

B. *Linguistic singularities.* Some of the interesting linguistic features of the two texts are best described as singularities; a brief description of these follows.

(1) The theme of 'the word' is an important one in Jonah, representing both Yahweh's command to Jonah which he seeks to escape, and Jonah's 'I told you so' to God in 4.2. In Ps. 55.21 we read that the faithless friend's speech was 'softer than oil', but like 'drawn swords'. I shall propose in due course that the faithless friend in Psalm 55 is analogous to the God of Jonah, whose words were undoubtedly dangerous to the prophet. There is a coda to this theme, in that the 'dove' in the psalm flees 'to the wilderness' (v. 7); we might, at a stretch, recognize a punning usage here given the similarity in Hebrew between *davar* ('word') and *midhbar* ('wilderness').

(2) Ps. 55.19 employs the verb *'anah* in its second meaning of 'to oppress, to humble', in parallel with the verb *shama'* ('to hear'). The same pairing is found in Jon. 2.2, which fits with the alternative reading of this verse which I proposed in Chapter 8.

(3) The verb 'to cover' (*kiseh*) refers in Jon. 3.6, 8 to the mourning garments worn by the king of Nineveh and all his subjects and animals, and in Ps. 55.5 to the horror which covers the psalmist in his fear.

(4) The repeated use of *miqedem* ('beforehand/eastward') in Jon. 4.2, 5, 8 could be understood ironically in relation to its use in Ps. 55.19: 'God, who is enthroned *from of old*, will hear and humble them – because they do not change, and do not fear God'. The transformation is ironic because it is precisely Jonah's point that God has refused to humble the Ninevites on the basis of what he (Jonah) deems to be a spurious conversion, thus revealing God's fickleness. It is *God* who has changed, thus denying God's unchanging character 'from of old'. From this derives Jonah's protest that he had to flee 'beforehand' to Tarshish, his deliberate decision to sit 'east' of the city, and the significance of the 'east wind' that causes him to faint.

C. *Linguistic links internal to Psalm 55.* It is suggestive for the discussion of structure in Psalm 55 that there are a number of interesting linguistic connections between sections A and C, and very few between either of these and section B. The exceptions, which I shall discuss below, are, first, echoes of vv. 12-14 in 20-21, and second, of vv. 16 in 23. In detail I note the following:

(1) The unusual phrase 'complaining (*siyach*) and moaning (*hom*)' in v. 2 is repeated in v. 17, 'I complain (*siyach*) and moan (*hamah*)'.[8]
(2) The verb *mot*, 'to stumble', is used in its normal sense in v. 22 (compare, for example, Ps. 121.3), and in a unique hiphil form in v. 3, where it must mean something like 'they bring evil tumbling upon me'.
(3) Another rare form – the hithpael of the root *'alam* ('to conceal oneself') – is found in v. 1, and is balanced by a contrasting instance of the derived form *'olam* 'for ever' in v. 22, where God's hiddenness is transformed into God's eternal reliability:

> Give ear to my prayer, O God;
>   do not <u>hide yourself</u> from my supplication.
> He will <u>never</u> permit
>   the righteous to be moved

---

8. These translations are from the New JPS <u>Tanakh</u>; the two verbs *hom* and *hamah* are formally close. The only other place where the pairing of either of these with *siyach* is found is Ps. 77.4 which JPS renders as 'I call God to mind, I moan / I complain, my spirit fails'.

(4) Though the root *'anah* ('to answer') is common in the Psalms (about 35 instances), its homonym, with the meaning 'to afflict, be humbled', is rarer, occurring some 15 times. Apart from 55.2, 19 the only other instance in the psalms where the two meanings come approximately together is Ps. 102.2, 23[9] – and in 102.23 the interpretation depends on a doubtful reading. In the light of (2) and (3) above, it is also of interest that Ps. 55.19 is the only example of a hiphil use of this verb in the Psalms.

(5) I note lastly a common word which gains some consequence from the context. In vv. 2-3 the psalmist is 'complaining and moaning at the <u>clamour</u> of the enemy'; in v. 17 we read, 'I complain and moan, and he hears my <u>voice</u>'. The same word, *qol*, is used in both verses; what is interesting is the contrast between the enemy's racket and the psalmist's voice.

D. *Structure in Psalm 55 in Relation to Jonah.* One of the fascinating features of Psalm 55 vis-à-vis Jonah is that they are, in a sense, the inversion of each other. The matter which in Jonah occupies chs. 1, 3 and 4, is found in Ps. 55.6-15, which we have designated B, while the hymn in Jonah 2 has its clearest parallels in 55.1-5, 16-23, referred to as A and C. This is the force of my comment above about the relative positioning of the significant language which is shared between Jonah and Psalm 55, where we found that linguistic features characteristic of Jonah 2 mapped to A and C, while features characteristic of the rest of Jonah [groups (1) and (2)] mapped to B.

The three divisions of Psalm 55 begin with a conventional supplication which, though intense, has no unusual features: it bemoans the strife caused by 'enemies' – a ubiquitous grievance in the psalms – and gives vivid expression to the writer's mental torture. It hints at a God who is prone to keep hidden (v. 1), and therefore multiplies verbs and nouns of address: 'give ear', 'my prayer', 'my supplication', 'attend to me', 'my complaint'. No response is forthcoming, and so the poet moves on to a flight (*sic*) of fantasy which takes the theme beyond that of the standard set of clichés into a new realm.[10]

---

9. I discount Psalm 119. Though both occur there, the instances of the second meaning are widely separated from those of the first.

10. The division I have opted for represents, of course, only one possible structure. My choice is determined by the linguistic points I have noted above concerning the internal links in Psalm 55 and the connections with Jonah.

Part B commences with a dove fleeing to the wilderness for safety; the scene then changes to the city, locus of incessant violence (the term *chamas* which I discussed in the Introduction) and oppression, a veritable no-go area; finally the psalmist takes up the theme of enemies once more, but with a significant twist: they are not (as we might have assumed) the pagan hordes or the apostate within Israel; rather they turn out to be our closest friends, with whom we regularly visited the sanctuary. For them, indeed, only the worst kind of punishment will suffice (v. 15):

> Let death come upon them;
> > let them go down alive to Sheol;
> > for evil is in their homes and in their hearts.

The final section, C, resumes the mode of prayer, though this time reported rather than directly addressed to God. A positive note of hope now emerges: 'the Lord will save me' (the only instance of the tetragrammaton in the psalm), 'he will hear my voice', 'he will redeem me unharmed'. As is to be expected in such psalms, the problems identified in the middle section are now disposed of, with the faithless companion consigned to 'the lowest pit'.

There is a reprise of the theme of the betrayer (vv. 12-15) in vv. 20-21, and the fate wished upon the psalmist's betrayers is fulfilled in v. 23. Unlike the other parallels I have noted within Psalm 55, this comparison operates almost wholly at a thematic level:

v. 15	v. 23
Let death come upon them (a);	
let them go down (b)	But you, O God, will cast them down (b)
alive to Sheol (c);	into the lowest pit (c);
for evil is in their homes	
and in their hearts (d)	the bloodthirsty and treacherous (d)
	shall not live out half their days (a)

While the only exact linguistic parallel is in (b), the pairing of 'pit' and 'Sheol', of 'Let death come upon them' with 'shall not live out half their days', and the immoral nature of the betrayers (d) are thematically exact.

Summing up the position with regard to the psalm itself, we find a tight structure in which a supplication and prayer, bound together both thematically and by specific linguistic features, brackets an unusual 'short story', a putative drama in which the oppressed writer wishes to flee 'like a dove' from the lawlessness of the city, only to discover that the enemy he fears is not some stranger or marginalized apostate, but his closest friend and companion. This story clearly has considerable dramatic potential, a potential, I claim, that was recognized by the author of Jonah who put it to good use in the construction of his best-selling (if I may be permitted a little academic licence) parable. The integrity of the psalm is clear from the two links between B and C which we noted in the preceding paragraph.

Conclusions

I believe that I have shown that in Psalm 55 there is a cleverly constructed dramatic poem which is both unique in important respects and of sufficient power to be a potential catalyst. We know of – or can guess at – other poetic catalysts of this kind: Exodus 15, discussed in detail above, and Judges 5 being the most impressive. I have demonstrated some important verbal connections between Jonah 1, 3 and 4 and Ps. 55.6-15 on the one hand and Jonah 2 and Ps. 55.1-5, 16-23 on the other. On the basis of these findings, I suggest that we have established a good case for a degree of knowingness regarding Psalm 55 on the part of the author of Jonah.

CODA

Jonah nowhere directly speaks of Israel's exodus experience which, together with the covenant, forms the two-fold foundation of the theological identity of Second Temple religious experience. What replaces any such commentary is a personal drama which, as we have seen, includes clear and frequent allusions to both direct Exodus traditions, and those of a secondary nature. What is of particular interest is that the personalised drama of Jonah is reflected in the 'narrative' psalms, Psalms 55 and 107, discussed above and which I have identified as important correlates to the book of Jonah. Psalm 107 speaks in general about 'the redeemed of the Lord' and can without difficulty be associated with Israel as a whole (assuming that everyone in Israel was deemed to have been redeemed!); Psalm 55, like the psalm in Jonah 2, is presented in first person. The implication is that one element of our ultimate reading of Jonah will have to take account of the elision of the boundary between national and personal identification with the foundation legend of the exodus.

Chapter 10

Jonah 3.1-10: An Innocent in Nineveh

¹The word of the Lord came to Jonah a second time, saying, ²'Get up, go to Nineveh, that great city, and proclaim to it the message that I tell you'. ³So Jonah set out and went to Nineveh, according to the word of the Lord. Now Nineveh was an exceedingly large city, a three days walk across. ⁴Jonah began to go into the city, going a day's walk. And he cried out, 'Forty days more, and Nineveh shall be overthrown!' ⁵And the people of Nineveh believed God; they proclaimed a fast, and everyone, great and small, put on sackcloth.
⁶When the news reached the king of Nineveh, he rose from his throne, removed his robe, covered himself with sackcloth, and sat in ashes. ⁷Then he had a proclamation made in Nineveh: 'By the decree of the king and his nobles: No human being or animal, no herd or flock, shall taste anything. They shall not feed, nor shall they drink water. ⁸Human beings and animals shall be covered with sackcloth, and they shall cry mightily to God. All shall turn from their evil ways and from the violence that is in their hands. ⁹Who knows? God may relent and change his mind; he may turn from his fierce anger, so that we do not perish.'
¹⁰When God saw what they did, how they turned from their evil ways, God changed his mind about the calamity that he had said he would bring upon them; and he did not do it.

It was my original intention to title this chapter 'A Navi' in Nineveh', tempted by the alliteration afforded by the use of the Hebrew term for prophet. But the need to explain the alliteration made it somewhat pointless; my final choice still alliterates, but is arguably both easier to understand, and apt in that it addresses a quality of the character of Jonah which is perhaps not often highlighted. He is surely an innocent, a naïf in the sense of an individual stumbling largely in the dark with only limited understanding of what is going on, yet determined to make his point as forcefully as he can. I suspect that this is one of the character traits which lies behind the way he reacts in ch. 4. For now, however, we return to his prophetic duty.

> ^{1}*The word of the* LORD *came to Jonah a second time, saying,*
> ^{2} *'Get up, go to Nineveh, that great city, and proclaim*
> *to it the message that I tell you'.*

[Compare 1.1-2: *Now the word of the* LORD *came to Jonah son of Amittai, saying, 'Get up, go*[1] *to Nineveh, that great city,* and cry out against it; for their wickedness has come up before me'[2]]

It is well known that the openings of the first and third chapters, verbally very similar but conveying a precisely opposite meaning, serve to divide the book into two clear episodes – the flight to Tarshish and its aftermath in the belly of the fish, and the journey to Nineveh and its sequel on a vantage point outside the city. We have already seen that these two consequences also reflect the two modes of destruction in Genesis: water and fire. A further parallel is striking: both sequels share a self-absorbed exchange between Jonah and Yahweh in the form of the psalm from the fish and the prayer from his position outside the city.

The vocabulary of these two introductions is very similar, but that very similarity – surely deliberate – serves to emphasise the differences, which need to be spelled out and (as it were) cross-examined. The first is probably the only one which has no immediate purpose: namely the omission of Jonah's patronymic 'son of Amittai'. Unless, of course, the putative meaning 'son of truth' signifies by its absence some kind of comment on the way the character of Jonah is being exposed to the reader. Be that as it may, the second change is the seemingly innocent addition 'a second time'. There is a slightly tetchy note to this expression, as though we are being invited to picture Yahweh stamping his foot ever so gently, as if to say to Jonah that one symbolic rebellion was just about tolerable, but now there is no choice left. More seriously, 'a second time' draws our attention to the semantic agreements with Jon. 1.1-2 because it clearly implies that he is back where he started, in his homeland, presumably Jerusalem; and whatever happened there on that previous occasion, we

---

1. I have amended the NRSV slightly here to show the similarity. Identical Hebrew is rendered by NRSV in 1.2 as 'Go at once' and in 3.2 as 'Get up, go'.

2. Phrases in italics are identical to those in 1.1-2.

are now primed to expect a different outcome. As experienced readers of narrative we are trained to look for development, and the author will not disappoint us.

The third modification is similarly subtle, being the mere substitution of the preposition 'to' for the original 'against'. The implication here is of a more ameliatory approach on Yahweh's part, especially when combined with the absence of any reference to the wickedness of Nineveh. If, as I have suggested, Jonah's original experience was flight from Jerusalem (aka Nineveh) following the predictably hostile response to his original message, we might speculate that the less aggressive oracle might elicit a better response. We are still left in the dark as to the content of any such oracle, but at least there is a divine undertaking that such will be provided: 'the message that I tell you'. In fact the Hebrew is more direct, for the verb form used (the participle) implies something like 'the message that I am telling you'. Did God whisper in Jonah's ear, leaving us tantalisingly in the dark?

> *³ᵃSo Jonah set out and went to Nineveh,*
> *according to the word of the LORD.*

The parallel sentence in 1.3 reads, 'But Jonah set out to flee to Tarshish from the presence of the LORD'. The opening four words in English render an identical Hebrew phrase, but then the action changes dramatically. No flight *from the presence of* the Lord; rather a journey *according to the word* of the Lord. The verb translated as 'set out' is *qum*, which strictly speaking indicates the action of arising, getting up which Hebrew regularly pairs with a following verb of movement. It is often found in positive responses by prophets and patriarchs to God's commands; Jonah's action in 1.3, where he does the opposite of what he is told, is the only place in Tanakh where such a response is recorded to God's direct instruction.[3]

Jonah's response contrasts strikingly with, for example, the instruction to Elijah in 1 Kgs 17.9 to 'get up and go to Zarephath in Sidon' on the unlikely assurance that a widow would feed him there. Sidon was, like Nineveh, a foreign location, though not one notorious as an enemy of Israel. On the other hand, it is associated with Tyre in the denunciatory oracles of Isaiah 23 and especially Ezekiel 26–28, the latter of which is also referenced by Jonah in ch. 1. Elijah, of course, obeys instantly and unquestioningly (17.10), unlike Jonah. My use of this comparison

---

3. Interestingly, the formula 'get up and go' is a lot less common than we might expect, and has links with Elijah. I will discuss this in more detail in Chapter 11.

is not accidental, for it is clear that the writer of Jonah alludes in ch. 4 to Elijah's dispiriting experiences in the aftermath of the contest with the prophets of Ba'al. There is a resultant irony in the fact that the obedience of the senior prophet does not protect him from precisely the same crushing despair that afflicts Jonah. Indeed, the referencing of Elijah invites closer comparisons to be drawn with Jonah. The former, despite having destroyed the enemies of God in 1 Kings 18, confronts his own inner demons when he flees to Beersheba and seeks death. The ensuing theophanic encounter on Mount Horeb, with its famously enigmatic 'sound of sheer silence' (19:12), appears to offer a critique of the violence of the previous chapter; yet that same divine appearance ends with a further promise of bloodshed and violence in the name of Yahweh (19:17-18). There are grounds for reading Jonah, then, as a commentary on the inscrutability, if not sheer perversity, of God in prophetic experience. I shall delay further explication of this observation at present, pending a discussion of the way that Jonah 4 taps into 1 Kings 19.

In each of chs. 1 and 3 the verb *qum* occurs three times and in the same verses (no doubt a coincidence, since the verse numbering is not original) – God's command to 'get up' in v. 2, Jonah's response in v. 3, and a third instance involving 'significant others' in v. 6. In 1.6 the sailors ask Jonah to get up and do something, while in 3.6 the king of Nineveh gets up and does something: he removes his robe, covers himself with sack-cloth, and sits in ashes (the verb *yashav* used here will pop up again in 4.5 when Jonah seats himself to the east of the city to view developments). There is a further suggestive link between these occurrences of 'to arise'. Just as Jonah's response in 1.3 is to defy God, equally in 1.6 he fails to respond to the sailors' request to him to get up and pray. And his positive response in 3.3 is reflected in the extravagant way that the king of Nineveh, immediately upon hearing Jonah's terse proclamation, renounces his throne and his robe of honour, puts on sackcloth, and squats in ashes.

A few other observations are in order regarding the opening words of v. 3. In 1.3 we are given a detailed description of the means by which Jonah fled the city to embark for Tarshish; now, however, Jonah arrives at Nineveh as if by magic (a magic carpet, perhaps?) – a difference which fits surprisingly neatly with conventions of magical realism which permeate the second half of the book.[4] In addition, there is no reiteration of the

---

4. Although the story of the storm, the whale, and the miraculous rescue of the ship and its crew is marvellous, it is not magical in its own cultural context. By contrast, even in its own terms, there are fantastical elements to the instantaneous transfer to

wickedness of Nineveh; an omission which may be inconsequential, but which could have a bearing on the action that follows, especially if the difference between 'against it' and 'to it' as we move from 1.2 to 3.2 represents a less aggressive stance by God towards Nineveh. This prompts a question – one to which Jonah will return in his closing debate with Yahweh. Is this change designed to persuade Jonah that his journey is not completely pointless, or is it a matter of emphasising God's freedom to undergo a change of mind in the face of compelling circumstances? Perry (pp. 43–5) seems to endorse the former interpretation when he suggests that whereas Jonah might out of pity for the Ninevites have refused a command to preach *against* them, to preach *to* them implies a different kind of mission. The latter reading leads to the thought that Yahweh is rubbing salt in Jonah's wounds. For if he believed that the original commission was justified, even if it was too dangerous to carry out, the change of policy has the effect (as we shall see) not of making God more approachable, but on the contrary of making him indefensibly fickle. In what follows – particularly in the almost contemptuous manner in which Jonah carries out his instructions – we catch a glimpse of a man seriously alienated from his God.

Interestingly, the subsequent occurrences of 'wicked' or 'evil' towards the end of ch. 3, where the Ninevite leadership takes the charge to heart, and in ch. 4 where they refer exclusively to Jonah's feelings about various matters, bear on the inner feelings of the participants rather than an objectified substance called 'wickedness' which, in Jon. 1.2, has the ability to 'rise up before God'. They are also similar to the use of the term in 1.7, 8 where it expresses the sailors' puzzlement as to why such 'evil' has befallen them, and suggests a meaningful parallel between Jonah and the sailors. Coupled with the way that Jonah's sacrifices and vows in 2.9 echo those of the sailors in 1.16 and his prayer in 4.2 opens (with one exception) with the same Hebrew as that of the sailors in 1.14,[5] we begin to see that a deeper connection is even to be found between seemingly peripheral characters and Jonah.

Nineveh, the conversion of the king, the Ninevites and their cattle, and the episodes that constitute ch. 4. Perhaps the message is that when human agents dare to apply reason and logic to Yahweh's seemingly outrageous demands, Yahweh's response is to upstage the whole rationalist argument by means of a virtuoso performance.

5. In 1.14 the sailors 'cry' to Yahweh; in 4.2 Jonah 'prays' to Yahweh.

> ^{3b}*Now Nineveh was an exceedingly large city,*
> *a three days' walk across.*

Like a good suspense writer, the author of Jonah now turns away from the promised content of the proclamation. Indeed, as we shall see, we never hear the words directly from God, for when they are spoken in v. 4 their terseness and uninformative character suggest strongly that Jonah has processed God's words and turned them into what must count as the prophetic oracle least likely to produce a response. The description of Nineveh, his supposed destination, as 'an exceedingly large city' represents a widely accepted interpretation of the literal Hebrew 'great to God' as an example of an idiomatic Hebrew phrase expressing extreme size which is found also in Gen. 1.2, where the 'mighty wind' which initiates creation is often translated literally as 'a wind from God'. The grammatical form used here is not identical to that in Genesis, and there may be a deliberate ambiguity which forces the parallel reading 'great [in the eyes of] God'. (See Sasson, 228–9 for a detailed discussion of this point.)

The introduction of a period of time – the first of two in this chapter, and an echo of the time supposedly spent in the belly of the whale – serves to link the two journeys: three days in a sea monster and three days to traverse a wicked city.[6] The fact that his second journey is cut short may represent a deliberate fracturing of an incipient pattern; for in a true folk tale there would be a series of 'threes' before the resolution. It may also serve a psychological purpose: Jonah wants rid of his edgy commission as soon as possible, so makes his proclamation not in the heart of Nineveh but presumably in the suburbs, if we take the narrative's geography on its own terms.

We noted the significance elsewhere in Tanakh of the number 3 in our discussion of 2.1-2 (Chapter 8); it is implied in Jon. 4.10 where the life-span of the qiqayon plant is referred to. References in other ancient Near Eastern sources seem sparse. There is one from Ugarit (*KTU* 1.20-22), which refers to redeemers and three days, but it is fragmentary and difficult to decipher.[7] There seems to be a reference to action being taken after 'three days and three nights' during Inanna's visits to the underworld.[8] Neither of these seems likely to have been available to the

---

6. Forget literality here. Ignore the NIV's quote from Tripadvisor: 'a city so big it would take three days to visit it [*sic*]'.

7. See http://www.baytagoodah.com/uploads/9/5/6/0/95600058/167256086-religious-texts-from-ugarit-whole.pdf pp. 314ff.

8. See 'The Descent of Innana' lines 173-75 at https://etcsl.orinst.ox.ac.uk/section1/tr141.htm

author of Jonah, let alone forming a source. They are admittedly limited, and the conclusion would seem to be that – unlike the significance of seven – this usage is not influenced by specific external traditions. The more important aspect is surely that of internal structuring: just as Jonah was trapped for three days in the belly of a 'great' fish, so he found himself trapped for three days in a 'great' city. And just as the fish was selected directly by God, so was Nineveh, as we have seen, both great 'as God' and deliberately chosen by God for this experiment in social-prophetic engineering – and further evidence, if we need it, of the integral nature of ch. 2 to the book as a whole.

⁴Jonah began to go into the city, going a day's walk. And he cried out, 'Forty days more, and Nineveh shall be overthrown!'

At last our hero enters Nineveh and proclaims the word of God. Or does he? As Trible (p. 180) astutely observes,

> Nowhere in the story has Yhwh given Jonah these exact words to speak. Is his prophecy, then, true or false? A contrast by omission also feeds doubt about the authenticity of the utterance. The storyteller declares that Jonah 'arose and went to Nineveh according-to-the-word-of Yhwh' (3.3a) but then does not use the phrase 'according-to-the-word-of Yhwh' when reporting what Jonah 'called and-said' (3.4b). Overall, the 'calling' abounds in unstable properties.

As well as raising doubts about the authenticity of this oracle, Trible hints at the still more disturbing possibility that Jonah is at best making it up, and at worst lying – the action of a false prophet. That may be to take the implication too far, but there is no doubt that a close reading of the form of words used in this verse suggests that the old Jonah, who dragged his feet with such spectacular effect in ch. 1, has reappeared. For a start, given that the author has made a point of the city being three days across, it is surely a pointed gesture that Jonah stops within the first day of his journey – in the outer suburbs, so to speak (moreover, he only 'begins' his journey). He then utters perhaps the briefest and least persuasive prophecy in Tanakh: 'Another forty[9] days and Nineveh will be destroyed'. Not even, 'Yahweh has said ....', no introduction or explanation. No suggestion that

---

9. Once again a significant number. Forty is closely associated with the Mosaic corpus and the giving of the law at Sinai, and we shall meet it in Chapter 11 in the matter of the Elijah pericope.

immediate repentance might mitigate the sentence. This is reminiscent of those government-sponsored invitations to consultation on sensitive planning issues which are posted on the least-read pages of obscure publications in order to minimise response. In short, it is arguable that Jonah's intention is to fulfil the letter of God's charge to him in such a way as virtually to guarantee the failure of his mission.

Even the terse sentence which Jonah utters contains a pregnant ambiguity: the verb in question does mean 'be destroyed', for example in relation to Sodom and Gomorrah (an outcome no doubt amenable to Jonah); but it can also mean 'be overturned' – and so, perhaps, transformed into another, or better place, which would suit God's apparent agenda. Historically – if history matters – there is no evidence that any repentance ever took place, and mute evidence on the ground that Nineveh's destruction (like that of every human creation) was accomplished. But these truisms have little bearing on the narrative under review, and even less on its meaning or message. What begins to become clearer as the story of Jonah proceeds is that this is a trial of strength between a man who believes himself to be in the right, and a God who quite unfairly holds all the aces. If this is a plausible analysis, we might propose a further analogy: there are suggestive similarities with the book of Job, hinting at a comedic approach in Jonah to what is a tragic narrative in Job. In the light of this observation, it is worth noting that both books end with the 'hero' rendered silent by Yahweh's deployment of the divine prerogative over the natural order. Job ends with the monstrous presence of Behemoth and Leviathan; the last two words in the book of Jonah are *behemah rabbah* – 'many cattle'. Did the author of Jonah know Job? Is there anything in Jonah that might hint at a parallel with Leviathan? Is Jonah a bathetic reduction of Job? The answers to these tentative questions are an equally tentative yes, as I have suggested in Chapter 6.

One last reflection before we turn to the equally abrupt and implausible response of the Ninevites: is this prophecy to be understood as Yahweh's word which Jonah got wrong (*he* thought – hoped – it prophesied the destruction of Nineveh; *God* intended it as a prediction of its conversion), or are Jonah's words ironically twisted by the God-directed events which ensued? That Yahweh manipulates events is one of the clear themes of the book of Jonah; moreover God manipulates events in all other cases exclusively to target Jonah, which entitles us to read what happens next in the light of the didactic purpose of the book as a whole (something I will return to in Chapter 13).

⁵And the people of Nineveh believed God; they proclaimed a fast, and everyone, great and small, put on sackcloth.

At first sight this is strange. If Jonah's oracle seems dismissive in the extreme, the immediate and fulsome response of the Ninevites is equally bizarre. A strange figure from a distant land suddenly appears. He speaks (presumably) some kind of Aramaic with a Hebrew accent, and proffers not advice, not a call to repentance, but a bald statement of apparent fact. And instantly the whole city decks itself in the symbolic dress of humiliation and begins a fast. Perhaps a contemporary parallel might be the speed with which a particular tweet might go viral, leading to a mass response; conceivably (in the light of the covid pandemic) some kind of mass hysterical episode. Just about plausible, I suppose. In the ancient world word-of-mouth would be the equivalent, with a viral panic being communicated through a gullible populace. Realistically, however, this superficially plausible scenario must be rejected. For one thing, hysterical mobs do not 'proclaim a fast'; for another, the autocratic and profoundly hierarchical society represented by Sennacherib's royal capital would be most unlikely to give rise to any such grass-roots protest. I propose to explore as an alternative an authorial technique which offers a better explanation.

The device in question appears first in ch. 1, where the *means* of Jonah's escape from drowning is announced in 1.17 before the extended hymnic account of the process Jonah went through before finally reaching dry land again. Thus ch. 2 provides an extended account of the process of redemption of Jonah from the sea which is summed up in the terse announcement of the arrival of the great fish which swallowed him. Similarly, ch. 4 introduces an extended process whereby Jonah awaits the outcome of his mission to Nineveh meanwhile taking the opportunity to berate God. All this despite the seeming fact that in 3.10 the matter appears already to have been settled. I shall designate this technique as a *proleptic summary*: as far as I am aware this is not a standard term in literary analysis, but it fits rather well a pattern in Jonah. The only other reference to this technique in Jonah that I have come across in Brichto (p. 75), where what I have called a *proleptic summary* is described as *gapping*; Brichto also uses the term *synoptic/resumptive-expansive* narrative technique. The current example of this technique is the digest provided in v. 5 of the process of humiliation before God adopted by all of Nineveh, followed by a clarification of that process in the detail of vv. 6-9. The effect of this device is to reinforce the sense of unreality which inhabits almost everything in the book of Jonah and at the same time to draw the reader's attention to the key moments in the fable: the psalm, the question of repentance, and the nature of Yahweh's mercy.

The opening phrase of v. 5 is a strong declaration: the people of Nineveh 'believed in God'. The wording here is especially potent: there is only one close parallel anywhere in Tanakh, and that is the central affirmation of belief that Abraham makes in Gen. 15.6 during the drama of the ritual in which Yahweh establishes the covenant with Abraham for the first time. The full verse merits quotation:

> And he [Abram] believed the LORD; and the LORD reckoned it to him as righteousness.[10]

For Abraham read 'the people of Nineveh'; and because they are not Israelites, and in keeping with a pattern in the book of Jonah, it is *'elohim* not *yhwh* in whom they believe. The uniqueness of this formulation, its high significance in Genesis, and the fact that Jonah makes extensive use of Genesis, means that there can be no doubt that we have here a clear and deliberate placement intended perhaps to shock, certainly to demand our attention. The consequence in Abraham's case was to have 'righteousness' attributed to him, clearly a symbolic token of his acceptance unreservedly by Yahweh. That such a definitive moment of the patriarchal story should be implicitly attributed to the repentance of the people of Nineveh is astonishing, if not close to blasphemous. Just how shocking this sequence is can be further illustrated by reminding ourselves that in prophetic terms also this episode is unmatched. The universal experience of other Hebrew prophets conforms to the Cassandra principle: fated to be right and never to be believed. What would an Isaiah or a Jeremiah not have given for this kind of instinctive and committed response? Their own impassioned pleas, couched in the most exquisite rhetoric, were delivered to their own people – yet these fell almost without exception on deaf ears. At one level what Jonah offers here is a *reductio ad absurdum* of the implied message of the prophetic books. This is a point that has often been made, but is nonetheless important for being commonplace. The problem with the prophets is that their bluff is never called, if I may put it somewhat crudely; that is, no-one ever tested the promise that repentance would lead to something better, and so they could be accused

---

10. Those interested might seek out my 1986 article in which I argued that this verse is exactly at the centre of an *ur*-text of the Abraham traditions and was placed there deliberately for both dramatic and theological purposes, analogous to the Pauline emphasis on salvation by grace through faith.

of occupying a spurious moral high ground. Jonah, on the other hand, had no doubt about the location of moral eminence. He was so sure that he felt no obligation to make more than the merest gesture towards the expression of God's message to Nineveh. The outcome, which we will confront shortly, will upend Jonah's certainties – but also pose a very serious challenge to the ethics by which Yahweh might be judged. Again, a matter for further reflection in due course. Incidentally, the postponement of God's response might constitute another example of a device which Magonet (pp. 73–4) identifies as one of the characteristic forms in which the author of Jonah deploys quotations: the separation of texts, that is, a clear use of an identifiable source (such as 1 Kings 19) which is divided between Jon. 1.5 and 4.2-8. Here a very obvious citation of Gen. 15.6 is split between 3.5 (the statement that the Ninevites 'believed God') and 3.10 (God's acceptance of this as evidence of a change of heart – righteousness).

> *⁶When the news reached the king of Nineveh,*
> *he rose from his throne, removed his robe, covered himself*
> *with sackcloth, and sat in ashes.*

In v. 6 we return to the natural order of things in hierarchical society. It is the king who takes the initiative, setting an example when he hears 'the word', donning sackcloth and sitting in ashes – another echo of the situation of Job at the beginning of his dispute with his neighbours (Job 2.8). I cannot resist quoting here Sherwood's delightful riff (pp. 264–5) on the question of what language was used in Jonah's Nineveh:

> [Jonah] encounters a King of Nineveh who (of all people and all places) is, uniquely for any foreigner in Tanakh, already in possession of, and familiar with, Scripture, and speaks the words of Jeremiah in perfect accentless Hebrew …. The fact that the King of Nineveh already possesses and quotes Scripture undermines any interpretation of Jonah as a book about mission-ising, or taking the Bible to the gentiles (since insofar as anyone 'has' 'the Bible' in the world of Jonah, everyone has it) and reinforces the pervasive atmosphere of the (literally) *unheimlich*, in which home and the 'bloody city' have changed places.

Sherwood is here referring to the words of the king in v. 9, and I shall return to the second part of her comment in Chapter 13. In the immediate context there is another interesting verbal play in this verse which points up a contrast between Jonah and the king in parallel with the contrast between Jonah and the sailors. As soon as the king of Nineveh knows the score he gets up and acts – in contrast with Jonah who 'got up and ran away' at the beginning of the story. The linguistic detail of his actions merits attention. I have already noted the significance of 'he got up' (*vayyaqom*); but this is not the end of the word-play, for in specifying that he got up 'from his throne and removed his royal cloak' at least three tantalising echoes are introduced. The throne (*kise'*) sounds very similar to the verb in the next clause: 'and he donned (*vayikas*) sackcloth'. Second, the root behind 'removed' is that used for crossing over from one place to another, suggesting that the king's action in some sense mirror's Jonah's epic journey from Judah to Nineveh. Thirdly, the word for cloak, *'adereth*, is often found in phrases suggesting that it is a symbolic garment. In particular it is Elijah's cloak which is used to pass on his prophetic calling to Elisha (1 Kgs 19.13, 19; 2 Kgs 2.8, 13, 14). Further prophetic connections are to be found in Zech. 11.3; 13.4, and in Mic. 2.8 it refers to a robe which is to be stripped 'from the peaceful'. The Elijah reference is plausibly part of Jonah's extensive use of that tradition; in sum it seems clear that the king is exchanging the symbol of his kingship for the humiliation of 'enthronement' (the word 'to sit' is the same as 'to be enthroned' in Hebrew) dressed in sacking amidst the ashes of mourning. It may be possible to find an echo here of the idea of the ritual humiliation of the king, familiar from the Mesopotamian Akitu Festival observed widely throughout the region, especially in Babylon, and adopted by Sennacherib in Assyria. Part of the ritual involved the humiliation of the king who was stripped of his insignia by a priest representing the God Marduk. There is no direct reference to this in Jonah, but the king's divesting himself of his ceremonial robe may suggest familiarity with the ritual. It was certainly widespread over many centuries, and it is not unlikely that literate scholars in the Judah of the Persian and Hellenistic periods would have been aware of its details.

> *⁷Then he had a proclamation made in Nineveh:*
> *'By the decree of the king and his nobles: No human being*
> *or animal, no herd or flock, shall taste anything.*
> *They shall not feed, nor shall they drink water. ⁸Human beings*
> *and animals shall be covered with sackcloth, and they shall cry*
> *mightily to God. All shall turn from their evil ways and from*
> *the violence that is in their hands.*

The NRSV translation of v. 7 is I think misleading The verb which opens this verse (*vayyaz'eq*) is often used to express a cry of anguish; it is used in 1.5 when the sailors cry out to their gods, and (paired with a near homonym with the same meaning) it is found in the refrain in Ps. 107.6,

13, 19, 28 – a psalm I have already identified as one of Jonah's influences.[11] It is true that there are two places where the verb seems best rendered as 'to call together',[12] but the most natural understanding of the opening of Jon. 3.7 is surely: 'Then he cried out and commanded Nineveh ...' (there are two separate verbs in this clause). Apart from being a better rendering of the Hebrew this reveals a meaningful parallel between the actions of the sailors in ch. 1 and the king in ch. 3. Accordingly I shall reword vv. 7-8 as:

> Then he cried out and commanded Nineveh: 'By the decree[13] of the king and his nobles: No human being or animal, no herd or flock, shall taste anything. They shall not feed, nor shall they drink water. Human beings and animals shall be covered with sackcloth, and they shall cry mightily to God. All shall turn from their evil ways and from the violence that is in their hands.

The 'nobles' here are literally 'the great men' – reminiscent of the frequent use of *gadhol* elsewhere in the book: 'great city' (1.2; 3.2, 3; 4.11); 'great wind' (1.4), 'great storm' (1.4, 12); 'great terror, awe' (1.10, 16); 'great fish' (1.17); 'important people' (3.5, 7); 'great misery' (4.1); 'great joy' (4.6); 'to make great' (4.10). The frequency is about three times as great as in its closest comparable book, Malachi. It is not entirely clear if this is significant or just an authorial 'tic'; it serves, I suppose, to emphasise the grotesquery of much of what is going on, at least on the surface.

The measures which the king and his court impose in vv. 7-8a are suitably over the top, introducing for the first time the notion that the city's flocks and herds are fully part of the process of mourning and repentance. It is probably not a coincidence that the verb for 'to graze' in v. 7 is a homophone with that for 'to do evil', as if the ban on sheep and cattle grazing is a kind of metaphor for the people's departure from the evil which prompted the description of Nineveh which opens the book of Jonah.[14] The compound 'man and beast' (*ha'adam vehabehemah*)

---

11. The two verbs in Hebrew are *za'aq* (Jon. 1.5; 3.7; Ps. 107.13, 19) and *tsa'aq* (Ps. 107.6, 28). They share a closely similar semantic range, and the use in Ps. 107 suggests that they may have been alternate spellings. Curiously the word for tempest or storm – *se'arah/sa'ar* – which we encountered in Jon. 1 (and also in Ps. 107.25, 29) is also found with two spellings: one where the opening 's' sound is the letter *samech* and the other *sin*.

12. Judg. 4.10, 13; 2 Sam. 20.4, 5.

13. Note that 'commanded' and 'by the decree of' use the same Hebrew verb, *'amar*.

14. The fact that this *double entendre* is intentional is shown by the five-fold repetition of this new root *ra'a'* in the next four verses (see Christensen).

reappears in v. 8 where, bizarrely, both people and animals together wear sackcloth and again, though the two are separated, in 4.11. Moreover the rest of the verse continues to associate the two groups in an act of repentance for the evil of their way and the violence (*chamas*) that is in their hands. More fluently, what they are to turn from is 'the evil of their way of life and the violence they are responsible for'. Again, we seem to be asked to attribute this to the animals as well – something that we might pedantically question were it not for 4.11.

Is this egregious anthropomorphism an example of early eco-sensitivity? At first sight this might seem unlikely, until we recall the words of Qoheleth, a commentator who could well be contemporary with our author, in the famous reflection on human fate in 3.19-21:

> For the fate of humans and the fate of animals is the same; as one dies, so dies the other. They all have the same breath, and humans have no advantage over the animals; for all is vanity. All go to one place; all are from the dust, and all turn to dust again. Who knows whether the human spirit goes upwards and the spirit of animals goes downwards to the earth?

It might seem an unlikely connection; however we know that the author of Jonah was very well read (if not well-travelled!), and there is nothing in the least improbable in the suggestion that they were near contemporaries. The manipulation by God of the elements in chs. 1 and 4 bears comparison with the Qoheleth's 'vanity' theme and the bleak picture of decay in Qoheleth 12. A more extensive treatment of this question will be found in Chapter 12.

> *⁹Who knows? God may relent and change his mind;*
> *he may turn from his fierce anger, so that we do not perish'.*
> *¹⁰When God saw what they did, how they turned from their evil ways,*
> *God changed his mind about the calamity that he had said*
> *he would bring upon them; and he did not do it.*

Jonah 3 concludes with a passage which taps into two significant prophetic themes: overtly, the question of the possibility of Yahweh's 'repentance', and implicitly the status of Yahweh's covenant with the people (a theme which will emerge once we have reviewed the evidence relating to the former). There is an abruptness to the treatment of the first question, a matter-of-fact pair of unnuanced sentences: 'Maybe God will have a change of mind' followed by 'Oh yes, he will!' There is no definitive position on this question to be found in Tanakh, as the following table of significant biblical witnesses (apart from Jonah) for and against shows. Of some interest is the fact that four of the five key expressions are found together in Jon. 3.9-10. Apart from the Exodus and Joel instances, I will not comment further on the individual examples; sufficient to note that – perhaps not surprisingly – the traditions are ambivalent on this question.

Table 11.1. *Does Yahweh Repent?*

FOR		AGAINST	
Key expressions		Key expressions	
Gen. 6.6-7	Repents making humans	Num. 23.19	(not) repent
Exod. 32.12-14	*See detailed comment to follow*	1 Sam. 15.29	(not) repent
1 Sam. 15.11	Repents choosing Saul	Jer. 4.26-28	Fierce anger; (not) repent or turn
2 Sam. 24.16 = 1 Chron. 21.25	Repents planning evil	Ezek. 24.14	(Does not) repent
Jer. 18.8, 10	Repents (for better or worse)	Zech. 8.14	(Does not) repent of evil
Jer. 26.3, 13, 19	Repents planning evil	Mal. 3.6	(Does not) change
Joel 2.13-14	*See detailed comments to follow*	Ps. 110.4	(Does not) repent
Amos 7.3, 6	Repents planning plagues		

repent = *nacham*   evil = *ra'ah*   change = *shanah*
fierce anger = *charon 'aph*   turn = *shuv*

Whatever one may think of the principle of God's freedom to change, it would seem to be a necessary condition of biblical prophecy that at the very least there should be the possibility that what is threatened will not occur. On that understanding oracles of doom are not predictions but warnings, and there is always the chance that repentance will avert disaster. To some extent that is true of biblical Israel's history: repeated failure, repeated forgiveness, repeated second chances. Oracles against non-Israelite nations might be construed differently – not least because (*pace* Jonah) no-one was making them aware of what God had planned.

Jonah is presented as a kind of moral hard-liner (of which more in the commentary on ch. 4) who believes that wrong-doing should earn punishment regardless of any possible future restoration. His approach is supported by the so-called Deuteronomistic theology[15] which interprets

---

15. For the benefit of any reader not familiar with this expression, it encapsulates a widely agreed understanding that the author(s) of the book of Deuteronomy had a defining influence on the books of Kings, the final form of Samuel, and the editing of Jeremiah at the very least.

the fall of Jerusalem and the exile as well-merited punishment for all kinds of sin (cf. Jer. 25.8-12; Deut. 8.11-20; 28.15-68). On this calculus, it is ethically abhorrent for the Ninevites (whoever they really are) to be let off the hook on the basis of a statement of intent and an ostentatious display of bad dress fasting. That said, the authorial position seems to favour an alternative view, that the deity represents a kind of work in progress rather than a set of predetermined positions, such that it is always open to frail humans to appeal to mercy when faced with judgement. There is some support for this understanding of Yahweh in some of the translations of Yahweh's gnomic self-definition in Exod. 3.14, 'I AM WHO I AM' (NRSV). Without labouring a point over which much scholarly ink has flowed, it seems that the phrase in question is a kind of folk-etymology of the mysterious name YHWH, a verbal form which is tolerant of readings such as 'I will be what I will be' (NRSV footnote), suggesting perhaps a conception of a god-in-process rather than an 'ancient of days' set in (tablets) of stone. The balance of passages alluded to in Jonah which deal with the possibility of a divine change of mind certainly favours this understanding, as we shall shortly see.

The defining expressions in Jon. 3.9-10 are:

'who knows' (*mi yodea'*)
'changing his mind' (*yashuv*)
'repenting' (*nicham*)
'fierce anger' (*charon 'aph*)
'calamity' (*ra'ah*)

There are three other passages in Tanakh where an association of at least three of these key terms is to be found within a brief compass. In Jer. 4.26-28, the only one which endorses the unchanging nature of God's punishment, the relevant terms are not used in a pattern at all similar to that of Jonah, However, the other two are highly significant: the aftermath of the Golden Calf episode in Exodus which also includes the 'mercy' formula of Exod. 34.6-7, and Joel's version of the same formula (2.12-13). The first of these is Exod. 32.12-14, in which Moses addresses Yahweh in an effort to ameliorate the threatened consequences of the people's idolatry:

> 'Why should the Egyptians say, "It was with evil intent (*ra'ah*) that he brought them out to kill them in the mountains, and to consume them from the face of the earth"? Turn (*shuv*) from your fierce wrath (*kharon appekha*); change your mind (*nakham*) and do not bring disaster (*ra'ah*) on your people. Remember Abraham, Isaac, and Israel, your servants, how you swore to them by your own self, saying to them, "I will multiply your

descendants like the stars of heaven, and all this land that I have promised I will give to your descendants, and they shall inherit it for ever".' And the LORD changed his mind (*nacham*) about the disaster (*ra'ah*) that he planned to bring on his people.

Chapters 32–34 of Exodus represent one of the most important theological developments in Tanakh, second only to the account of the establishment of God's personal covenant with Abraham in Genesis 15. I do not discount the Noahic covenant spoken of in Gen. 6.18 and 9.8-17, but it is of lesser significance in the biblical account of God's dealings with Israel. We have already seen that the confession of faith by the Ninevites points strongly to Abraham's in Gen. 15.6; it is therefore to the point that the allusion in Exod. 32.13 to the covenant with the patriarchs is part of Moses' prayer. The importance of the Golden Calf legend and its aftermath is, as Erich Zenger (2018) has convincingly demonstrated, the establishment of the principle that Yahweh's covenant with Israel can neither be abrogated nor superseded, whatever calamity may befall the people or whatever faithlessness they may show. Zenger's analysis is set against the background of Jewish–Christian relations and the scandal of Christian appropriation of the covenant to the detriment of the Jews; but its truth is of general application. At which point we might reasonably ask why the author of Jonah at this point associates the repentance of the Ninevites with the enduring covenant between Yahweh and Israel: a question I shall take up in due course.

The passage in Joel which I considered when looking at the possible dating of Jonah also has significant verbal links with the conclusion of ch. 3:

> Return to the LORD, your God,
>   for he is gracious and merciful,
> slow to anger (*'aph*), and abounding in steadfast love,
>   and relents (*nacham*) from punishing (*ra'ah*).
> Who knows (*mi yodea'*) whether he will not turn (*shuv*) and relent (*nacham*).

As we noted earlier, there is surely some kind of dependence between Jon. 3.9 with 4.2 and Joel 2.12-13. I believe the balance lies in favour of Jonah's use of Joel, a conclusion which is strengthened when the likely connection with Exod. 32.12-14 is taken into account. Clearly, then, these two closing verses of Jonah 3 pack a tremendous theological and historical punch, none of which bears directly on the historical Nineveh, its ruler Sennacherib, or the marauding Assyrian Empire. Rather it speaks to the covert theme which I noted at the start of this section: the status of Yahweh's covenant with the people of Israel.

One last literary note is in order here. I alluded earlier to Magonet's device of the 'separation of texts' which he finds several times in Jonah's use of sources. I noted then that the borrowing from Gen. 15.6 which marks the opening of v. 5, 'and the people of Nineveh believed God', is one example. Its completion is in fact to be found in v. 10 when we read that 'God changed his mind' and refrained from the intended overthrow of Nineveh. But this is not the end of the device, for this is also a borrowing, from Joel 2.12-13, and the second part of that quotation is in turn delayed until we come to Jonah's dispute with Yahweh in 4.2.

The narrative consequence of these moves is shocking. Based on nothing but the outward performance of humility and fasting, God accepts the Ninevite's repentance at face value. This is cheap grace if ever something deserved that title: unearned repentance in the face of simple fear – a paradigm of the death-bed scenario beloved of Victorian evangelists. I can just imagine Isaiah and Jeremiah and Amos heading the queue of protestors at this devaluation of the honour and standing of Yahweh. This is almost at the level of sympathetic magic: because the people (and their herds) said they had abandoned evil, God agreed to cancel the 'great evil' planned for the city. But it gets worse, for God's evidence is their 'deeds' (but what, the honest evangelist and prophet might ask, did they actually do?), in return for which God repents of what God planned to 'do' and 'does not do' it. And that's that. As a more recent celebrity often remarked, 'You cannot be serious'. Can you?

Coda

The 'failure' explicitly to cite the covenant reaches a crisis in this chapter where, as we have seen, at least three profoundly important 'moments' in the *Heilsgeschichte* are found to be implicit in the choice of references the author has made: Abraham's faith (Gen. 15) which leads to the first formulation of the covenant with Yahweh; the aftermath of the Golden Calf which results in Moses impassioned plea to Yahweh to 'repent'; and the mercy formula from Exod. 34.6-7 mediated through Joel's novel claim that Yahweh 'relents from punishing'.

I have posed more than once the question, 'What has all this to do with Nineveh?' The answer is, I propose, rather obvious: nothing whatsoever. All of the subtexts, the coding, the insistent subterranean drumbeat of the covenant, are constantly present even if (especially because?) they are never openly allowed. The writer of this book is subtle and persuasive. We are being led, just as Jonah was led, to conclusions which we may not wish to hear.

Chapter 11

JONAH 4.1-11: ON BEING ELIJAH THE TISHBITE

The title of this chapter is a deliberate tribute to Charlie Kaufman's cult film *Being John Malkovitch* in which the central character literally inhabits the mind of the eponymous actor. The allusions to the Elijah legend in Jonah are numerous, and appear throughout the text, to the extent that we might think of Jonah as *channelling* Elijah.

> **¹But this was very displeasing to Jonah, and he became angry. ²He prayed to the L**ORD **and said, 'O L**ORD**! Is not this what I said while I was still in my own country? That is why I fled to Tarshish at the beginning; for I knew that you are a gracious God and merciful, slow to anger, and abounding in steadfast love, and ready to relent from punishing. ³And now, O L**ORD**, please take my life from me, for it is better for me to die than to live.' ⁴And the L**ORD **said, 'Is it right for you to be angry?'**

Verses 1-4 describe, it seems, Jonah's response to Yahweh's decision in 3.10 to waive the punishment of Nineveh. There are, however, at least two narrative problems with this assumption. One is that 3.10 belongs to the voice of the 'omniscient narrator', and there is no obvious way that Jonah could have been privy to this opinion. The second is that, even assuming that somehow he sensed what was in store, in his own words forty days had to elapse before the final outcome could be determined; his anger is premature. Some commentators offer to resolve the difficulty by proposing that v. 5 has been displaced from a position originally at the beginning of ch. 4, or after 3.9; this however leaves an equally incoherent narrative which separates Jonah's construction of his shelter in 4.5 from Yahweh's subsequent actions in v. 6:

3.9 Who knows? God may relent and change his mind; he may turn from his fierce anger, so that we do not perish'

4.5 Then Jonah went out of the city and sat down east of the city, and made a booth for himself there. He sat under it in the shade, waiting to see what would become of the city.

3.10 When God saw what they did, how they turned from their evil ways, God changed his mind about the calamity that he had said he would bring upon them; and he did not do it.

4.1 But this was very displeasing to Jonah, and he became angry. ²He prayed to the LORD and said, 'O LORD! Is not this what I said while I was still in my own country? That is why I fled to Tarshish at the beginning; for I knew that you are a gracious God and merciful, slow to anger, and abounding in steadfast love, and ready to relent from punishing. ³And now, O LORD, please take my life from me, for it is better for me to die than to live'. ⁴And the LORD said, 'Is it right for you to be angry?'

4.6 The LORD God appointed a bush, and made it come up over Jonah, to give shade over his head, to save him from his discomfort; so Jonah was very happy about the bush.

Since there seems to be no plausible reason why an original text such as this might have been re-arranged, nor is there any ancient evidence for it, the better approach is to seek to understand the text as we have it. To those not familiar with the habits of biblical criticism this may seem to be a matter of stating the blindingly obvious; others will recognize that, just as with any ancient source, many of the biblical texts show signs of accidental misprisions – perhaps caused by scribal fallibility, or by natural damage to fragile materials. The state of most of the Dead Sea Scrolls testifies to the latter hazard while simultaneously offering a third problematic: the existence in antiquity of diverse forms of materials which now constitute biblical books. It is therefore not irrational to ask whether the text of Jonah could have been similarly modified in transmission. There is scant objective evidence for these problems: the psalm in ch. 2 is the most frequently canvassed candidate for an add-on, but the increasing consensus is, as I have already observed, to accept its original integrity as part of the book.

The apparent problem is open to more than one interpretation without requiring any adjustment to the text. The first is the device I described in Chapter 8 in my discussion of Jon. 3.5: the proleptic summary. At the narrative level, 3.10 serves as a summary in advance of God's ultimate decisions regarding Nineveh, while 4.1-5 encapsulates Jonah's response in advance of what he presumes will happen; an anticipatory expression of Jonah's feelings – perhaps gaining urgency from the craven failure of God to smite the Ninevites immediately for their evident hypocrisy (exacerbated, for sure, by their ironic extension of the visible signs of repentance to the beasts of the field). Looked at from Jonah's point of view this is a veritable rubbing of salt into the wounds on his already bruised ego. Hence his immediate angry response, before he has time to leave the city, and his bitter rejection of the God whom he believed had betrayed him. It is when that preliminary exchange is over that Jonah settles down to wait out the statutory period before finalising his grievance; and it is that waiting period that Yahweh uses to teach Jonah a lesson, or to heap further humiliation upon him, depending on how we read the final verses of the book. The twist is that we are never shown directly what the outcome is. The narrator has Jonah 'waiting to see what would become of the city' (v. 5), while the last words on the subject attributed to God are 'should I not be concerned about Nineveh, that great city?' The book in effect stops abruptly with no resolution, no closure. Perhaps a second series was envisioned, but never commissioned!

But there is another, more subtle way to read the sequence from 3.10 to 4.5. Ask yourself the question, precisely what is it that was 'displeasing to Jonah'? Remember that 3.10 is in the voice of the narrator: it is decidedly *not* a divine communication to Jonah. All *he* knows is that all the inhabitants of the city, from the king down to the lowliest citizens and their domestic animals, have adopted the forms of penance and have expressed the hope that God might relent. These are the only public events in Jonah 3: logically, therefore, it is these which have incensed Jonah – not any evidence that Nineveh has been spared. I want now to look more closely at these opening verses of ch. 4.

¹But this was very displeasing to Jonah, and he became angry.

This searing account of Jonah's anger represents a range of relevant terms: the root for 'evil' twice; the key adjective 'great' and the impersonal verb *charah*, 'to burn with anger'. There can be no doubt that this is deliberate. The frequent use of 'evil' in 3.7-10, the diagnostic role that 'great' plays in the book as a whole, and the fact that Jonah's anger is cognate with Yahweh's burning anger in 3.9 which the Ninevites hope by their actions to forestall, combine to demonstrate the fierce emotion packed into this brief sentence. The semantic play on *ra'ah* is of central importance: it is translated by the NRSV in Jonah as wickedness (1.2), calamity (1.7, 8;

3.10), displeasure (4.1), punishment (4.2), and discomfort (4.6); the adjectival form *ra'* is rendered 'evil' in 3.8, 10; and the verbal form *ra'a'* as 'to be displeasing' in 4.1. If we perhaps mischievously adopt an English term with a similar sound, we find that the book is suffused with 'rage' and 'outrage', and (stretching things a little!) 'tragedy'. Here are the relevant passages re-translated using this device:

> Go at once to Nineveh, that great city, and cry out against it; for their *outrage* has come up before me. (1.2)

> The sailors said to one another, 'Come, let us cast lots, so that we may know on whose account this *tragedy* has come upon us'. So they cast lots, and the lot fell on Jonah. Then they said to him, 'Tell us why this *tragedy* has come upon us'. (1.7, 8)

> Human beings and animals shall be covered with sackcloth, and they shall cry mightily to God. All shall turn from their *outrageous* ways and from the violence that is in their hands. (3.8)

> When God saw what they did, how they turned from their *outrageous* ways, God changed his mind about the *tragedy* that he had said he would bring upon them; and he did not do it. (3.10)

> But Jonah was *outraged*, filled with *rage*, and he became angry. (4.1)

> He prayed to the LORD and said, 'O LORD! Is not this what I said while I was still in my own country? That is why I fled to Tarshish at the beginning; for I knew that you are a gracious God and merciful, slow to anger, and abounding in steadfast love, and ready to relent from *deadly rage*. (4.2)

> The LORD God appointed a bush, and made it come up over Jonah, to give shade over his head, to save him from his *umbrage*;[1] so Jonah was very happy about the bush. (4.6)

This is one angry man – and on the face of it he has a case: why should it even be theoretically possible for those guilty of such outrageous behaviour to escape without consequence? What moral universe encompasses on the one hand Yahweh the God of the Israelites who regularly visits all manner of disasters upon them in consequence of their unfaithfulness, and on

---

1. Clutching at straws here! I think it possible that there is a hint that God is distracting Jonah from his complaints at this point. The lack of shade (umbra) would be a good pretext for his next grumble; hence my punning '*umbr*age'.

the other the merciful being who invites Bonhoeffer's 'cheap grace' as a means (perhaps?) of recruiting adherents at any cost? Or is the issue that of the definition of what is right, what constitutes morality? Are we to assume that if Yahweh acts, that act is *by definition* good; or is good an objective fact to which Yahweh is also subject? Genesis 1 is potentially biblical evidence for the latter: 'God saw that it was good' – not God *said* that it was good, or defined it as good, but having brought the various elements of creation into being, became aware that these were good things. A similar expression of trust in Yahweh's adherence to natural justice and goodness is to be found in Psalm 145. Equally, however, the former view is implicit in some of the biblical stories which imply an arbitrary or high-handed God whose commands and desires defy customary morality. Perhaps the most striking of these is the story in 1 Kgs 13.11-25 of the old prophet and a younger one. The tale is complex; neither prophet is named, and the full story is lengthy, stretching over the whole of 13.1-32. Its fundamental premise is that the word of God comes in ambiguous forms: getting it wrong can cost you your life even if your intentions are good and your actions entirely innocent. Let me give arbitrary names to these people in order to set out the bones of the story: I will call the older prophet Elias and the younger Jonas.

(1) The story begins with Jonas prophesying to Jeroboam the future birth of Josiah the king of Israel under whom the altar at Bethel will be polluted.
(2) Jeroboam stretches out his hand to denounce Jonas, but instead his hand is withered.
(3) Jeroboam pleads with Jonas to intercede with Yahweh to cure him. He does so and the king's hand is restored.
(4) In gratitude Jeroboam invites Jonas to dine with him, but the prophet refuses, explaining that he was commanded by the word of the Lord 'not [to] eat food or drink water, or return by the way that [he] came'.
(5) Jonas sets out by a different route.
(6) Meanwhile Elias, informed by his sons of what Jonas has done, sets out to find him. He discovers him 'sitting under an oak tree'.
(7) Elias invites Jonas to come home with him and share food.
(8) Jonas refuses, with the same explanation he gave to Jeroboam.
(9) Elias then declares: 'I also am a prophet as you are, and an angel spoke to me by the word of the LORD: Bring him back with you into your house so that he may eat food and drink water'.
(10) The narrator comments: 'But he was deceiving him'.

(11) Jonas is persuaded (perhaps by Elias's greater age and status) and breaks his earlier oath by sharing food with him.
(12) Elias then receives a <u>word from the Lord</u> and prophesies that Jonas will die before he reaches his home.
(13) Jonas leaves for home, but is killed by a lion on the way.
(14) Elias, hearing this news, brings Jonas's body back to his town, gives him an honourable burial, and mourns him, exclaiming 'Alas, my brother!'
(15) Elias's concluding words are:

> When I die, bury me in the grave in which the man of God is buried; lay my bones beside his bones. For the saying that he proclaimed by the <u>word of the LORD</u> against the altar in Bethel, and against all the houses of the high places that are in the cities of Samaria, <u>shall surely come to pass</u>.

There are some nice parallels with the book of Jonah. Jonas also travels from Judah to prophesy to a foreign king (Jeroboam of Israel).[2] His commission is not without danger, and he is given curious instructions by 'the word of the Lord'. Elias finds him sitting under a tree (a motif found in both Jon. 4 and the Elijah episode in 1 Kgs 19). The 'word of the Lord' is clearly a highly ambiguous form of communication (as it may also be in Jonah): whose word is genuine? Is the Lord issuing contradictory messages to test/confuse Jonas? Is Elias a liar (as the narrator suggests), or is the narrator's opinion merely an attempt to make sense of a murderously deceptive deity? Elias's final actions might suggest this explanation. The final words 'shall surely come to pass' nicely anticipate the final uncertainty in Jonah, where we are left in the dark precisely on this question.

As a footnote to this fantasy retelling I must record the delightful and equally fanciful genealogy conjured in antiquity to link Elijah to Jonah. Youngblood (p. 116) reports a legend found in the pseudepigraphical *Lives of the Prophets* that the widow's son whom Elijah resuscitated in Zarephath (1 Kgs 17.17-24) was in fact Jonah; he further connects this legend with the prayer of Eleazar in *3 Macc.* 6.8: 'And Jonah, wasting away in the belly of a huge, sea-born monster, you, Father, watched over and restored unharmed to all his family': perhaps the legend was known to the author of *3 Maccabees*.

---

2. Recall that Jonah ben Amittai prophesied in the reign of Jeroboam II according to 2 Kgs 14.25.

The sailors in 1.14 also lean towards this concept of a rather arbitrary deity when in their prayer they declare that 'you, O Lord, have done as it pleased you'. Such a resigned approach to the fickleness of the gods was normal in the world of antiquity: Greek and Roman gods were not renowned for their adherence to proper standards of morality or ethics. The turn of phrase used here is only found in two other places: Ps. 115.3 and Ps. 135.6. Both Magonet and Sasson note this link, but without exploring the implications to any extent. The former is a member of the Hallel sequence which later became an essential part of the liturgy, while the latter includes formalised historical references, particularly to Egypt and the entry into Canaan. The setting in Ps. 135.5-7 is rather apt:

> For I know that the LORD is <u>great</u>;
>   our Lord is above all gods.
> <u>Whatever the LORD pleases he does</u>,
>   in <u>heaven</u> and on earth,
>   in the <u>seas</u> and all <u>deeps</u>.
> He it is who makes the clouds rise at the end of the earth;
>   he makes lightnings for the rain
>   and brings out the wind from his storehouses.

The underlined words are also found in Jonah, and suggest that we have here one of the book's allusive uses of familiar material: a deliberate echo, but put to a distinctive use. For the phrase in question seems to convey a benign sense in both of the psalms. In Psalm 115 Yahweh, unlike dumb idols, actually does things. In Psalm 135 Yahweh's subsequent actions, while harsh in relation to Egypt and the kingdoms of Canaan, are beneficial to Israel, and the psalm repeats with considerable similarity of terminology the motif of the useless idols of the nations (135.15-18; cf. 115.4-8). Jonah, of course, refers to 'vain idols' at the end of ch. 2, but it is the sailors – presumably the sort of collection of non-Israelites envisaged by these two psalms – who appeal to Yahweh. They appear to acknowledge that 'to do what you please' is a natural divine prerogative, so that their prayer takes the form of a kind of hedging of bets based on a depressingly realistic assessment of the behaviour of the gods (Yahweh included).

It is interesting that whether God is seen as arbitrary depends on the perspective of the victims of divine action. Jonah, in fact, appears not to question Yahweh's propriety in sending the storm and endangering the lives of the crew. From his limited perspective he deserved punishment for his act of defiance. But limited it is, since the question of collateral damage or innocent bystanders is not raised. Similarly, and unlike

Abraham when faced with Yahweh's intended annihilation of Sodom, Jonah does not query the morality of the utter destruction of Nineveh regardless of (for example) the innocence of children and animals. If we are correct in reading this as the nature of Jonah's protest and the source of his rage, then his position becomes almost toxic in demanding of Yahweh the kind of integrity which we might be tempted to associate with the more dirigiste forms of Calvinism.

While these are philosophical conundrums of long standing which we cannot deal with at any length here, it is of interest that the character of Jonah, already presented as somewhat determined, if not intransigent, should appear in the defence of an absolute idea of justice and righteousness to which even Yahweh ought to be subject. There is simply no point in an all-powerful God who swings this way and that and turns out to be every bit as changeable as the beings who were created by and are subject to him.

> ²*He prayed to the* LORD *and said, 'O* LORD!
> *Is not this what I said while I was still in my own country?*
> *That is why I fled to Tarshish at the beginning;*
> *for I knew that you are a gracious God and merciful,*
> *slow to anger, and abounding in steadfast love, and ready*
> *to relent from punishing.'*

Time for a prayer. Just as Jonah prayed to Yahweh from the belly of the fish (2.1) so now he prays (the verb used is the same) from the depths of his frustration. The verbal form of this prayer also reminds us of the prayer of the sailors in 1.14 when they were seeking exemption from responsibility for the death of Jonah. The same plea is entered, an emphatic form of the vocative 'O Yahweh' (*'annah yhwh*), followed by the substance of the prayer. In the present case, ironically, the outcome demanded by Jonah is that he be allowed to die, while the sailors longed passionately to survive. The reader may suspect that this is a hopeless request: what tempests, foreign sailors, and a whale were unable to accomplish is surely not going to be granted at this late stage. Jonah needs to be kept alive to serve as an example – though of what, we are not yet clear.

The first claim in the prayer is that Jonah already made this point when he was 'still in my own country'. The Hebrew actually has 'on my own land (or property)', a phrasing which does not really support the implication of the NRSV and other versions that Jonah was then in a different political realm. The NIV is good here: it has 'when I was at home', which fits much better with the way that *'adhamah* with a personal pronoun is predominantly used in Tanakh,[3] namely as something like one's home ground, or farmstead, or living arrangements. As is frequently the case in Jonah, the form with the first person singular 'my land' is virtually unique (there is one instance, in 2 Chron. 7.20, where Yahweh speaks of 'My land which I gave you'). I labour this point because it contributes to my thesis that Nineveh is 'really' Jerusalem and Jonah never went anywhere near Assyria (even in the Jonah-narrative).

The next point is the curious assertion that 'this is what I said ...'. We have no record of Jonah having said anything at the beginning of ch. 1, where the narrative presents us with a prophet fleeing immediately. While I have already suggested that something unrecorded might have happened before the journey to Tarshish, I will here note another possible explanation which has been put forward more than once. Sasson has 'I was of the opinion' which quite neatly resolves the apparent problem. In fact the Hebrew literally reads 'this was my word (*davar*)'. The expression *davar* covers a very wide semantic range, to some extent overlapping with the equally indefinable Greek *logos*, but also sharing much of the sense in which modern speakers of English use the term 'thing'. In this context, then, there is much to be said for a translation which avoids the overly literal 'word': Sasson's suggestion is helpful, but I think it needs a stronger formulation, perhaps along the lines of 'This was my issue when I was still at home' or even 'this was my *thing*' if a modern colloquialism is fitting.

As if these niggles were not enough, there is one more enigma in Jonah's account of his prior actions. The term for taking flight is the same as in 1.3, but it is prefaced not with a reiteration of something like 'I set out to flee', but introduces a verb which belongs to the same root as the 'east wind' in 4.8 and 'east of the city' in 4.5. What it signifies is not easy to ascertain. To some extent it presents as a punning usage stretching the regular meaning which, in most other places, has to do with bringing or coming forward, either to meet someone or to present something. Sasson's 'this is why I planned to flee' is helpful, but does not quite represent the sense of 'coming forward' which is there in most of the other instances of this verb. Perhaps the RSV's 'hastened to flee' is after all as close as we can get, recognising a piece of wordplay which is simply untranslatable. If there is an interpretative clue it may lie in the direction of several hints at a kind of instability or tendency to instinctive and impulsive action on the part of the character Jonah, combined with a rigorous attachment to

---

3. Frequently as 'the property on which one lives' and with reference to 'the fruits or produce of one's property', most often relating to Israel, but with a few references to land belonging to others. The only writer who uses the term territorially is Ezekiel who has *'adhmath yisrael* ('the land of Israel') 16 times.

prior positions: something which becomes evident in the next stage of this verse.

In the Introduction I considered the relationship to Joel 2.13 of Jonah's citation of the ubiquitous Exodus 'mercy formula', the only other place where the phrase 'ready to relent from punishing' is found. My judgement is that Joel is primary, and that this is one more example of the intertextual technique of the author of Jonah. The signal importance of this version of the formula is the omission of the second part of the Exodus original referring to the insistence on punishment for the guilty and their descendants. Undoubtedly Jonah is shown to disapprove of the leniency implied by this change: it is his core objection to what he believes Yahweh intends, and it is given additional prominence both by the retrospective explanatory device here deployed, and the (to Jonah) scandalous use of the same words by the Ninevites in 3.9.

The words of Exod. 34.6-7, in various forms, recur so frequently throughout Tanakh that we can surely accept that they were widely known and respected; perhaps a regular feature of liturgies. It is impossible to identify any original form of the saying, and probably wrong to give priority to Exodus simply because of its placement in the canon. In some ways Exod. 34.7 is like a commentary on, or expansion of, the core blessing, and its purpose might have been to dispose of any idea that the blessing is a kind of freedom card carrying no responsibilities. A short review of the main parallels will help to elucidate this point and contextualise the form used in Jonah and its implications. In each case the themes represented in Exod. 34.7 are italicised:

Exod. 20.5-6   *I the* LORD *your God am a jealous God, punishing children for the iniquity of parents, to the third and the fourth generation of those who reject me,* but showing steadfast love to the thousandth generation of those who love me and keep my commandments.

Exod. 34.6-7   The LORD, the LORD, a God merciful and gracious, slow to anger,
and abounding in steadfast love and faithfulness,
keeping steadfast love for the thousandth generation,
forgiving iniquity and transgression and sin,
yet by no means clearing the guilty,
but visiting the iniquity of the parents
upon the children
and the children's children,
to the third and the fourth generation.

Num. 14.18	The L<small>ORD</small> is slow to anger, and abounding in steadfast love, forgiving iniquity and transgression, *but by no means clearing the guilty,* *visiting the iniquity of the parents* *upon the children* *to the third and the fourth generation.*
Deut. 5.9	*I the L<small>ORD</small> your God am a jealous God, punishing children for the iniquity of parents, to the third and fourth generation of those who reject me.*
Jer. 32.18	You show steadfast love to the thousandth generation, *but repay the guilt of parents into the laps of their children after them.*
Joel 2.13	Return to the L<small>ORD</small>, your God, for he is gracious and merciful, slow to anger, and abounding in steadfast love, and relents from punishing. Who knows whether he will not turn and relent, and leave a blessing behind him,
Jon. 4.2	a gracious God and merciful, slow to anger, and abounding in steadfast love, and ready to relent from punishing.
Nah. 1.3	The Lord is slow to anger but great in power, he will by no means clear the guilty.
Ps. 86.5, 15	For you, O Lord, are good and forgiving, abounding in steadfast love to all who call on you. But you, O Lord, are a God merciful and gracious, slow to anger and abounding in steadfast love and faithfulness.
Ps. 103.8-9	The L<small>ORD</small> is merciful and gracious, slow to anger and abounding in steadfast love. He will not always accuse, nor will he keep his anger for ever.
Ps. 145.8	The L<small>ORD</small> is gracious and merciful, slow to anger and abounding in steadfast love.

Neh. 9.17, 31	But you are a God ready to forgive, gracious and merciful, slow to anger and abounding in steadfast love, and you did not forsake them. Nevertheless, in your great mercies you did not make an end of them or forsake them, for you are a gracious and merciful God.
2 Chron. 30.9	For the LORD your God is gracious and merciful, and will not turn away his face from you, if you return to him.

What is striking about this arrangement is that the principal negative voices are from Torah. The other two negative witnesses (Jer. 32.18 and Nah. 1.3) only glancingly advert to the central motif – and Nahum makes no mention of grace or mercy. A question naturally arises: does Torah represent a more rigorous interpretation of an earlier blessing, or have a diverse range of other tradents (Psalmists, the Chronicler and the Ezra–Nehemiah source, and Joel) elected to soften the blessing? When I put it in that way, I am tempted to regard the 'kinder' saying as prior, since the three Torah instances are clearly interdependent and probably reflect just one (hard-line?) position. But then I note that Joel appears actively to modify the Torah form, rather than simply reporting the rather bland formulation found in Psalms, Chronicles and Nehemiah. This might hint at a more complex development in which Joel represents a rejection in turn of Torah's insistence on formal judgement. One obstacle to this might be that it is somewhat counter-intuitive to propose a Torah perspective dependent on, at the earliest, Psalm 86. This objection can be somewhat softened by the recognition that Exodus 32–34 may be amongst the later strands in the book's composition.[4] Happily we do not need to resolve this question for the purposes of our understanding of Jonah's point of view, which can be taken as a rejection of Joel's position. The wider context is informative for it implies that there lies behind the book of Jonah a sharper divergence about the significance of the mercy formula in antiquity than is often supposed.

To sum up: Torah imposes a limit on the mercy formula, reserving Yahweh's right to punish those who are 'guilty' to three or four generations – an expression unique to Exod. 20.5; 34.7; Num. 14.18; and Deut. 5.9. The simple statement of Yahweh's mercy and grace is found in

---

4. Dozeman provides a very detailed analysis of the compositional history of Exod. 32–34 in which he broadly concludes that much of this material (including the mercy formula) is from a later strand familiar with both Deuteronomy and Kings. See especially pp. 575–80, 688–700, and 735–6.

Psalms, Chronicles and Nehemiah. And a further version, in Joel and Jonah, has the appearance of a deliberate attempt to reverse the express purpose of the Torah category by allowing Yahweh to 'repent' of the imposition of punishment (*ra'ah*). Jonah, of course, firmly rejects that amelioration, a fact that surely indicates some kind of current dispute or disagreement amongst Jonah's fellow religious experts in Jerusalem. Or, more accurately, amongst the religious compatriots of the author of Jonah. For this to have the consequence which follows in v. 3 must imply more than a nice theological debating point: to which we shall return.

> ³'*And now, O* LORD*, please take my life from me,*
> *for it is better for me to die than to live'.*
> *And the* LORD *said, 'Is it right for you to be angry?'*

At this point, unlike 3.10, we are presented with a direct communication between Yahweh and Jonah in response to Jonah's death-wish. The thought that it would be better to die than live is not exactly paralleled anywhere else, though there are a number of expressions of a similar kind. Job and Jeremiah both deplore their birth, in various ways cursing that unfortunate event (Job 3.11; 10.18; Jer. 15.10; 20.14-18), and Job directly expresses a desire for death (7.15-16; cf. 9.21; 10.1). The idea that something might be better than their present circumstances is found in Exod. 14.12 where the Israelites complain that it would be better to serve Pharaoh than die in wilderness, and twice in Qoheleth (4.2: the dead, who have already died, are more fortunate than the living; 7.1-3: mourning and death are better than life and laughter). The second of these is the most striking:

> A good name is better than precious ointment,
>   and the day of death, than the day of birth.
> It is better to go to the house of mourning
>   than to go to the house of feasting;
> for this is the end of everyone,
>   and the living will lay it to heart.
> Sorrow is better than laughter,
>   for by sadness of countenance the heart is made glad.

While there is no question of a direct borrowing in either direction, the fourfold repetition of the adjective 'good/better' (*tov*) and the use of the verb 'to make glad' (*yatav*) has a suggestive similarity to the use of 'better' (*tov*) and 'to be right' (*yatav*) in Jon. 4.3.

Yahweh's question remains unanswered, though its reiteration in a more specific form in v. 9 does elicit a response. One subtle verbal feature stands out: Jonah's (unique) protest that it is *better* (*tov*) to die is picked up in Yahweh's 'Is it right?'. The Hebrew here is literally 'Is it good?', using a verbal form of the adjective 'good'. The NRSV's 'Is it right?' implies a moral dimension which is not obviously present in the text. In which case the conversation might go along the lines of:

> JONAH: I bitterly resent, Yahweh, your leniency towards wrongdoers. It would be better to die than go on living with such moral laxity.
>
> YAHWEH (*rather avoiding the question*) Is it really appropriate for you to be so angry?

Perhaps Jonah's silence at this point is a well-merited snub: Yes, Lord, you know what's at stake and my anger is entirely fitting!

On Elijah

At this point the nods in the direction of the legends associated with Elijah which have appeared at several points become full-blown reference, and the linking of the two figures takes on a compelling force. Because this is a theme which has been frequently described in detail[5] and about which there is little controversy, I shall set out concisely the relevant coincidences for my purpose, which is to imagine that the author presents Jonah as in some sense 'channelling' Elijah (to use a concept no doubt alien to the original readers), but with significant differences. Why Elijah serves this purpose will be examined in due course.

(a) Even the very first words of Jonah provide a hint, though not uniquely, at the author's purpose. As Wolff points out in his commentary (pp. 97–8), the pattern 'the word of Yahweh came to X, saying' is a form characteristic of Hebrew prophetic narrative. It is found frequently in Jeremiah and Ezekiel, and five times in Zechariah. Its use elsewhere is limited to nine examples – 1 Sam. 15.10; 1 Kgs 6.11; 12.22; 16.1; 17.2, 8; 18.1; 21.17, 28 – and it may be significant that five of these are found in the Elijah traditions. What seems to be happening here is not that the author of Jonah 'quoted' this aspect of these traditions, but rather that the many other indications of their use influenced (perhaps unconsciously) the adoption of this particular formula to set Jonah's story in motion.

---

5. For example Wolff (pp. 168, 172), Sasson (pp. 284–5), Youngblood (p. 168).

However there is one further dimension which is pertinent, namely that the Elijah cycle (1 Kgs 17–19, 21) and the Jonah story are the only two narrative sequences in Tanakh which use this specific introductory formula, and use it more than once.

(b) The phrase 'Get up and go' in Jon. 1.2 is a lot less common than we might expect, as I observed in Chapter 10; so much so that there is good reason to believe that Jonah here is explicitly calling as witness the behaviour of Elijah in 1 Kgs 17.9-10. There are only a few other examples of this imperative combination of verbs (though various forms of 'he, she, they' got up and went are found). In Num. 22.20-21 a very similar construction is used of God's instruction to Balaam to go to Moab, while in Jer. 13.4, 6 the prophet is told to 'get up and go' to the Euphrates, followed in 13.5, 7 by his positive response (both of these are clear parallels to 1 Kgs 17.9, 10). In a different mode, in Mic. 2.10 it is the prophet who seems to be instructing the wicked to depart; there is no evidence that they obeyed. In the Song of Songs (2.10, 13) the lover twice demands of his beloved, 'Arise my love, my fair one, and come away'. Finally, there is the plaintive demand made of God repeatedly in the Psalms: 'Rise up, O Lord' (Pss. 3.7; 7.6; 9.19; 10.12; 17.13; 74.22; 82.8; 132.8 = 2 Chron. 6.41) which is as much a liturgical set piece as a real prayer expecting an immediate answer. In short, Jonah is clearly aligned with Elijah, with perhaps a glance at Jeremiah. The case of Balaam, who is summoned from the Euphrates to pronounce a curse against the invading Israelites, affords an interesting contrast: the opposite direction of travel, a curse instead of a call to repentance, and the instruction comes from a Moabite king rather than Israel's god.

(c) The next hint lies in Jonah's flight – the first of two. On the surface this is presented as a flight from the burden of carrying out Yahweh's unreasonable demands; I have already suggested, however, that there may be another way to see this: as an escape from an irate audience not best pleased by being tarred as guilty of 'great wickedness'. Such a reading would bring Jonah's flight here into a much closer parallel with that of Elijah, fleeing for his life from the wrath of Jezebel.

(d) Jonathan Magonet builds one of his allusive sequences on the image of Jonah fast asleep in the hold of the ship, finding a suggestive connection with the similar scene in which Elijah falls asleep under the broom tree. He points out that the phrase 'he lay down and slept' (1 Kgs 19.4) is similar to that in Jon. 1.5, though the latter uses the rarer verb *radam*, as I noted in Chapter 2. It is of interest that Jonah is *not* said to sleep beneath the gourd, even though the context of 4.6-7 seems to imply that he would have. Magonet sees this as an example of the author's distribution of source material across diverse parts of the book. In another contrast we find that Elijah's 'normal' sleep led to a vision (1 Kgs 19.5b-7) whereas Jonah's 'visionary' sleep let to a rude awakening by the sailors.

(e) Both prophets are found in places of shelter at different points in their stories: Elijah under a broom tree, Jonah under a gourd; Elijah in a cave, Jonah in a booth which he made for himself.[6] Jonah additionally sleeps in the hold of the ship, and finds refuge inside the whale. This need for security, to use a modern psychological trope, is in the case of both prophets a response to their dispiriting experiences of the impenetrable divine will. Elijah, seemingly the victor in his contest with the prophets of Ba'al, suffers crushing despair as his triumph turns to ashes, while Jonah, as we have seen, believes himself to have been forced against his will by the unreliable God he is nevertheless compelled to serve. Elijah confronts his own inner demons when he flees to Beersheba and seeks death. I commented above (p. 178) on the way that this theophanic experience on Mount Horeb at the same time both condemns implicitly the violence of Elijah's treatment of the prophets of Baal and yet concludes with the intimation of yet further bloodshed and violence in Yahweh's cause (1 Kgs 19.17-18). Further evidence, if we need it, of the apparently perverse character of God, the inscrutable subject of much of the prophetic witness. I shall delay further explication of this observation at present, pending a discussion of the way that Jonah 4 taps into 1 Kings 19.

(f) In Jonah 3, despite the size of the city having been given as three days' wide, he only journeys one day into Nineveh; similarly Elijah journeys just one day into the wilderness (1 Kgs 19.4). However, he takes forty days and forty nights to reach Horeb. Compare Jonah's forty days' warning of God's impending punishment on Nineveh.

(g) After the story of Naboth's vineyard, Elijah pronounced an oracle damning Ahab and Jezebel (1 Kgs 21.20-24); on hearing this Ahab put on sackcloth and fasted (v. 27). As a result God promised to delay the 'disaster' (*ra'ah*) until the reign of Ahab's son. There are surely some parallels with Jonah 3.[7]

(h) The close similarity between Jonah's death wish (4.3, 8, 9) and that of Elijah (1 Kgs 19.4) has long been noted. The wording of 4.8 is closest to 1 Kgs 19.4. The point is once again that the author of Jonah makes explicit use of 1 Kgs 19.4 while adding a unique twist which – though it sounds familiar and obvious, is entirely characteristic of this work.

(i) Youngblood (p. 164) sets out in tabular form a list of five comparisons between 1 Kings 19 and Jonah 4. Only two have not yet been noted. One is the fact that in both accounts God/Yahweh poses the same question

---

6. The Hebrew is *sukkah*, which gives its name to the Feast of Sukkot in Judaism.
7. I am indebted to Cary, p. 114 for this observation.

twice. 'What are you doing here, Elijah?' (1 Kgs 19.9, 13), eliciting the response that his enemies seek to take his life; and 'Is it right for you to be angry?' (Jon. 4.4, 9).

(j) Finally, in both stories the deity communicates with Elijah/Jonah by means of natural phenomena: wind, earthquake and fire on the one hand (1 Kgs 19.11-12), and a bush, a worm and a burning easterly wind (Jon. 4.6-8) on the other.

I submit that there is a powerful case for the sequence of Elijah legends as an important source for the form and content of Jonah, and that this further must have substantive implications for our ultimate reading of the book, since it is clear that we are being directed to view Jonah sub specie Elijah. I will take this up again at the end of this chapter, and in my conclusions in Chapter 13.

> **⁵Then Jonah went out of the city and sat down east of the city, and made a booth for himself there. He sat under it in the shade, waiting to see what would become of the city. ⁶The LORD God appointed a bush, and made it come up over Jonah, to give shade over his head, to save him from his discomfort; so Jonah was very happy about the bush. ⁷But when dawn came up the next day, God appointed a worm that attacked the bush, so that it withered. ⁸When the sun rose, God prepared a sultry east wind, and the sun beat down on the head of Jonah so that he was faint and asked that he might die. He said, 'It is better for me to die than to live'.**

This section of the final encounter encompasses the remaining 'appointments' by Yahweh and Jonah's final despair. It is worth noting that while the ostensible purpose of Jonah's new location is to await the outcome of the events of ch. 3, this objective is quickly forgotten – another of the author's pointed gaps within which we as readers will be expected to seek meaning.

> *⁵Then Jonah went out of the city and sat down east of the city, and made a booth for himself there. He sat under it in the shade, waiting to see what would become of the city.*

At this point Jonah's 'exile' from the city seems relatively peaceful. Having made his case to Yahweh, and seemingly resigned to the fact that he can do nothing, he makes a 'booth' in which to shelter. As with most of the language of Jonah, the booth – *sukkah* – is a word pregnant with meaning, and by now we can be sure that the author wants us to recognize that fact. The commonest meaning is in relation to the autumn festival (fifteen times), with another five represented by poetic language such as darkness or thunder as God's canopy (2 Sam. 22.12 = Ps. 18.11; Job 36.29) or a protective divine covering (Ps. 31.20; Isa. 4.6). Any reader at all familiar with the Hebrew scriptures would identify with these references, suggesting that Job's shade here has a deeper religious meaning. Reinforcing this cultic dimension, 2 Sam. 11.11 refers to the Ark being in booths, while Amos 9.11 looks forward to the eschatological restoration of 'the booth of David' – whatever that may be. There are two instances of what looks like an agricultural practice of setting up shelters in which watchers could protect the ripening fruit in autumn (Isa. 1.8;[8] Job 27.18) and an etymology in Gen. 33.17 which appears to use the term with the meaning of 'cattle-shed'. It has been suggested in the past that the festival use is based on such agricultural practices, but these three instances are really too limited to form the basis of any such theory. I would conclude that Jonah here is almost challenging God to rise to the occasion: 'Here I am in your symbolic shelter: what will you do now?'

I must, however, report one last usage. In 1 Kgs 20.12 and 16 we find a description of Ben-hadad of Syria relaxing during a military campaign:

> When Ben-hadad heard this message – now he had been drinking with the kings in the booths – he said to his men, 'Take your positions!' And they took their positions against the city.
> They went out at noon, while Ben-hadad was drinking himself drunk in the booths, he and the thirty-two kings allied with him.

Perhaps, after all, there is no cultic significance to all this. Jonah just went down the pub for a couple of pints while awaiting God's verdict!

> [6]*The* LORD *God appointed a bush, and made it come up over Jonah,*
> *to give shade over his head, to save him from his discomfort;*
> *so Jonah was very happy about the bush.*

What happens now is interesting, for the two main players seem at this point to lose interest in 'the city', preferring to wage their own peculiar war of nerves. Yahweh's first move is to disconcert the grumpy prophet by making his shelter even more comfortable. The idea of a living plant[9]

---

8. It may be relevant to the wider discussion in this book that Isa. 1.7-9 has already been noted in the context of the Sodom and Gomorrah theme. It has more than a purely agricultural reference.

9. I do not propose to enter into any discussion here of the qiqayon's identity, following Good's wise advice (p. 51) that 'It does not matter, and we would as soon get satisfaction by trying to identify the variety of Jack's beanstalk.'

growing up around the *sukkah* fits well within the background of the way that the Feast of Sukkot was celebrated – very much a harvest event given historical emphasis by means of the 'reminder' that (Lev. 23.43) 'I made the people of Israel live in booths when I brought them out of the land of Egypt'.[10] We should not imagine that the author of Jonah was familiar with Sukkot as described in the Mishnah, some 500 years at least after his time, but as one of the three central festivals of Second Temple Jerusalem he must have known its significance.

A reminder: the English translation above is rather anodyne. Yahweh is *rescuing* Jonah from his *calamity* (that word *ra'ah* again); and it might be closer to the mark to say that Jonah was *ecstatic*. The adjective 'great' is used here and 'sang for joy'. These details would make the festival context still clearer to a Hebrew reader. Just as the Israelites were redeemed out of Egypt, so is Jonah saved from his affliction. The comparison is, of course, bathetic. Jonah is being set up, his rather narrow focus on his own probity and comfort due for a well-deserved fall. At least he will have one good night's sleep before God appoints the next instrument of Jonah's misery.

> *⁷But when dawn came up the next day, God appointed a worm that attacked the bush, so that it withered. ⁸When the sun rose, God prepared a sultry east wind, and the sun beat down on the head of Jonah so that he was faint and asked that he might die. He said, 'It is better for me to die than to live'.*

Enter a worm. Whether or not this was the little creature which I included in my *dramatic personae* is of no matter. God could have brought this unique insect into being *sui generis* to gorge itself at Jonah's expense then die (that being the only plant in the vicinity). Just what sort of plant this was that could grow and disappear so quickly has of course been the subject of much speculation. I will content myself here with just one: Pyper (pp. 343–4) suggests that the *qiqayon* is a concretisation of the seaweed in 2.5. 'The weed crops up in the story of the plant that grows to shade Jonah in 4.6. Weeds are literally wrapped around or covering his head in this strange episode'. He further proposes a pun: that *qiqayon* relects the *qi'* of the whale's vomiting in 2.10. The real point is 'I told you so!' If Jonah thinks God is fickle and inconsistent, let him suffer the consequences of his own belief. The kind of God whose putative forgiveness

---

10. There is no reference to any such practice in Exodus, During their sojourn in the wilderness the people no doubt sheltered in tents (Hebrew *'ohel*; also one of the terms for the 'tabernacle', the portable wilderness shrine, also referred to as *mishkan*).

of Nineveh is a mere whim certainly cannot be relied on to keep Jonah comfortable. There is an ironic consistency here: if Jonah wants to stick to his high principles, let him live (or die) with them. Yahweh is certainly happy to oblige in the form of an object lesson in real time.

Yahweh's mind games here belong to the same category as the mystifying events experienced by Elijah on another mountain. The prophet who had used fire and bloody slaughter to teach the prophets of Ba'al – and their sponsor Jezebel – a lesson they would never forget is discomfited when the God he thought he knew frankly eschews storm and earthquake and fire in favour of a sound so faint it was little better than the hint of a murmur. You surely don't, in Elijah's world, confront the enemies of Yahweh by whispering to them. Do you? You surely don't, in Jonah's world, deal with the wickedness of the great city by letting them off with a first oral warning. Do you?

Whether or not Elijah actually got that message is a discussion for a different book. What seems clear, however, is that Jonah didn't get it. As the bush withers and the sun beats down and the hot wind scours his exposed flesh, Jonah's response is utterly self-absorbed. The reader gets the message: we read that Yahweh *appoints* both the worm and the wind – just as he had appointed the gourd and the whale – and just as the worm *attacks* the plant, so the sun *attacks* Jonah's head. Jonah faints from heatstroke, and even here the author plays with the sounds of words. The word used for 'to faint' is very rare, and is not the same as the synonymous term used in 2.7, 'my life *ebbed away*'. This should alert us to the possibility of a deliberate choice: so it is not surprising to find that there is in Hebrew a pronounced assonance amongst the words *come up* (v. 6, of the plant), the *worm* (v. 7), the *rising* of the sun (v. 7), and Jonah's *fainting* (v. 8).

Jonah is of course in no position to appreciate the finer points of literary technique; all he can do is reiterate his earlier complaint. 'I'd rather be dead than go on living like this'. But the context makes a significant difference, which will play into Yahweh's hands, for what troubles Jonah now is no high ideal, no moral principle, but simple personal distress. And even comparisons with Job which are sometimes made are inappropriate: the loss of one's entire family and property and an affliction of painful boils surely puts into the shade (*sic*) the discomfort of sunburn. I may do Jonah something of an injustice, but there is an important point here: Yahweh has reduced Jonah to the point of mere self-pity, and will use that humiliation to complete the lesson.

⁹But God said to Jonah, 'Is it right for you to be angry about the bush?' And he said, 'Yes, angry enough to die'. ¹⁰Then the LORD said, 'You are concerned about the bush, for which you did not labour and which you did not grow; it came into being in a night and perished in a night. ¹¹And should I not be concerned about Nineveh, that great city, in which there are more than a hundred and twenty thousand people who do not know their right hand from their left, and also many animals?'

⁹But God said to Jonah, 'Is it right for you to be angry about the bush? And he said, 'Yes, angry enough to die'.

Yahweh puts the question to Jonah a second time, but with a difference. Now it is not anger in some principled form that Jonah is accused of, but rage at the dying of a bush. How fitting is such anger? How *good* is it for Jonah to feel like this? To which his response is something like 'I do well to be angry enough to die'. There is a hint of resignation about Jonah's last words, as though he now understands what God is up to. The fight's gone out of him, and all he can do is hear God out.

As we approach the conclusion of the book of Jonah I would like to draw attention to another two structural points. One concerns the name which the author uses to refer to the deity. As we might expect, there is a fair degree of consistency of usage: thus Yahweh, the personal name peculiar to Israel, is used in the narrative itself where we understand Jonah's god to be the prime mover (1.1, 3, 4, 17; 2.1, 10; 3.1, 3; 4.2, 4, 6, 10). It is also used by Jonah (1.9; 2.2, 6, 7, 9; 4.2, 3), and by or in respect of the sailors after Jonah has revealed his religious identity to them (1.10, 14, 16). The generic word for God (*'elohim*) is used by the sailors (1.5, 6) and by the Ninevites (3.5, 8, 9), and in tandem with Yahweh (e.g. Yahweh my God etc.) in 1.9; 2.1, 6; 4.6. A third term, *'el* is found once, in 4.2 in the quotation of the mercy formula – probably because this is the form used in Exod. 34.6. So far this usage is perfectly logical on the assumption that God's special name is reserved for Israelite use.

There are two interesting variations on this pattern. The first is in 3.10 where we are told of the divine change of mind with regard to Nineveh. Although this is part of the narrator's text, the term *'elohim* is used: perhaps to draw attention to the unusual application of the principle of the God of mercy beyond the boundaries of Israel. The second is more striking, for in 4.7, 8 and 9 it is *'elohim* who appoints the worm and the east wind, and who challenges Jonah for the second time. I do not believe this is accidental, though its purpose is not fully clear. My best suggestion is a deliberate sign that a degree of alienation has found its way into the discourse between Jonah and his god, a proposal reinforced by the observation that while it was 'Yahweh Elohim' who (kindly) provided the bush, it was 'Elohim' who destroyed it. If so, this is modified in the end, for the final speech is given once more to Yahweh.

The second structural point concerns the distribution of material in ch. 4, and was pointed out by Sasson (p. 317). On a word count (and bearing in mind the uncertainties of such estimates) Jonah's monologue in vv. 2-3 and Yahweh's in vv. 10-11 each have 39 words. Perhaps this helps to emphasise the importance of these two closing speeches – one for the prosecution, perhaps, the other for the defence. The central section, vv. 5-8, consists of a 'worked example', the literal trial of Jonah's patience and his commitment in the face of God's relentless teasing by first easing Jonah's condition and then causing him dis-ease. Bracketing that passage are the two questions from God to Jonah about the appropriateness of his anger (vv. 4 and 9), the second of which elicits a grudging response from him.

The proposal that we can think of Jonah 4 as in some fashion a legal proceeding is not unprecedented. For example, Job's rhetoric often resorts to a quasi-legal challenge: 'Speak to me, Lord, so that I can challenge you to explain yourself' being a typical refrain, and the concluding chapters have been understood as a speech by Yahweh as defendant, prosecutor and judge rolled into one. Looked at in this light, Jonah opens his case by charging Yahweh with culpable leniency and seeks a remedy, which is to be freed from his insufferable life. He then retires to consider whether his charge will be proven by Yahweh's forgiveness of the city. But the defence has other weapons in its armoury: hence the drama of the booth, the bush, the beetle and the blazing sun. Classic diversionary tactics which force Jonah to take the stand again with a much-weakened case: fainting from exposure to the elements he can only whisper 'It would be better for me to die than live'.

The cross-examination then begins with God's reiteration of his insistent question, 'Do you do well to be angry' – though now God adds 'about the bush', which reduces Jonah's complaint to something less than momentous. All this opens the way to Yahweh's concluding peroration, that notoriously open-ended declaration which brashly exacerbates the original charge by suggesting that the divine ethic demands automatic care for those who have no way of knowing what the issues of right and wrong entail. The verb used here (*chus*) is interesting. It is not that common, and in most cases (sixteen in number) it has a negative use: a stern refusal of compassion or pity for those who are Israel's enemies or those who have sinned, and the subject is most often God. If the word was familiar to ancient readers, its application in a positive sense might have seemed somewhat disruptive, adding to the now familiar sense that the author is intent on wrong-footing readers. Of the five more positive instances, where someone pities someone else, two are of particular interest as having a bearing on Jonah. In Ps. 72.13, a prayer for the king, the psalmist asks that he might 'have pity on the weak and the needy'. And in Joel 2.17 – in the same context as that prophet's version of the mercy formula – we find this prayer: 'Let the priests, the ministers of the Lord weep. / Let them say, "Spare your people, O Lord"'.

I shall pass over the question of the size of Nineveh's population,[11] since it was either unknowable to the author, or is in fact a guess (almost certainly wildly exaggerated) at the number of inhabitants in Jerusalem at the time of writing. As to the matter of whether people knew their right from their left hand, there is no obvious consensus. Some have suggested that the reference is to children – a most unlikely reading since it would imply an enormous number of pre-teens in Nineveh. Others go for a meaning somewhere in the field of knowing right from wrong, but this also leads to the assumption of a vast number of ignorant, or morally illiterate, citizens. Sasson (pp. 314–15) covers most of the options in his commentary, pointing in particular to the one place (in Qoh. 10.2) where a specific connection is made between right and left on the one hand and wisdom and folly:

> The heart of the wise inclines to the right,
>   but the heart of a fool to the left.

The implication would be that the people of Nineveh as a whole were pushed to tell the difference between sense and nonsense: bear in mind that this is a population which dressed its cattle in sackcloth and instructed them to fast! It is tempting to add this to our steadily growing set of associations between Jonah and Qoheleth, but caution reminds me that these rather loose links could be established with a little ingenuity between many otherwise unrelated materials.

The conclusion is not provided. We are being invited, I think, to infer in the first place that Yahweh favours mercy over strict justice and pity over punishment, and in the second that (contrary to most legal codes) ignorance of the law is a proper defence. Does this mean that the author of Jonah is in turn proposing what we might term a liberal theological agenda?

---

11. I will have more to say about both the numbers of inhabitants and the 'right hand/left hand' question in Chapter 12.

I will stop for now on that unanswered question, just as the book itself ends on a similar note. Indeed it is one of only two books in Tanakh which ends thus,[12] the other being Nahum: 'For who has ever escaped your endless cruelty?' (3.19). That Nahum is one of the possible source texts for Jonah, and that its oracle is ostensibly against Nineveh, provides a poignant pairing. On the one hand, (the book of) Nahum asks rhetorically if anyone can escape the cruelty of Assyria; on the other, (the book of) Jonah asks, also rhetorically(?), whether Yahweh should not take pity on Nineveh, that great city.

Coda

The Mercy Formula

There is I believe an inner-Judaic argument about the precise character of the mercy formula and its application. Is it only pertinent to Israel, or does is have a wider remit? The setting in Exodus and Deuteronomy is firmly within the special covenant of Yahweh with Israel: does Jonah's careful avoidance of the term $b^e rit$ imply a deliberate challenge to that assumption on the part of the author? Further, the evidence of disagreement about the existence of and extent of any punishment which might qualify the bare statement of mercy points to a lively debate within the religious circles from which the author came.

Elijah

We must surely accept that the pairing of Jonah and Elijah is central to the book. Elijah, like Jonah, seems to have been a flawed, combative individual unable to accept compromise and with a clear sense of his own worth and importance. Both he and Jonah are confronted by Yahweh in ways that fundamentally challenge their sense of calling and identity, and do so in the direction of a more generous, rather more gentle understanding of the nature of Yahweh.

---

12. Some have argued that the lack of a direct signifier for a question in this final verse means that it is in fact a direct statement that Yahweh should not be concerned for Nineveh and its inhabitants. Thus Cooper and Guillaume; the latter insisting that the final meaning of the book is that, contrary to the expectations of the naïve reader, Yahweh is indeed a God whose decrees cannot be manipulated. Jonah's initial mission was true.

The Open-ended Conclusion
If the book is in some sense a contribution to a debate rather than a piece of polemic, we might read it as a provocative but nonetheless orthodox essay in setting out religious and ethical choices and dilemmas. The ending in that case hands the judgement over to the 'jury' – the readership both then and through the ages.

Chapter 12

THE LORD'S FONDNESS FOR LIVESTOCK*

My aim in this chapter is to offer a more leisurely review of the treatment of animals in Tanakh; in particular, those we think of as domestic cattle. We are prone to think of their part in Jonah as strange or eccentric, bordering on the merely whimsical: a judgement, I suspect, based on a rather traditional view of animals as being without feelings or intelligence, belonging to a radically different order from ourselves. Despite the lessons of Darwinism, it remains the case that advocates of animal rights, better treatment for our fellow creatures, and entailed forms of human consumption such as vegetarianism and veganism are mostly at best tolerated or regarded with condescending humour, and at worst seen as dangerous fanatics.

In a review of the role of animals in Jonah, Yael Shemesh (pp. 2–4) identifies the singularity of that book's approach in the context of a centuries-long and persistent anthropomorphising of animals which, at best, values them only for their relevance to the human condition. She observes (pp. 4–5):

> The anthropocentrism that excludes animals from the ethical domain casts light on the extent to which the final words of the book of Jonah, 'and many beasts,' are not self-evident and may even be unexpected. Nevertheless, not only is the idea that the Lord has compassion for animals expressed in the Bible, it is particularly appropriate for the book of Jonah.

Her article addresses a number of the specific points touched upon in this work, and broadly supports my own conclusion that we cannot simply dismiss Jonah's language about animals as a mere quirky device, but rather as the reflection of a much more serious ethical position.

* The content of this chapter is drawn mainly from Hunter (2016), and is used here with permission.

The Treatment of Animals in Tanakh

The most obvious first place to go for a parallel to Jonah's fixation with cattle is Qoheleth, where we find a seeming elision of whatever difference we may like to imagine exists between humankind and the rest of the animal kingdom. I refer of course to Qoh. 3.18-22:

> I said in my heart with regard to human beings that God is testing them to show that they are but animals. For the fate of humans and the fate of animals is the same; as one dies, so dies the other. They all have the same breath, and humans have no advantage over the animals; for all is vanity. All go to one place; all are from the dust, and all turn to dust again. Who knows whether the human spirit goes upwards and the spirit of animals goes downwards to the earth? So I saw that there is nothing better than that all should enjoy their work, for that is their lot; who can bring them to see what will be after them?

In Jonah – leaving aside the whale and the worm – the focus is on cattle (*behemah*), but another term is also widely used with a broadly similar reference, namely *chayyah*, literally 'living creatures': these two will define the boundaries of this enquiry. Both of these terms refer almost exclusively to four-footed creatures,[1] and *behemah* seems to refer to larger, possibly domesticated animals. This is the usage which seems to be implied in Jonah, but we may note, however, that the famous discussion in Qoh. 3.18-22 does not necessitate that restriction. *Chayyah* has an obvious etymology in the root *chayah*, 'to be alive', and includes both wild animals ('the beasts of the fields') and domesticated herds. There is no known etymology for *behemah*, though older grammars used to postulate an otherwise unknown related verb *baham* with the supposed meaning 'to be mute'. Perhaps the thought was that cattle are 'dumb animals' – a categorisation most today would find offensive; there is no support for this biblical usage beyond the well-known declaration in Isa. 53.7:

> ... yet he did not open his mouth;
> like a lamb that is led to the slaughter,
> and like a sheep that before its shearers is silent,
> so he did not open his mouth.

---

1. It is clear that there are many other life-forms named in Tanakh, things that creep, crawl and slither, and things that fly or swim. These belong to separate categories, and are not part of the present discussion. Indeed, some of the dietary and purity rules make it clear that they occupy a separate cultural niche.

Whatever this metaphor means, it cannot surely be literal dumbness; more likely the sense is that, just as animals cannot articulate their feelings in any language we as humans can understand, so the servant chose(?) to suffer without protest. While on the subject of spurious etymology, I cannot resist pointing out the rare form *bahemmah* ('with *or* by means of them', Exod. 30.4; 36.1; Hab. 1.16) and suggesting, mischievously, that the animals are named *behemah* because they are our close companions.

Since it is the term *behemah* that is found in Jonah and Qoheleth, my primary concern is to elucidate further its use and meaning in Tanakh more widely.

The first possibility to dispose of is the natural hypothesis that the latter term is more general – that the class of *behemah* forms a subset of all *chayyot*, specifically referring to domestic animals. There are undoubtedly places where this is so, and Modern Hebrew usage follows this line. But it is by no means the only, or the most dominant, usage in Tanakh, and it is important to examine these others more closely. The results are rather surprising.

Semantic Equivalence and Difference

(1) There are a number of passages where the two terms seem more less equivalent. The most striking are Gen. 3.14, where they are in parallel, and 1 Sam. 17.44 and 46 where very similar phrases are repeated using first *behemah* and then *chayyah:*

> Gen. 3.14: The LORD God said to the serpent, 'Because you have done this, cursed are you among all animals (*behemah*) and among all wild creatures (*chayyath*); upon your belly you shall go, and dust you shall eat all the days of your life'.

> 1 Sam. 17.44 and 46: The Philistine said to David, 'Come to me, and I will give your flesh to the birds of the air and to the wild animals of the field (*behemah*)' ... 'This very day the LORD will deliver you into my hand, and I will strike you down and cut off your head; and I will give the dead bodies of the Philistine army this very day to the birds of the air and to the wild animals of the earth (*chayyah*), so that all the earth may know that there is a God in Israel.'

While the Samuel passage is a simple equation of terms, the Genesis case raises other intriguing possibilities. The fact that the serpent is to 'eat dust' is not unrelated to the 'dusty' conclusion of all life, and the fact that Eve, whose name in Hebrew can be connected to the same root as *chayyah*, is the mother of all life (Gen. 3.20), both serve to strengthen the already strong likelihood that there are links between Gen. 3.19 and Qoheleth.

They suggest two things: that Adam is one of the animals, and that the use of *behemah* in Qoheleth is not restricted to cattle.

(2) A related pairing is found in Gen. 8.19 and 20. In v. 19 *chayyah* refers to 'every animal' (but not creeping things and birds) emerging from the ark after the flood, while in v. 20 *behemah* is used in a general sense to refer to all *clean animals*. While this might imply that *behemah* is a sub-category of *chayyah*, in Lev. 11.26-27 in a passage discussing *unclean* animals both terms are used with that meaning. Even more confusingly, there is a set of passages where *behemah* refers to both clean and unclean animals (Gen. 7.2, 8; Lev. 7.21; 20.25; 27.11; Deut. 14.6; Ezek. 8.10; 44.31).

(3) Lastly under this heading I note a number of examples of the use of *behemah* to refer to animals in general – though always distinct from creeping things and birds. Loosely associated with the creation and flood themes we find Gen. 6.7, 20; 7.23; 1 Kgs 4.33; Ps. 8.7. The last of these is of some interest because it seems to class these creatures with other domestic breeds:

> all sheep and oxen,
> > and also the beasts of the field;

unless, of course, the second line is contrastive rather than complementary! For there are also a number of explicit references to *behemah* as 'wild animals': thus Deut. 28.26; Job 35.11; Prov. 30.30; Isa. 18.6; Jer. 7.33; 15.3; 16.4; 19.7; 34.20; and Mic. 5.7. Apart from Prov. 30.30 and Mic. 5.7, these all use 'beasts of the land' rather than 'beasts of the field' which might suggest that the balance in Ps. 8.7 is in favour of the reading 'domestic beasts'.

The conclusion of this review is that there is no real support for interpreting these two terms as anything other than synonyms in Biblical Hebrew usage. I now turn to other specific ways in which *behemah* is used, some of which will be of relevance to its deployment on Jonah.

Cultic and Prophetic Uses
References to *behemah* in cultic contexts include some quite suggestive parallels. Thus they are included in the ban on working on Sabbath (Exod. 20.10; Deut. 5.14); they can be stoned for encroaching on the sacred mountain (Exod. 19.13); and they are found praising God, with *chayyim* and other created life, in Ps. 148.10. Negatively, the ban on bestiality (Exod. 22.18 and parallels) suggests a conception of a shared nature which is consonant with widespread cultural myths about the offspring of the miscegenation of humans and animals. All of these imply a oneness

of essence not unlike that which I shall argue is presupposed by both Qoheleth and Jonah. Add to these verses like Ps. 36.6 'you save (*yasha'*) humans and animals alike, O Lord', or Pss. 50.10 and 104.14, which express God's care for both humans and animals; in this regard, Joel 2.21-24 is particularly striking:

> Do not fear, O soil;
> be glad and rejoice,
> for the LORD has done great things!
> Do not fear, you animals of the field
> for the pastures of the wilderness are green;
> the tree bears its fruit,
> the fig tree and vine give their full yield.
> O children of Zion, be glad
> and rejoice in the LORD your God;
> for he has given the early rain for your vindication,
> he has poured down for you abundant rain,
> the early and the later rain, as before.
> The threshing-floors shall be full of grain,
> the vats shall overflow with wine and oil.

The theme of animals apparently in mourning, which is such a striking feature of Jon. 3.7-8, can be found also in Judith (4.10-11), where the mistaken information that Nebuchadnezzar was king of Assyria (Jdt 4.1) might hint at an allusion to Jonah:

> They and their wives and their children and their cattle and every resident alien and hired labourer and purchased slave – they all put sackcloth around their waists. And all the Israelite men, women, and children living at Jerusalem prostrated themselves before the temple and put ashes on their heads and spread out their sackcloth before the Lord.

Joel 1.18-20 also deploys a similar motif, and our discussions of influences between Joel and Jonah make this a particularly useful parallel:

> How the animals groan!
>   The herds of cattle wander about
> because there is no pasture for them;
>   even the flocks of sheep are dazed.
> To you, O LORD, I cry.
> For fire has devoured
>   the pastures of the wilderness,
> and flames have burned
>   all the trees of the field.

> Even the wild animals cry to you
> > because the watercourses are dried up,
>
> and fire has devoured
> > the pastures of the wilderness.

Perry (pp. 47–8) notes a number of the points raised in this section, though his final note is somewhat pessimistic: 'If the Ninevites have quite correctly appealed to the principle of solidarity between humans and animals, however, their general imposition of penance upon the general populace ... has a sinister side. For one might ask: even if the general public is guilty of "evil", what about the innocent? What about children, who have not reached the age of responsibility, and animals, who may not be even capable of evil?' An Augustinian approach to 'original sin' might deal with the former objection, while Perry's citing of Montaigne's discussion of animals in his 'Apology for Raymond Sebond' (*The Complete Essays of Montaigne* [trans. Donald Frame, Stanford 1976], pp. 330–58) addresses the latter at least to the extent that Montaigne (*Essays*, p. 353) famously attributes to animals the powers of repentance, acknowledgement of faults, and clemency amongst other moral values!

Less directly, but still carrying something of the same implication, we find parallels between the treatment of the firstborn of both humans and animals in Lev. 27.26-27; Num. 3.13; 8.17; 18.15; Neh. 10.37; and note also the tenth plague (Exod. 11.5; cf. Ps. 135.8: 'He it was who struck down the firstborn of Egypt, both human beings [*'adam*] and animals'). Further, the ban on likenesses (Deut. 4.17) could be interpreted on the same lines, as could the assumption that they are suitable for substitutionary sacrifice.

Jeremiah 27.5-6 (with a parallel in 28.14 which uses *chayyah*) affords a curious link to the association of subject animals in the kingdoms of Mesopotamia. No doubt this is a coincidence – but it is a tempting one. It refers to Babylon under Nebuchadnezzar, but that scarcely affects the general point, that this affords yet another plausible connection to the book of Jonah:

> It is I who by my great power and my outstretched arm have made the earth, with the people and animals that are on the earth, and I give it to whomsoever I please. Now I have given all these lands into the hand of King Nebuchadnezzar of Babylon, my servant, and I have given him even the wild animals of the field to serve him.

There is no need to argue for direct influence at this point; it is enough that the 'strange' ideas about cattle in Jonah are in fact attested at several points elsewhere in Tanakh.

Animal Intelligence

Behind the various themes adumbrated above lurks a possibly disturbing question: are the 'beasts' sentient? Do they share with us awareness, knowledge, pain, emotional distress and pleasure, and some kind of ability to communicate? Is there, to be blunt, no categorical difference between us beyond the accident of evolutionary happenstance? Two final passages force us to look at this theme not just as a modern sensibility but rather as one which was already adumbrated in antiquity.

Job 12.7-10 is an intriguing passage. Whether it pertains to our subject is moot – but it is worth reproducing to illustrate the kind of ambiguity which surrounds the subject of the boundaries and distinctions between the animal and human realms:

> But ask the animals, and they will teach you;
> the birds of the air, and they will tell you;
> ask the plants of the earth, and they will teach you;
> and the fish of the sea will declare to you.
> Who among all these does not know
> that the hand of the LORD has done this?
> In his hand is the life (*nephesh*) of every living thing
> and the breath (*ruach*) of every human being.

Presumably this passage is metaphorical – certainly the idea of birds, plants and fish literally 'teaching' is not one which we would normally entertain; nevertheless the conclusion, that everything living knows that *nephesh* and *ruach* are ultimately in God's power is clearly a *shared* knowledge. Incidentally, the use of the verb *yada'* in the context of animals is rare: apart from this instance, Qoh. 3.21 and Jon. 4.11, it is only found in Pss. 50.10-11 and 73.22; the Job passage is the only one which attributes 'knowing' directly to non-human life; however, I shall modify this point in the concluding commentary.

Lastly in this survey I submit a verse which is beloved of animal rights campaigners: Prov. 12.10, which seems to come some way towards expressing a contemporary sensitivity to animals. Since it is isolated, not too much weight should be placed on it; nonetheless it is intriguing:

> The righteous know the needs of their animals,
> but the mercy of the wicked is cruel.

In fact the Hebrew is even more surprising, for the English 'know the needs of their animals' renders the Hebrew phrase *yodea' ... nephesh behemto* which might signify an understanding of a beast's appetite, but could equally mean 'understand the very life of their animals', indicating empathy rather than 'mere' sympathy. The effect of the contrasting second stich is to imply that those who lack empathy with their fellow-creatures are equally likely to show little mercy to fellow-humans. A very contemporary assessment. Clearly there is no actual equality; indeed, on some readings human attitudes to *behemah* are more abusive because of the closeness (their use for sacrifice, for instance).

I conclude that there is much more to *behemah* in Tanakh than our modern clear-cut species distinctions allow for, and that in short there is plenty of evidence for the possibility that Jonah is in fact very far from satire in his incorporation of animals into the salvation story of Nineveh and the reluctant prophet. I hope this does not disappoint: it is a shame, I suppose, to lose Jonah's wonderfully bizarre conclusion. By way of consolation, I remind you that in a world of plural readings I have not displaced one with another, merely added to the rich stock of available interpretations.

This is perhaps the place to record a seemingly dissonant voice. Thomas Bolin (2010) argues that contrary to modern thought (which sees the end of Jonah as evidence of God's universal concern) the proper ancient context is that of ritual sacrifice. Thus the links between *'adam* and *behemah* in Jonah (twice in 3.7-8 and again in 4.11) belong to a deliberate authorial attack on sacrifice. References to sacrifice in Jon. 1.17, 2.10 and Gen. 8.20 are designed to emphasise that God does *not* need them, for 'they are not demanded by God, nor is their efficacy automatic or guaranteed' (pp. 105–6). Bolin's case seems to be that we should understand the *behemah* as objects of sacrifice, mimetically clothed in sackcloth in preparation for their substitutionary sacrifice. All this is no doubt to the point, but it remains arguable that their suitability for sacrifice lies precisely in their being perceived to be rather close to *'adam* in nature. Indeed, in his conclusion Bolin seems to admit this when he observes:

> As domestic beasts, the animals of Nineveh are not under Yahweh's control and indeed, they are the only non-human living thing in the book of Jonah that is not the object of the verb *manah* with God as its subject.

Bolin makes this comment in the context of a note to the effect that Yahweh cannot control, but can only coerce his human subjects; it seems the same is true of his beastly subjects.

Understanding the Beasts in Jonah

Armed with the information gleaned above, we can now approach the heart of the matter. Jonah 4.11 is my starting point:

> And should I not be concerned about Nineveh, that great city, in which there are more than a hundred and twenty thousand people who do not know their right hand from their left, and also many animals?

The subordinate clause in this verse contains two tantalising statements and poses a syntactic puzzle. What is the significance of the claim that such a large number of people 'do not know their right hand from their left'? Why are 'many animals' listed? And finally, are the animals an afterthought or should they be included in the class of ignorant beings? There is a suggestive chiastic structure to the clause which might support the contention that people and animals are in a state of shared ignorance. I can show this more clearly by setting out this verse in a manner that reveals the pattern of A-B-C-B'-A' more clearly:

> *More than a hundred and twenty thousand* **people**
>   who do not know their right hand from their left
> **and animals**   *in great number.*

The outer inclusio is a pair of large numbers ('More than a hundred and twenty thousand' :: 'in great number'); inside that is a second inclusio ('people' :: 'animals'); and the centre a statement about (their?) condition of not knowing their left hand from their right. Given the care with which the language of Jonah has been crafted it is not unreasonable to interpret this chiasmus as part of an intentional coda to the book, a deliberate extension of the inclusion of *behemah* in the ritual mourning instructed by the king of Nineveh in the previous chapter, in effect the only other reference in Tanakh (alongside Job 12.7-10) that animals might have some kind of knowing.

That said, there are aspects to this verse which challenge our ability to read it by appealing to other biblical texts. For one thing, nowhere else is there a challenge to distinguish between right and left – the middle term of the chiasmus is unique. Secondly, the phrase 'many animals' has no specific parallels, apart from one or two places where people are described as owning large flocks or herds (without the use of the word *behemah*). And thirdly, this is the only occasion where the inhabitants of a city are specifically numbered.[2] The importance of the final phrase in its setting is precisely not that it identifies the people of Nineveh as being cattle-rich;

---

2. Three other cities are described as 'large': Calah, in Gen. 10.12; Gibeah in Josh. 10.2; and Jerusalem in Neh. 7.4, where it is described as 'wide and large' but with few people and no houses. Apart from these, I can find no significant parallels to the enumeration of the population of Nineveh.

what it identifies is the presence of an equally important population of animals – specifically *behemah* – in the city.

A consideration of the pairing of 'right and left' in Tanakh shows that by far the most common uses are (a) to make it clear that some thing or some effect is present[3] either on two sides or, in some cases, to the north and the south, and (b) to express either literal or metaphorical deviation (including a choice between options). The second of these has some bearing, since it usually refers to disobedience or moral vacillation,[4] which might be thought to be the point of Jon. 4.11. In two places the reference is to a source of blessing – Isaac's contrary blessing of Ephraim and Manasseh in Gen. 48.13-14, and Wisdom holding long life in her right hand and riches in her left (Prov. 3.16). The residue consists of two passages which I want to look at more closely: Isa. 30.20-21, where the idea of moral choice is reinforced by means of a figure described as 'your Teacher' (*morekha*), and Qoh. 10.2, where the wise choose the right and the foolish the left. Isaiah 30.20-21 is tempting, but in the end it is more likely to belong with those passages which guard against deviation to the left or the right:

> Though the Lord may give you the bread of adversity and the water of affliction, yet your Teacher will not hide himself any more, but your eyes shall see your Teacher. And when you turn to the right or when you turn to the left, your ears shall hear a word behind you, saying, 'This is the way; walk in it'.

The figure of the Teacher is somewhat mysterious – is he someone different from Yahweh? (cf. the 'man of God' in Judg. 13.8 and other similar instances) – but in the end his purpose is to keep the people of Zion on the right path. The reference to not hiding himself bears comparison with Job 23.9; interestingly, the only other instance of the title 'teacher' for God is also in Job, at 36.22.[5]

Having identified these preliminary data, let me turn to a closer examination of the final chiasmus of Jonah. I shall adopt as a working hypothesis

---

3. In Job 23.9 God *cannot* be found either on the left or the right.
4. Thus Deut. 5.32; 17.11, 20; 28.14; Josh. 1.7; 23.6; 2 Sam. 14.19; 2 Kgs 22.2; 2 Chron. 34.2; Prov. 4.27.
5. The other occasions where God teaches, using the verb *yarah*, are in Exod. 4.12, 15 (God teaching Moses and Aaron what to say), 24.12 (the stone tablets 'for teaching them'); 1 Kgs 8.36 (= 2 Chron. 6.27) (Solomon refers to God's teaching Israel 'the good way in which they should walk'); Isa. 2.3 (= Mic. 4.2); 28.9, 26; Pss. 25.8, 12; 27.11; 32.8; 86.11; 119.33, 102; Job 6.24; 34.32.

the proposal that we should take seriously the claim that 120,000 *'adam* and many *behemah* share a failure to know the difference between right and left. In the setting of Jonah, what does this failure imply? I think we can at once rule out literal uses: the author of Jonah is not interested in literal wandering from a path, or in the precise placement of things. On the other hand, it seems certain that the element of choice is central to Jonah – the prophet's choice whether to obey Yahweh or not, the Ninevite's choice whether to repent or not, even God's choice about what to do with recalcitrant humans, whether prophets or Ninevites. It follows that even those passages which imply a moral deviation (listed in n. 4) are only of incidental interest. While they confirm that 'right and left' is regularly used in the realm of ethics, the predominant reference is the unacceptable nature of deviation in either direction from a strict code. Of the remaining passages, the only one which provides in the end a helpful parallel is Qoh. 10.2. But what an interesting passage it is – particularly given the other connection to be made between Qoh. 3.18-21 and Jonah:

> The wise man's mind is of the right hand, the fool's of the left.

A very clear moral distinction, and one that is (surprisingly) unique in Tanakh: only here are right and left invested with specific moral values, so that it matters that a person should be able to tell the difference. Of course, wisdom literature and Psalms are replete with references to wisdom and the wise, and folly and the fool. To cite just one striking example, Proverbs 9 dramatises the competing attractions of the Goddesses Folly and Wisdom, inviting the reader by implication to make his or her choice. Qoheleth, notoriously, challenges himself to investigate the relative merits of the two and seems – at times – to conclude that there is little advantage in the long run (2.12-26). Despite this, he never quite abandons his belief that it is, all things being equal, preferable to be wise (and, of course, to eat, drink and be merry).

A Brief Digression: Qoheleth and Jonah

Can this understanding of Qoh. 10.2 be applied to Jonah? To answer that question we need to take seriously the question of some kind of relationship between the two books. There is admittedly little or nothing in the way of direct citation of Qoheleth in Jonah, an awkward fact that stands in contrast with the undoubtedly extensive evidence of intertextual connections between Jonah and many other books – Genesis, 1 Kings, Ezekiel, Joel and Psalms, to list just a few. This would, I think, rule out any possibility that Jonah was later than Qoheleth. Qoheleth is surely a late composition, something agreed upon by the great majority of commentators. It may at first sight seem improbable that Jonah belongs in some kind of literary ensemble with Qoheleth. Nevertheless I find the proposal interesting enough to pursue a little further. In favour of some kind of intersection I note the following:

(1) Both are pseudonymous on the basis of a character from Kings, though admittedly the fame of Solomon is vastly superior to that of the obscure prophet from Gath-hepher.
(2) Both undermine the credibility of their eponymous authors: Qoheleth by his radical questioning of the value of wisdom; Jonah by his undermining of the authority of the prophet.
(3) Both address the problem of trust in God: Qoheleth by proposing a remote, arbitrary and inscrutable deity kept emphatically at arms length, and the resulting ethical dilemmas; Jonah in his encounter with an all-too-predictable God whose direct interference in the affairs of individuals and empires poses intractable ethical dilemmas.
(4) Both introduce animals, using the specific term *behemah* in surprising ways: Qoheleth by insisting on the essential similarities of humans and animals; Jonah by seemingly including them as part of the repentant population of Nineveh.
(5) Both introduce a moral dimension to the choice between right and left, and are in fact the only two biblical books to do this.
(6) Note also the intriguing use of *hevel* in Jon. 2.9 with reference to 'vain idols'. *Hevel* in Qoheleth is of course one of its key motifs, representing the 'vanity' of life.

To these I want to add one highly speculative, but interesting coda. There is in Qoh. 9.12-16 a curious little parable which has echoes of Jonah. The core of the parable (vv. 14-15) is as follows: 'There was a little city with few people in it. A great king came against it and besieged it, building great siege-works against it. Now there was found in it a poor, wise man, and he by his wisdom delivered the city. Yet no-one remembered that poor man.' For the purposes of my analysis I will set out the full context I have underlined the expressions which I wish to consider in more detail:

> For no one can anticipate the time of disaster. Like <u>fish</u> taken in a <u>cruel net</u>, and like birds caught in a snare, so mortals are snared at a time of <u>calamity</u>, when it suddenly <u>falls</u> upon them.

> I have also seen this example of wisdom under the sun, and it seemed <u>important</u> to me. There was a <u>little city</u> with <u>few people</u> in it. A <u>great king</u> came against it and besieged it, building <u>great siege-works</u> against it. Now there was found in it a poor, wise man, and he by his wisdom delivered the <u>city</u>. Yet no one remembered that poor man. So I said, 'Wisdom is better than might; yet the poor man's wisdom is despised, and his words are not heeded.'

I note the following points:

(1) The adjective 'great' (*gadhol*), which is remarkably frequent in Jonah, is hardly visible in Qoheleth, but three of its four occurrences are in this brief pericope. One is to be found in v. 13 ('it seemed important ["great"] to me'); and two in v. 14 ('a great king'; 'great siege works').

(2) The combination of 'little city' and 'great king' is striking. Bearing in mind that one of the likely contexts for Qoheleth is the beginning of the Seleucid period when Syrian rulers were taking a disturbing interest in the Levant, it is tempting to see in this combination one of the sieges experienced in Jerusalem at that time. The echo of Jonah's dealings with Nineveh is palpable – is he to be understood as the 'poor, wise man' here?

(3) The terms translated as 'cruel' and 'calamity' are from the verbal root *ra'ah* which is another key expression in Jonah, especially in relation to the character of the 'great city' and its wickedness.

(4) The Hebrew terms for both the net in which the fish are caught and the siege works in which the city is about to be trapped come from the same verbal root (*tsod*); it is a curious coincidence that in Gen. 10.8-12 where Nimrod is presented as the founder of the 'great city' Nineveh, he is described (v. 9) as a mighty 'hunter' (*tsayid* – from the same root).

(5) There are not many references to a 'great city' in Tanakh. Apart from Jonah, Gen. 10.12, and Gibeon in Josh. 10.2, and the implication of the etymology of the name *Rabbah* (great?) in 2 Samuel 11, there is one intriguing description of Jerusalem in Neh. 7.4: 'The city was wide and large, but the people within it were few …',[6] reflecting the state of affairs when the first group of exiles returned. The lack of inhabitants contrasts with the large numbers given in Jonah.

---

6. Note in contrast Isa. 49.20, where the children born in exile complain of Zion, 'The place is too crowded for me'.

The coming together of so many allusions which chime with the language and themes of Jonah, particularly ch. 3, is suggestive. My subjective response is to find here a writer playing knowingly with a familiar disruptive source and shaping it to their own equally subversive purposes. So, did Qoheleth and Jonah know each other? I suspect that there is some crossover – and if I were to hazard a guess it would be that Qoheleth, already familiar with Jonah's deconstruction of the high claims of prophets and prophecy, took on as a parallel endeavour a similar undermining of the unquestioned authority of kings and the received wisdom of the sages. In doing so he did not copy Jonah, but emulated him, planting for our pleasure the odd incident in 9.12-16 and extending to its logical conclusion his understanding of the nature of animals.

Behold Behemoth

Returning to the main argument of this chapter, I believe that there a strong case for linking the way in which animals are regarded in Jonah and Qoheleth, and that this reinforces the proposal that they are to be understood as having a form of existence which is not wholly other than that of humankind. This means that they can indeed be understood to experience innocence and guilt, that they can be faced with moral choice, and that it therefore makes sense for the king of Nineveh to include them in the rites of repentance, bizarre though it may appear to our modern sensibilities. This also suggests that whatever we mean by the 'spirit' (*ruach*) of humankind it is the same as that of the animals, and suffers the same fate.

Qoheleth's position is reinforced by his deliberate citation of Gen. 3.19 through which he implicitly extends the rubric 'dust to dust' to animals as well as humans.[7] In turn this association suggests that the use of *behemah*

---

7. There is, incidentally, considerable reluctance in some circles to recognize this connection. Despite the fact that it is the closest parallel to the Genesis saying anywhere in Tanakh, the cross-reference edition of the NRSV allows no link at all. It offers Job 10.9 and Ps. 103.14 as parallels to Gen. 3.19. Qoh. 12.7 (a much less radical statement of the same theme) is allowed as a parallel to Ps. 103.14 and to Gen. 2.7 – but not, incidentally, to 3.20! The only direct parallel indicated is to Sir. 16.30 – and there, at last, the assiduous explorer will find the following list of parallels. Gen. 3.19; Job 34.15; Ps. 104.29; and Qoh. 3.20 and 12.7. The whole process reminds me of childhood game in which you start with a word, look up its definition in the dictionary, and then repeat the process with that definition as starting point to see where you end up – either in a circle, back at the word of origin, or (preferably) at some quite unexpected conclusion. I confess that the principles underlying the

in Gen. 3.14, which we noted earlier, might for Qoheleth have been more inclusive than we normally take it to be. The serpent – who, after all, has the gift of speech – is counted amongst all *behemah*; Eve is 'the mother of all that live', a self-aware biblical pun (Gen. 3.20) which connects Eve's Hebrew name – *chawwah* – with the word for 'living being' – *chayyah*. In fact both names are punning references to the origins of life, for *'adam* was literally shaped by God (Gen. 2.7) out of dust from 'the ground' – *'adamah*. He is quite literally a part of the Hebrew earth. Right from the start, if we read Genesis correctly, the first couple symbolise the dust of the earth and the breath that gives them life. There is no difference in essence between them and all living creatures.

The proposition which these various observations lead to is that there is a case for taking Jonah's references to animals literally, rather than (or in addition to) modern sensibilities which are inevitably drawn to explanations such as hyperbole, satire, or irony. There is an interesting precedent in Greek thinking, which the writers of Jonah and Qoheleth may well have been aware of: namely, the Pythagorean concept of transmigration of souls and the one-ness of human and animal souls. The date and cultural milieu of both books renders this at least possible, suggesting that the chiasmus in Jon. 4.11 is not simply a throw-away parting shot, but a reminder that in the eyes of God the king of Nineveh (and the prophet of Yahweh) belong to the same moral universe as the lowly *behemah*.

If, then, Qoheleth and Jonah between them have succeed in reducing human pretensions by emphasising their oneness with animals, perhaps there is comfort to be drawn from the magnificent presence of the semi-divine *Behemot* of Job 40.15-24. The first of God's great acts (v. 19), just like Wisdom herself (Prov. 8.22), this mighty creature challenges our own pretensions to supremacy, and reminds us that Jonah's conclusion is not after all so odd: there is a commonality to life, both in its everyday needs and in its divine aspects, that we do well to remember.

Coda

Recent publications have raised the profile of the importance not just of animals for our understanding of ancient Hebrew and other cultures, but of what can best be described as 'the whole Earth'. The 'Earth Bible

---

process of cross-referencing seem at best unclear, and at worst to exemplify (at least in this instance) a theologically influenced choice. NIV isn't much better – though it does allow a link between 3.20 and Gen. 2.7. (Another interesting example of interpretative cross-referencing from the same context is the linking of Gen. 3.15 with Rom. 16.21, which succeeds in introducing Satan to Eden by a sleight of hand.)

Project' hosted by Normal C. Habel is only one – albeit high-profile – example from which a stream of publications has issued (see https://www.sbl-site.org/publications/article.aspx?articleId=291). One monograph in particular, Mari Joerstad's *The Hebrew Bible and Environmental Ethics* (2019), takes the 'person-ness' of inanimate entities wholly seriously in a wide-ranging reflection on their shared participation biblical thought in their own right, and not simply as metaphors for human experience. She cites recent work on 'new animism' as one context for her analysis. There is much food for thought in these developments, though not in the present volume.[8]

---

8. In this context I note a recent publication of which I have only been able to see a review: Jione Havea's *Jonah: An Earth Bible Commentary* (Earth Bible Commentary; London: T&T Clark, 2020).

Inconclusions

The author of Jonah wisely fell silent just when the book's readers might reasonably have expected closure. The gap thus created has been a fruitful source of putative completions – as the author may well have intended. None of these have proved to be conclusive, nor have any won wholehearted support; again, one might guess, as the author hoped. I see no reason not to follow in an honourable tradition in this final chapter. In recognition of the inevitable futility of what follows, however, I have elected to describe these musings as *inconclusions*, a word which nicely comprehends both the validity of the enterprise and its inherent failings.

Inconclusion One: The City and the City

Throughout this book I have returned regularly to the centrality of Jerusalem and its educated elite as the primary, if unspoken focus of the book of Jonah. My starting point was Marian Kelsey's important recognition of the way that Nineveh constitutes a surrogate for Jerusalem. On the basis of her insight I propose to redefine Jerusalem not just as the implied metaphoric reference of Nineveh but as the actual but 'unseen' referent of the book as a whole. Such a reading is at first sight counterintuitive, given the explicit nature of the plot and its overt references. However, there are many indications in support of such an approach, and I have indicated these at numerous points in the foregoing chapters – sometimes in the form of occasional codas at the end of certain chapters.

A key symbolic move is my deployment of the fictional work of China Miéville, one of whose books has inspired the title of the present section. More importantly, his insights into urban forms of being seem to me to offer a fruitful metaphoric key to what is going on in the book of Jonah. Specifically, I refer to the psychogeographical dimension of many of his books, a reminder that literate urban experience is not an objectively defined relationship between intellectuals and fixed and inanimate built environments, but rather a mutually reinforcing – and constantly renewed – interaction between *two* fluid realities. Miéville's most explicit realisation of this relationship is to be found in his eponymous *The City and the City* (see my acknowledgement in the Prologue, and the passage on Psychogeography and the Coda in Chapter 1).

In particular I turn to his fascinating idea of 'unseeing', which seems to me to have much wider application than its use as a technical device in Miéville's book. I do not intend to misrepresent what he has achieved – of course the device has profound implications for both the ambience and the plotting of *City* – I simply mean to suggest that what is a seemingly alien stratagem in the book can be readily applied to 'normal' lived experience. It serves, in short, to explain the apparent gap between the 'overt' and the 'covert' in the book of Jonah. I shall have more to say on this topic in Inconclusion Three; for now I simply want to insist that the first readers of Jonah would not have been in the least baffled by its apparent – but entirely misleading – concern for the conversion of the citizens of a long-vanished city, and would have been perfectly capable of 'seeing' the other city occupying the same space as that Mesopotamian ruin.

Sandor Goodhart offers an interesting Jewish-perspective example of this congeries of approaches. His thesis is that the rabbis were not mistaken in associating Jonah with Yom Kippur because the central theme of Jonah is in the end the rejection of idolatrous sacrifice in favour of that associated with the mercy of Yahweh. But that very rejection can itself become idolatrous if it is regarded as a protected merit confined only to the Israelites. The choice of Nineveh is not accidental: the Hebrews originally (in the biblical tradition) came from Mesopotamia, and risk a metaphoric return if they fetishize their special position before Yahweh. Sandor interprets the qiqayon as a symbol of the intention to guard or protect this privilege; Jonah's response to its destruction is no mere petulant rage over his personal discomfort, but anger at the loss of his (i.e. Israel's) special position. Israel *was* Nineveh; in becoming Israel it eschewed idolatrous sacrifice. But it becomes Nineveh again by making an idol out of their having become Israel. 'Israel is what Ninevah (*sic*) is becoming as it turns away from the idolatrous sacrificial ways of its past, and, moreover, what it is in danger of becoming once again should it make an idol of that transformation itself. … Jonah is the Israelite who would reserve the revelation of the law of anti-idolatry for himself and God's interaction with him serves to deconstruct that position … in two distinct ways: in such a way that Jonah can understand it …, and in such a way that through Jonah's recognition we can see it as well' (p. 56). This is a subtle, interesting, and not insignificant reading; but it nevertheless constrains the book by forcing Jonah into an allegorical straightjacket and risking the pejorative conclusion – even if it nowhere expresses this explicitly – that somehow the religion of post-exilic Israel is at risk of falling into an introspective exclusivism.

More generally, those for whom the reading they took from the book was uncomfortable or unacceptable had the option to 'unsee' their own city and to focus exclusively on the 'what if' of the fishy tale of the prophet sent by Yahweh to Nineveh. It is instructive to note that most of the history of the reception of Jonah, certainly in Christianity, falls firmly into that category in its insistence that the conversion of the pagan Ninevites is the main point upon which any meaning must centre. Whether it is a lesson about the breadth of God's mercy and the intransigence of Israel, or about the struggle within Jerusalem over a narrow *versus* a broad understanding of Yahweh's remit, or even a moral tale about prophetic obedience and the ineluctable word of God, it matters for most of these readings that a city full of non-Israelites repented and thereby earned God's forgiveness.

My proposal is to accept that both for modern 'sophisticated' readers and for ancient 'educated elites' in Jerusalem the story is equally preposterous and self-evidently demanding of a reading informed by the very many clues planted in the text for those with the knowledge and the will to see them. This is, of course, the burden of my commentary, informed throughout as it is by its deep and pervasive intertextuality. There is hardly any phrase, scarcely any word, which would not have sounded loudly in the ears of those who first encountered this material. This is the burden of my work of contextualisation in the Introduction: I shall have more to say about readers, authors, narrators and characters in Inconclusion Two. For now I will end this reflection by turning back to a comment of Sherwood's which I used in Chapter 10:

> The fact that the King of Nineveh already possesses and quotes Scripture undermines any interpretation of Jonah as a book about missionising, or taking the Bible to the gentiles (since insofar as anyone 'has' 'the Bible' in the world of Jonah, everyone has it) and reinforces the pervasive atmosphere of the (literally) *unheimlich*, in which home and the 'bloody city' have changed places. (p. 265)

Just as Miéville's two cities are alienated from each other and must be consciously and mutually *unseen*, so, to use Sherwood's terminology, Nineveh and Jerusalem are mutually *(un)heimlich*. Yet both, in the end, are one.

Inconclusion Two: Voices

In the Coda to Chapter 5 I commented briefly on the hierarchy of voices in Jonah. By 'voices' I mean three things: those responsible for the text; those participating in the text; and those reading (or otherwise receiving) the text. In summary they are:

The narrator (*not* to be confused with the author).
Yahweh; the Word of God; Jonah; the ship's captain and crew; the
    King of Nineveh and his spokesperson.
The original 'audience'.
The author of this book.

It should be noted that the third group is usually subdivided into such notional figures as 'the intended reader', 'the implied reader', 'the actual first readers', and any other identifiable groups in time by whom the text is read. This last category might include persons such as 'Gospel writers', 'Church Fathers', 'Rabbinic scholars', 'Reformation figures', 'academic scholars' and 'individual readers of a religious bent'. This is obviously not a complete list, but insofar as such figures might comment on or contribute to the understanding of the text we call the book of Jonah, they have a legitimate role. A few observations are in order: (1) none of these groups can be recovered or identified objectively; (2) circular argumentation is unavoidable, particularly regarding the first three categories, since the text itself is a material witness to their identity; and (3) the remaining groups are largely known by their commentaries, sermons, fictions, etc., and are in modern parlance covered by the field of *reception history*. I intend to confine myself to a consideration of 'the actual first readers', in line with much of what I had to say in the Introduction.

In the book of Jonah the text is distributed across the six speakers listed above and the narrator. The pattern is suggestive, particularly (as we shall see) when it is compared with a similar text. There may be a number of possible candidates for such a comparison, such as other books in the collection of Twelve Prophets, or embedded prophetic cycles in the historical material, of which the Elijah sequence (1 Kgs 17–19, 21) is the most obvious. I propose that the criteria should include, in addition to the presence of a key prophetic figure: (a) similar length; (b) dating in the same era; (b) the inclusion of a substantial narrative dimension; and (c) evidence of some concern around issues relevant to the post-Ezra period. A tempting option is the story of the birth and coming to maturity of Samuel in 1 Sam. 1.1–4.1, which has the further advantage of the inclusion of a 'psalm' passage in the form of Hannah's prayer; in another context, with more space to develop this theme, it would be worth looking more closely at both this sequence and the Elijah traditions. However, it is questionable whether they are close enough in date to Jonah, and the central cultic questions seem somewhat remote from the Persian period. I confine myself, therefore, to others of the Twelve. Here I think there is one clear front-runner: the book of Haggai. It is of approximately the same length as Jonah, includes significant narrative matter, contains in outline at least a plot concerning the rebuilding of the temple, and features a prophet (Haggai) about whom nothing is known, and whose name is somewhat strange. The name appears to relate to a verb meaning 'to dance' or 'to celebrate a festival': not normal terms for a personal name. The work's likely composition date is in a range similar to that of Jonah, and the central concerns of each book were crucial to the postexilic Jerusalem community. In the case of Haggai, we note that the re-establishment of the temple – the only specific cultic locus which is named also in Jonah – was of supreme importance in the defining of what we might legitimately designate *New Israel* as the second temple inheritors of the pre-exilic religious traditions. And in Jonah the question of how to understand the Exodus mercy formula is ultimately the central question.

The comparison that follows is based upon words in the NRSV version, admittedly a fairly crude unit of measurement, but sufficient for the purpose of a broad overview.

Jonah (1355 words)	Haggai (1348)
Narration: 589 words (43.5%)	Narration: 578 words (42.9%)
Prophet's speech: 329 words (24.3%)	Prophet's speech: 51 words (3.7%)
Other speakers: 312 words (23%)	Other speakers: 5 words (0.4%)
Divine speech: 125 words (9.2%)	Divine speech: 714 words (53%)

Two features stand out: the proportion given to narration is almost the same in both, but there is a huge difference in the relative allocation to human and divine speech. If we discount the poem in ch. 2 of Jonah, an interesting parity emerges in that Jonah's words (158) and those of Yahweh and 'the word of the Lord' (125) become much more proportionate. Indeed, as Sherwood (p. 273) notes regarding ch. 4 (her word count is based on the Hebrew text),

[a]t the very heart of the book of Jonah's reputation as a strange interloper in the biblical is the *equity* and *legitimacy* given to Jonah's voice. Jonah's words and Yhwh's words are split with mathematical precision: in a pedantic commitment to dialogism they get absolutely equal air-time, and thirty-nine words, or pieces, each. ... [A]s they set out their words, God and Jonah suddenly seem more like fellow-disputants (or yeshiva partners), than (gigantic) God and (baby) man, and the text that at first looked like a strategy game for one begins to change to something more like a chess board.

The difference between Haggai and Jonah, then, is one of *authorial* choice. Whereas Yahweh's speeches – albeit mediated by the narrator, Haggai, and 'the word of the Lord' – dominate the former, they form less than a fifth of that total in Jonah. And, in consequence, the proportion of speech allocated to human voices is in Jonah twelve times what it is in Haggai. We are directed in our reading to the stand-off between Jonah and Yahweh in Jonah, while Haggai is used merely as a rather traditional prophetic cipher. In addition, we are presented with non-Israelite voices – again a rather rare feature, certainly in the prophetic books – who demonstrate a familiarity with Tanakh. I submit, therefore, that, in addition to what we have already identified as characteristics of the author in our earlier discussion, we now know that the author's agenda includes a deliberate distortion in favour of a face-to-face confrontation between Jonah and Yahweh. Moreover, that confrontation is further emphasised through the way that the alien parties both demonstrate familiarity with Tanakh and a readiness to fall in line with Yahweh. Note that, despite the tendency to confuse author and narrator in a number of studies, all of this demonstrates a clear authorial *and not narratological* purpose[1].

---

1. Craig's otherwise useful study of the poetics of Jonah suffers significantly in this regard. Thus (p. 46), 'The narrator in Jonah could, if he chose, undertake to tell us what any of the characters felt at *any* moment, but consistently conveys information at the moment which suits his strategy best'. Cf. p. 94: 'The author seems to delight in creating discrepancy in awareness both among characters on the one hand and the audience on the other'. Similarly Person devotes a chapter to 'Narrative in the Book of Jonah' which has many merits, but also seems to elide any difference between narrator and author. Thus p. 83, 'The narrator in the book of Jonah is clearly omniscient. ... In fact, his explicit references to omitted dialogue suggest that this narrator even likes to flaunt his power and control over the material.' But then, p. 89, 'In summary, the author of the Jonah narrative has crafted a text which utilizes various strategies in the development of the different narrative elements'. It is perhaps not surprising, then, that Levine (1996, p. 177) observes that the author is '*universally* overlooked by students of the Book of Jonah'.

The significance of this is that – perhaps unlike Haggai – the authorial presence is strongly felt in the sense that it by no means results from a merely editorial function. Rather, authorial intention is a palpable driving force. Incidentally, if this is not a circular observation, it suggests a further reason to be sceptical about redactional stages or inserted material in some imagined *ur*-Jonah.

Given that the author chooses both the characters and the form of the narrative, what role can be imputed to that mysterious figure, the narrator? The most pressing question is undoubtedly, 'Why does this figure exist?' The narrator is not omniscient, has no privileged insights into character, and as a character cannot be questioned as to authorial intention or divine purpose. My proposal is that we see this persona as analogous to that of the trickster in legendary material, a figure whose effect is to confuse and disconcert, and through whom the fundamental oddness of the relationship of humankind to the gods is revealed. Tanakh is not without such figures: characters in the Jacob traditions are the most obvious candidates, but we might think also of the serpent in Eden and aspects of the Samson tales.[2] A core function of the trickster is misdirection, a phenomenon which is striking in the book of Jonah; but it is noteworthy that the victim of the narrator's trickery in this case is not another character, but the reader, whose entirely justifiable expectations are repeatedly disappointed. And the final twist, the final disappointment, comes right at the end when the character Yahweh poses that notorious unanswered/unanswerable question. As we have already seen, the narrator's deceptions include the omission of key information, disruption of chronology, turns in the narrative counter to genre expectations, and a seeming disregard for propriety – which last phenomenon has prompted many to find satire, irony or pastiche in the book.

If this is an accurate perception, the question then begged is why the author might engage in such a contorted process. Pyper (p. 358) hints at this in his brief characterisation of the author: 'Jonah is the work of a poet, a rereader of difficult texts, a master of the techniques of serious play with his material, who manages both to acknowledge and satirise the power of the tradition and the misreadings that it spawns', and Ben Zvi (p. 101) reminds us that the first readers and the author almost certainly moved in the same social group and shared a similar education and world views. But to go further requires a considerable effort of imagination, not to mention speculation, since the answer can only lie in what the author wished to achieve, who were the readers whose expectations were frustrated, and what discourse might have been anticipated as a result.

2. See further Hunter (2006, pp. 251–5).

I will return to these questions under Inconclusion Four, though it is worth reiterating that author and original readers were almost certainly drawn from the same intellectual and cultural milieu. I agree with Ben Zvi in rejecting the common perception (see for example Burrows p. 105) that the most likely intended readers were the conservative reform followers of Ezra and Nehemiah. Thus Ben Zvi (pp. 99–101):

> Contrary to the still common idea that the book is a kind of satire that comes from a particular group or groups and is aimed at other contemporaneous groups in society ... [I argue] that the book of Jonah reflects and carries a message of inner reflection, and to some extent critical self-appraisal of the group within which and for which this book was written. ... It follows that they would have construed the implied author in a way that resembled the actual author, and would not have identified him/her with a group they were vehemently opposed to.

And further, Person (pp. 95–6; he is discussing *implied* readers):

> [A]n author, who writes within a particular literary tradition, crafts the text according to some generic standards with a particular range of readers in mind. ... What readers bring to interactions between texts and themselves can be understood as simply the other side of the interaction. That is, if authors draw from literary traditions and history in the construction of texts, then readers bring their particular knowledge of their tradition (and possibly others) based upon their own experiences.

My only mild dissent from these opinions is that I am not convinced of the need to differentiate between a 'real' and 'implied' author on the one hand, or between 'real' and 'implied' readers on the other. The distinction seems to suggest that we might be better placed to find the 'implied' versions in each case; I am of the opinion that they are equally (in)accessible and so for practical purposes can be merged into one 'reader' and one 'author' *simpliciter*.

Turning finally in this inconclusion to the voices of the characters, I want to distinguish the two major proponents, Yahweh and Jonah, from the others. Craig (p. 64) points out that the 'story's principal characters, Jonah and the Lord, are the only ones who have a name and therefore an identity'.[3] This is an interesting suggestion, but I wonder if it is entirely

---

3. He cites here Meir Sternberg's argument that if 'for a biblical agent to come on stager nameless is to be declared faceless, then to bear a name is to assume an identity: to become a singular existent, with an assured place in history and a future in the story'.

plausible. Certainly the Ninevites and their rulers are little more than caricatures, but surely the sailors are shown to have real human feelings and natural reactions. This is perhaps best seen in the way that the term for fear, *yara'*, is used in an increasingly intense fashion: in v. 5 they are 'afraid'; in v. 10 they are 'even more afraid'; and in v. 16 they fear Yahweh with a great fear (NRSV. 'the men feared the Lord even more'[4]). And surely, even within the limits of the book's fantastical framework, readers would empathise with the very real threat faced by this innocent crew, and the way that they engage in increasing panic with the probable source of their troubles: thus the captain's urgent plea in 1.4, followed by the sailors' direct questioning of Jonah (1.8-10), their attempt to find a solution in the face of the mounting storm (1.11), their brave efforts to save the situation despite Jonah's advice (1.13), and finally their guilt-ridden acceptance of what appears to them in the end to be inevitable (1.14-15).

Both the ship's crew and the Ninevites have ruling figures – the captain and the king – and in both cases it is the more anonymous group which initiates action. The actions of the captain and the king (through his herald), while important, are not by themselves enough to ensure the desired result: the ship's crew elicit responses from Jonah and carry out the deed which saves the ship; the people of Nineveh respond to Jonah and initiate the action which saves the city. Also the speeches given to these figures include material crucially dependent on a knowledge of Tanakh: thus 1.14 and 3.8b-9. Moreover, there is no dimension of conflict between them and Yahweh: they accept both the reality of Yahweh and accept without question the validity of the divine will. Interactions between Jonah and these figures are also non-confrontational, at least as far as the overt narration reveals. Many commentators suggest that Jonah's proclamation to Nineveh in 3.4 must have been either derisory or provocative, but the narrator's voice at this point is perfectly neutral, and the people's response is of unquestioning acceptance.

I submit, therefore, that in terms of the text as presented the distinction between the named and unnamed groups lies not so much in their having clear identities (after all Jonah is largely a psychological enigma and Yahweh is in essence a mystery, as Exod. 3.13-14 shows), but rather in the nature of their relationship *within the text*. That this is ultimately of the essence is seen in the pattern of responses throughout,

---

4. See Trible, p. 151, for a clear exposition of the escalating nature of the Hebrew text in this manner.

whose culmination in ch. 4 is the singular face-to-face confrontation between Jonah and Yahweh. That pattern can be set out schematically as follows:

A	1.1-2	The word of Yahweh speaks to Jonah	no response
	2.2-10	Jonah's prayer to Yahweh	no response
	3.1-2	The word of Yahweh speaks to Jonah	no response
B	1.6-14	The captain, the sailors and Jonah	many responses
	3.4-9	Jonah's prophecy	the king's proclamation
C	4.1-11	Jonah and Yahweh	many responses

What is unique in the end is that *only* Jonah has any active interaction with Yahweh, and this is emphasised by two things: the fact that Jonah interacts with others at earlier stages, and the fact the Jonah and Yahweh effectively ignore each other at earlier stages.

Enter Elijah. At the end of Chapter 11 I wrote:

> We must surely accept that the pairing of Jonah and Elijah is central to the book. Elijah, like Jonah, seems to have been a flawed, combative individual unable to accept compromise and with a clear sense of his own worth and importance. Both he and Jonah are confronted by Yahweh in ways that fundamentally challenge their sense of calling and identity, and do so in the direction of a more generous, rather more gentle understanding of the nature of Yahweh.

This is important for our understanding of the voices in Jonah, for it is beyond doubt that the author expected readers to be fully aware of Jonah's channelling of the older prophet. In addition to the numerous similarities reviewed in Chapter 11, one other merits particular attention. A close reading of the dramatic episode on Mount Carmel in 1 Kgs 18.20-40 shows that nowhere does Yahweh directly instruct the mass slaughter of the prophets of Ba'al. The only direct instruction to Elijah is in 18.2, 'Go, present yourself to Ahab; I will send rain on the earth'. In the drama itself undoubtedly Yahweh is presented as answering Elijah's prayer by sending fire to consume the altar and the sacrifice as a demonstration of divine power. But that is all. The prophet's actions in v. 40 – the gruesome killing of the prophets of Ba'al – is strictly his own initiative. In sum, then: to all the other parallels between the two we must add the charge of an arrogant usurpation of divine authority. Both Jonah and Elijah believe they know better than Yahweh, and both are shown to have to pay in consequence, and that consequence is played out in the paired passages 1 Kings 19 and Jonah 4.

Inconclusion Three: Unseeing

The dimension of *unseeing* in the book of Jonah is remarkable. Almost every important motif from the religious and social history of Israel as transmitted in Tanakh is blanked in Jonah. Including Israel, as Ben Zvi (p. 62 n. 78) notes: 'Jonah is the *only* prophetic book in the Hebrew Bible that contains no reference to Israel at all'. Jerusalem is unnamed – despite the inclusion of three other urban centres. There is no mention of the covenant, though its existence is loudly indicated in the intertext. And the Exodus, though discernible in the interplay of ch. 2, is skilfully masked. All of these I have treated in detail in earlier chapters; at this point I want to reflect not on the fact of unseeing but its significance.

In *The City and the City*, unseeing is willed and personal, as well as being enforced by quasi-legal constraints. No-one is unaware of the alternative presence, equally no-one publicly admits it. The manner in which the book of Jonah is constructed invites, indeed persuades, the literate and knowledgeable reader to see behind the artifice and to make the appropriate adjustments; to 'see' in fact that the focus is Jerusalem, the people are Israel, and the sins which rise up to Yahweh are their own. The dilemma which then presents is how to relate to Jonah himself – a conundrum which has foxed readers for more than two millennia. The core problem is that we know next to nothing about his motivations: the only exception being the famous explanation after the event in 4.2. And even that is ambiguous. It is commonly read as a sign that Jonah was a hard-liner, in that he resented any possibility that Yahweh might relent. But suppose that Jonah in this speech is applying the maxim to himself; that is, he felt free to flee to Tarshish in the confident expectation that Yahweh would not hold it against him. Subsequent events have shown that he was seriously mistaken, so that now he finds himself alienated both from God and from the city – whatever the result of his proclamation – and death is the only way out. This interpretation is not incompatible with my argument in Chapter 11 that Jonah's anger is in part prompted by the facile and cynical 'repentance' of Nineveh. It is a case of 'heads you win, tails I lose' in that Jonah failed to be shown the compassion which he now suspects is about to be granted to the worthless people of the city. How galling is that – and we can surely find some sympathy for him in his confusion, and understand that (a) he thought (back home) that Yahweh's mission was likely to end like this, and (b) he fled thinking (wrongly) that

God would be consistently compassionate. On this understanding Jonah is a realist rather than intolerant, but is also naïve as regards the God he serves.

The drama of Jonah's experience in the depths makes Jonah the focus of a retelling of the cultic history of Israel as a personal story of condemnation, punishment and redemption. As I have shown in earlier chapters, the flood, the legend of Sodom and Gomorrah as a symbol of punishment for evil, and the exodus as Israel's redemptive myth are recognisably 'unseen' in Jonah. Opening one's eyes to these themes is to accept (as a Second Temple Jerusalemite) that there is no easy road to the recovery of the covenant relationship with Yahweh. Unbreakable it no doubt is, from the divine perspective; but it is also impossibly demanding from a human point of view. So this reading of the character of Jonah comes at a high cost, but it is a noble vision, encouraging the response: 'Yes, we are Jonah, we too have plumbed the depths and lived the sacred history'.

But the author has set a trap: for the instinct which quite properly admires the psalm and its suffering servant must then deal with the equally full-on portrait of Jonah as a man clearly in the wrong, opposed to Yahweh, who must in the end be humiliated. No matter how we read the character of Jonah, this is someone who keeps getting it wrong: wrong in his reading of the original commission, wrong in his understanding of the mercy formula, wrong in his belief that Yahweh would stand by him whatever happened, and wrong to imitate Elijah's desire for death only to end up in a bathetic stand-off with Yahweh.

So, yes 'We are Jonah'; but that is not a boast but a confession. And if the well-being of the city rests with us it is surely in the most fragile of hands. For the salvation of the city (in one possible reading of the open ending) is that without Jonah's public admission that he was wrong, the fate of Nineveh/Jerusalem remains unresolved. In the fourth inconclusion I will return to this paradox, for it is tied up with the unresolvable issue of the morality of God and the uncomfortable truth that Jonah, for all his stubborn recalcitrance and his apparent refusal of the mercy code, is an honourable man who is (on one reading) badly treated by (not to mince words) a bullying deity.

But now comes another twist, deriving from my thoughts on the banishment of Jonah in the Codas to Chapters 5 and 8. Linking the strange urgency of Jonah's headlong flight at the beginning of the story with the word used in ch. 2 to describe that episode, I concluded first of all, that

> Jonah's home is either in or close to Jerusalem. Flight to Yapho and hence across the sea is then, obviously but surprisingly, an escape from Jerusalem. The passionate nature of his prayer [in Jonah 2] falls into place when we

realise that he did not run from Jerusalem to escape God or avoid Nineveh, but because he understood the meaning of the great and sinful city, and feared the consequences of proclaiming to his own people a message that might effect a radical change.

In Chapter Eight I took this argument a stage further, noting that the word used to express his having been 'banished' has a particular theological resonance which implies not *flight* per se, but *being put to flight against one's will*. From that starting point I then suggested that one of the narrator's 'gaps' occurs between 1.2 and 1.3, and that accordingly 'Jonah did *not* reject God's first instruction. Indeed, he preached against Jerusalem, that great and wicked city, and was in consequence banished for his pains – a fate not unknown in prophetic experience. Verse 3 then should be read as 'So Jonah set out to flee …' rather than 'But …' (both are true to the Hebrew). The words of the psalm turn out then to be a true reflection of Jonah's experiences and an accurate depiction of his faith'. The plot thickens as we try to sum up Jonah. An honest man, a mistaken man, a disappointed man, a brave man, a man willing to stand by his beliefs whatever the cost? Or a weak man, a coward with no thought for others, an embittered and envious prophet, a fool who clings to the impossible long after others have thought better? Maybe we would, on reflection, be better advised to unsee.

Inconclusion Four: A Moral Dilemma

It is a fact not often enough admitted that Tanakh is a remarkably moral collection. Not in every aspect, of course, and not always a morality that would be recognized as appropriate in the post-Enlightenment world, but a morality nonetheless which is humanly directed. A perhaps facile comparison with the Greek gods might make the point. There is nothing in Tanakh which matches the rivalry, squabbling and pettiness of the Olympians, whose treatment of humans is always in the interests of their own concerns. Maybe the Greeks were in fact closer to a pragmatic understanding of the reality of the human condition with its arbitrariness and casual, meaningless suffering – at least from a sceptical point of view. Nevertheless there is much in the Hebrew tradition which indicates a real concern not just with the demands of Yahweh, but with the desire to reach an ethical explanation of these. The book of Job, obviously, and Ecclesiastes from a more jaundiced perspective are immediately obvious; but there are also many smaller units with similar concerns. Abraham's pleas on behalf of Sodom, for instance, or Nathan's parabolic judgement of David; Solomon's decision on the matter of disputed parenthood, or the justice meted out to the elders who molested Susannah. And central to it all, the mercy formula in which Yahweh sets out the divine credentials in terms of mercy, faithfulness and love.

The book of Jonah has often been used as a source of moral teaching, though not always advisedly, in that the lessons advocated tend to make broad conclusions about God's universal love and the mission of the Jews to bring that knowledge to the wider world, coupled with salutary warnings about national self-interest, narrow-mindedness and bigotry.[5] These are too often linked to an overt or implied assumption that Christianity has a more enlightened view than that of the Jews to whom Jonah was addressed. I have already referred to this problem *en passant* and will not comment further now.

As regards the ethics *of* Jonah rather than those supposedly deriving *from* the book, Handy (pp. 98–109) reviews the range of moral positions which might have been expected in the time and society from which the book emerged. This is useful, if somewhat reductive in that it largely confirms the surface conventions of the narrative. While these may well have been popular current moralities, it is my judgement, and the thrust of this whole book, that the author of the book of Jonah is driving at something much more subtle and complex. At various points I have had occasion to comment on ethical problems as they arise in the course of the narrative: I shall return these as I develop the theme of this section. I begin with a statement of the obvious: can we differentiate between the human drive to behave ethically and the freedom of God in the context of ethical absolutes. Even to state this in such a stark fashion is to raise immediately a whole series of consequent issues; nevertheless it constitutes a useful starting point. Both human and divine characters in Jonah face moral dilemmas – the difference being that for the most part the former recognize them as such, while Yahweh remains blithely indifferent. Thus I note in Chapter 5 that the sailors are manifestly uneasy about the deal that Jonah offers them, as their prayer in mitigation when they finally throw him overboard reveals. The narrative device does not require this passage: a simple equation and an unceremonious denavistration[6] would have sufficed. Let us mark this as a plus for humankind!

Jonah himself, though seemingly untroubled at first, recognizes the causes and effects and the fatal arithmetic of Yahweh's actions. His

---

5. That such views are by no means extinct is evidenced by the following sentiment from Rosa Ching Shao's *Jonah* (Langham Global Library, 2019), p. 7: 'One important purpose of [this] book is to address this deep-seated Jewish particularism and rebuke Jewish narrow-mindedness'.

6. See Chapter 1 n. 7 on this neologism.

acceptance of his role as sacrificial victim is (in terms of the beliefs of his time) a moral decision, and I have no doubt that the narration nudges us to accept it as such. For if we take the tale on its own terms, it takes real courage to accept both that responsibility and its consequences. The sea was a real threat to ancient mariners – which is not to say that the threat is not still real, but only to highlight the fragility of ancient ships and the complete lack of either communications in situations of distress or rescue facilities. Storms such as this are not comic-book effects. They come (literally) from God knows where and suck everything down to a watery grave, the kind so vividly described in Jonah 2. It would be churlish, then, to dismiss what Jonah does as mere posturing or some kind of effete death wish. He was in flight from the fear of death already, and if he was ready to accept death (which is by no means the same as seeking it) it was because he saw the moral good in letting one man go for the sake of the many. This too I record in humanity's favour.

Jonah 2 raises more complex matters, and is commonly associated with Jonah's supposed hypocrisy – a charge which, if proven, would considerably qualify the assessment I have just made. My discussion in Chapter 8, which examined Jonah 2 in some detail, sought to answer this accusation, and raised at the same time concerns about Yahweh's actions and motives which have a bearing on the question of what ethical principles are at stake. Further, Jonah 2 brings us both literally and thematically to the core of the book, as I observed in the Coda. The status of Yahweh and the theme of God's mercy and trustworthiness will engage us in the last part of this chapter, and so I shall for the moment move directly to Jonah 3. If Jonah 1 hints at the finer features of human morality, it seems that ch. 3 is determined to travel in the opposite direction. Jonah himself is now a blank figure: he makes a mysteriously trouble-free journey to the ends of (his) earth and fulfils his mission (barely) with no sign of either engagement or conviction. The correlates of the captain and the crew in chapter 1 are the king and people of Nineveh. Unlike the former, they face no urgent danger, since the warning given by Jonah is for some future time, even if it is credible. At the moral level one has the sense of folk taking steps to protect themselves just in case, a suspicion reinforced by the generic language of the king's proclamation. I have elsewhere characterised this move as a form of cheap grace, angling as it were for forgiveness on the basis of saying the right thing and performing the expected rites. If this reading is fair, we find chapters 1 and 3 in ethical tension with each other, illuminating human morality and cynicism through narrative means.

So far I have not remarked on Yahweh's ethical stance, though I have commented in passing at various stages on the intractability of this subject, rooted as it is in the paradox that if good is defined as what Yahweh defines to be good, then our innate ethical sense is offended, but if good is something by which the gods themselves are constrained, it seems that they must inexorably be diminished. As Wagner (rightly?) saw, one consequence of this, if taken to its logical/absurd limits, is the *Götterdämmerung* – the point at which the gods, having done their worst, step aside (are pushed aside?) to allow humankind its moment of folly. Of course the author of the book of Jonah had no such vision to work with; but the underlying absurdity is not a recent discovery – as Job certainly knew, and Qoheleth must have suspected. As we approach Jonah 4 it is no longer possible to postpone an enquiry into Yahweh's ethics, the stand-off between Jonah and his God being that chapter's central feature.

At the core of the debate in Jonah around Yahweh's behaviour is the mercy formula from Exodus 34, and in particular that version of it which seems to indicate a readiness – perhaps even eagerness – on Yahweh's part to forgive. All of the protagonists hint at this one way or another: the ship's captain, the king of Nineveh, and (famously) Jonah. The first of these is indeed just a hint which in other contexts would not be noteworthy, but two features of it suggest something afoot. The first is that his plea, 'Perhaps the god will spare us a thought[7] so that we do not perish', employs a verb for 'perish' which is used again by the sailors in v. 14, and repeated verbatim in the king of Nineveh's proclamation in 3.9. And secondly, the captain and the sailors both express a hope that 'the god' will somehow relent, a hope which is pinned firmly to the mercy formula in the Ninevite prayer in 3.9, 'Who knows? God may relent and change his mind ... *so that we do not perish*' (emphasis added).

Though Jonah will address the formula directly in his confrontation with Yahweh, his earlier allusion in 2.8 is pointed though indirect: 'Those who are heedful of vain lies forsake their true loyalty' (my translation). In the context of the psalm this seems at first sight to be directed against Jonah's enemies in the city; but in this book nothing is to be taken purely at face value. The key term 'loyalty' (*chesed*) is of course also a divine attribute much celebrated in the mercy formula. That this verse is also physically central to the book gives it an added force, and we do well to consider this: might Jonah be here preparing his argument for later use,

---

7. The word used is very rare, and is commonly taken to be an Aramaism. It is of some interest that one of the only two occurrences of a derived form which means something like 'thoughts' is in Ps. 146.4, where it also paired with the same verb 'to perish'.

as a lawyer perfecting his brief. Is it not possible that in retrospect we hear at this point an anticipation of what Jonah will later accuse Yahweh of: forsaking the divine *chesed* by being heedful of vain lies – namely, the hollow and deceitful protestations of the rulers of Nineveh and their people? As an incidental consequence, reading 2.8 in this way lends some tentative support to Jonah's claim in 4.2 that his opinion on this matter should already have been clear to Yahweh.

And in-Conclusion

It is time to engage with the closing arguments. I am persuaded that there is much to be said for decoding chapter 4 in terms of an informal legal contest, a point I made in my commentary on 4.9. I remarked then on the fact that Jonah and Yahweh are allocated almost exactly the same number of words in their speeches in this chapter, as though some kind of equal opportunity principle has been adopted. The legal format is explicitly referenced by Levine's 1996 article 'The Case of "Jonah" vs "God"'. That said, he does not really develop the motif formally, but rather engages in a philosophical and judicial examination of the essential problem which Jonah elucidates. This is of course the problem of evil and the ethical problems associated with any understanding of God's response to it, given that 'Biblical literature describes a God who is both *ex hypothesi* and *ex professo* perfect in justice and goodness, hence any perceived contradiction is a moral dilemma and demands ethical explanation' (p. 187). According to Levine (pp. 174–6) the ancients understood three ways to correct evil – (1) appropriate punishment; (2) performance of an equally weighty good deed; and (3) a ritual of propitiation – and observes that none of these occurs in Jonah. Since the 'mercifulness of God was axiomatic in biblical thought' (p. 190) it follows that the dilemma is fundamentally unresolvable. In his summing up, Levine (p. 197) observes that, rather than reaching any facile conclusion which slides over the historical reality, '[i]t is the grappling with the consequences of values and actions that gives Jonah the man his stature and Jonah the book its cogency'.

But the court is once again in session and the case being presented is that:

> The god, commonly known as Yahweh, knowingly and with aforethought did presume upon a reputation for mercy and readiness to forgive, with the intention of misleading the plaintiff Jonah to his grievous physical and emotional harm, by (firstly) forcing him under false pretences to preach against his own people aka Nineveh, (secondly) in pursuance of said Jonah

who took justifiable flight in fear for his life, imposing upon him violence likely to lead to his severe physical harm, and (thirdly) cavalierly resiling from the divine obligation to punish wrongdoing by granting, on no proper evidence provided, a full amnesty to a guilty collective, aka Nineveh. Furthermore said Yahweh did thereby contradict that same reputation by contradicting the divine prerogative for absolute justice, without which mercy and forgiveness are nugatory, by receiving improper petitions from unauthorised parties, to wit, a company of sailors and a self-styled 'king' of Nineveh, and by showing to these same parties favours above and beyond the constraints of divine duty. The plaintiff appears in his own behalf and the defendant has waived any right to legal representation.

One curious feature of this case is that after the plaintiff presents his opening arguments and Yahweh briefly replies (4.2-4), the court adjourns to a location outside the city to await further evidence. This proves to be a rather pointless exercise, since nothing germane to Jonah's plea emerges. The latter, however, rather damages what appeared at first to be a strong argument by returning to his earlier position of affecting a desire to die. This provides an opening to the defendant, who presents, it must be admitted, a powerful argument in mitigation (4.10-11), in effect countering the plaintiff's core argument with an assertion that, in the longer term, mercy cannot be constrained by the short-term desire for 'justice' on merely human terms. Since, as Yahweh points out, created things without the ability to control their own being suffer good and ill arbitrarily, why should a collective of people and animals under similar constraint not experience divine mercy? In other words, must the letter of justice always trump the expression of God's pity. Unfortunately the court record comes to an abrupt end at this point, and we can only surmise what verdict the judges might have reached.

This is of course a fantasy. What remains is the sense of an un-ending, one moreover that is surely intended. The readers, those intelligentsia of Jerusalem who have no illusions about the real references at work, whose textual knowledge enables them to spot the many allusions which we modern exegetes have to work so hard to uncover, these readers are left with the debate unresolved and asked, not to vote but to reflect. We can only imagine how that discussion might proceed, and how it might be focused. Would it have centred on the generosity of Yahweh – too generous perhaps for some? Or perhaps on the problem of ethics confronted by good and evil – does a good God do the kind of things that Yahweh does in this story? Crouch (p. 112) hints at the thought of a weak and vulnerable deity with this proposed reader's concluding words for Jonah:

> O Yahweh, do you have eyes to see but cannot see and ears to hear but cannot hear? Nineveh has not repented. They, as I in the belly of the great fish, are only afraid of dying at your hands. They have manipulated your soft heart just as I have. I remain unrepentant and so do they. O great and mighty Elohim, you have thought nothing about destroying countless cities through the ages – are you, in this circumstance, really that gullible?

To which the reader might reply: 'Yes – yes, Yahweh is'.

But then there is issue of our own complicity, reserving the cultic privilege to an elite, guarding the covenant by keeping silent about its real purpose? Or might it even have been a quasi-Rabbinic debate about the mercy formula and its various manifestations whose complexity and paradoxical character has been so deftly picked apart by the author – whose identity they may well have been able to discover?

I am tempted to end with a famous conclusion reached by Abraham Heschel:[8]

> God's answer to Jonah, stressing the supremacy of compassion, upsets the possibility of looking for a rational coherence of God's ways with the world. History would be more intelligible if God's word were the last word, final and unambiguous like a dogma or an unconditional decree: once wickedness had reached its full measure, punishment would destroy it. Yet, beyond justice and anger lies the mystery of compassion.

And the author? Are we any closer to him (or her)? My last word is that the more I have engaged with this story the more I am persuaded that the spirit of the author is to be found above all in Jonah the character: a stubborn, courageous, knowledgeable, puzzling (and puzzled) witness to a God whom he would rather were more straightforward, but whose inconsistencies he is willing to challenge, even if in the end he must admit defeat and self-imposed silence.

---

8. Cited in Burrows, pp. 99–100.

Bibliography

Abela, Anthony A. 2001. 'When the Agenda of an Artistic Composition is Hidden: Jonah and Intertextual Dialogue with Isaiah 6, the "Confessions of Jeremiah", and other texts'. Pages 1–30 in *The Elusive Prophet*. Edited by Johannes C. de Moor. OTS XLV. Leiden: Brill.

Ackerman, James S. 1981. 'Satire and Symbolism in the Song of Jonah'. Pages 213–46 in *Tradition and Transformation*. Edited by B. Halpern and J. Levenson. Winona Lake, IN: Eisenbrauns.

Adams, Colin E. P. 2001. 'There and Back Again: Getting Around in Roman Egypt'. Pages 138–66 in *Travel and Geography in the Roman Empire*. Edited by C. E. P. Adams and R. Laurence. London & New York: Routledge.

Barstad, Hans M. 1996. *The Myth of the Empty Land: A Study in the History and Archaeology of Judah During the 'Exilic' Period*. Symbolae Osloensis Supp. 28. Oslo: Scandinavian University Press.

Ben Zvi, Ehud. 2003. *Signs of Jonah: Reading and Rereading in Ancient Yehud*. JSOTSup 367. Sheffield: Sheffield Academic Press.

Berlin, Adele. 1985. *The Dynamics of Biblical Parallelism*. Bloomington: Indiana University Press.

Bewer, Julius A. 1912. *Jonah*. ICC. Edinburgh: T. & T. Clark.

Bolin, Thomas M. 1995. '"Should I Not Also Pity Nineveh?": Divine Freedom in the Book of Jonah'. *JSOT* 67: 109–20.

Bolin, Thomas M. 2010. 'Jonah 4,11 and the Problem of Exegetical Anachronism'. *SJOT* 24: 99–109.

Bonhoeffer, Dietrich. 1959. *The Cost of Discipleship*. London: SCM Press.

Brichto, Herbert C. 1992. *Towards a Grammar of Biblical Poetics: Tales of the Prophets*. New York: Oxford University Press.

Burrows, Millar. 1970. 'The Literary Category of the Book of Jonah'. Pages 80–107 in *Translating and Understanding the OT*. Edited by T. H. Frank and W. L. Reed. Nashville: Abingdon Press.

Cary, Phillip. 2008. *Jonah*. SCM Theological Commentary on the Bible. London: SCM Press.

Casson, Lionel. 1971. *Ships and Seamanship in the Ancient World*. Princeton, NJ: Princeton University Press.

Christensen, Duane L. 1983. 'Anticipatory Paronomasia in Jonah 3.7-8 and Genesis 37.2'. *RB* 90: 261–3.

Cooper, Alan. 1993. 'In Praise of Divine Caprice: The Significance of the Book of Jonah'. Pages 144–63 in *Among the Prophets: Language, Image and Structure in the Prophetic Writings*. Edited by P. R. Davies and D. J. A. Clines. JSOTSup 144. Sheffield: JSOT Press.

Craig, Kenneth M., Jr. 1993. *A Poetics of Jonah: Art in the Service of Ideology*. Columbia, SC: University of South Carolina Press,.

Crouch, W. B. 1994. 'To Question an End, to End a Question: Opening the Closure of the Book of Jonah'. *JSOT* 62: 101–12.

Dobbs-Allsopp, F. W. 2015. *On Biblical Poetry*. Oxford: Oxford University Press.

Dozeman, Thomas B. 2009. *Exodus*. Eerdmans Critical Commentary. Grand Rapids, MI: Eerdmans.

Elata-Alster, Gerda, and Rachel Salmon. 1989. 'The Deconstruction of Genre in the Book of Jonah: Towards a Theological Discourse'. *Literature and Theology* 3: 40–60.

Finkelstein, Israel. 2018. *Hasmonaean Realities behind Ezra, Nehemiah and Chronicles*. Atlanta: SBL Press.

Good, Edwin M. 1965. *Irony in the Old Testament*. London: SPCK.

Goodhart, Sandor. 1985. 'Prophecy, Sacrifice and Repentance in the Story of Jonah'. *Semeia* 15: 43–63

Guillaume, Phillipe. 2006. 'The End of Jonah is the Beginning of Wisdom'. *Bib* 87: 243–50.

Handy, Lowell K. 2007. *Jonah's World: Social Science and the Reading of Prophetic Story*. London: Equinox.

Huguenin, Justin. N.d. *The Tobiads and the Maccabees*. https://kb.osu.edu/bitstream/handle/1811/54608/The_Tobiads_and_the_Maccabees.pdf.

Hunter, Alastair G. 1986. 'Father Abraham: A Structural and Theological Study of the Yahwist's Presentation of the Abraham Material'. *JSOT* 35: 3–27.

Hunter, Alastair G. 2001. 'Jonah from the Whale: Exodus motifs in Jonah 2'. Pages 142–58 in *The Elusive Prophet. The Prophet as a Historical Person, Literary Character & Anonymous Artist*. Edited by J. C. de Moor. OTS XLV. Leiden: Brill.

Hunter, Alastair G. 2002. 'Creating Waves: Why the Fictionality of Jonah Matters'. Pages 101–16 in *Sense and Sensitivity. Essays on Reading the Bible in Memory of Robert Carroll*. Edited by A. G. Hunter and P. R. Davies. Sheffield: Sheffield Academic Press.

Hunter, Alastair G. 2006. *Wisdom Literature*. London: SCM Press, 2006.

Hunter, Alastair G. 2007. 'Inside Outside Psalm 55: How Jonah Grew Out of a Psalmist's Conceit'. Pages 129–39 in *Psalms and Prayers*. Edited by B. Becking and E. Peels. OTS 55. Leiden: Brill.

Hunter, Alastair G. 2016. 'An Awfully Beastly Business: Some Thoughts on *behēmāh* in Jonah and Qoheleth'. Pages 82–94 in *Goochem in Mokum: Wisdom in Amsterdam*. Edited by G. W. Brooke and P Van Hecke. OTS 68. Leiden: Brill.

Joerstad, Mari. 2019. *The Hebrew Bible and Environmental Ethics: Humans, Nonhumans, and the Living Landscape*. Cambridge: Cambridge University Press.

Kelsey, Marian. 2018. 'Jonah: Co-Texts and Contexts'. Ph.D. Diss., The University of St. Andrews.

Kugel, James. 1981. *The Idea of Biblical Poetry*. New Haven: Yale University Press.

Levine, Étan. 1975. *The Aramaic Version of Jonah*. Jerusalem Academic Press.

Levine, Étan. 1996. 'The Case of "Jonah" vs. "God"'. *Proc. AAJR* 62: 165–98

Limburg, James. 1993. *Jonah*. OTL. London: SCM Press.

Lipschits, Oded, and Joseph Blenkinsopp, eds. 2003. *Judah and the Judeans in the Neo-Babylonian Period*. Winona Lake, IN: Eisenbrauns.

Magonet, Jonathan D. 1983. *Form and Meaning: Studies in Literary Techniques in the Book of Jonah*. 2nd ed. Bible and Literature 8. Sheffield: Almond Press.

McCarter, P. Kyle. 1973. 'The River Ordeal in Israelite Literature'. *HTR* 66, no. 4: 403-12.

Perry, Theodore A. 2006. *The Honeymoon is Over: Jonah's Argument with God.* Peabody, MA: Hendrickson.
Person, R. F., Jr. 1996. *In Conversation with Jonah.* JSOTSup 220. Sheffield: Sheffield Academic Press.
Salters, R. B. 1994. *Jonah and Lamentations.* OT Guides. Sheffield: JSOT Press.
Sasson, Jack M. 1990. *Jonah.* AB 24B. New York: Doubleday.
Shemesh, Yael. 2010. '"And Many Beasts" (Jonah 4:11): The Function and Status of Animals in the Book of Jonah'. *Journal of Hebrew Scriptures* 10: 1–26.
Sherwood, Yvonne. 2000. *A Biblical Text and its Afterlives: The Survival of Jonah in Western Culture.* Cambridge: Cambridge University Press.
Trible, Phyllis. 1994. *Rhetorical Criticism: Context, Method and the Book of Jonah.* Guides to Biblical Scholarship. Minneapolis: Fortress Press.
Vayntrub, Jacqueline. 2019. *Beyond Orality: Biblical Poetry on its Own Terms.* London & New York: Routledge.
Watts, James W. 1992. *Psalms and Story: Inset Hymns in Hebrew Narrative.* JSOTSup 139. Sheffield: Sheffield Academic Press.
Wolff, Hans Walter 1986. *Obadiah and Jonah.* Translated by M. Kohl. Minneapolis: Augsburg.
Wyatt, Nicholas. 1987. 'Sea and Desert: Symbolic Geography in West Semitic Religious Thought'. *UF* 19: 375–89.
Youngblood, Kevin J. 2013. *Jonah: God's Scandalous Mercy.* Hearing the Message of Scripture. Grand Rapids, MI: Zondervan.
Zenger, Erich. 2018. 'Gottes Ewiger Bund mit Israel'. Pages 47–64 in *Gottesrede: gesammelte Aufsätze von Erich Zenger zum jüdisch-christlichen Dialog.* Edited by R. Kampling and I. Müllner. Stuttgarter Biblische Aufsatzbände Altes Testament 65. Stuttgart: Bibelwerk.

Index of References

Hebrew Bible/		4.16	113	9.6	115
Old Testament		6	115	9.8-17	118, 191
Genesis		6.2-4	55	10–19	34
1–2	106, 107	6.3	112	10	42
1	62, 86, 107	6.5–8.22	106	10.4	100
		6.5-13	32	10.8-12	230
1.1-2	103	6.5	32, 114	10.9	230
1.1	81	6.6-7	189	10.12	226, 230
1.2	112, 113, 159, 180	6.7	221	11.6	33
		6.11-13	32	12–19	116
1.7	103	6.11	114	12	116
1.9	157	6.13-22	115	12.1-3	117
1.10	157	6.13	114	12.10-20	117
1.11-12	113	6.17	112	13.1-13	117
1.16	104	6.18	118, 191	13.3-13	116
1.24-25	113	6.20	221	13.13	116
1.26-27	108	7.2	221	13.14-18	117
1.26	110, 111, 120	7.8	221	13.14-16	116
		7.11	159	14	58, 116, 117
1.28	110, 120	7.15	112		
2.4	81	7.22	112	14.13	78
2.7	50, 231, 232	7.23	221	14.19	81
		8.1-12	154	14.22	81
2.8	113	8.1	112	15	117, 191, 192
2.21	111	8.2	159		
3.8	58, 60, 113	8.3	89	15.1-21	117
		8.5	89	15.6	184, 185, 191, 192
3.14-19	108	8.8	48, 69		
3.14	220, 232	8.9	48	15.9	48
3.15	232	8.10	48	15.12	111
3.19	220, 231	8.11	48, 69	15.18	118
3.20	220, 232	8.12	48	16	116
3.24	113, 140	8.17	116	16.4	69
4	50	8.19	221	16.5	69
4.1-16	108	8.20	221, 225	17	116, 117
4.11	225	9.1-7	116	17.4-6	50
4.14	140	9.2	110	18.1-15	117

18.12	50	2.13	78	15.13	159
18.16–19.29	106	3.1–4.18	11	15.19	109, 157
18.16-33	117	3.1-6	63	15.22	124, 157
19	34, 36, 37, 40, 116	3.6	158	16.15	121
		3.13-15	77	16.31	121
19.1-29	117	3.13-14	242	16.33	121
19.21	34, 35	3.14	51, 190	16.35	121
19.24-29	35	3.16	78	17.7	80
19.24-26	123	3.18	78, 124	18	162
19.25	34	4.9	109, 110, 157	18.22	69
19.29	34			19.10-11	124
19.30-38	117	4.12	227	19.13	221
20.13	167	4.15	227	19.19	89
21.3-6	50	5.3	78, 124	20.5-6	202
21.12	91	6.1	140	20.5	204
21.14	167	7.8-13	122	20.10	221
22	91, 147	7.16	78	20.11	81
22.4	124	8.27	124	20.18-19	63
24.3	81	9.1	78	21.2	78
24.7	81	9.13	78	22.5	53
33.17	210	10.3	78	22.15	60
37.15	167	10.11	140	22.18	221
37.25-28	164	10.19	157	23	124
37.35	164	10.22	124	23.1	32
39.1	164	11.1	140	23.10	131
39.14	78	11.5	223	23.28-31	139
39.17	78	12.39	140	23.31	157
40	124	13.18	157	24.9-11	63
41.7	122	14–15	157, 162	24.12	227
41.12	78	14.6	160	24.15-18	63
41.24	122	14.8	160	30.4	220
42.38	164	14.9	160	31.17	81
44.29	164	14.12	205	32–34	191, 204
44.31	164	14.16	109, 157	32.12-14	189–91
48.13-14	227	14.21	160	32.13	191
48.16	119	14.22	109, 157	34	66
49.25	159	14.23	160	34.6-7	26, 28, 190, 192, 202
		14.29	109, 157		
Exodus		15	33, 157, 159, 165, 174	34.6	3, 26, 56, 131, 146, 160, 163, 213
1.15	78				
1.16	78				
1.19	78	15.1-13	155, 157, 160		
2.3	36, 158				
2.5	158	15.2	159	34.7	26, 131, 202, 204
2.6	78	15.4	157		
2.7	78	15.5	158–60	34.10-28	118
2.11	78	15.8	159		

Leviticus
1.14	48
5.7	48
5.11	48
7.21	221
11.26-27	221
12.6	48
12.8	48
14.22	48
14.30	48
15.14	48
15.29	48
16.7-10	74
20.25	221
21.7	140
23.43	211
27.11	221
27.26-27	223

Numbers
3.13	223
6.10	48
8.17	223
14.18	203, 204
14.25	157
16.30-34	154
16.30-35	121
18.15	223
21.4	157
22.20-21	207
23.19	189
25.6-13	17
26.10	121
33.10	157
33.11	157

Deuteronomy
1.40	157
2.1	157
4.15-18	108
4.17	223
5.9	203, 204
5.14	221
5.32	227
7.7-8	66
8.7	159
8.11-20	190
11.4	157
11.6	121
14.6	221
17.11	227
17.20	227
28.14	227
28.15-68	190
28.20	131
28.26	221
29	36
29.22-23	35
31.24-29	16
32.8-9	55
32.21	131, 132
32.31-32	38, 42
33.2	55
33.13	159

Joshua
1.7	227
1.11	124
2.10	157
4.22	109, 157
4.23	157
10.2	226, 230
19.46	100
23.6	227
24.6	157

Judges
4–5	162
4.10	187
4.13	187
4.21	111
5	174
6.12-24	11
9.41	140
11.2	140
11.7	140
11.16	157
11.29-40	86
13.8	227
19.1	70

1 Samuel
1.1–4.1	238
1	68
2	68
2.6	164
4.6	78
4.9	78
9.20	124
10.3	124
10.9-13	76
13.3	78
13.7	77, 78
13.19	78
14.11	78
14.21	78
14.52	50
15	72
15.10	206
15.11	189
15.29	189
17.44	220
17.46	220
18.11	64
20.30	69
20.33	64
26	111
26.12	111
26.19	140
28	125
29.3	78

2 Samuel
2.10	50
10.3	34
11	230
11.11	210
12.25	50
14.19	227
20.4	187
20.5	187
22	155, 162
22.12	210
24.12-13	124
24.16	189

1 Kings
2.27	140
4.33	221
6.9	97
6.11	206

6.15	97	21.17	206	20.37	101
8.36	227	21.20-24	208	30.9	204
9.26	157	21.27	208	34.2	227
10.22	101	21.28	206	36.23	81
12.4	69	22	55, 56, 89		
12.9	69	22.5-12	76	*Ezra*	
12.10	69	22.7	101	1.2	81
12.22	206	22.17	25	3.7	27, 100
13.1-32	197			6.20	16
13.11-25	197	*2 Kings*		7.5	17
16.1	206	2.1-12	63	8.2	17
16.13	132	2.1	63	8.33	17
16.26	132	2.8	186	9–10	16, 54
17–22	62	2.11	63		
17–19	47, 56,	2.13	186	*Nehemiah*	
	207, 237	2.14	186	1.4	81
17.2	206	2.15 18	76	1.5	81
17.8	206	3–6	76	2.4	81
17.9-10	207	6.11	63	2.20	81
17.9	53, 177,	6.25	48	3.28-32	14
	207		14	4–6	14
17.10	53, 207		166	6.17-19	14
17.17-24	198	14.25	2, 27, 29,	7.4	226, 230
18	40, 68, 178		47, 198,	8	18
18.1	206		995	9	9
18.2	243	17.15	132	9.2	16
18.17–19.18	12	19.23	70	9.6	82
18.20-40	243	19.36	42	9.9-11	155, 157,
18.27	71	22.1–23.30	27		160
18.40	243	22.2	227	9.9	157
19	112, 163,	*1 Chronicles*		9.11	109, 157,
	178, 185,	2–9	22		158, 160
	198, 208,	8.33	50	9.17	204
	244	9.39	50	9.20	121
19.4	207, 208	19.3	34	9.31	204
19.5-7	208	21.25	189	10.37	223
19.9-11	51			12.30	16
19.9	51, 209	*2 Chronicles*		12.45	16
19.11-12	209	2.12	81	13.1-3	16
19.11	51	2.16	27, 100	13.9	16
19.12	178, 208	6.27	227	13.15-22	16
19.13	186, 209	6.41	207	13.22	16
19.17-18	178, 208	7.20	201	13.23-31	16
19.19	186	9.21	101	13.30	16
20.12	210	11.5-12	22		
20.16	210	20.11	140		
21	207, 237	20.36-37	101		

Esther
3.7	74
9.24	74

Job
1–2	55
1.13-19	56
2.7-8	56
2.8	185
4	106
4.13	111
6.24	227
7.3	120
7.9	164, 165
7.15-16	205
7.16	132
9.21	205
9.29	132
10.1	205
10.9	231
10.18	205
11.8	138
12.7-10	224, 226
13.2	80
14.13	138
23.9	227
26.6	138
27.18	210
27.20	63
28	152
28.14	159
33.9	80
33.15	111
34.15	231
34.32	227
35.11	221
36.22	227
36.29	210
38.1	63
38.7	55
38.16	159
38.30	159
40.6	63
40.25	105
40.15-24	232
40.19	232
41.16	160
41.31	105, 158
41.32	159

Psalms
3.7	207
3.8	149
3.9	5
5	142
5.7	141, 142
5.8	5, 141
7.6	207
8	108
8.7	221
8.8	110, 120
9.19	207
10.12	207
11	142
11.4	141
11.5-6	41
16.5	74
17.13	207
18	155, 161
18.4-6	122
18.5	5
18.11	210
19	161
22.6	5
24.4	131, 132
25.8	227
25.12	227
27.11	227
29.1	55
29.3-4	138
29.10	138
30.3	164, 165
31.6-7	131
31.6	132
31.7	5
31.20	210
31.23	5
32.8	227
33.7	159
36.6	159, 222
39.5	131, 132
39.6	132
39.11	131, 132
42.7	159
42.8	5
48	101
48.3	70
48.7	101
50.3	63
50.10-11	224
50.10	222
50.14	5
55	33, 49, 155, 163, 169–71, 173, 174
55.1-5	170, 172, 174
55.1-2	33, 170
55.1	171, 172
55.2-3	172
55.2	171, 172
55.3	171
55.4	33
55.5	170
55.6-15	170, 172, 174
55.6	50
55.7	48, 169, 170, 996
55.8	64, 169, 170
55.9	33, 170
55.10-12	169
55.12-15	173
55.12-14	171
55.12	170
55.13-15	169
55.15	33, 170, 173
55.16-32	170
55.16-23	170, 172, 174
55.16-19	170
55.16	169, 171
55.17-20	169
55.17	171, 172
55.19	170–2
55.20-21	171, 173
55.21	170
55.22-23	170

55.22	171	79	142	107.15-16	167
55.23	171, 173	79.1	141	107.19	187
55.24	169	82	55, 163	107.21-22	167
56	48	82.1	55	107.23-32	155, 156, 160, 167
56.13	5	82.6-7	55		
58.1	55	82.8	207	107.23-30	156, 168
58.9	63	83.15	63	107.24	158, 168
61.7	114, 120	86	204	107.25	64, 187
62.9	132	86.5	203	107.26	159
66.6	109, 157	86.11	227	107.28	187
68.18	48	86.15	203	107.29	64, 187
68.22	158	88.3	5	107.31-32	167
69	155, 156	88.6	158	107.43	167
69.1-3	155	89.5-12	107	110	16
69.1-2	156, 160	89.6	55	110.4	189
69.1	156	89.22	50	115	199
69.2	5, 155, 156, 158	89.35	91	115.3	199
		94.11	132	115.4-8	199
69.3	5	95.5	109, 157	116.1	5
69.8	156	102.2	5, 172	116.3	5
69.13-15	155, 160	102.23	172	116.16	5
69.14	156	102.35	82	116.17	5
69.15	122, 155, 156	103.4	5	116.18	5
		103.8-9	203	119	18, 172
69.16	5, 158	103.14	231	119.33	227
69.21	156	103.20-21	55	119.102	227
69.22	156	104.6	159	119.161	18
69.31	156	104.14	222	119.164	18
69.43	156	104.26	104, 105	119.23-24	18
71.20	159	104.29	231	119.37	132
72.10	101	105-107	167	119.46	18
72.13	215	105	160, 167	120.1	6
73	163	105.29	110	120.11	6
73.22	224	106	167	121.2	81
74.12-18	86	106.7	157	121.3	131, 171
74.12-17	107	106.9	157, 159	121.4	131
74.12-15	138	106.17-18	121	121.5	131
74.14	104	106.22	157	121.7	131
74.19	48	106.30	17	121.8	131
74.22	207	107	155, 156, 158, 163, 167–9, 174, 187	124.1-8	138
76	111			124.8	81
76.5	111			127.1	131
77.4	171			127.2	131
77.16	159	107.1	167	128.3	70
78	160	107.6	186, 187	132	163
78.15	159	107.8-9	167	132.8	207
78.33	132	107.13	187	134.3	81

Psalms (cont.)

135	199	16.33	74	3.8-9	39
135.5-7	199	19.15	111	4.6	210
135.6	159, 199	21.6	132	5.7	68
135.8	223	23.34	159	5.14	122
135.15-18	199	30.19	159	6.5	11
136.13	157	30.30	221	7.18	50
136.15	157			13	37
138	142	*Qoheleth*		13.1	11
138.2	6, 141, 142	1.2	131	13.19-20	36
139.7-12	95, 165	3.18-22	219	14	165
139.8	138	3.18-21	108, 228	14.13	70
140	33	3.19-21	112	14.14-15	164
140.1-4	33	3.20	231	14.15	165
142.4	6	3.21	224	17.14	74
143.4-5	6	4.2	205	18.6	221
144.4	132	7.1-3	205	19.6	158
145	197	9.12-16	229, 231	22.17-18	64
145.8	203	9.13	230	23	177
145.19	6	9.14-15	229	23.1	101
146.4	249	9.14	230	23.2	101
146.5-6	81	10.2	215, 227, 228	23.6	101
148.2	55	12	188	23.8	101
148.7	159	12.7	231	23.10	101
148.8	63			23.14	101
148.10	221	*Song of Songs*		23.18	101
		1.15	48	28.2	63
Proverbs		2.10	207	28.9	227
1–9	20	2.12	48	28.26	227
1.12	122	2.13	207	29.6	63
2.12-26	228	2.14	48	29.10	111
3.16	227	4.1	48	30.20-21	227
3.19	82	5.2	48	30.28	132
3.20	159	5.12	48	34	37
4.16-17	33	6.9	48	34.9-10	36, 41
4.27	227			34.17	74
5.5	122	*Isaiah*		37.37	42
7.27	122	1.1	11	38	155
8.22-31	82	1.7-10	39	38.14	48
8.22	232	1.7-9	210	40.9	25
8.24	159	1.8	210	40.24	63
8.27	159	1.13	132	41.16	63
8.28	159	2	166	41.27	25
9	228	2.1	52	42.5	82
10.5	111	2.2	11	43.1-21	107
12.10	224	2.3	227	44.3-4	109
15.11	138	2.16	101	44.3	157
				44.24	82

44.28–45.1	53	16.13	64	13.13	63		
45.12	80, 82	18.8	189	16.46-58	40		
45.18	82	18.10	189	17.10	177		
49.4	132	18.15	132	24.6	74		
49.20	230	19.7	221	24.14	189		
50.2	110	20.1-2	12	24.15-17	12		
51.10	159	20.14-18	205	26–28	177		
51.13	82	20.15	37	26.19	159		
52.7	25	22.26-28	64	27	97, 98, 163		
53.7	219	23.13-14	40	27.4	159		
54.9	64	23.13	40	27.8-9	996		
54.11	64	23.19	63	27.8	97		
57.6	74	25.8-12	190	27.9	97		
57.13	132	25.32	63, 70	27.12	101		
57.20	141	26.3	189	27.15	101		
59.6-7	32	26.10-11	12	27.16	101		
59.11	48	26.13	189	27.18	101		
60.8	48	26.19	189	27.21	101		
60.9	101	27.5-6	223	27.25-29	996		
63.13	159	28.14	223	27.25	97, 101, 159		
66.19	101	30.23	63				
		31.8	70	27.26	101, 159		
Jeremiah		32.17	81	27.27	97, 159		
1.1-2	11	32.18	203, 204	27.28	97		
1.4-10	11	34.20	221	27.29	97		
1.11-12	59	38.1-6	167	28.2	159		
2.5	132	38.6	12	28.13	101		
4.26-28	189, 190	43.1-7	12	29.4	110		
5.17	101	48.28	48	29.5	110		
6.7	32	49.17-18	37	31.4	159		
6.22	70	49.21	157	31.15	159		
7.10-25	89	50.39-40	37	32.4	64		
7.33	221	50.41	70	32.23	70		
8.7	48	51.15	82	38.6	70		
8.19	132	51.34	104	38.15	70		
10.8	132	51.44	122	38.20	110		
10.9	101			39.2	70		
10.12	82	*Lamentations*		44.31	221		
13.4	207	4.6-8	38, 39	47.9	110		
13.5	207			47.10	110		
13.6	207	*Ezekiel*					
13.7	207	1.4	63	*Daniel*			
13.25	74	7	33	1	54		
14.22	132	7.16	48	1.5	120		
15.3	221	7.23-24	32	1.10	120		
15.10	205	8.10	221	1.11	120		
16.4	221	13.11	63	2.25	79		

Daniel (cont.)		Jonah		1.6-14	243
7.9-10	55	1	32, 33, 49,	1.6	83, 111,
8.18	111		83, 87, 90,		137, 178,
10.9	111		97, 98,		213
11.40	63		137, 140,	1.7-12	156
			144, 145,	1.7-10	73
Hosea			159, 163,	1.7	74, 87,
1.1	11		166, 168,		168, 179,
4.3	110		172, 174,		195, 196
6.1-2	124		177, 178,	1.8-10	242
7.11	48		181, 183,	1.8	83, 151,
9.15	140		187, 188,		168, 179,
11.8-9	40		248		195, 196
11.11	48	1.1-3	46	1.9	8, 69, 71,
13.3	63	1.1-2	176, 243		77, 79, 81,
13.14	138	1.1	11, 51, 52,		82, 84, 87,
			71, 213		94, 109,
Joel		1.2	57, 61, 64,		151, 157,
1	11		71, 74,		166, 168,
1.18-20	222		151, 168,		213
2.12-13	190–2		170, 176,	1.10	64, 69, 75,
2.13-14	189		178, 179,		83, 94,
2.13	3, 56, 202,		187, 195,		109, 119,
	203		196, 207,		187, 213,
2.14	3		246		242
2.17	215	1.3	11, 58, 59,	1.11-16	85
2.21-24	222		61, 69, 71,	1.11-13	170
3.3	74		83, 100,	1.11	64, 88,
			144, 151,		156, 168,
Amos			156, 168,		242
1.14	63		177, 178,	1.12	8, 64, 69,
4.11	38		201, 213,		151, 156,
6.3	32		246		168, 187
6.10	70	1.4-6	62	1.13	64, 88,
7.3	189	1.4	62, 64, 87,		109, 156,
7.4	159		94, 112,		157, 166,
7.6	189		113, 168,		168, 242
7.14	11		170, 187,	1.14-15	242
8.1-2	59		213, 242	1.14	72, 90,
8.8	141	1.5-7	97		168, 179,
9.2	164	1.5	61, 83,		199, 200,
9.11	210		97, 111,		213, 242,
			165, 168,		249
Obadiah			185–7,	1.15-16	166
11	74		207, 213,	1.15	69, 144,
			242		161, 168

1.16	64, 68, 83, 92–4, 148, 156, 179, 187, 213, 242, 997	2.3-10 2.3-7 2.3-6 2.3	168, 170, 213 150 161 138 49, 77, 105, 129, 143, 144, 156, 158, 159, 168	3	3, 32, 54, 57, 67, 144, 149, 163, 172, 174, 178, 179, 187, 191, 195, 208, 209, 231, 248, 993
1.17–2.10	119				
1.17–2.1	125				
1.17	47, 64, 93, 110, 114, 119, 120, 139, 149, 156, 160, 183, 187, 213, 225	2.4	29, 122, 130, 137, 139, 143, 145, 150, 156, 159	3.1-10 3.1-2 3.1 3.2	175 243 213 11, 57, 64, 170, 176, 179, 187
2	32, 33, 49, 57, 58, 64, 68, 90, 92, 95, 103–5, 115, 119, 120, 122, 126, 137, 138, 140, 143, 144, 150, 152–5, 157–65, 167, 181, 183, 199, 244, 245, 248, 993	2.5-6 2.5 2.6 2.7-9 2.7 2.8-9	6, 138, 142 129, 142–4, 156, 168, 211 61, 105, 137, 142–5, 156, 159, 168, 170, 213 144 142, 145, 159, 168, 212, 213 114, 140, 161	3.3 3.4-9 3.4 3.5 3.6-9 3.6 3.7-10	64, 99, 170, 178, 181, 187, 213 243 8, 87, 181, 242 183, 184, 187, 192, 213 183 170, 178, 185 195
2.1-2	170, 180				
2.1	47, 68, 110, 119, 120, 137, 200, 213	2.8	94, 131–3, 135, 137, 148, 150, 156, 159, 249, 250	3.7-8 3.7 3.8-9	187, 222, 225 64, 186, 187 242
2.2-10	243				
2.2-9	8, 123, 126, 128, 136, 161, 163	2.9	94, 148, 150, 156, 159, 170, 179, 213, 229	3.8 3.9-10 3.9	114, 170, 196, 213 189 72, 185, 191, 193–5, 202, 213, 249
2.2-6	144				
2.2-4	139	2.10	110, 125, 126, 149, 157, 166, 211, 213, 225		
2.2-3	122, 137, 170			3.10	166, 168, 183, 185, 193–6, 205, 213
2.2	123, 129, 137, 139, 156, 161,				

Jonah (cont.)		4.6-8	209	Nahum	
3.11	205	4.6-7	207	1.3	26, 63, 203, 204
3.19-21	188	4.6	59, 61, 64, 113, 120, 121, 168, 187, 193, 194, 196, 211-13, 999		
4	32, 41, 57–9, 107, 113, 120, 121, 123, 137, 163, 166, 172, 174, 176, 178, 179, 183, 188, 189, 193, 195, 198, 208, 214, 243, 249, 250			1.15–2.2	28
				1.15	25
				1.16	220
				2.2	26
				2.7	48
				2.8	25
		4.7-8	994	3.7	25
		4.7	59, 113, 120, 121, 168, 212, 213	3.8-10	25
				3.9	27
				3.10	74
				3.18	25
		4.8-9	8	3.19	216
		4.8	61, 101, 112, 113, 120, 121, 168, 171, 201, 208, 212, 213, 994		
				Habakkuk	
4.1-11	193, 243			1.14	108, 110, 111
4.1-5	195				
4.1-4	193			2	142
4.1	64, 74, 75, 168, 170, 187, 194, 196			2.5	122
				2.20	141, 142
		4.9	206, 208, 209, 213, 214, 250	3.10	159
				3.14	63
4.2-8	185				
4.2-4	251	4.10-11	214, 251	Zephaniah	
4.2-3	8, 214	4.10	72, 170, 180, 187, 213	1.3	110
4.2	3, 11, 26, 56, 58, 66, 68, 87, 113, 156, 163, 166, 170, 171, 179, 191, 192, 196, 203, 213, 244, 250			2.4-15	27
				2.9	41
		4.11	47, 64, 170, 187, 188, 224, 225, 227, 232	2.12	27
				2.13	26
				Haggai	
				2.10-14	19
		Micah		Zechariah	
		1	142	1.8	158
4.3	74, 112, 168, 205, 208, 213	1.2	141, 142	6.10-14	14
		2.8	186	8.14	189
		2.10	207	10.2	132
4.4	209, 213, 214	4	166	10.11	158
		4.2	227	11.3	186
4.5-8	214	5.7	221	13.4	186
4.5	29, 113, 168, 171, 193–5, 201	7.19	158		

Malachi
1.4	101
2.11-12	17, 19
3.6	189

NEW TESTAMENT
Matthew
8.23-27	112
12.38-42	4, 24

Luke
1	68
2	68
11.29-32	24

John
18.14	90

Acts
7.14	63
9.14	63
12.1	82
27	68
27.18-19	68
27.23	68

1 Corinthians
1.18-25	87

Hebrews
7.17	16

Romans
16.21	232

APOCRYPHA
Tobit
14.4	3

Judith
4.1	222
4.10-11	222

Ecclesiasticus
16.30	231
24	19, 20
45.23-24	17
49.10	3
49.11-12	20
49.13	20

PSEUDEPIGRAPHA
3 Maccabees
6.8	3, 198

BABYLONIAN TALMUD
Baba Meşia
59b	147

MIDRASH
Genesis Rabbah
56.8	91

OTHER JEWISH WORKS
Pirke Avot
1	30

INSCRIPTIONS
Descent of Innana
ll. 173-75	180

KTU
1.20-22	180

QURAN
10	102
37	102
37.139-147	102

Index of Authors

Abela, A. A. 11, 15
Ackerman, J. S. 149
Adams, C. E. P. 99

Barstad, H. 54
Ben Zvi, E. 10, 16, 43, 52, 240, 241, 244
Berlin, A. 161
Bewer, J. A. 2, 126, 144
Blenkinsopp, J. 54
Bolin, T. M. 3, 153, 154, 225
Bonhoeffer, D. 66, 88, 197
Brichto, H. C. 1, 65, 153, 183
Burrows, M. 1, 241, 252

Cary, P. 2, 208
Casson, L. 98, 99
Christensen, D. L. 150, 187
Cooper, A. 216
Craig, K. M., Jr. 239, 241
Crouch, W. B. 251

Dobbs-Allsopp, F. W. 161
Dozeman, T. B. 204

Elata-Alster, G. 106

Finkelstein, I. 21–3

Good, E. M. 1, 50, 210
Goodhart, S. 235
Guillaume, P. 216

Handy, L. K. 7–10, 86, 247
Huguenin, J. 14
Hunter, A. G. 86, 106, 124, 152, 169, 218, 230, 240

Joerstad, M. 233

Kelsey, M. xii, 43, 44, 234
Kugel, J. 161

Levine, É. 119, 239, 250
Limburg, J. 2, 126
Lipschits, O. 54

Magonet, J. D. 3–7, 31–5, 42, 44, 97, 106, 111, 112, 114, 123, 127, 156, 163, 169, 185, 192, 199, 207
McCarter, P. K. 161, 164

Perry, T. A. 59–61, 65, 66, 85, 91, 121, 141, 179, 223
Person, R. F., Jr. 239, 241

Salmon, R. 106
Salters, R. B. 2, 126
Sasson, J. M. 2, 57, 65, 78, 98, 100, 120, 127, 130, 144, 150, 152, 154, 156, 180, 199, 201, 206, 214, 215
Shemesh, Y. 104, 218
Sherwood, Y. xii, 30, 65, 66, 100, 102, 104, 185, 236, 238

Trible, P. 181, 242

Vayntrub, J. 34, 162

Watts, J. W. 152, 161
Wolff, H. W. 2, 87, 100, 126, 144, 206
Wyatt, N. 164

Youngblood, K. J. 2, 99, 198, 206, 208

Zenger, E. 191

Index of Subjects

LITERARY ASPECTS OF JONAH
allegory 57, 166, 235
allusion 5, 104–5, 138, 140, 156, 169174, 191, 193, 199, 207, 222, 231, 249, 251
audience 2, 5, 7–9, 43, 64, 81, 237, 239
author xiii–xiv, xvi, xviii, xix, 1–5, 7–9, 11–12, 23, 25, 27–9, 31, 34, 41, 44, 45, 57, 64, 65, 67, 69, 73, 76, 79, 81, 83, 85, 89, 93, 94, 96, 97, 99, 100, 103–5, 107, 121, 122, 124, 125, 129, 137–40, 144, 145, 150–3, 159, 163, 174, 177, 180–92 (passim, 206–9, 212, 213, 215, 216, 228, 229, 234, 237, 239–41, 245, 247, 249, 252
channelling 6, 193, 206, 243
elite 7–9, 26, 38, 42, 234, 236, 252
folk-tale 1, 56, 59, 85, 86, 124, 180
forty (folk motif) 115, 167, 181, 208
intellectual etc. xii, 5, 9, 13, 19, 241, 251
intertext etc. 3, 5, 6, 8, 9, 13, 24, 26, 31, 35, 47, 49, 57, 106, 107, 111, 113, 118, 121, 154, 202, 228, 236, 244
irony 1, 2, 66, 70, 73, 77, 80, 87, 94, 114, 138, 139, 141, 146, 148, 161, 171, 178, 182, 195, 200, 212, 232, 240
literary etc., literati xii, 1, 7, 8, 10, 13, 18, 22, 86, 94, 96, 103, 138, 152, 186, 192, 229, 241, 244
morality tale xii, 145, 236
myth, mythic xi, xiii, xvi, 4, 55, 86, 103, 104, 106, 108, 117, 123–5, 143, 149, 156, 158–60, 165, 166, 245
narrative, narrator xi, xiii, 3, 5, 6, 8–11, 15, 16, 20, 27, 30–5, 50, 52, 57, 58, 67, 69, 72, 78, 81, 83, 88, 92, 96, 99, 101, 109, 110, 112, 116, 121, 125, 126, 128, 129, 135, 137, 140, 146, 149–54, 156, 160–3, 165, 166, 169, 174, 177, 180, 182, 183, 192–5, 197, 198, 201, 206, 207, 213, 236–40, 242, 246–8

parable 1, 13, 42, 51, 58, 90, 174, 229
pastiche 5, 10, 57, 58, 113, 154, 161, 240
polemic 13, 217
proleptic summary 183, 194
prophecy (literary genre) xii, 128, 149, 206, 225, 231, 236–9, 244
psychogeography 28, 29, 44, 234, 235
quotation 5, 6, 108, 123, 185, 206, 213, 236
reader xiii, xviii, xix, 4, 5, 8, 13, 17, 29–31, 34, 35, 40, 42–6, 58, 64, 73, 78, 79, 85, 87, 89, 91, 96, 107, 108, 113, 137–9, 158, 159, 166, 176, 177, 184, 209–12, 214–16, 234–7, 240–4, 251, 252
register 34, 42, 105, 156
satire xii, 1, 2, 10, 26, 57, 94, 145, 154, 225, 232, 240, 241
scribe 7–10, 13, 18, 22, 23
three (folk motif) 4, 59, 124, 125, 180, 181
unsee (*sic*) xxi, 44, 45, 234–6, 244–6
voice (literary theory) 31, 96, 122, 128–30, 193, 195, 237–43 (passim)
wisdom 19, 20, 58, 82, 87, 124, 215, 227–32
translation xxiii, 30, 51, 52, 71, 75, 77, 84, 88, 92, 93, 97, 98, 104, 105, 126–38 (passim), 141, 161, 171, 186, 190, 201, 211, 249

THEOLOGICAL AND ETHICAL ISSUES
barrenness: see *empty land*
blessing 3, 41, 118, 202–4, 227
booth (cf. Sukkot) 208–11, 214
covenant, silence of 9, 16, 18, 20, 21, 30, 33, 66, 67, 115, 117, 118, 131–3, 165, 174, 184, 188, 191, 192, 216, 244, 245, 252 (**Heb *berit*, 21, 118, 216**)

creator 1, 9, 49, 50, 60, 62, 64, 65, 69, 70, 79–82, 84, 103, 106, 117, 121, 140, 154, 157, 159, 165, 166, 197, 200
cult 9, 15, 16, 18, 21, 27, 29, 58, 108, 124, 210, 221, 238, 245, 252
death-wish 6, 30, 49, 57, 58, 60, 70, 85, 90, 91, 112, 121, 122, 124, 125, 144, 145, 158, 159, 163–5, 168, 173, 178, 192, 200, 205, 208, 244, 245, 248
empty land 31, 35–7, 54, 70
ethics 12, 13, 55, 56, 75, 89, 93, 115, 185, 190, 199, 214, 217, 218, 228, 229, 246–51
evil 3, 24, 31, 33, 74, 75, 87, 175, 179, 187–90, 192, 194–6, 223, 245, 250, 251 (**Heb *ra'ah*, 6, 31, 74, 189–91, 195, 205, 208, 211, 230**)
exile 14, 17, 21, 22, 48, 49, 53, 54, 81
exodus 6, 9, 29, 86, 107, 109, 125, 126, 140, 155–7 (passim), 174, 244, 245
grace 9, 11, 26, 66, 88, 134, 146, 147, 191–4, 197, 202–4, 248
grace, cheap 66, 146, 147, 192, 197, 248
idol 94, 108, 131–5, 150, 199, 229, 235 (**Heb *shave', hevel*, 131–4, 150, 229**)
loyalty 94, 114, 131, 133–5, 148, 151, 156, 159, 160, 249
maker 79, 82, 94
mercy 9, 26, 47, 66, 114, 133, 134, 141, 146, 158, 163, 166, 184, 190, 192, 197, 202, 204, 213, 215, 216, 235, 236, 238, 245, 247–52
mercy/blessing formula 118, 190, 192, 202, 204, 213, 215, 216, 238, 245, 247, 249, 252 (**Heb *chesed*, 131, 133–5, 148, 156, 160, 249, 250**)
moral xiv, 12, 56, 88–91, 93, 94, 146, 165, 185, 189, 196, 197, 200, 206, 207, 212, 227–9, 231, 232, 245–8, 250
prayer 11, 29, 67, 68, 72, 83, 90–2, 95, 115, 119, 120, 127, 129, 136, 137, 144–6, 151, 171–3, 176, 178, 179, 197–200, 207, 247, 249 (**Heb *tephillah*, 68, 71, 137**)
repentance (Nineveh/Jonah) xiii, 12, 31, 44, 47, 75, 87, 88, 145, 146, 181–4, 187, 188, 191, 192, 195, 228, 229, 231, 236, 244, 252
suicide 65, 85
Sukkot/sukkah 208–9, 211

temple (destroy/rebuild) 20, 42, 54, 100, 238,
temple (cult) 8, 9, 18, 22, 29, 49, 115, 130, 136, 137, 139–45, 148
theophany 62, 63, 89, 124, 178, 208
vow xvii, 67, 90, 92, 94, 148, 149, 179
wickedness 6, 11, 32, 33, 40, 44, 46, 52, 55, 57, 58, 61, 74, 114, 115, 163, 169, 170, 176, 177, 179, 195, 207, 212, 230, 252
Yahweh's punishment xiv, 3, 11, 26, 28, 41, 65, 72, 89, 115, 146, 149, 189–92, 199, 202–5, 208, 215, 216, 245, 250–2
Yahweh's repentance 83, 89, 188, 189, 192, 205
Heb *nacham* 189, 191
Yahweh's unpredictability:
ambiguity 146, 197, 198, 252
ambivalence 55
arbitrariness 28, 51, 55, 89, 199, 229, 246, 251
fickleness 66, 114, 171, 179, 199, 211
unreliability 87, 146, 208
Yahweh's word xiv, 51, 52, 74, 113, 170, 180–2, 197, 198, 201, 206, 236–9, 252
Heb *davar* 51, 170, 201

DIVINE INTERVENTIONS
Appoint 41, 70, 102, 110, 114, 119, 120, 165, 166, 209, 211–13 (**Heb *manah*, 113, 114, 120, 149, 166, 225**)
cetacean xiii, xviii, 86, 103
cucumber 59, 107, 121 (**Heb *qiqayon*, xx, 59–61, 65, 72, 113, 180, 210, 211, 235**)
fire 34, 35, 42, 114, 117, 166, 176, 209, 212, 243
plant xx, 59, 60, 70, 107, 120, 121, 166, 180, 210–12, 224
whale xi, xvii, xviii, 86, 92, 102, 103, 115, 120, 121, 125, 137, 138, 143, 144, 147, 149, 178, 180, 200, 208, 211, 212, 219
wind 12, 32, 41, 59, 62–5, 70, 101, 102, 112, 113, 117, 120, 121, 131, 132, 166, 170, 171, 180, 187, 201, 209, 211–13 (**Heb *ruach*, 101, 112, 117, 225, 231**)
worm (insect, beetle) xx, 12, 30, 59, 70, 89, 107, 113, 120, 121, 166, 211–14, 219

Index of Subjects

CREATION MOTIFS
animal 32, 37, 47, 60, 65, 67, 108, 111–13, 115, 116, 170, 188, 195, 196, 200, 218–32 (passim), 251 (**Heb** *behemah, chayyah,* **60, 182, 219–21, 223–9, 231, 232**)
cattle xix, 32, 59, 60, 89, 92, 115, 182, 187, 215, 218, 219, 221–3
dry land xiii, 6, 29, 64, 79–81, 84, 88, 94, 107, 109, 110, 117, 143, 149, 157, 160, 165, 166, 183 (**Heb** *yavashah, yavash, yibbashah, yibbesheth,* **6, 81, 109, 110, 117, 143, 149, 154, 157**)
heaven 29, 35, 67, 79–82, 84, 87, 107, 166

JONAH'S TRIALS AND TRIBULATIONS
ascending: see *up*
banishment 79, 140, 151, 245, 246 (**Heb** *garash,* **139**)
commission 9, 11, 24, 54, 55, 99, 179, 180, 198, 245
descending: see *down*
dispossessed 139, 140
dove 48, 49, 51, 154, 169, 170, 173
down xiii, 6, 33, 60, 61, 69, 125, 142–5, 159, 164–6, 168–70, 173, 248 (**Heb** *yarad,* **xiii, 60, 61, 143, 145, 164**)
exile (Jonah) 49, 51, 140, 151, 190, 209
flee etc. 58, 59, 80, 85, 113, 169, 170, 171, 173, 208
flight xvi, 29–31, 49, 50, 52, 58, 83, 95, 144, 146, 147, 151, 154, 163, 166, 176, 177, 201, 207, 245, 246, 248, 251
get up 52, 53, 71, 137, 176, 177, 207 (**Heb** *qum,* **177, 178**)
journey xiii, xiv, 3, 28, 29, 31, 44, 58–60, 75, 76, 99, 124, 143, 144, 164, 166, 167, 176–81 (passim), 186, 201, 208, 248
presence 11, 52, 55, 57–9, 63, 71, 115, 139, 141, 142, 177
prophet (Jonah) xi, xiii, xv, 2, 3, 8, 10–13, 24–31, 37, 42–4, 47, 48, 52–4, 59, 62, 75, 76, 87, 89, 95, 112, 113, 151, 153, 176–8, 180–2, 184, 188–9, 197, 198, 201, 207–9, 228, 229, 243, 246
sleep 6, 61, 68–72, 111–13, 117, 151, 169, 207, 208 (**Heb** *tardemah, radam,* **6, 70, 111, 117, 202**)

travel xiii, xiv, xvi, 8, 11, 29, 31, 44, 70, 75, 76, 99, 164, 198, 207, 248
up xiii–xv, 11, 52, 53, 55, 57, 58, 60, 61, 69, 71, 143, 145, 164–6, 176–9, 186, 207, 212 (**Heb** *'alah,* **xiii, xiv, 60, 103, 164**)
victim 12, 64, 65, 121, 148, 199, 248

THE TERRORS OF THE DEEP
abyss xiii, xvi, 6, 143
deeps 103, 105, 122, 129, 137, 138, 143, 156, 158–60, 168
depths xiii, 32, 65, 70, 103, 115, 142–4, 150, 156, 158, 164, 165, 245 (**Heb** *mitsulah,* **105, 122, 143, 156, 158, 160**)
flood xvi, 6, 31–5, 42, 48, 49, 65, 89, 106, 109, 112, 114–18, 154, 221, 245
hurl 62, 64, 69, 87, 92, 105, 139
ordeal 30, 148, 161, 163, 164, 166
storm xiii, 62–5, 68, 69, 71, 80, 85, 89, 91, 105, 112, 113, 121, 138, 151, 156, 187, 199, 242, 248
tempest 64, 105, 169, 187, 200
water xiii, xvi, 31, 32, 34, 62, 64, 77, 89, 103, 105, 107–10, 112–15, 117, 138, 143, 156, 157, 159, 161, 166, 176, 248
whirlwind 63, 65 (**Heb** *sa'ar,* **62, 63, 175**)

THE SEA, THE SEA
behemoth 182, 232
captain xvi, 71, 75, 88–90, 96–8, 237, 242, 243, 248, 249
crew xvi, xvii, 67, 70, 71, 74, 75, 83, 84, 88, 90, 97, 98, 146, 199, 237, 242, 248
fish xi, xvii, 4, 47, 53, 64, 68, 70, 89, 92, 102–4, 110–13, 119–21, 123–7, 138, 144, 149, 161, 165, 166, 176, 181, 183
leviathan xviii, xx, 103–5, 182
mariners xvi
sailor xiii, 29, 47, 60, 64, 65, 67–73, 75, 76, 79–81, 83–91, 93, 94, 96, 99, 101, 109, 113, 115, 121, 135, 138, 140–2, 145, 146, 148, 149, 151, 166, 178, 179, 185–7, 196, 199, 200, 208, 213, 242, 243, 247, 249, 251
sea xiii, xvi, xviii, 6, 29, 32, 33, 37, 47, 49, 59–62, 64, 65, 69, 75, 77, 79–82, 86–8, 92–5, 117, 123, 138, 139, 142, 143, 148, 156, 161, 163, 164, 166, 168, 180, 183, 198, 248

sea creatures 86, 102–5, 121, 180, 198
seafaring xvi, 67, 159
seamen 153
ship xvi, xvii, 12, 48, 49, 58–62, 65, 67–72, 75, 87, 88, 93, 95–8, 100–2, 105, 111, 112, 121, 138, 140, 143, 151, 159, 163 165, 166, 178, 207, 208, 242, 248, 249
swallow xi, 102, 104, 121, 122, 124, 139, 149, 154–6, 183 (**Heb** *bala'*, **121, 139, 149, 155, 156**)
Tannin 103–5, 121, 122
Tiamat 86, 103, 105, 143

DATING JONAH
chronology 54, 107, 137, 161, 162, 240
dating 2–5, 7, 9, 13–15, 17, 22, 25, 26, 28, 49, 74, 79, 104, 150, 162, 163, 169, 232, 237 238
Hellenistic Period 3, 8, 9, 13, 15, 19, 21–4, 27, 186
historical 2, 3, 5, 21, 22, 25, 47, 76, 100, 106, 107, 250
history 7, 27, 47, 182
Persian Period 7–9, 13, 14, 16, 21, 22, 24, 27, 98, 186, 238
purity 16, 19, 27, 219
sects 8, 15–17, 23, 133

MISCELLANEOUS KEY EXPRESSIONS
awe 62, 68, 80, 81, 83, 94, 121, 142
east 29, 44, 59, 65, 101, 102, 113, 120, 121, 171, 178, 209, 213 (**Heb** *qedem*, **113, 171**)

fear xvii, 62, 64, 68, 69, 81, 83–5, 87, 94, 143, 156, 158, 166, 170, 171, 242 (**Heb** *yara'*, **68, 69, 242**)
good xiv, 1, 11, 13, 25, 28, 50, 54, 58, 74, 76, 101, 109, 124, 128, 138, 140, 145, 147, 162, 164, 166, 167, 174, 180, 196, 197, 200, 203, 205–7, 210, 211, 213, 227, 248–51 (**Heb** *tov*, **205, 206**)
great 43, 46, 52, 53, 64, 67, 78, 83, 87, 94, 95, 104, 116, 121, 149, 151, 175, 176, 180, 181, 183, 187, 192, 195, 196, 207, 211, 213, 216, 226, 229, 230, 242, 246, 252 (**Heb** *gadhol*, **64, 94, 105, 116, 187, 230**)
overthrow 6, 31, 34–9, 115, 117, 192 (**Heb** *hapakh*, **31, 34–6, 41**)
rabbinic 4, 13, 14, 18, 20, 30, 53, 60, 65, 72, 74, 91, 110, 119, 120, 123, 125, 137, 147, 150, 235, 237, 252
sacrifice xvii, 21, 48, 49, 70, 84–6, 91, 92, 94, 114, 117, 118, 146–9, 156, 179, 223, 225, 235, 243
terror xvi, 62, 63, 70, 83, 94, 121, 123, 138, 143, 187
violence 31–3, 41, 83, 88, 114, 115, 117, 159, 173, 175, 178, 186–8, 208, 251 (**Heb** *chamas*, **6, 31, 173, 188**)